SAP PRESS Books: Always on hand

Print or e-book, Kindle or iPad, workplace or airplane: Choose where and how to read your SAP PRESS books! You can now get all our titles as e-books, too:

▶ By download and online access
▶ For all popular devices
▶ And, of course, DRM-free

Convinced? Then go to **www.sap-press.com** and get your e-book today.

ABAP® Development for SAP HANA®

 **PRESS**

SAP PRESS is a joint initiative of SAP and Galileo Press. The know-how offered by SAP specialists combined with the expertise of the Galileo Press publishing house offers the reader expert books in the field. SAP PRESS features first-hand information and expert advice, and provides useful skills for professional decision-making.

SAP PRESS offers a variety of books on technical and business-related topics for the SAP user. For further information, please visit our website: *www.sap-press.com*.

Dr. Berg and Penny Silvia
SAP HANA: An Introduction (2nd Edition)
2013, 527 pp., hardcover
ISBN 978-1-59229-865-5

Jonathan Haun, Chris Hickman, Don Loden, and Roy Wells
Implementing SAP HANA
2013, 837 pp., hardcover
ISBN 978-1-59229-856-3

Tanmaya Gupta
Function Modules in ABAP: A Quick Reference Guide
2014, 977 pp., hardcover
ISBN 978-1-59229-850-1

Rich Heilman and Thomas Jung
Next Generation ABAP Development (2nd Edition)
2011, 735 pp., hardcover
ISBN 978-1-59229-352-0

Thorsten Schneider, Eric Westenberger, and Hermann Gahm

ABAP® Development for SAP HANA®

Galileo Press

Bonn • Boston

Galileo Press is named after the Italian physicist, mathematician, and philosopher Galileo Galilei (1564–1642). He is known as one of the founders of modern science and an advocate of our contemporary, heliocentric worldview. His words *Eppur si muove* (And yet it moves) have become legendary. The Galileo Press logo depicts Jupiter orbited by the four Galilean moons, which were discovered by Galileo in 1610.

Editor Laura Korslund
Acquisitions Editor Kelly Grace Weaver
German Edition Editor Janina Schweitzer
Translation Lemoine International, Salt Lake City, UT
Copyeditor Laura Schreier
Cover Design Sabine Reibeholz, Graham Geary
Photo Credit Fotolia/33788629/© lassedesignen
Layout Design Vera Brauner
Production Graham Geary
Typesetting Publishers' Design and Production Services, Inc.
Printed and bound in the United States of America, on paper from sustainable sources

ISBN 978-1-59229-859-4
© 2014 by Galileo Press Inc., Boston (MA)
1st edition 2014
1st German edition published 2013 by Galileo Press, Bonn, Germany

Library of Congress Cataloging-in-Publication Control Number: 2013043363

Contents at a Glance

Dear Reader,

Rarely has an SAP technology generated so much discussion in recent times as SAP HANA. The in-memory database promises enormous improvements in terms of application performance and opens up completely new dimensions in data processing, thus paving the way for new types of business processes that would have been inconceivable previously. However, what do these developments mean for you as a programmer? Which changes do you and your established procedures need to adapt to? Are there any areas that require you to think differently in order to optimize or reprogram your applications for use with SAP HANA?

To answer all of these questions, Thorsten Schneider, Eric Westenberger, and Hermann Gahm have put everything you need to know into this book. Not only have they provided clear examples to demonstrate what ABAP development on SAP HANA entails in comparison to development on traditional databases, but they have also outlined its many new possibilities. Ultimately, they will make you a confident user of the SAP HANA development environment and show you how to access SAP HANA objects within ABAP programs.

Your comments and suggestions are the most useful tools to help us improve our books. We encourage you to visit our website at *www.sap-press.com* and share your feedback about *ABAP Development for SAP HANA*.

Thank you for purchasing a book from SAP PRESS!

Laura Korslund
Editor, SAP PRESS

Galileo Press
Boston, MA

laura.korslund@galileo-press.com
www.sap-press.com

Contents

PART III Advanced Techniques for ABAP Programming for SAP HANA

Foreword

Today, less than four years after we officially commenced development of SAP HANA, and over ten years after we envisaged the first precursors to the technology, column-based *main memory databases* is now a very hot topic, and one that is rapidly gaining a market presence.

We could not have foreseen this development back in 2002 when we integrated the first version of a pure main memory-based (non-transactional) column store into the TREX search engine. For the document world, column-based storage of metadata (author, creation date, and so on) delivered added value because it was possible to add metadata in a flexible and easy manner, and to query this data very efficiently.

Things became very interesting when we started to use the technology to aggregate large volumes of data. Initial performance results were phenomenal and produced an air of disbelief within SAP, quickly followed by immense euphoria. Production continued until 2005 when we delivered SAP NetWeaver Business Warehouse Accelerator (BWA) as an accelerator for our BW systems. The benefits were obvious: No additional database aggregates, as well as extremely good and above all, consistent access times because the risk of accessing undefined aggregates, had disappeared.

The major breakthrough in relation to main memory-based column stores occurred in 2009 when Hasso Plattner had the vision to postulate joint column storage for OLAP (reporting) queries and the OLTP load. This proposal was revolutionary for two reasons: Firstly, because of Hasso's suggestion to place OLAP and OLTP in one system, and secondly, to supplement this system with database storage in the form of a main memory-based column store. At first the research community was very skeptical, but soon after, the sheer number of high-quality publications on this topic made it clear that it had well and truly arrived.

In order to productize this vision, HANA was established as an organization in 2009 when three groups (P*Time, MaxDB, and TREX) were merged and later joined by the Sybase team. The goal was—and remains—to build a database management platform that offers much more than traditional databases, and to make this platform available to a wide range of applications, including SAP application platforms. At the end of 2010, the first "data-mart variant" of HANA was delivered, followed by HANA for B1 and HANA for SAP NetWeaver BW. A major event and final confirmation of Hasso's vision was the announcement of SAP Business Suite on HANA in January of this year and its delivery to our customers.

Our customers, partners, and internal development groups can now implement a large range of options that incorporate HANA's speed and functionality into their applications, and thus reap the rewards of deploying SAP HANA. ABAP is, without doubt, one of the key development environments for SAP HANA. However, developers must think a little differently in order to realize the full potential of HANA. This book will certainly help them in this regard.

SAP HANA will continue to be SAP's innovation platform. We can therefore all look forward to exciting times ahead—with lots of new features, innovations, and the opportunity to build new types of as-yet inconceivable applications.

Franz Färber
Executive Vice President, SAP PI HANA Platform, SAP AG

Preface

SAP HANA will soon celebrate its second birthday. Hard to believe, but this technology has been on the market for almost two years now. During this time, its use potential increased significantly: From an in-memory database for data marts, which supplements SAP NetWeaver Business Warehouse and the SAP Business Suite, to all types of data warehouse applications and a platform for analytical and transactional systems. Today, SAP HANA is a complete, high-end database for all SAP applications and, at the same time, an innovation platform for completely new types of real-time applications (in the area of healthcare, for example).

I had the opportunity to actively accompany this rapid development, from its origins in the SAP NetWeaver Business Warehouse environment right up until the present day, and to do so from the perspective of an internal user. Never before had I witnessed the energy within the walls of SAP that greeted the arrival of SAP HANA. And the best thing about it is that this is just the beginning. Anyone who has experienced this enthusiasm from customers, partners, and employees—or seen the wealth of ideas for developing completely new applications for the software—will know exactly what I mean.

SAP NetWeaver Business Warehouse (since the end of 2011) and the SAP Business Suite (since the start of 2013) can now run productively on SAP HANA. Porting and optimizing these systems for the in-memory database technology was one of SAP's key strategic projects in recent years. In parallel, and as an additional support for this project, we developed a new SAP NetWeaver release, namely SAP NetWeaver 7.4, in mid-2012. As part of this development, we systematically optimized ABAP technology for use with SAP HANA and ported the Java-based SAP NetWeaver Hubs (for example, SAP NetWeaver Portal and SAP NetWeaver Business Process Management) to SAP HANA in particular, thus giving each and every customer the opportunity to run SAP NetWeaver productively on SAP HANA—a key milestone for not only SAP but our customers, as well.

The new features in SAP NetWeaver AS ABAP 7.4 support the application developers at SAP in optimizing existing ABAP programs for SAP HANA and implementing completely new applications based on SAP HANA. Of course, our customers and partners can also benefit from these opportunities. A non-disruptive way of migrating existing business processes to SAP HANA, while at the same time developing completely new applications, now exists for the entire ABAP ecosystem.

In this book, Thorsten Schneider, Eric Westenberger, and Hermann Gahm describe the importance of SAP HANA for ABAP development, as well as the new opportunities presented by ABAP 7.4 in the context of in-memory database technology. Thorsten, Eric, and Hermann not only discuss program acceleration as a result of moving the calculation logic to the database, but also the innovative features that SAP HANA makes available to you—thus making this book a must-read for every single ABAP developer.

I hope that you enjoy reading this book.

Andreas Wesselmann
Vice President, SAP PI HANA Platform Extensions, SAP AG

Introduction

Today's business world is extremely dynamic and subject to constant change, with companies continuously under great pressure to innovate. SAP HANA's vision is to provide a platform that can be used to influence all business processes within a company's value chain in real time. However, what does this key term *real time* mean for business applications?

In technological terms, it describes, in particular, the availability of essential functions without *unwanted* delays. The environment in which a technology is used and the time when this occurs strongly influences the functions needed and what is deemed to be an *acceptable* delay. Before we discuss the software currently used for enterprise management, we wish to illustrate this using an example from daily life, namely telecommunications.

Early forms of communication (for example, telegraphs) were very limited in terms of their usage (range, availability, and manual effort). At that time, however, it was an immense improvement in terms of the speed at which messages were previously exchanged. Then, with advent of the telephone, it became possible to establish flexible connections over long distances. Once again, however, users of this technology had to allow for various delays. Initially, it was necessary to establish a manual connection via a switchboard. Later, and for a very long time after, there were considerable *latencies* with overseas connections, which affected and complicated long-distance telephone conversations. Today, however, telephone connections can be established almost anywhere in the world and done so without any notable delay. Essentially, every leap in evolution has been associated with considerable improvement in terms of *real-time quality*.

Example: real time in telecommunications

In addition to a (synchronous) conversation between two people, asynchronous forms of communication have always played a role historically (for example, postal communication). In this context, the term *real time* has a different meaning because neither the sender nor the receiver needs to actively wait. Asynchronous communication has also undergone immense changes in recent years (thanks to many new variants such as email, SMS, and so on), which, unlike postal mail, facilitates a new dimension of real-time communication between several people. Furthermore, there is an increasing number of non-human communication users such as devices with an Internet connection, which are known as *smart devices* (for example, intelligent electricity meters).

Most people will testify to the fact that, nowadays, electronic communication is available in real time. Nevertheless, in our daily lives, some things still cannot occur in real time despite the many advances in technology (for example, booking a connecting flight during a trip). It is safe to say that in the future, many as yet inconceivable scenarios will be so widespread that currently accepted limitations will become completely unacceptable.

Real time in business
The above example of telecommunications technology contains some basic principles that can also be applied to business software. On the one hand, there are corporate and economic developments such as globalization and the increasing mobility of customers, and employees who are the driving forces for new types of technology. Companies operate globally and interact in complex networks. Furthermore, customers and employees expect to be able to access products and services at all times, from anywhere in the world.

On the other hand, there are technological innovations that pioneer new paths. The Internet is currently a catalyst for most developments. Enormous volumes of data are simultaneously accessible to a large part of the world's population (that is, *in real time*). The Internet also provides a platform for selling all types of products and services, which has led to a phenomenal increase in the number of business transactions conducted each day. Companies can gain a massive competitive advantage each time a business process (for example, procurement, production, billing, and so on) is optimized. In most industries, there is great potential here, which can be realized by establishing a closer link between operational planning and control in real time.

Today's customers also expect greater customization of products and services to their individual wishes (for example, to their personal circumstances). In particular, companies that are active in industries subject to major changes (for example, the energy industry, financial providers or specific forms of retail) are under a great deal of pressure to act.

The term *real time* shapes the evolution of 40 years of SAP software. Even Real time at SAP the letter "R" in SAP's classic product line, R/3, stood for *real time*. SAP's initial concepts in the 1970s, which paved the way for the development of R/1, facilitated the on-screen entry of business data, which, compared to older punch card systems, provided a new quality of real time. Consequently, processes such as payroll accounting and financial accounting were the first to be mapped electronically and automated. With SAP R/2, which was based on a *mainframe* architecture, SAP added further ERP modules (*Enterprise Resource Planning*), for example, Materials Management, to these applications areas. As part of this release, SAP introduced the reporting language ABAP. (Originally, ABAP stood for *Allgemeiner Berichtsaufbereitungsprozessor*, which means "General Report Creation Processor," but this was later changed to *Advanced Business Application Programming*). ABAP *reports* were used to create, for example, a list of purchase orders, which was filtered according to customer and had *drilldown options* for line items. Initially, this was available in the background only (*batch* mode). However, it later became available in *dialog* mode.

Thanks to the *client/server architecture*, in particular, and the related scaling options in SAP R/3, it was possible for a large number of users within a company to access SAP applications. Consequently, SAP software, in combination with consistent use of a database system and an ever-growing number of standard implementations for business processes, penetrated the IT infrastructure of many large companies, thus making it possible to use an integrated system to support transactional processes in real time (for example, a *just-in-time production process*).

Parallel to these developments is the fact that, over the past 20 years, Importance of business intelligence it has become increasingly more important to analyze current business processes, the purpose of which is to continuously obtain information in order to make better operational and strategic decisions. Within this *business intelligence trend*, however, it soon became clear that in many situations, it is technically impractical to perform and integrate the required analyses into a system that already supports business processes. Parallel processing of analyses and transactions involving extremely large amounts of data overloaded most systems, with the database, in particular, emerging as a limiting factor. This was one of the reasons why SAP created a specialized system for analytical scenarios, which you currently know as

SAP NetWeaver Business Warehouse (*BW*). In addition to new options for consolidating data from multiple systems and integrating external data sources, the use of the data warehouse system for operational scenarios is, unfortunately, fraught with losses when data is processed in real time. First of all, data needs to be extracted and replicated, which, in practice, can cause a time delay, ranging from several hours up to one week, until the current data is available at the correct location. This was SAP's starting point for SAP HANA; in other words, no more delays in receiving key information for a business decision.

SAP HANA as a database | SAP likes to describe SAP HANA as a platform for real-time data management. To begin with, SAP HANA is a high-end database for business transactions (*Online Transaction Processing*, OLTP) and reporting (*Online Analytical Processing*, OLAP), which can use a combination of in-memory technology and column-oriented storage to optimize both scenarios. In the first step, SAP HANA was used as a *side-by-side scenario* (that is, in addition to an existing traditional database) to accelerate selective processes and analyses. Soon after, it was supported as a new database for SAP NetWeaver BW 7.3. In this way, SAP demonstrated that SAP HANA not only accelerates analytical scenarios, but that it can also be used as a primary database for an SAP NetWeaver system. With the announcement of *SAP Business Suite powered by SAP HANA*, it is now also possible for customers to fully benefit from SAP HANA technology within standard SAP applications. The new SAP NetWeaver release 7.4 underlying this constellation (in particular, SAP NetWeaver Application Server (AS) ABAP 7.4) will therefore play a key role in this book. Furthermore, the sample programs in this book require ABAP 7.4. However, we will always indicate which functions you can also use with earlier releases of SAP NetWeaver. A cloud-based trial version of ABAP 7.4 on SAP HANA is available. For more information, see Appendix E.

SAP HANA as a platform | Furthermore, SAP HANA provides many more functions that go beyond the usual range of functions associated with a database. In particular, these include extensive data management functions (replication, extraction – transformation – load (ETL), and so on) and data analysis functions (for example, *data mining* by means of a *text search* and *predictive analysis*). Many of these technologies and functions are not exclusively available to SAP HANA. In fact, many software systems now manage data in the main memory or use column-oriented displays. SAP itself developed and used in-memory technology long before SAP HANA came into being (for example, in *SAP NetWeaver BW Accelerator*). Similarly, a number of software manufacturers (including SAP itself) are involved in data analysis, especially in the context of business intelligence and information management solutions. One key benefit of SAP HANA is the fact that it offers this function in the same system in which business transactions are running. If, for example, you want to run SAP Business Suite on SAP HANA, these enhanced functions are available to you immediately, without the need to extract data. Furthermore, since SAP HANA incorporates the key data structures of the SAP Business Suite, installed functions already exist for some standard operations (for example, currency conversion).

Therefore, what does SAP HANA mean for standard SAP applications that run on the ABAP application server? What changes are occurring in ABAP programming? What new options does SAP HANA open up in terms of ABAP-based solutions? These three questions will be at the heart of this book. Furthermore, we will always use examples to explain the relevant technical backgrounds and concepts, rather than simply introducing you to the technology behind the new tools and frameworks. In particular, we will focus on the basic functions of ABAP development and database access via ABAP. We will introduce existing or planned supports for SAP HANA in ABAP-based *frameworks* as an overview or outlook because a detailed description would generally require an introduction to how these components work. (Examples here include *Embedded Search* and *BRFplus*.) In the examples contained in this book, we will use simple ABAP reports as the user interfaces, for the most part. In two detailed examples, however, we will also create web-based interfaces with Web Dynpro ABAP and HTML5.

ABAP development on SAP HANA

We made the decision to divide this book into three parts. In Part I, "Basic Principles," we will introduce you to the basic principles of in-memory technology. Here, you will get to know the development tools as well as refresh your knowledge of ABAP database programming. In **Chapter 1**, "Overview of SAP HANA," we will start with an overview of the components of SAP HANA and potential usage scenarios in conjunction with ABAP. In **Chapter 2**, "Introducing the Development Environment," we will introduce you to the development environment, which comprises

Structure of the book: Part I

SAP HANA Studio and the ABAP development tools for SAP NetWeaver (also known as ABAP in Eclipse). **Chapter 3**, "Database Programming using SAP NetWeaver AS ABAP," will discuss the use of Open SQL and Native SQL to access the HANA database from ABAP programs.

Part II In the second part of the book, "Introduction to ABAP Programming with SAP HANA," you'll learn how to store data from an ABAP application (for example, certain calculations) in SAP HANA, thus achieving considerably better performance. Here, the focus will be on programming and modeling SAP HANA, as well as accessing SAP HANA from ABAP programs. In **Chapter 4**, "View Modeling in SAP HANA Studio," we will discuss the various ways in which you can create data views, which can then be used to conduct calculations and analyses in relation to ABAP table content. Then, in **Chapter 5**, "Programming Options in SAP HANA," you will learn about SQLScript, which is the programming language for database procedures in SAP HANA. You'll also learn how to use ABAP to access these procedures. In **Chapter 6**, "Application Transport," we will explain how you can transport ABAP development objects alongside the objects contained in the SAP HANA Repository. Together with the tools in **Chapter 7**, "Runtime and Error Analysis on SAP HANA," you now have the basic tools that we, as ABAP developers, believe you need to know within the context of SAP HANA. Part II of this book will conclude with **Chapter 8**, "Sample Scenario: Optimizing an Existing Application," where we will use the technologies and tools introduced earlier in this book to optimize an existing ABAP implementation for SAP HANA, step by step.

Part III In Part III of this book, "Advanced Techniques for ABAP Programming for SAP HANA," we will introduce you to some advanced SAP HANA functions, which are not available in classic ABAP development. Even though the chapters contained in Part III of this book are based on the content of the preceding part, Part III can be read in isolation. In **Chapter 9**, "Text Search and Analysis of Unstructured Data," we will start by describing the *fuzzy search* in SAP HANA and we will show you how you can use it to improve, for example, input helps within an ABAP application. Then in **Chapter 10**, "Integrating Analytical Functionality," we will introduce you to the capabilities of the embedded SAP NetWeaver BW technology in conjunction with ABAP developments on SAP HANA and existing SAP Business Intelligence products. You can then use decision tables, whose usage we will discuss in **Chapter 11**, "Decision Tables in SAP HANA," to use rules that enable you to design parts of an application in a very flexible manner. As a final element, we will show you in **Chapter 12**, "Function Libraries in SAP HANA," how you can, for example, incorporate statistical functions for *predictive analysis* into an ABAP application. In **Chapter 13**, "Sample Scenario: Development of a New Application," we will create a small sample application that connects innovations achieved with SAP HANA to ABAP transactions. The book concludes with **Chapter 14**, "Practical Tips," which contains our recommendations for optimizing ABAP applications on SAP HANA as well as some new developments in relation to ABAP applications on SAP HANA.

As you will see while reading this book, the HANA platform provides a whole host of options. You do not necessarily have to use all of the elements introduced here in ABAP custom developments on SAP HANA. For some new types of functions, the use of *low-level technologies*, which you may only have used occasionally in the past, is currently necessary in the ABAP application server (for example, Native SQL). However, we are convinced that the use of new options holds great innovation potential in terms of new developments. For this reason, we strive to adopt a certain pioneering approach, which is evident in some of the examples provided in this book.

Deploying new technologies

As an example, we will use the *flight data model* in SAP NetWeaver (also known as the SFLIGHT model), which was and remains the basis for many training courses, documentation, and specialist books relating to SAP ERP. Thanks to its popularity, the new features and paradigm shifts involved with SAP HANA can be explained very well using this example. The underlying business scenario (airlines and travel agencies) is also very well suited to explaining aspects of real time because, in recent years, the travel industry has been subject to great changes as a result of globalization and the Internet. Furthermore, the volume of data in the context of flight schedules, postings, and passengers has continued to grow.

Sample data model

Throughout this book, you will find several elements that will make it easier for you to work with this book.

How to use this book

Highlighted information boxes contain helpful content that is worth knowing, but lies somewhat outside the actual explanation. In order to help you immediately identify the type of information contained in the boxes, we have assigned symbols to each box:

[+] Tips marked with this symbol will give you special recommendations that may make your work easier.

[»] Boxes marked with this symbol contain information about additional topics or important content that you should note.

[!] This symbol refers to specifics that you should consider. It also warns about frequent errors or problems that can occur.

[Ex] Examples marked with this symbol make reference to practical scenarios and illustrate the functions shown.

In addition, you will find the code samples used throughout as a download on this book's web page at *www.sap-press.com*.

We hope that, with this book, we can give you a comprehensive tool that will support you in using the HANA technology in ABAP programs. Finally, we hope that you enjoy reading this book.

Acknowledgments

We wish to thank the following people who supported us by partaking in discussions and providing advice and feedback during the writing of this book:

Arne Arnold, Dr. Alexander Böhm, Ingo Bräuninger, Ralf-Dietmar Dittmann, Franz Färber, Markus Fath, Dr. Hans-Dieter Frey, Boris Gebhardt, Dr. Heiko Gerwens, Dr. Jasmin Gruschke, Martin Hartig, Vishnu Prasad Hegde, Rich Heilman, Thea Hillenbrand, Dr. Harshavardhan Jegadeesan, Thomas Jung, Bernd Krannich, Dr. Willi Petri, Eric Schemer, Joachim Schmid, Sascha Schwedes, Christiaan Edward Swanepoel, Welf Walter, Jens Weiler, Stefan Weitland, Tobias Wenner, and Andreas Wesselmann.

Thank you so much—this book would not have been possible without your help.

Thorsten Schneider, **Eric Westenberger**, and **Hermann Gahm**

PART I
Basic Principles

The first part of the book provides an overview of the SAP HANA database. We'll present all software components of the database and explain the basic principles and architecture of the in-memory technology. Moreover, you'll see typical application cases for SAP HANA. Following this section, you'll find an introduction to the new development environment. This section provides an overview of Eclipse, and you'll learn how to install the development environment. In this context, we'll explain how to get started using the ABAP Development Tools for SAP NetWeaver and SAP HANA Studio. The third chapter provides an overview of the architecture, the database interface, and the database usage by the application server. This information forms the basis for the subsequent detailed explanation of database access from ABAP.

SAP HANA is more than just a database. In fact, SAP HANA provides an application development platform and includes tools for data replication. Using SAP HANA, you can thus optimize existing applications as well as develop new applications from scratch.

1   Overview of SAP HANA

SAP HANA stands for *High Performance Analytical Appliance*. This flexible *appliance* (combination of hardware and software) runs independently of the data source and can be used to analyze large data volumes in real time within the main memory (*in-memory* technology). The SAP HANA appliance is provided by leading SAP hardware partners and comprises several SAP software components, in particular a full relational database.

Organizations can use SAP HANA for more than just data analysis. In addition to analytical applications, transactional applications can also benefit from SAP HANA. This means that both SAP NetWeaver Business Warehouse (BW) and the SAP Business Suite can use the SAP HANA database and benefit from the advantages it provides.

In the first part of this chapter, we introduce the software components of SAP HANA. We'll then describe the basic principles of the in-memory technology and the architecture of the SAP HANA database. To conclude this chapter, we'll present application cases for SAP HANA and explain the impact SAP HANA has on application development.

1.1   Software Components of SAP HANA

SAP HANA is comprised of the following software components, which will be explained in greater detail in the following sections (see Figure 1.1):

- **Core components**
  SAP HANA database, SAP HANA Studio, SAP HANA Client, SAP HANA Application Function Libraries (AFL—an optional component)

- **Software for data replication**
  SAP LT Replication Add-on and Server, SAP HANA Direct Extractor Connection (DXC), SAP BusinessObjects Data Services

- **Software for direct data preparation**
  SAP HANA Client Package for Microsoft Excel, SAP HANA User Interface for Information Access (INA), SAP HANA Information Composer

- **Lifecycle management components**
  SAP Host Agent, Software Update Manager for SAP HANA, SAP Solution Manager Diagnostics Agent

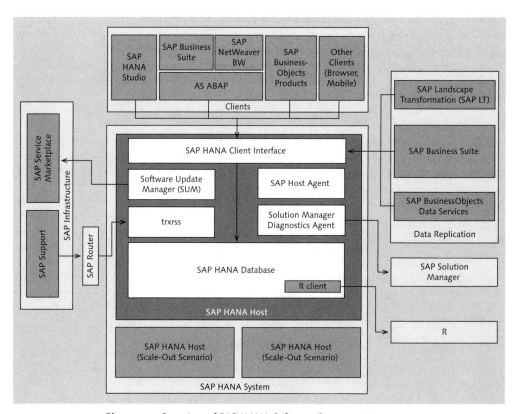

Figure 1.1 Overview of SAP HANA Software Components

The following sections explain the structure of these components and their usage. In this context, we'll focus on aspects that are relevant for application development.

1.1.1 SAP HANA Database

As a full relational database, SAP HANA provides functions similar to other relational ("traditional") databases that are supported by SAP. Like these traditional databases, SAP HANA provides functions for data backup and recovery, supports the SQL standard (SQL 92 Entry-Level and some SQL 99 extensions), and guarantees data consistency by following the ACID principle (atomicity, consistency, isolation, durability) when executing transactions.

Relational database

In contrast to other relational databases, SAP HANA can place all relevant business data in the main memory. It combines row-, column-, and object-based database technologies and was optimized for the usage of parallel processing functionality provided by modern hardware technologies. With this, you can use multi-core and multi-CPU architectures to their fullest potential. You can thus optimize existing applications for the new technology and develop applications that you could only dream of with traditional database technologies.

The SAP HANA database provides its own programming language (*SQLScript*) that can be used to express data-intensive application logic. In addition to SQLScript, SAP HANA provides highly optimized libraries for specific *business functions* or *predictive analyses*. The functions of these libraries can be called using SQLScript (see Section 1.1.4). Moreover, for statistical calculations there is a connection to the R software system (see *http://www.r-project.org/*).

Functionality

The internal architecture of the SAP HANA database is explained in more detail in Section 1.3.

1.1.2 SAP HANA Studio

SAP HANA Studio is comprised of the administration and development environment. This solution is based on the Eclipse platform, which is SAP's strategic choice for new development tools. An Eclipse-based development

Eclipse development environment

environment is now also available for ABAP (*ABAP Development Tools for SAP NetWeaver*). We'll particularly use this environment for the tasks described in this book.

[»]

> **Note: Eclipse and its Significance for SAP**
>
> Eclipse is a platform for development tools and environments (e.g., for Java, C/C++, or PHP). It is maintained and further developed by the Eclipse Foundation (see *http://eclipse.org*). As an active member of the Eclipse Foundation, SAP supports the organization in several projects.
>
> In addition to SAP HANA Studio and the ABAP Development Tools for SAP NetWeaver, the following SAP development environments are based on Eclipse:
>
> ▶ SAP NetWeaver Developer Studio (Java)
> ▶ SAP Eclipse Tools for SAP HANA Cloud Platform
> ▶ SAP UI Development Tools for HTML5
> ▶ SAP NetWeaver Gateway Plug-in for Eclipse
>
> One of the main advantages of the Eclipse platform is the ability to integrate different tools into one installation so that the user benefits from a homogeneous development environment. Particularly useful is the possibility to install the ABAP Development Tools in SAP HANA Studio, which is described in Section 2.4.

SAP HANA Studio: usage areas

As an example, administrators can use SAP HANA Studio for the following tasks:

▶ Starting and stopping database services
▶ Monitoring the system
▶ Specifying system settings
▶ Maintaining users and authorizations
▶ Configuring the audit log

Administering SAP HANA will not be the focus of this book. Please refer to the documentation at *http://help.sap.com/hana_appliance*. As a developer, however, you can create so-called *content* (in the form of views or database processes, for example) using SAP HANA Studio. These development artifacts are stored in the *repository* of the SAP HANA database. The development environment of SAP HANA Studio is explained in detail in Chapter 2, Chapter 4, and Chapter 5.

1.1.3 SAP HANA Client

Using the SAP HANA Client, you can connect to the SAP HANA database via a network protocol. The following standards are supported (see Figure 1.2): Connection protocols

- *ODBC* (Open Database Connectivity) and *JDBC* (Java Database Connectivity) for SQL-based access
- *ODBO* (OLE DB for OLAP) for *MDX*-based access (multi-dimensional expressions)

Internally, in particular the proprietary *SQLDBC library* (SQL Database Connectivity) from SAP is used.

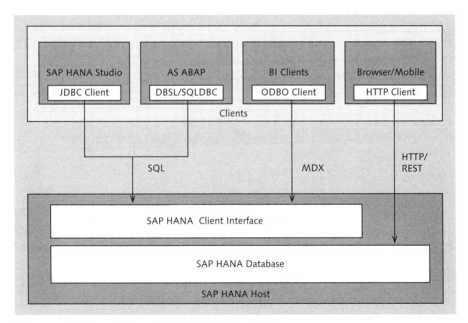

Figure 1.2 Options for Accessing SAP HANA via Clients

As the Eclipse platform is Java-based, SAP HANA Studio uses the JDBC client to establish the connection. This variant is also used in Java-based application servers.

The SAP NetWeaver Application Server (AS) ABAP uses the so-called *Database Specific Library* (DBSL) (which is embedded in the SQLDBC client) to Connecting AS ABAP connect to the SAP HANA database. The database interface architecture of the AS ABAP is explained in detail in Chapter 3.

BI clients Special *BI* clients (business intelligence), such as add-ins for Microsoft Excel, typically use MDX-based access for multi-dimensional queries that are executed via the ODBO client. In addition, SAP HANA offers direct HTTP access using the *XS Engine*, which is explained in Section 1.3.

1.1.4 SAP HANA Function Libraries

Application Function Libraries The functional scope of SAP HANA can be extended using special function libraries (*Application Function Libraries, AFL*) written in C++. With the current release level SAP HANA SPS5, these libraries must be installed manually using the SAP HANA on-site configuration tool after installing the database (see Section 1.1.6).

SAP HANA currently provides two application function libraries: the *Business Function Library* (BFL) with its own standard business functions, and the *Predictive Analysis Library* (PAL) for data mining and predictions based on existing historical data.

The usage of these function libraries is described in greater detail in Chapter 12.

1.1.5 Software for Data Replication

Initial and delta load For many application scenarios (for instance, the *side-by-side scenarios* described in Section 1.4), you must use data from existing systems in SAP HANA. The process of first replicating data structures and then an existing data set (*initial load*) is called *data replication*. If the data is subsequently changed in the original system (for example, after creating a new business partner), the mirrored data is updated as well (*delta load*). The existing systems can be systems of the SAP Business Suite, SAP NetWeaver BW, or any other data source.

Options for data replication Depending on the data source and usage scenario, different mechanisms and tools can be used for replication. Within the scope of this book, setting up or executing data-replication functions will not be explained in further detail. Table 1.1 provides a short overview of the replication options that are currently supported by SAP HANA.

Replication via	Technical Details	Usage Scenarios
SAP Landscape Transformation Replication Server (SAP LT)	▶ Table replication based on database triggers ▶ Minimal time offset (near real-time)	Table-based replication from SAP Business Suite to SAP HANA
SAP Data Services	▶ ETL-based replication (extraction, transformation, load) using a design tool for data-flow modeling ▶ Time offset, depending on the job server configuration	Flexible use of SAP and non-SAP data with additional data-management capabilities
Direct Extractor Connection (DXC)	▶ Direct ETL-based replication (no middleware) ▶ Time offset, depending on the job scheduling	Connecting existing data extractors, e.g., from the SAP Business Suite

Table 1.1 Overview of Replication Options

For extensive, up-to-date technical information on these variants and their usage scenarios, please see the SAP HANA Master Guide.

1.1.6 Software for Direct Data Access

For easy, direct access to data models in SAP HANA, SAP offers several tools that are introduced in this section.

To directly access analytical models in SAP HANA from Microsoft Excel for simple reporting scenarios, you can use the *SAP HANA Client Package for Microsoft Excel*. This package uses the ODBO client internally for MDX-based access to SAP HANA (see Section 1.1.3). In the following chapters, this variant is primarily used for testing our analytical models.

Client Package for Microsoft Excel

Using the *SAP HANA UI for Information Access*, you can easily create browser-based user interfaces for searches that can be executed directly on tables or data models in SAP HANA.

UI for Information Access

Information
Composer

And finally, the *SAP HANA Information Composer* provides an alternative method for creating simple, analytical views based on imported, external data; this method is primarily intended for end-users, while the modeling options in SAP HANA Studio are instead designed for developers. To use this tool, a separate Java application server is required. We will not examine this tool in any detail within the scope of this book.

1.1.7 Lifecycle Management Components

For the sake of completeness, this section briefly describes the SAP HANA components used for landscape integration and *Application Lifecycle Managements (ALM)*.

On-site
configuration tool

SAP HANA is usually installed by a certified SAP hardware partner. To change the configuration of the SAP HANA appliance after installation, system administrators use the *on-site configuration tool*. Using this tool, you can set up additional SAP HANA systems on the same appliance, rename systems, set up a connection to SAP Solution Manager, or install an additional function library (as mentioned in Section 1.1.4), to name a few examples.

SAP Host Agent
and SUM

Each SAP HANA host runs the *SAP Host Agent,* which makes it possible to monitor the individual hosts and their corresponding instances; this information is then made available for central monitoring via web services (e.g., via the *SAP Management Console*).

Using the *Software Update Manager for SAP HANA (SUM)*, you can download and automatically install new *support packages* (SPs) of the installed components from the *SAP Service Marketplace*.

Support

In case of an error, you can run an analysis by setting up a connection between your SAP HANA installation and the SAP Support that provides restricted access via the SAP standard support infrastructure (especially *SAProuter*). Using the *Diagnostics Agent* on the SAP HANA appliance, SAP Solution Manager moreover provides comprehensive options for technical monitoring of your SAP HANA system in the context of standard ALM processes (e.g., *root cause analysis* or *SAP EarlyWatch Alert*).

1.2 Basic Principles of In-Memory Technology

This section describes some of the basic principles of the in-memory technology and special innovations in SAP HANA with regard to both hardware and software. Although not all of these aspects have a direct impact on the development of ABAP applications for SAP HANA, we consider it important to explain the basic concepts of SAP HANA and their implementation, since this will help you understand some of the design recommendations within this book.

In recent years, two major hardware trends dominated not only the SAP world, but the market as a whole:

Hardware trends

▶ Instead of further increasing the clock speed per CPU core (central processing unit), the number of CPU cores per CPU was increased.

▶ Sinking prices for the main memory (random access memory, RAM) have led to increasing memory sizes.

Section 1.2.1 further explains the hardware innovations of SAP HANA.

For software manufacturers, stagnating clock speeds are somewhat problematic at first. In the past, it could be assumed that clock speeds would increase in the future, so software code would be executed faster on future hardware. With the current trends, however, you can't safely make that assumption. Since you can't increase the speed of sequential executions simply by using future hardware, you instead have to run software code in parallel to reach the desired performance gains. Section 1.2.2 introduces such software optimizations in SAP HANA.

Software optimizations

1.2.1 Hardware Innovations

To benefit from these hardware trends, SAP has been working in close cooperation with hardware manufacturers during the development of SAP HANA. Consequently, the SAP HANA database currently only runs on hardware certified by SAP.

Hardware partners

Certified Hardware for SAP HANA [«]

The currently certified hardware for SAP HANA is listed in the Product Availability Matrix (PAM) of the SAP Service Marketplace under *http://service.sap.com/pam*. To view this list, search this site for *SAP HANA*.

This hardware list currently includes the Intel Westmere-EX architecture (Intel XEON Processor E7 family) which contains up to 8 CPUs per server node with 10 CPU cores each. Older systems still use the Nehalem-EX architecture (Intel Xeon Processor X75xx family) with up to eight CPUs and 8 cores each. A server node provides up to four TB RAM.

The number of both CPUs and CPU cores, as well as the RAM size, might be increased in the future (often referred to as *scale-up*). For early 2014, for instance, usage of the announced Intel Xeon Processor E7 V2 family (Ivy Bridge EX) will provide a significantly higher number of cores and bigger main memory size.

Scale-out
For SAP NetWeaver BW (see Section 1.4), a so-called *scale-out* is possible, where up to 16 server nodes (some manufacturers even allow for up to 56 server nodes) can be combined with one TB RAM. This way, systems with up to 128 CPUs, 1,280 CPU cores, and 16 TB RAM can be set up. For internal tests, systems with up to 100 TB RAM and 4,000 CPU cores are currently already combined.

Access times
Due to the large RAM size, the I/O system (persistent storage) is basically no longer accessed for reading accesses to SAP HANA (at least, not if all data is loaded into the main memory). In contrast to traditional databases, data transport from the I/O system to the main memory is no longer a bottleneck. Instead, with SAP HANA the speed of the data transport between the main memory and the CPUs via the different *CPU caches* (there are usually three cache levels) is of central importance. In the following sections, these access times are discussed in more detail.

Hard disks
Current hard disks provide 15,000 rpm. Assuming that the disk needs 0.5 rotations on average per access, two milliseconds are already needed for these 0.5 rotations. In addition to this, the times for positioning the read/write head and the transfer time must be added, which results in a total of about six to eight milliseconds. This corresponds to the typical hard-disk access times if the actual hard disk (i.e., not a cache in the I/O subsystem or on the hard disk) is accessed.

Flash memory
When using Flash memory, no mechanical parts need be moved. This results in access times of about 200 microseconds. In SAP HANA, performance-critical data is placed in this type of memory and then loaded into the main memory.

Access to the main memory, (or DRAM, dynamic random access memory) is even faster. Typical access times are 60 to 100 nanoseconds. The exact access time depends on the access location within memory. With the *NUMA architecture* (non-uniform memory access) used in SAP HANA, a processor can access its own local memory faster than memory that is within the same system but is being managed by other processors. With the currently certified systems, this memory area has a size of up to four TB.

Main memory

Access times to caches in the CPU are usually indicated as *clock ticks*. In case of a CPU with a clock speed of 2.4 GHz, a cycle takes about 0.42 nanoseconds. The hardware certified for SAP HANA uses three caches, referred to as *L1 to L3 cache*. L1 cache can be accessed in three to four clock ticks, L2 cache in about ten clock ticks, and L3 cache in about 40 clock ticks. L1 cache has a size of 64 KB, L2 cache of 256 KB, and L3 cache of 30 MB. Each server comprises only one L3 cache which is used by all CPUs, while each CPU has its own L2 and L1 cache. This is illustrated in Figure 1.3. Table 1.2 lists the typical access times.

CPU cache

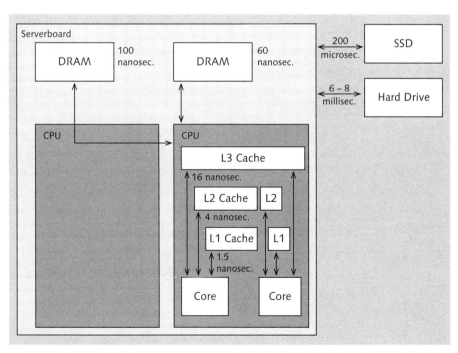

Figure 1.3 Access Time

Memory	Access Time in Nanoseconds	Access Time
Hard disk	6,000,000–8,000,000	6–8 milliseconds
Flash memory	200,000	200 microseconds
Main memory (DRAM)	60–100	60–100 nanoseconds
L3 cache (CPU)	16 (about 40 cycles)	16 nanoseconds
L2 cache (CPU)	4 (about 10 cycles)	4 nanoseconds
L1 cache (CPU)	1.5 (about 3–4 cycles)	1.5 nanoseconds
CPU register	< 1 (1 cycle)	< 1 nanosecond

Table 1.2 Typical Access Times

The times listed depend not only on the clock speed, but also on the configuration settings, the number of memory modules, the memory type, and many other factors. They are provided only as a reference for the typical access times of each memory type.

Main memory as the new bottleneck

When sizing an SAP HANA system, enough capacity should be assigned to place all data in the main memory so that all reading accesses can usually be executed on this memory. When accessing the data for the first time (e.g., after starting the system), the data is loaded into the main memory. You can also manually or automatically *unload* the data from the main memory. This can be necessary if, for example, the system tries to use more than the available memory size.

In the past, access to the hard disk was usually the performance bottleneck; with SAP HANA, however, main memory access is now the bottleneck. Even though these accesses are up to 100,000 times faster than hard-disk accesses, they are still four to 60 times slower than accesses to CPU caches, which is why the main memory is the new bottleneck for SAP HANA.

Memory algorithms

The algorithms in SAP HANA are implemented in such a way that they can work directly with the L1 cache in the CPU wherever possible. Data transport from the main memory to the CPU caches must therefore be kept to a minimum—which has major effects on the software innovations described in the next section.

1.2.2 Software Innovations

The software innovations in SAP HANA make optimal use of the previously described hardware. This is done through two ways: By keeping the data transport between the main memory and CPU caches to a minimum (e.g., by means of compression), and by fully leveraging the CPUs using parallel threads for data processing.

SAP HANA provides software optimizations in the following areas:

- Data layout in the main memory
- Compression
- Partitioning

These three areas are discussed in more detail in the following subsections.

Data Layout in the Main Memory

In every relational database, the entries of a database table must be stored in a certain *data layout*—independent of whether this representation is done in the main memory (as in case of SAP HANA) or by following the traditional approach using a physical medium. Basically, two completely different options are available for this: *row-based* and *column-based* data storage. SAP HANA supports both approaches. The concepts and their differences are explained next.

We'll first take a look at row-based data storage in the row store of SAP HANA. In this store, all data pertaining to a row (e.g., the data in Table 1.3) is placed next to each other (see Figure 1.4) which facilitates access to entire rows. Accessing all values of a column is a little more complex, however, since these values cannot be transferred from the main memory to the CPU as efficiently as in the case of column-based data storage. Data compression, which will be explained in the next section, is also less efficient with this storage approach.

Row store

41

Name	Location	Gender
...	...	...
Brown	Chicago	M
Doe	San Francisco	F
Smith	Dallas	M
...	...	...

Table 1.3 Sample Data to Explain the Row and Column Store

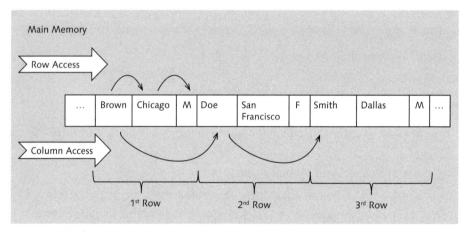

Figure 1.4 Illustration of Row-Based Data Storage in the Row Store

Column store Let's now take a look at column-based data storage in the column store. Column-based data storage is nothing really new; rather, this type of storage was already used in Data Warehouse applications and analysis scenarios in the past. In transactional scenarios, however, only row-based storage had been used thus far (such as in the row store described already).

Figure 1.5 shows a schematic representation of the sample data from Table 1.3 in a column-based storage. The contents of a column are placed next to each other in the main memory. This means that all operations accessing a column will find the required information nearby, which has favorable effects on the data transport between the main memory and the CPU. If a lot of data or all data from a row is needed, however, this approach is disadvantageous because this data is *not* nearby. Column-based data storage facilitates efficient compression and aggregation of data based on a column.

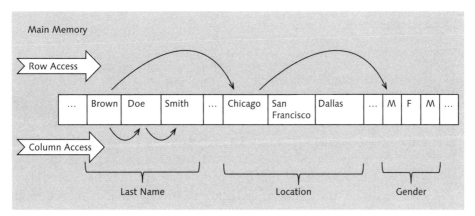

Figure 1.5 Illustration of Column-Based Data Storage in the Column Store

As you can see, both approaches have advantages and disadvantages. With SAP HANA, you can specify the storage approach to be used for each table. Business data are almost always placed in column-based storage, since the advantages of this approach outweigh its disadvantages. However, some tables (or their main access type) require row-based data storage. These are primarily either very small or very volatile tables where the time required for write accesses is more important than the time required for read accesses, or in technical tables where single-record accesses (e.g., via ABAP command SELECT SINGLE) are the main access pattern.

Flexible data storage

Compression

The SAP HANA database provides a series of compression techniques that can be used for the data in the column store, both in the main memory and in the persistence. High data compression has a positive impact on runtime, since it reduces amount of data that needs to be transferred from the main memory to the CPU. SAP HANA's compression techniques are very efficient with regard to runtime, and can provide an average compression factor of five to ten compared to data that has not been compressed.

The compression techniques listed next are based on dictionary encoding, where the column contents are stored as encoded integers in the

Dictionary encoding

attribute vector. In this context, encoding means "translating" the content of a field into an integer value.

To store the contents of a column, the SAP HANA database creates a minimum of two data structures:

- a dictionary vector
- an attribute vector

Dictionary vector

The *dictionary vector* stores each value of a column only once. This means that the GENDER column for our sample data from Table 1.3 only contains the values "M" and "F" in the corresponding dictionary vector. For the LOCATION column, there are three values: Chicago, San Francisco, and Dallas. The contents of the dictionary vector are stored as sorted data. The position in the dictionary vector maps each value to an integer. In our example, this is 1 for gender "M" and 2 for gender "F". In the dictionary vector for the location, integer 5 stands for Chicago, integer 6 for San Francisco, and integer 7 for Dallas. As this value can implicitly be derived from its position (first value, second value, etc.), no additional storage is required.

The dictionary vectors for the sample data from Table 1.4 are displayed in the upper half of Figure 1.6. Only the data shaded in gray is explicitly stored in memory.

Record	Last name	Location	Gender
...	...	...	...
3	Brown	Chicago	M
4	Brown	San Francisco	F
5	Doe	Dallas	M
6	Doe	San Francisco	F
7	Smith	Dallas	M
...	...	...	...

Table 1.4 Sample Data for Dictionary Encoding and Compression

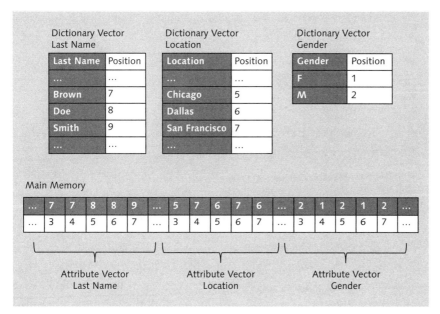

Figure 1.6 Dictionary Encoding

The attribute vector now only stores the integer values (the position in the dictionary). As in case of traditional databases, the order of the records is generally not defined.

Attribute vector

The last name "Smith" was placed in the dictionary vector for last names. From its position in this vector, a value can implicitly be derived (the value 9 in our example). This value, again, is now always stored at the position for the last name "Smith" in the attribute vector for the last name; in our example, this is the seventh record of the sample data from Table 1.4. Another example is the location "San Francisco", which is stored at position 7 in the dictionary vector for the location and appears for rows 4 and 6 in the attribute vector for the location (Table 1.4). The attribute vectors are shown in the lower part of Figure 1.6. In this figure, all three attribute vectors are shown consecutively to show that all data (also the dictionary vectors) is stored in a "data stream" in the main memory and addressed via memory references and offsets. Here, only the sections shaded in gray in Figure 1.6 are actually stored in the main memory. The row numbers displayed below those sections do not need any storage space and are again implicitly derived from their position in the attribute vector. They correspond to the position in our sample Table 1.4 (first record, second record, etc.).

Advantages of storing integer values

The fact that the data is only stored as integer values in the attribute vectors provides the following advantages:

- Lower storage requirements for values that occur several times
- Accelerated data transfer from the main memory to CPU caches since less data needs to be transported
- Faster processing of integer values (instead of strings) in the CPU

Moreover, additional compression techniques can be used for both dictionary vectors and attribute vectors. These are introduced in more detail later on.

Delta compression

For the dictionary vector, *delta compression* is used for *strings*. With this compression technique, every character from a string in a block with 16 entries (for example) is stored only once in a delta string. Repeated characters are stored as references. Other data types are maintained as sorted arrays.

[Ex]

Delta Compression

The following entries are present: Brian, Bus, Britain, Brush. After delta compression, this results in: 5Brian12us34tain23ush. The first digit indicates the length of the first entry (Brian = 5). The digit pairs between the other entries contain the information for reconstruction. The first digit indicates the length of the prefix from the first entry, the second digit indicates the number of characters that are appended by the subsequent part. Consequently, "12us" means that one character from "Brian" is used and that two more characters are added ("us"); "34tain" means that the first three characters from Brian ("Bri") are used and that four more characters are added ("tain"). And "23ush" finally means that the first two characters from "Brian" are used and three more characters ("ush") are added.

Compression in the attribute vector

For the attribute vector, one of the following compression techniques can be used:

- **Prefix encoding**
  Identical values at the beginning of the attribute vector (prefixes) are left out; instead, a value and the number of its occurrences is stored only once.

- ▸ **Sparse encoding**
  The individual records from the value with the most occurrences are removed; instead, the positions of these entries are stored in a bit vector.

- ▸ **Cluster encoding**
  Cluster encoding uses data blocks of perhaps 1,024 values each. Only blocks with a different value are compressed by storing only the value. Information on the compressed blocks is then stored in a bit vector.

- ▸ **Indirect encoding**
  Indirect encoding also uses data blocks of 1,024 values each. For every block, a mini-dictionary is created that is similar to the dictionary vector in the dictionary encoding described above. In some cases, a mini-dictionary may be shared for adjacent blocks. This compression technique provides another level of abstraction.

- ▸ **Run-length encoding**
  With run-length encoding, identical successive values are combined into one single data value. This value is then stored only once together with the number of its occurrences.

SAP HANA analyzes the data in a column and then automatically chooses one of the compression techniques described. Table 1.5 presents a typical application case for each compression technique.

Automatic selection of the compression technique

Compression Technique	Application Case
Prefix encoding	A very frequent value at the beginning of the attribute vector
Sparse encoding	A very frequent value occurring at several positions
Cluster encoding	Many blocks with only one value
Indirect encoding	Many blocks with few different values
Run-length encoding	A few different values, consecutive identical values
Dictionary encoding	Many different values

Table 1.5 Overview of Compression Techniques

Read-optimized main store

The memory structures presented so far (consisting of sorted dictionary vectors and attribute vectors with integer values), which might still be compressed in some cases, are optimized for read access. These structures are also referred to as the *main store*. They are not optimally suited for write accesses, though. For this reason, SAP HANA provides an additional area that is optimized for write access: the *delta store*. This store is explained in detail in Appendix C. In this appendix, another memory structure is also described: indexes. Moreover, Appendix C explains why SAP HANA is called an *insert-only database*.

Partitioning

Let's now take a look at the third area of software innovation: partitioning. Partitioning is used whenever very large quantities of data must be maintained and managed.

Advantages of partitioning

This technique greatly facilitates data management for database administrators. A typical task is the deletion of data (such as after an archiving operation was completed successfully). There is no need to search large amounts of information for the data to be deleted; instead, database administrators can simply remove an entire partition. Moreover, partitioning can increase application performance.

Partitioning variants

There are basically two technical variants of partitioning:

▶ With *vertical partitioning*, tables are divided into smaller sections on a column basis. For a table with seven columns, column 1 to 5 could perhaps be stored in one partition, while column 6 and 7 are stored in a different partition.

▶ With *horizontal partitioning*, tables are divided into smaller sections on a row basis. Rows 1 to 1,000,000 are then perhaps stored in one partition, while rows 1,000,001 to 2,000,000 are placed in another partition.

SAP HANA supports only horizontal partitioning. The data in a table is distributed across different partitions on a row basis, while the records within the partitions are stored on a column basis.

The example in Figure 1.7 shows how horizontal partitioning is used for a table with the two columns *Name* and *Gender* in case of column-based data storage. On the left side, the table is shown with a dictionary vector (DV) and an attribute vector (AV) for both the column *Name* and the column *Gender*. On the right side, the data was partitioned using the round-robin technique, which will be explained in more detail next. The consecutive rows were distributed across two partitions by turns (the first row was stored in the first partition, the second row in the second partition, the third row again in the first partition, and so on).

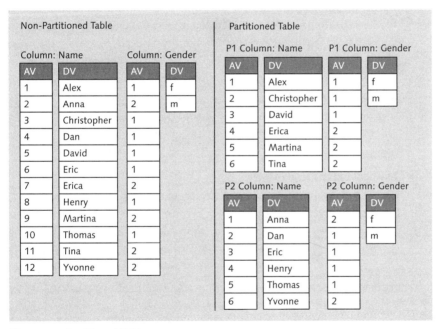

Figure 1.7 Partitioned Table

Partitioning should be used in the following application scenarios:

▶ **Load distribution**
If SAP HANA runs on multiple servers, the data from very large tables can be distributed across several servers by storing the individual partitions of the tables on different servers. Table queries are then distributed across the servers where a partition of the table is stored. This

way, the resources of several computers can be used for a query and several computers can process the query in parallel.

▶ **Parallelization**

Parallelization is not only possible across multiple servers, but also on a single server. When a query is run, a separate process is started for each partition and these processes are processed in parallel in the partitions. Please note that parallelization across partitions is only one variant of parallelization in SAP HANA. There are other types of parallelization that can be used independent of partitioned tables.

▶ **Partition pruning**

With partition pruning, the database (or the database *optimizer*) recognizes that certain partitions do not need to be read. Example: If a table containing sales data is partitioned based on the column *Sales organization* so that every sales organization is stored in a separate partition, only a certain partition is read when a query is run that needs data just from the sales organization in that partition; the other partitions are not read. This process reduces the data transport between the main memory and CPU.

▶ **Explicit partition handling**

In some cases, partitions are specifically used by applications. Example: If a table is partitioned based on the column *Month*, an application can create a new partition for a new month and delete old data from a previous month by deleting the entire partition. Deleting this data is very efficient, since administrators do not need to search for the information to be deleted, but can simply delete the entire partition using a *DDL statement* (*data definition language*).

[»] | **Partitioning to Circumvent the Row Limit**

The SAP HANA database currently has a limit of two billion rows per table. If a table should comprise more rows, it must be partitioned. Each partition must again not contain more than two billion rows. The same limit currently applies to temporary tables that are, for example, used to store interim results. SAP is working on increasing these limits.

Now that you are familiar with the concept of partitioning and suitable application scenarios, we'd like to introduce the types of partitioning available in SAP HANA:

- ▶ **Hash partitioning**
  Hash partitioning is primarily used for load distribution, or in situations where tables with more than two billion records must be maintained. With this type of partitioning, data is distributed evenly across the specified number of partitions based on a calculated key (*hash*). Hash partitioning supports partition pruning.

- ▶ **Round-robin partitioning**
  With round-robin partitioning, data is also distributed evenly across a specified number of partitions so that this type is also suitable for load distribution or for very large tables. Round-robin partitioning does not require a key; instead, the data is simply distributed in sequence. If a table is divided into two partitions, for example, the first record is stored in the first partition, the second record is stored in the second partition, the third record is again stored in the first partition, and so on (see Figure 1.7). Round-robin partitioning does not support partition pruning.

- ▶ **Range partitioning**
  With range partitioning, the data is distributed based on values in a column. You can, for example, create a partition for every year of a column *Year* or create a partition for three months of a column *Month*. In addition, you can create a partition for *remainders* if records are inserted that do not belong in any of the ranges of the partitions you created. Range partitioning supports partition pruning.

These partitioning types can be combined in a two-step approach. For instance, you could use hash partitioning in the first step and then, in a second step, use range partitioning within this hash partitioning.

1.3   Architecture of the In-Memory Database

This section introduces important aspects of the SAP HANA database architecture. Figure 1.8 shows the main components of the architecture.

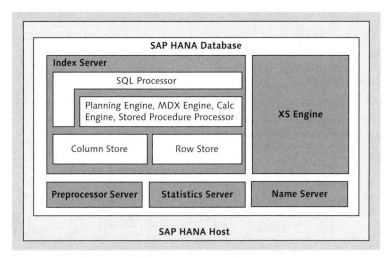

Figure 1.8 Architecture of the SAP HANA Database

Server and engine components

The following section provides a detailed description of all of these architecture components, which can be subdivided into two component types:

- **Server**
  Server components are processes and services that are run on the operating system.

- **Engines**
  Engines are functional components within a server that are used to handle certain queries.

Index server

The SAP HANA database comprises several servers; the most important one is the *index server,* which is used to process SQL commands. The index server itself contains several components: The *SQL processor* receives and accepts the SQL commands and either runs them directly or forwards the commands to a subordinate component. These subordinate components can be either a central data storage (i.e., the column store or the row store) or one of the engines. All data that is currently being used is either stored in the column store or in the row store. This data is read directly from these stores or, in case of complex queries, processed via one of the engines. There are multiple engines that can be used for activities such as planning functions, for multidimensional expressions (MDX), or for database procedures (*stored procedures*). These engines all were optimized for special data processing tasks that can be called if required.

The *preprocessor server* is used for the text-search function integrated in SAP HANA and primarily analyzes text data. If needed, this server is called by the index server.

Preprocessor, statistics, and name server

The *statistics server* is used for monitoring the SAP HANA database. It collects information on status, performance, and resource consumption of the individual components, and it creates historical views based on this data. SAP HANA Studio accesses this information via the statistics server.

The *name server* maintains the information on the topology of the SAP HANA database, or information regarding the distribution of the software components and data.

To provide a complete list of the SAP HANA database servers, we'll now describe the *XS* Engine (*SAP HANA Extended Application Services*). This engine is a simple application server that can be accessed directly via HTTP/a web browser. Using the XS Engine and server-side JavaScript, you can currently develop web applications that access things such as data models or text searches in SAP HANA and expose them as *RESTful Services* (representational state transfer). In this context, the OData and HTML5 are used. Section 10.2.1 provides a brief overview over OData and HTML5.

SAP HANA Extended Application Services

1.4 Application Cases for SAP HANA

This section explains the different application cases for SAP HANA. These application cases can be subdivided into two groups:

- **Side-by-side scenarios**
  In a side-by-side scenario, SAP HANA is implemented in addition to an existing traditional database (*primary database*). Certain applications read the data needed from SAP HANA instead of the primary database. In this case, SAP HANA is used as a *secondary database* and comprises data that was replicated from the primary database. Using this approach, access times can be significantly improved.

- **Integrated scenarios**
  In an integrated scenario, existing applications are migrated to SAP HANA and the traditional database is replaced with SAP HANA. SAP HANA becomes the primary database.

Figure 1.9 shows two typical side-by-side scenarios: *accelerators* and *SAP HANA applications*.

Accelerator scenarios

In an *accelerator scenario*, the data from the traditional database is replicated to an SAP HANA database. Certain reading database accesses within existing applications are redirected to SAP HANA. This can be done using different procedures. In most cases, this redirection is done via separate database connections and small changes to the ABAP source code.

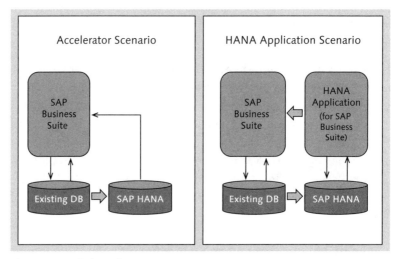

Figure 1.9   Side-by-Side Scenarios

> **[Ex]   SAP CO-PA Accelerator**
>
> The SAP CO-PA Accelerator (cost profitability analysis) is used to implement an accelerator scenario and is probably one of the best-known examples of a side-by-side scenario. However, there are further examples from finance and controlling, or customer relationship management (CRM). An overview can be found in SAP Note 1761546.

You can also redirect customer-developed ABAP programs using an accelerator scenario, and thus implement them in a side-by-side scenario. For the *SAP Business Application Accelerator powered by SAP HANA* (see Appendix D), redirection is done via a special SAP kernel and adjustments in Customizing; please note that it is not necessary to change ABAP source code for this accelerator.

Other side-by-side scenarios are new applications in the context of the SAP Business Suite that were developed for SAP HANA. These are applications that use SAP HANA functions and other modern technologies like HTML5. They are based mainly on data that was replicated from the SAP Business Suite and can write back result data via remote-enabled interfaces. Examples are the segmentation of CRM customer data on SAP HANA and the creation of campaigns in CRM. In addition to those applications, there are new applications that are not based on existing data from the SAP Business Suite, but are run on SAP HANA as stand-alone applications with their own data basis instead. Amongst others, these include applications for utilities working with *smart meter data*, for example from smart electricity meters.

SAP HANA applications

In an integrated scenario, application packages are run entirely on SAP HANA. These can for example be SAP Business One, the SAP Business Suite, or SAP NetWeaver BW. One of the innovations in the SAP Business Suite on SAP HANA is the *virtual data model* (*VDM*). VDMs are analytical models that make data from the SAP Business Suite available for reporting purposes in a consistent manner and via open interfaces. This scenario does not require data replication and SAP HANA is implemented as the primary database.

Integrated scenarios

Figure 1.10 illustrates this scenario: all applications or application packages are run directly on SAP HANA.

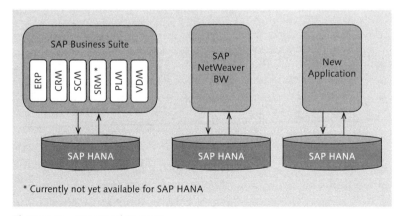

Figure 1.10 Integrated Scenario

You should now have an overview of the application options of SAP HANA. The following section explains what moving to SAP HANA means for developers.

1.5   How SAP HANA Affects Application Development

Having explained the basic principles of the in-memory technology and the architecture of the SAP HANA database, you may now be asking yourself how the described hardware and software innovations affect application development with ABAP. This question will be answered in the following sections.

Many rules are still valid
Note the following: Not everything changes when implementing SAP HANA. Like in the past, you can develop powerful applications using ABAP even if these applications use SAP HANA as a database. Many of the rules for ABAP programming that you are familiar with (e.g., the rules for efficient database access—also known as the *five golden rules*, see Section 14.4) will essentially still be valid.

So what changes for application development in ABAP? In the following section, we'll describe the technical options that benefit ABAP developers when using SAP HANA and we'll explain the *code pushdown* concept. You'll learn why the database can no longer be considered a *black box* in the future, and which skills you should acquire.

1.5.1   New Technical Options

Optimization potential
Using SAP HANA, you can support several application scenarios—as described in Section 1.4. From an ABAP developer's point of view, using SAP HANA provides the following new technical options:

- ▶ **Accelerate**
  Using SAP HANA, you can accelerate existing ABAP programs. On the one hand, this allows you to significantly reduce the time needed to run background jobs. On the other hand, you can improve the

immediate response time for queries triggered by end-users within dialog transactions.

▶ **Extend**

You can use SAP HANA to customize and extend existing applications in a way that goes beyond solely accelerating these applications. Some ABAP programs that could only be run as background jobs in the past due to their response behavior can now be converted into interactive dialog transactions with SAP HANA. Moreover, you can enhance usability and functionality of ABAP dialog transactions by implementing SAP HANA. Such improvements include embedded analyses and fault-tolerant full-text searches.

▶ **Innovate**

Finally, you can develop new, innovative applications and application types using ABAP and SAP HANA. In this context, convergence of *online transactional processing* (OLTP) and *online analytical processing* (OLAP) and so-called *hybrid applications* are often mentioned. Hybrid applications combine transactional and analytical functions within a single system so that end-users can take direct steps based on insights they gained in real time from data analyses (for example, supported by statistical algorithms for predictions based on historic data).

1.5.2   Code Pushdown

For applications that take advantage of the hardware and software innovations in SAP HANA described in Section 1.2, at least part of the application logic must be executed in the database. This is especially important if complex calculations with large data amounts have to be performed. The process of moving application code from the application layer to the database layer is often referred to as *code pushdown*.

Traditionally, ABAP-based applications use the so-called *data-to-code paradigm*. Applications optimized or developed specifically for SAP HANA, however, use the *code-to-data paradigm*. The following section describes the differences between the two paradigms (see Figure 1.11).

Different paradigms

57

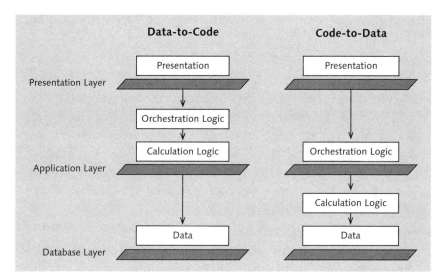

Figure 1.11 The Code Pushdown Principle

Data-to-code As you can see in Figure 1.11, the application data is placed in the database layer when using the data-to-code paradigm. Basically, the application logic–comprised of orchestration logic and calculation logic—is executed entirely in the application layer. The presentation logic is executed in the presentation layer.

[»] **Elements of the Application Logic**

In the following, the application logic is subdivided into two sections:

▸ The *orchestration logic* controls business processes and the data flow and determines how calculation results are combined and further processed.

Example: Once a flight booking is saved, the system automatically sends an email to the traveler.

▸ The *calculation logic* identifies algorithms used to perform calculations based on the application data.

Example: To suggest the "best" flight to a traveler, the system analyzes historical flight and booking data prior to a booking and then calculates a score per flight.

For ABAP programs, this means: A data-to-code application reads the records from the database. The records are then often buffered in internal tables of the application server. The application logic is implemented based on this principle. For presentation, the records or the data calculated based on these records are transferred to the front-end—SAP GUI, SAP NetWeaver Portal, or SAP NetWeaver Business Client. With this procedure, it's possible to send millions of records from the database to the application server, even though only a few hundred calculated key figures will be displayed for the end user.

When using the code-to-data paradigm, the application data is also placed in the database layer. However, some of the application logic is executed in the application layer, while some of it is implemented in the database layer. In an extreme case, the entire application logic can be executed in the database layer. Nothing fundamentally changes in the execution of the presentation logic.

Code-to-data

When applying this paradigm to an ABAP program, this means: The data of a code-to-data application is stored in the database. The orchestration logic is implemented on the application server. The calculation logic is usually executed in the database. The more complex a calculation is and the more records needed for the calculation, the more valuable is the execution in the database. With this approach, the amount of data transferred from the database to the application server can be kept to a minimum. Even if millions of records are needed for a calculation, the system only transfers the few hundred calculated key figures that the user should see.

1.5.3 Database as Whitebox

Thanks to the architecture of the SAP NetWeaver AS ABAP and the database independence of *Open SQL*, you can develop ABAP applications without knowing database-specific details. Section 3.2 describes all important elements of database access from ABAP applications in detail.

Using Open SQL, you can perform operations on the database of the application server. Open SQL provides a unified syntax and unified semantics for all database systems supported by SAP. The result of the operations and potential error messages are independent of the database system. This means that programs that only use Open SQL can be run on all database systems supported by SAP.

Open SQL

Native SQL
In addition to Open SQL, *Native SQL* can also be used. With Native SQL, you can use database-specific operations that are not supported by Open SQL. However, the disadvantage of Native SQL is that programs using database-specific operations cannot be run on all database systems supported by SAP. This is probably the reason why you only used Native SQL and database-specific operations in exceptional cases in the past. The database was usually a *black box*, or a closed system with an internal structure that did not need to be considered.

From a blackbox to a whitebox
However, if the application logic, or at least part of it, is now to be executed (and possibly also implemented) in the database, knowledge of database-specific (or better, SAP HANA-specific) details is imperative. To really benefit from SAP HANA and achieve optimum performance, the database must become a *white box*. In particular, you must understand the following aspects:

▸ How can application code be moved from the application layer to the database layer?

▸ To what extent is moving the application code possible when using Open SQL?

▸ What options are provided by the SQL standard and SAP HANA-specific extensions in this regard (e.g., modeled or implemented SAP HANA Views and SQLScript)?

▸ How can you use these options in ABAP?

The risk of complexity
When optimizing programs for SAP HANA, you should always ask yourself if these programs should also be used on different database systems (which often is the case). If a program is to be used not only on SAP HANA but also on other systems, you carefully need to weigh the pros and cons of optimizing it with SAP HANA Views or SQLScript (as you had to when using Native SQL in the past). You could, for example, have a significantly better performance. A disadvantage, however, is the database-dependent application code that results from this optimization.

In general, you should only use Native SQL, SAP HANA Views, and SQLScript if optimization using Open SQL does not result in the desired outcome (e.g., with regard to the response behavior); see Chapter 14.

Within a program—or generally speaking, within modularization units— you can distinguish between application code for SAP HANA and application code for other database systems using case distinctions, i.e. by using IF... ENDIF. In some cases, if the application code would otherwise become too complex, it may also be necessary to create several alternative implementations of a modularization unit. In the extreme case, you have to develop a separate program for every database system.

Modularization units

Alternative Implementations   [Ex]

Alternative implementations for a modularization unit could look as follows:

▶ One implementation for SAP HANA that uses SAP HANA-specific options and one Open SQL-based implementation for all other database systems supported by SAP.

▶ One implementation for SAP HANA, one implementation for Oracle, one implementation for IBM DB2, etc. With this approach, each implementation is optimized for the respective database system.

Code pushdown might lead to greater complexity of programs that are to support both SAP HANA and other database systems. This is discussed in detail in Section 14.1.2.

1.5.4 Required Qualifications for Developers

How should ABAP developers deal with the impact of SAP HANA on application development? It's certainly not enough to simply understand the impacts described. To be able to optimize existing applications and develop new applications or application types based on ABAP and SAP HANA, developers need to gain expertise. And you should make sure to acquire this knowledge at an early stage.

From our point of view, you should gain detailed knowledge of Open SQL (if you are not already highly skilled in this language), but should also familiarize yourself with technologies of the SQL standard and the SAP HANA database that go beyond Open SQL. You should know how to model SAP HANA Views and how to use SQLScript for more complex requirements both in SAP HANA Views and within database procedures.

SQL and SAP HANA

Performance analysis and optimization

To optimize existing applications for SAP HANA—especially with regard to their performance—you need to know which programs and *code patterns* within these programs are particularly suitable candidates. You should familiarize yourself with the development tools used to identify suitable programs for code pushdown. And you should be able to perform a run-time analysis to thoroughly examine the identified programs.

Altogether, we assume that sound knowledge in the areas of performance analysis and performance optimization with regard to the in-memory technology will become (even) more important than in the past and than in case of traditional databases.

New UI technologies

To develop new applications that process large data amounts using SAP HANA, the application architecture must be designed accordingly from the start. The performance of SAP HANA must be noticeable for the end-user. It might not be sufficient to simply perform calculations with a high performance. The results of these calculations must also be displayed to the user very quickly and in simple and intuitive views. You should therefore also familiarize yourself with technologies for developing modern user interfaces.

Old and new rules

And finally, you should understand the impact SAP HANA has on the known rules of ABAP programming. As already mentioned at the beginning of Section 1.5, many rules are essentially still valid. However, some rules now have a different priority, for instance, compared to using traditional databases they are now more or less important when implementing SAP HANA. Example: Avoiding many individual SQL statements (such as in a loop) is now more important than in the past.

At the same time, new guidelines will help you to create several alternative implementations of a modularization unit so that a program can be run optimally, for example, both on the SAP HANA database and on traditional databases. ABAP developers should be familiar with those new guidelines as well. Details on all of these guidelines can be found in Chapter 14.

ABAP development for SAP HANA is closely linked to SAP's latest development tools, which are based on the Eclipse platform. ABAP developers require a basic understanding of this platform and, in particular, should become familiar with both the ABAP Development Tools for SAP NetWeaver and SAP HANA Studio.

2   Introducing the Development Environment

In the past, ABAP developers would have used the SAP GUI-based *ABAP Workbench* to develop, adjust, and test programs. However, SAP's new development tools are based on the *Eclipse platform*. Furthermore, SAP is migrating some of its existing development tools to Eclipse.

At the start of this chapter, we will explain Eclipse and the significance of this platform for SAP. We will then introduce you to the *ABAP Development Tools for SAP NetWeaver*—which is the new Eclipse-based development environment for ABAP—as well as *SAP HANA Studio*, which is the administration and development environment for the HANA database. We will also discuss how to install these development environments.

2.1   Overview of Eclipse

Eclipse is an open source framework that, in principle, can be used to develop all types of software. Eclipse was originally developed by IBM but has been maintained and further developed by the Eclipse Foundation (*http://eclipse.org*) since 2004. In particular, Eclipse is known as a platform for development tools and environments.

Open source framework

A key strength of Eclipse is its ability to integrate different development tools (for example, *Java Development Tools (JDT), C/C++ Development Tools*

(CDT), or ABAP Development Tools for SAP NetWeaver) into one installation, and therefore provide users with a homogenous development environment.

Extension points and plug-ins In technical terms, Eclipse defines *extension points* that *plug-ins* can use to integrate themselves into Eclipse. A plug-in enhances the functional scope of Eclipse.

Each plug-in is described by an XML file (known as a *manifest*) and implemented in Java. Furthermore, each plug-in can provide extension points for other plug-ins that are based on it.

Eclipse SDK Eclipse provides the *Eclipse Software Development Toolkit* (Eclipse SDK) for the development of plug-ins (and Java applications in general).

Figure 2.1 provides a schematic representation of the structure of the Eclipse SDK and shows how extension points are used to facilitate the multilevel integration of different tools into Eclipse. In this figure, you see that the Eclipse SDK comprises the following three components:

▸ The Eclipse platform

▸ The Plug-In Development Environment (PDE)

▸ The Java Development Tools (JDT)

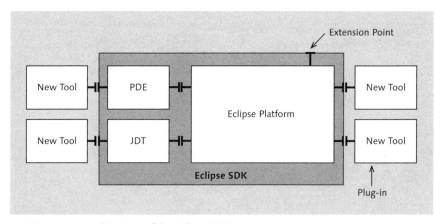

Figure 2.1 Architecture of the Eclipse SDK

The Eclipse platform provides a framework for development tools and contains reusable user interface modules. This is helpful, for example, when implementing help systems and connecting version control systems.

You use the Plug-In Development Environment to create the manifest for a plug-in, while you use the Java Development Tools to implement the plug-in in Java (and also for Java development in general). Technically, the Plug-In Development Environment and the Java Development Tools are also implemented as plug-ins for Eclipse.

The Eclipse Foundation coordinates the maintenance and further development of Eclipse. In particular, it handles the following:

▶ IT infrastructure

▶ Copyright

▶ Development process

▶ Ecosystem

The Eclipse Foundation organizes the development process on the basis of projects. These projects, known as *Eclipse projects*, handle the further development of the Eclipse platform, PDE, and JDT, among other things. There are also a number of other projects (for example, the *Eclipse Modeling Project*, the *Mylyn Project*, and the *Eclipse Web Tools Platform Project*). We will not examine these projects here. However, further information is available at *http://www.eclipse.org/projects/*.

Each year, in an effort to synchronize the various projects, the Eclipse Foundation releases all projects at the end of July in one composite release (known as the *Eclipse Release Train*). The current composite release is called *Juno*. Figure 2.2 provides an overview of the past six composite releases and their scope in terms of the number of projects involved and the number of program lines (*lines of code*, LOC). This information was obtained from the *2012 Annual Community Report* by the Eclipse Foundation.

The composite releases are important for ensuring that all development tools based on Eclipse can work together without any problems (at least while they follow the Eclipse Foundation's development process).

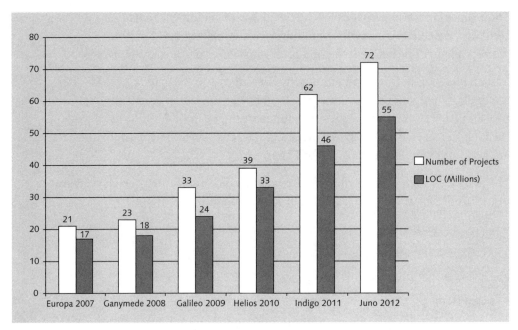

Figure 2.2 Composite Releases by Eclipse

2.2   SAP's Eclipse Strategy

Heterogeneous tools

Ten years ago, IBM's ever-increasing range of products created a challenge: The company was faced with different development tools that did not interact with one another. Its response was to develop Eclipse. Today, SAP faces the same challenge because to some extent, developers have to work with different tools to develop SAP applications. Occasionally, these tools don't follow the same operating concept, are based on different lifecycle management concepts, and do not work well together.

Eclipse as a strategic platform

To pave the way for highly standardized operating and lifecycle management concepts for all development tools used in a particular SAP context — and to integrate these in the best possible manner — SAP has decided to use the Eclipse platform as a strategic basis for new development tools. SAP is also migrating some of its existing development tools to Eclipse.

Unfortunately, the issue of heterogeneous tools is not solved solely by deciding to use Eclipse as the basis for new tool developments. It is great when different development tools are based on Eclipse and possibly even follow the same operating concept. If, however, the tools use different versions of Eclipse, users are forced to have multiple Eclipse installations. For this reason, SAP plans to provide a composite release in the future—the *SAP Release Train for Eclipse*—which will be similar to what's released each year by the Eclipse Foundation.

SAP Release Train for Eclipse

The purpose of the SAP Release Train for Eclipse is to ensure that different development tools can coexist in a single Eclipse installation, to guarantee the unbundling of Eclipse and SAP software, and to make a central update site available for installing and updating development tools.

2.2.1 Unbundling of Eclipse and SAP Software

So far, SAP frequently delivers Eclipse-based development tools in the form of installation programs, which generally do not make it possible to integrate different development tools into one Eclipse installation. Instead, each installation program generates its own Eclipse installation and, as a result, the user has to switch between multiple development environments to use different tools (even if the tools are based on the same version of Eclipse).

Problem with installation programs

However, the use of other installation mechanisms, specifically a *repository* or update site, will enable Eclipse and SAP software to be unbundled. Consequently, all of the tools following the SAP Release Train for Eclipse will be available, in the medium to long term, in one development environment.

2.2.2 Central Update Site

Equinox P2 is a platform for adding or updating software components in an existing Eclipse installation (see also *http://projects.eclipse.org/projects/rt.equinox.p2*). The basic concept here is that a software component is stored in a self-descriptive repository that is typically made available as an *update site* on an HTTP server. However, it can also be stored in a file

Equinox P2 Update Sites

system as a compressed archive file. If the Eclipse installation recognizes the repository, it can install or (automatically) update the software from there. If Eclipse identifies dependencies on software components stored in another known repository during the process of adding or updating software, it can automatically download these from the repository. Figure 2.3 provides a graphical representation of the update site concept.

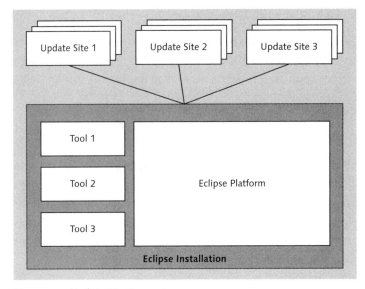

Figure 2.3 Update Site Concept

SAP provides the following central update site for tools associated with the SAP Release Train for Eclipse: *https://tools.hana.ondemand.com/*. To some extent, however, you can also download the repositories for the development tools from SAP Service Marketplace (and then run your own update site, for example).

Development tools   At present, the following development tools are affiliated with the SAP Release Train for Eclipse:

▶ ABAP Development Tools for SAP NetWeaver

▶ SAP HANA Cloud Tools

▶ UI Development Toolkit for HTML5

▶ SAP NetWeaver Gateway Productivity Accelerator

2.3 Installing the Development Environment

Now that we have given you some background information about Eclipse and its significance for SAP, we'll explain how you can set up a development environment for ABAP development for SAP HANA, and what you should keep in mind when doing so. We will consider the installation of a development environment only conceptually. In other words, our explanations will in no way replace the installation guides valid at the time of installation.

First, we will explain the installation of SAP HANA Studio. Then, we will explain the installation of ABAP Development Tools for SAP NetWeaver. Since SAP HANA Studio is installed using an installation program and the ABAP Development Tools are installed using a repository or update site, you must install the tools in this sequence in order to obtain a homogeneous development environment (as of June 2013).

Installation sequence

As already mentioned in the introduction, our consideration is based on the following: SAP NetWeaver Application Server (AS) ABAP 7.4 (Support Package 2), ABAP Development Tools for SAP NetWeaver 2.7, and SAP HANA 1.0 (Support Package Stack 5). We will assume that the ABAP application server and the SAP HANA database have already been installed.

Technical requirements

2.3.1 Installing SAP HANA Studio

At present, you can install SAP HANA Studio in the following system environments:

Availability of SAP HANA Studio

▶ Windows XP, Vista, and 7 (32-bit or 64-bit)

▶ SUSE Linux Enterprise Server 11 x86 (64-bit)

SAP HANA Studio is currently based on Eclipse 3.8 and requires the *Java Runtime Environment* 1.6 or 1.7 (as of June 2013).

The following two installation mechanisms are available:

Installation and update

▶ Installation in the form of a graphical installation program (`hdbsetup`, which is the installation mechanism currently recommended by SAP).

▶ Installation via the command line (program `hdbinst`).

You can also use the same programs to update an existing SAP HANA Studio installation. This is always necessary if you or an administrator update the HANA database because, from our experience, SAP HANA Studio should always have the same Support Package (or, in HANA terminology, the same *revision*) as the HANA database.

Alternatively, you can also use a repository or update site to update SAP HANA Studio (see Section 2.2). This enables companies to automatically update a large number of SAP HANA Studio installations and easily synchronize the versions of SAP HANA Studio and HANA database.

Working with multiple revisions

If you want to establish a connection to *different revisions* of different HANA databases from either your PC or laptop, we currently recommend that you install multiple versions of SAP HANA Studio on your PC or laptop, and establish a connection to the compatible version in each case. In this case, each installation should use a separate *workspace*. For information about these workspaces, see Section 2.4.1.

SAP HANA client software

When you install SAP HANA Studio, we recommend that you also install the SAP HANA client software, which includes not only support for the interfaces SQLDBC, ODBO, ODBC, and JDBC, but also the *SAP HANA Repository Client*. You require this, among other things, in order to work with the SAP HANA DEVELOPMENT perspective (For more information, see Section 5.2.). Use the program `hdbsetup` or `hdbinst` to install the SAP HANA client software.

More detailed information and a step-by-step guide to installing SAP HANA Studio and the SAP HANA client software is available at *http://help.sap.com/hana_appliance*.

2.3.2 Installing the ABAP Development Tools for SAP NetWeaver

Availability of ABAP Development Tools

ABAP Development Tools for SAP NetWeaver are currently available for the following system environments:

▶ Windows XP, Vista, and 7 (32-bit or 64-bit)

▶ Mac OS X 10.6 (64 bit)

▶ Linux (see also *http://scn.sap.com/docs/DOC-8760*)

They support Eclipse 3.7–4.2 and require Java Runtime Environment 1.6 or higher, as well as Microsoft Runtime DLLs VS2010 (in the case of an installation on Windows).

Unlike SAP HANA Studio, there is no installation program for the ABAP Development Tools. A repository or update site is used to install these tools. Furthermore, you must have a compatible Eclipse installation on your PC or laptop.

Installation and update

For ABAP development on SAP HANA, we recommend that you use the SAP HANA Studio installation (in other words, that you install the ABAP Development Tools on SAP HANA Studio). Later on, you can complete all necessary ABAP and SAP HANA development tasks within a single development environment.

The ABAP Development Tools for SAP NetWeaver comprise the following components:

Components

▶ **ABAP Core Development Tools (mandatory)**
This toolkit contains editors for editing ABAP source code, debuggers, transport connections, and so on.

▶ **Web Dynpro ABAP Tools (optional)**
Tools for developing user interfaces with Web Dynpro ABAP.

▶ **ABAP Development Tools for SAP HANA (optional)**
Tools for ABAP development on SAP HANA.

▶ **ABAP Connectivity and Integration Development Tools (optional)**
Tools for integrating systems.

To install the ABAP Development Tools, you must perform the following two steps:

Installation steps

1. First, make sure that all of the Eclipse functions required by the ABAP Development Tools have been installed. If necessary, you can install these retroactively from the Eclipse update site.

2. Then, maintain the repository or update site for the ABAP Development Tools in Eclipse and, from there, install the necessary software components for ABAP development.

If companies want to have a large number of ABAP Development Tools installations, an administrator can perform both steps once and then set up a company-specific update site that contains both the necessary Eclipse functions and the software components of the ABAP Development Tools. When required, the installations can be updated from this update site.

Working with multiple releases
If you want to establish a connection between your PC or laptop and different versions of SAP NetWeaver AS ABAP, this is easily done. The ABAP Development Tools are downward compatible to older releases. This means that, in the Eclipse-based development environment, you can connect both to the current release (or Support Package) as well as all older releases of the ABAP application server. The ABAP Development Tools recognize if certain functions are not available in an older release and then do not provide them. The minimum requirement for using the ABAP Development Tools is SAP NetWeaver AS ABAP 7.03/7.31, Support Package 4.

More detailed information and a step-by-step guide to installing the ABAP Development Tools for SAP NetWeaver is available at *http://service.sap.com*.

2.4   Getting Started in the Development System

Now that you have set up a development environment for ABAP development on SAP HANA, you can get started in the system. We will therefore provide you with sample developments that you can install on SAP NetWeaver AS ABAP 7.4 (by using the description provided in Appendix E).

If this is your first time working with Eclipse, we recommend that you take a look at other sources of information in addition to this book. We will refer you to these additional sources at the relevant stages in this section.

2.4.1   Basic Principles of Eclipse

Start the newly set up development environment as described in Section 2.3. Execute the program `hdbstudio`, which is located in the installation directory of SAP HANA Studio, independent of the ABAP Development Tools.

Workbench
If the WELCOME tab page is displayed when you start the program, use the button at the top right of the screen to navigate to the WORKBENCH.

Choose the menu path WINDOW • OPEN PERSPECTIVE to open the ABAP perspective. You should now see a screen similar to that shown in Figure 2.4. We'll use this figure to explain the key elements of the Eclipse development environment.

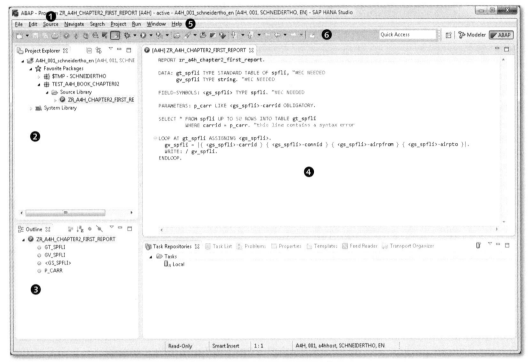

Figure 2.4 Eclipse Workbench (with the ABAP Perspective Opened)

In Eclipse, you can work with one or more *windows* in parallel. If you want to open an additional window, choose the menu option WINDOW • NEW WINDOW.

Windows and perspectives

Within a window, Eclipse only ever shows exactly one *perspective* at any given point in time. The name of the perspective currently displayed by the system is shown in the window's title bar ❶. A perspective describes the layout of screen elements for a particular purpose. For example, the ABAP perspective is available for ABAP development, while the JAVA perspective is available for Java development.

In the following text, we'll discuss in detail the most important screen elements within a perspective, namely:

▶ Views ❷ and ❸

▶ Editors ❹

▶ Menu bars ❺

▶ Toolbars ❻

Eclipse automatically saves any changes that you make to the screen elements of a perspective (for example, layout and size). If you exit a perspective and then open it again (via the menu path WINDOW • OPEN PERSPECTIVE), the perspective will look exactly as it did when you exited it.

If you want to reset a perspective to its original state, choose the menu option WINDOW • RESET PERSPECTIVE.... You can also create your own perspectives, if necessary. To do this, use the menu option WINDOW • SAVE PERSPECTIVE AS...

Views and editors A *view* (❷ and ❸) makes certain information available to you. For example, the PROBLEMS view displays warnings and errors that occurred when you activated a program. You can view the properties of a program (for example, title, package, and original system) in the PROPERTIES view, and change them to some extent. To open a view, choose the menu option WINDOW • SHOW VIEW.

Editors An editor ❹ is used to edit a development object. Editors are frequently *source code-based*. However, *form-based* editors also exist.

[»] | **Differences between Views and Editors**

When developers work with Eclipse for the very first time, they often ask the following question: What is the difference between a view and an editor?

The main differences between views and editors are as follows:

▶ Within a window, a view can only be opened once, while an editor can be opened several times (for example, to edit different programs in parallel).

▶ Unlike a view, an editor cannot be positioned anywhere.

▶ When an editor is open, it can be viewed in every perspective.

▶ Changes within a view are saved immediately. Changes within an editor must be saved explicitly.

Further information is available at *http://wiki.eclipse.org*.

Menu bars and toolbars contain commands that you can execute in the current context (for example, saving a program or activating a program). The main menu bar ❺ is located at the very top of the Eclipse development environment. Views and editors can have additional menus, especially context menus (which you call using the right mouse button). However, you can also add additional commands to the main menu bar.

Menu bars and toolbars

The main toolbar is located below the main menu bar ❻. Frequently used commands are located there. Views and editors can have additional toolbars. You can also add additional commands to the main toolbar.

We now wish to briefly discuss the workspaces already mentioned in Section 2.3.1. Put simply, a workspace is a directory on your computer's hard drive in which Eclipse stores your personal settings (for example, layout and size of the screen elements in a perspective) and your project data (for example, system connections to the ABAP application server).

Workspaces

Eclipse only ever works with exactly one workspace at any given point in time. In the case of workspaces, you can configure the following settings:

- You can use the file *eclipse.ini* (or *hdbstudio.ini* in the case of SAP HANA Studio) to control which workspace Eclipse will automatically open at startup.

- You can configure Eclipse in such a way that, at startup, you are asked which workspace you want to use. This is Eclipse's default behavior. If, however, you do not do anything, this is overridden by SAP HANA Studio. In Windows, SAP HANA Studio uses the directory *hdbstudio* within your user profile by default (for example, *c:\Users\<user name>\ hdbstudio*).

- You can change the workspace within Eclipse at any time. To do this, choose the menu option FILE • SWITCH WORKSPACE.

Further information about Eclipse is available at *http://www.eclipse.org/ documentation/*.

2.4.2 ABAP Development Tools for SAP NetWeaver

We will now discuss the ABAP Development Tools for SAP NetWeaver in more detail. When working with the ABAP Development Tools, use the following perspectives:

Available perspectives

▶ **ABAP**

You use this perspective to edit development objects (for example, programs, classes, and interfaces). You can also perform code checks and module tests here.

▶ **ABAP Connectivity & Integration**

You use this perspective to develop integration between systems.

▶ **ABAP Profiling**

You use this perspective to conduct performance analyses.

▶ **Debug**

You can use this perspective to analyze program errors. (The DEBUG perspective is not delivered with the ABAP Development Tools. Rather, it is a standard component of Eclipse and is also used, for example, to debug Java programs or SQLScript.)

Authorizations   In the ABAP backend, you require the relevant authorizations for working with the ABAP Development Tools. The following authorization roles are available by default:

▶ SAP_BC_DWB_ABAPDEVELOPER

Put simply, this role enables you to create, change, activate, and delete development objects.

▶ SAP_BC_DWB_WBDISPLAY

This role enables you to display development objects.

Both roles contain the authorization object S_ADT_RES, which is needed for working with the Eclipse-based development environment. If you want to use your own roles to assign authorizations to ABAP developers, make sure that these roles consider the authorization object S_ADT_RES.

We will now explain the steps involved in creating a program with the ABAP Development Tools. We will provide some background information for each step.

Creating a Project

Connection to the   In order to be able to work with the ABAP Development Tools, you require
ABAP backend   an *ABAP project* that connects the Eclipse-based development environment with the ABAP backend. To create an ABAP project, choose the menu path FILE • NEW • ABAP PROJECT. Then, provide the following information:

▸ A connection from the *SAP Logon Pad*

▸ Logon client and language

▸ User name and password. (You only enter the password if single sign-on is not set up for the connection from the SAP Logon Pad. Since the password is not saved, you must enter it again any time you restart Eclipse.)

▸ A list of your favorite packages (optional). (You should always include the package TEST_A4H_BOOK here, which you will use in conjunction with this book. To install the package, refer to the information contained in Appendix E.)

The project data is saved to your current workspace (see also Section 2.4.1). You can create any number of projects within a workspace and therefore work with multiple ABAP backends simultaneously.

After you have saved the project data, the ABAP project is displayed in the PROJECT EXPLORER view (❷ in Figure 2.4). A tree structure is displayed below your project, and the uppermost level of this tree structure contains the following two nodes:

Project Explorer

▸ Your FAVORITE PACKAGES and their development objects.

▸ The SYSTEM LIBRARY, which you use to access all packages and their development objects on the connected application server.

If you double-click a development object in PROJECT EXPLORER, the relevant editor opens. In addition, the OUTLINE view ❸ displays the structure (for example, the global variables and methods for a program), while the PROPERTIES view displays the properties of the development object.

Editors and SAP GUI integration

Not all development objects have an editor that is implemented natively in Eclipse. If a development object does not have an editor, the SAP GUI opens. In the case of a data element, Transaction SE11 (ABAP Data Dictionary) opens, for example. The OUTLINE and PROPERTIES views are not available in this case.

You can use SAP GUI integration to execute any development objects in the SAP GUI, even if they are not displayed in the PROJECT EXPLORER view at present. To do this, choose the menu option RUN • RUN ABAP APPLICATION. Then, select the relevant development object. This is particularly useful if you want to execute a standard program or transaction (for example, SM50).

ABAP resource URLs

ABAP resource URLs are an interesting function for all development objects, irrespective of whether the ABAP Development Tools provide native editor development objects. They enable you to generate hyperlinks for development objects and to integrate them into websites or emails, for example. You can click the hyperlink to open the relevant development object directly in the ABAP Development Tools.

To generate an ABAP resource URL, choose the menu option EDIT • COPY ABAP RESOURCE URL. Note that you will not be able to open a development object via a hyperlink unless you have registered your Eclipse installation. Keep reading for more information.

No check-in/ check-out

Unlike other Eclipse-based development tools, the ABAP Development Tools do not use a *check-in/check-out mechanism*. As a result, you cannot work with the ABAP Development Tools *offline* (that is, without a connection to the ABAP backend). As soon as you edit a development object, this is automatically locked against editing by another user. Therefore, unlike in the SAP GUI, you do not explicitly toggle between DISPLAY and CHANGE. The following tasks always occur in the ABAP backend: save, perform syntax check, and activate.

User-Specific Settings

You should be familiar with using the menu option UTILITIES • SETTINGS to configure user-specific settings in the ABAP Workbench, and therefore adjust the (SAP GUI-based) development environment to your personal requirements.

General settings

In Eclipse, user-specific settings are available in the menu under WINDOW • PREFERENCES. Many of the options provided here are general settings for Eclipse. They are not specifically used for ABAP development, but influence it nonetheless.

ABAP Development Tools

The specific settings for the ABAP Development Tools are available under the ABAP DEVELOPMENT node (see Figure 2.5). You should be familiar with the following setting options:

▶ Directly on the ABAP DEVELOPMENT node, you can set the OPEN ABAP RESOURCE URLs from external documents in this installation of SAP HANA Studio checkbox. You cannot use ABAP resource URLs (see the previous section) unless this checkbox is set.

▶ You can use the DEBUG node to configure settings for debugging ABAP programs.

▶ The PROFILE node enables you to parameterize performance analyses.

▶ You can use the SOURCE CODE EDITOR node to manage code templates, among other things.

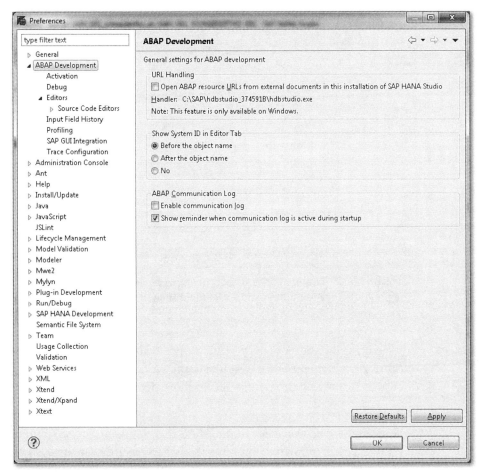

Figure 2.5 User-Specific Settings for ABAP Development Tools

Creating a Program

The next step is to create a new development object under the menu path FILE • NEW. If you want to create a program that outputs the flight schedule for a given airline, for example, choose FILE • NEW • ABAP PROGRAM. Then enter the program name, title, and package. Select a transport request, if necessary.

Editing the source code

The editor for the program now opens. As an example, insert the source code from Listing 2.1:

```
REPORT zr_a4h_chapter2_first_report.
DATA: lt_spfli TYPE STANDARD TABLE OF spfli, "#EC NEEDED
      lv_spfli TYPE string. "#EC NEEDED
FIELD-SYMBOLS: <ls_spfli> TYPE spfli. "#EC NEEDED
PARAMETERS: p_carr LIKE <ls_spfli>-carrid OBLIGATORY.
SELECT * FROM spfli UP TO 50 ROWS INTO TABLE lt_spfli
        WHERE carrid = p_carr. "this line contains
                               "a syntax error
LOOP AT lt_spfli ASSIGNING <ls_spfli>.
  lv_spfli = |{ <ls_spfli>-carrid } | &&
  |{ <ls_spfli>-connid } { <ls_spfli>-airpfrom } | &&
  |{ <ls_spfli>-airpto }|.
  WRITE: / lv_spfli.
ENDLOOP.
```

Listing 2.1 Simple ABAP Program

[»]

Note on Listing 2.1

To restrict the program runtime, use the UP TO n ROWS addition. Consequently, the program does not output the entire flight schedule. Instead, it outputs a maximum of 50 connections.

Editing functions

When editing the source code, you are supported by numerous functions in ABAP Development Tools (just like in the SAP GUI). We now wish to discuss the following three functions in more detail:

▶ **Code completion**

You can use *code completion* in the ABAP Development Tools. You can use the key combination Ctrl + Space to ensure that the system proposes valid keywords and identifiers at a particular location within the source text.

▶ **Code templates**

You can also use the key combination ⎡Ctrl⎤ + ⎡Space⎤ to insert code *templates* in the source code. Alternatively, this also works by using drag-and-drop to drag templates from the TEMPLATES view to the editor. You can also define your own code templates in the TEMPLATES view. These are then saved to your current workspace.

▶ **Pretty Printer**

The *Pretty Printer* helps you to standardize source text formatting (especially with regard to upper/lower case and indentations). As is the case in the SAP GUI, you use the key combination ⎡Shift⎤ + ⎡F1⎤ to call the Pretty Printer in the ABAP Development Tools.

When editing the source text, you can perform a syntax check at any time. The easiest way to do this is using the key combination ⎡Ctrl⎤ + ⎡F2⎤.

Check

As shown in Figure 2.6, warnings and errors are displayed in both the PROBLEMS view and in the editor (specifically in the left and right column spaces). For Listing 2.1, the syntax check should issue a reminder about an error in program line 11. Correct this error.

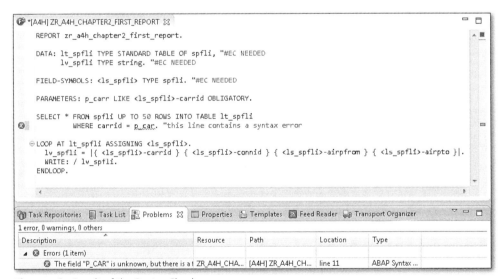

Figure 2.6 Result of the Syntax Check

If you want the source text to undergo more extensive checks, you can use the *ABAP Test Cockpit* for this purpose. To do this, call the context menu in your program: RUN AS • ABAP TEST COCKPIT.

Saving and
activating
programs
Following a successful syntax check, choose the menu path FILE • SAVE to save your program (in principle, you can also save erroneous development objects). When you save your program, an inactive version of the program is generated in the ABAP backend.

If you then choose the menu path EDIT • ACTIVATE ABAP DEVELOPMENT OBJECT to activate the program, an active version of the program is generated in the ABAP backend (assuming that the program does not contain any syntax errors).

As a result of your work with the ABAP Workbench, you have no doubt become familiar with—and have come to appreciate—the extensive navigation options available there. Forward navigation and the where-used list are also available to you in the Eclipse-based development environment.

Forward navigation
For forward navigation, select an identifier in the source text. Then, choose the menu path NAVIGATE • NAVIGATE TO (or press the ⌐F3⌐ key). For our sample program, you can execute the following actions:

▶ Forward navigation to the variable LV_SPFLI in program line 15: The system navigates to the definition of the variable in program line 4.

▶ Use the mouse pointer to select the database table SPFLI and then press the ⌐F3⌐ key: The system opens the definition of the database table in the SAP GUI.

Where-used list
The where-used list works in the same way. First, select an identifier in the source text. Then, choose GET WHERE-USED LIST... in the context menu. The result of the where-used list is displayed in the SEARCH view (see Figure 2.7).

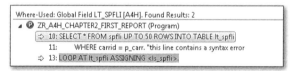

Figure 2.7 Result of the Where-Used List

You can double-click a line in the result to navigate to where the object is used. You can also use the context menu to generate an ABAP resource URL.

Executing the Program

Now that you have learned how to create a program and are familiar with the editing options available in the ABAP Development Tools for SAP NetWeaver, you will most likely want to execute the program for testing purposes. To do this, choose the menu option RUN • RUN ABAP APPLICATION... and execute the sample program in Listing 2.1. The selection screen for the program is then displayed in the SAP GUI. Here, enter the code of an airline. If you then press [F8], the corresponding flight schedule is displayed.

Executing the program in the SAP GUI

If you want to debug a program in order to analyze program errors, you can set one or more breakpoints in the ABAP Development Tools. Here, you can choose between static and dynamic breakpoints:

Debugging

- ▶ *Static breakpoints* refer to a specific program line. You set a static breakpoint by double-clicking the left column space in the editor.
- ▶ *Dynamic breakpoints* refer to a specific ABAP statement or exception class. To set a dynamic breakpoint, choose RUN • ABAP BREAKPOINTS.

Figure 2.8 shows how static breakpoints are displayed in the left column space in the editor and in the BREAKPOINTS view. Dynamic breakpoints are displayed in the BREAKPOINTS view only.

From a technical perspective, the ABAP Development Tools work with *external breakpoints*. These apply to all programs in your current user session, which are executed under your user on one of the application servers on the ABAP backend (defined by the system and client in the ABAP project).

External breakpoints

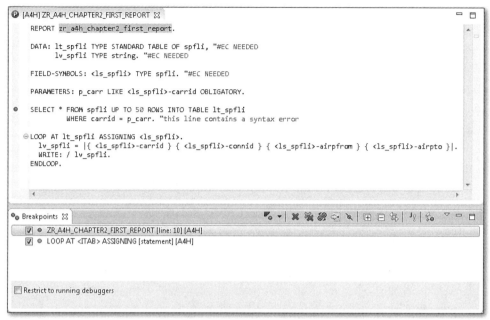

Figure 2.8 Displaying Breakpoints that Have Been Set

If the system encounters a breakpoint when executing a development object, it automatically opens the DEBUG perspective. Here, you can (similar to the SAP GUI-based debugger) analyze the call hierarchy and the contents of the variables, as well as debug the source code step by step. Figure 2.9 shows the DEBUG perspective for our sample program.

Additional
information

We now wish to give you some additional sources of information in relation to the ABAP Development Tools:

- If this is your first time working with the ABAP Development Tools, we recommend that you complete the tutorials in the SAP Community Network: *http://scn.sap.com/docs/DOC-31815*.

- You can call the online documentation at any time. To do this, choose the menu path HELP • HELP CONTENT.

- SAP has provided some *cheat sheets* to help you get started with the ABAP Development Tools. They are located under HELP • CHEAT SHEETS...

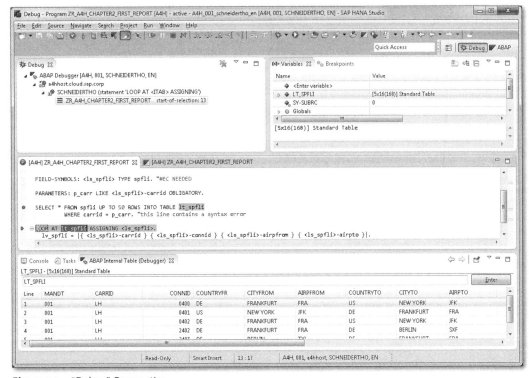

Figure 2.9 "Debug" Perspective

You are now ready to use the ABAP Development Tools for SAP NetWeaver. In the next section, we will introduce you to SAP HANA Studio.

2.4.3 SAP HANA Studio

Just like the ABAP Development Tools for SAP NetWeaver, SAP HANA Studio also comprises different perspectives, namely:

Available perspectives

► **Administration Console**
In this perspective, you or an administrator can monitor the system, configure system settings, and manage users and authorizations, among other things.

► **Modeler**
In the modeler, you can access the database catalog and create views and database procedures in the *SAP HANA Repository*.

▶ **SAP HANA Development**
The SAP HANA DEVELOPMENT perspective is used for development in SAP HANA. In particular, it is intended for *SAP HANA Extended Application Services*. It communicates with the SAP HANA Repository.

Authorizations for
SAP HANA Studio

Similar to working with SAP NetWeaver AS ABAP, you require the relevant authorizations for working with SAP HANA Studio, specifically in the HANA database.

[»]

Authorizations in SAP HANA

The authorizations in SAP HANA are divided into the following areas:

▶ *Analytical authorizations* control access to attribute views, analytic views, and calculation views.

▶ *SQL authorizations* define specific authorizations that users have for particular database objects.

▶ *System authorizations* define the system operations that users are permitted to perform.

▶ *Package authorizations* control access to the packages in the SAP HANA Repository.

Authorizations can be grouped into roles or assigned directly to users.

We won't discuss the authorization concept for the HANA database in detail here. Instead, we wish to focus on the authorizations that you, as an ABAP developer, require in order to work with SAP HANA Studio.

ABAP_DEV and
ABAP_READ

If you are already working with ABAP release 7.4 and using the HANA database as primary persistence, you can use the following standard roles to assign authorizations to ABAP developers who will work with SAP HANA Studio:

▶ ABAP_DEV
Put simply, this role enables you to edit development objects in the SAP HANA Repository.

▶ ABAP_READ
This role enables you to display development objects.

Otherwise, you must create your own roles. When doing so, you can base them on the two aforementioned roles. Figure 2.10 provides a schematic representation of the structure of the role ABAP_DEV.

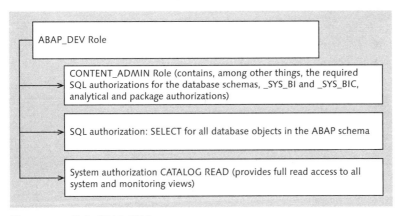

Figure 2.10 Role ABAP_DEV

In this section, we will focus on the MODELER perspective, which is relevant for you as an ABAP developer. You will obtain further information in Chapter 4 and Chapter 5. In Chapter 5, you will also learn about the SAP HANA DEVELOPMENT perspective.

Creating a System Connection

To work with SAP HANA Studio, you require a system connection between SAP HANA Studio and the HANA database. You can create a system connection in the MODELER perspective, for example. In the NAVIGATOR view, use the ADD SYSTEM... option in the context menu for this purpose. Then, provide the following information for the system connection:

Connecting to the database

- ▶ Server name and instance number.
- ▶ Description.
- ▶ User name and password (unlike the ABAP Development Tools, SAP HANA Studio stores both the user and password).

The system data is saved to your current workspace (see also Section 2.4.1). You can create any number of system connections within a workspace. This enables you to work with multiple databases simultaneously.

After you have saved the system data, the system connection is displayed in the NAVIGATOR view (see Figure 2.11).

Navigator

Figure 2.11 Modeler Perspective in SAP HANA Studio

A tree structure is displayed below your system connection, and the uppermost level of this tree structure contains the following four nodes:

- The CATALOG node ❶ contains *database objects,* such as database tables, views, and database procedures.
- The BACKUP node is used for data security purposes.
- You manage roles and users under the SECURITY node.
- The CONTENT node represents the packages ❸ in the *SAP HANA Repository,* which is used for development organization.

User-Specific Settings

Settings in the Modeler perspective
Similar to the ABAP Workbench or ABAP Development Tools, you can also configure some user-specific settings in SAP HANA Studio.

The relevant settings for the MODELER perspective are located under WINDOW • PREFERENCES • MODELER. Of particular interest here are the data preview settings (under the DATA PREVIEW node) and the rules for validating development objects (under the VALIDATION RULES node).

Working with the Database Catalog

The database catalog in the HANA database has a similar structure to the catalogs in other databases. It manages the database objects in *database schemas* (❷ in Figure 2.11). A schema groups logically related database objects together (comparable with a *namespace*). In principle, each database user has his own database schema.

Database schemas

The ABAP application server generally uses exactly one technical database user to communicate with the database. This user also has a corresponding database schema, known as the *system schema* or *ABAP schema* (for more information, see Section 3.1.2). In Figure 2.11, this is schema SAPH74.

Some database schemas are used internally by the HANA database. In particular, these include the database schema SYS and all database schemas that start with _SYS.

Technical schemas

Technical Database Schemas in SAP HANA   [«]

Immediately after the installation, SAP HANA contains a set of database schemas that play a major role in different scenarios. We therefore wish to give you some background information about some of the schemas used internally by the HANA database:

▶ SYS
This schema contains technical tables and views for managing and monitoring the system. It does not play any role in application development.

▶ _SYS_AFL
Database objects for function libraries are stored here. The schema is first created when function libraries are installed (see Chapter 12).

▶ _SYS_BI
This schema contains special tables and views for analysis scenarios (for example, fiscal year data).

▶ _SYS_BIC
When you activate development objects, the associated runtime objects are generated in this schema (we will discuss this in more detail next).

▸ _SYS_REPO
The development objects for the SAP HANA Repository are stored here (we will also discuss this in more detail below).

▸ _SYS_XS
This schema is used by the XS Engine.

Database objects

Database schemas contain database objects. The HANA database recognizes the database objects listed in Table 2.1.

Object	Description
Column view	Column views are special views in SAP HANA. They are based on tables in the column store and are usually created in the SAP HANA Repository.
Function	A *user-defined function* performs calculations and can be integrated into SELECT statements.
Index	An index facilitates searches and sorting. Please note the information about indexes in Chapter 9 and Chapter 14.
Procedure	You can use database *procedures* to encapsulate and reuse algorithms that are to be executed in the HANA database. Further information is available in Chapter 5.
Sequence	You can use a *sequence* to generate unique, consecutive numbers in accordance with certain rules. This concept is very similar to number ranges in ABAP.
Synonym	*Synonyms* can be defined as aliases for database tables, data views, procedures, and sequences. We will discuss these later in this chapter.
Table	Data is saved to database *tables*. As part of your ABAP development work in SAP HANA, you frequently use the ABAP Data Dictionary to create database tables.
Trigger	Database *triggers* are functions that are called for certain changes made in the database.
View	Put simply, *views* are saved queries (across one or more tables), which can be called via SQL in the same way as a database table.

Table 2.1 Objects in the Database Catalog

As part of your ABAP development work in SAP HANA, you will generally not create any database objects directly in the catalog. You'll typically create objects only indirectly, for example, via the ABAP Data Dictionary, SAP HANA Repository, or SAP Landscape Transformation Replication Server. In certain circumstances, however, you may want to view database objects directly in the catalog. We will now use the example of the table SPFLI, which you already used in Listing 2.1, to explain how this works.

Open the ABAP schema under the CATALOG node. Here, you see nodes for the different database objects. If you want to search for a specific database table, choose the FIND TABLE option in the context menu for the TABLES node. Then, enter "SPFLI" in the search dialog box. Make sure that the SHOW DEFINITION checkbox is set and choose OK.

Table definition

The system now opens the table definition (see Figure 2.12). Here, you see that the table SPFLI uses *column-oriented data storage* (known as the *column store*). You can also check columns, indexes, and runtime information for the database table, among other things.

	Name	SQL Data Type	Dim	Column Store Data Type	Key	Not Null	Default	Comment
1	MANDT	NVARCHAR	3	STRING	X(1)	X	000	
2	CARRID	NVARCHAR	3	STRING	X(2)	X		
3	CONNID	NVARCHAR	4	STRING	X(3)	X	0000	
4	COUNTRYFR	NVARCHAR	3	STRING		X		
5	CITYFROM	NVARCHAR	20	STRING		X		
6	AIRPFROM	NVARCHAR	3	STRING		X		
7	COUNTRYTO	NVARCHAR	3	STRING		X		
8	CITYTO	NVARCHAR	20	STRING		X		
9	AIRPTO	NVARCHAR	3	STRING		X		
10	FLTIME	INTEGER		INT		X	0	
11	DEPTIME	NVARCHAR	6	STRING		X	000000	
12	ARRTIME	NVARCHAR	6	STRING		X	000000	
13	DISTANCE	DECIMAL	9,4	FIXED		X	0	
14	DISTID	NVARCHAR	3	STRING		X		
15	FLTYPE	NVARCHAR	1	STRING		X		
16	PERIOD	SMALLINT		INT		X	0	

Figure 2.12 Table Definition Using the Example of Table SPFLI

Similar to the table definition, you can also use the FIND TABLE option in the context menu to display the table contents. Alternatively, you can use the context menu for the TABLES node to set a filter for the table name. The NAVIGATOR view then displays only those tables that satisfy the filter condition. You can now right-click to select the OPEN CONTENT option in the context menu. Note that the system displays only the first 1,000 data records (and not the entire contents of the database table).

Table contents and data preview

Data preview You can use the *data preview* to analyze more than 1,000 data records. To access the data preview, choose the OPEN DATA PREVIEW option in the context menu. Figure 2.13 displays the data preview using the example of the table SPFLI.

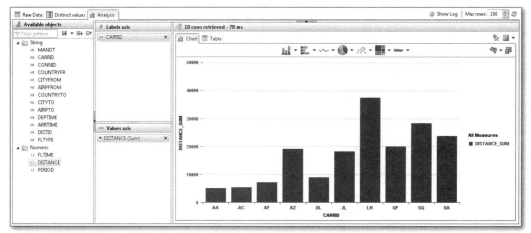

Figure 2.13 Data Preview Using the Example of Table SPFLI

The data preview comprises the following tab pages:

▶ The RAW DATA tab page displays the table's raw data. Here, you can filter, sort, and export the data, among other things.

▶ On the DISTINCT VALUES tab page, you can analyze which different values exist for a field in the database table and the frequency with which these values occur, thus enabling you to draw conclusions in relation to data distribution.

▶ The ANALYSIS tab page has a similar structure to a pivot table. You can create simple analyses here. Both a tabular and graphical display are available here.

SQL console We'll now introduce you to one more tool that can be very useful when working with the database catalog—namely, the *SQL console*. This enables you to quickly and easily execute read and write SQL statements on the HANA database. If, for example, you want to add the name of an airline to the flight schedule from Section 2.4.2, you can use a *join* (see Chapter 3). You can test the JOIN statement (see Listing 2.2) in the SQL console. To open the SQL console in the NAVIGATOR view, choose the SQL CONSOLE option in the context menu for the ABAP schema. You can then enter the relevant SQL statement. Similar to the ABAP Development Tools, you can also use ⎡Ctrl⎤ + ⎡Space⎤ to revert to code completion and templates.

```
select spfli.carrid, scarr.carrname, spfli.connid,
       spfli.airpfrom, spfli.airpto
       from spfli
       join scarr on scarr.carrid = spfli.carrid;
```

Listing 2.2 Simple Join

Then, choose EXECUTE to execute the SQL statement. The result is shown in Figure 2.14. In addition to the result list, the system provides some information about the runtime and number of data records read.

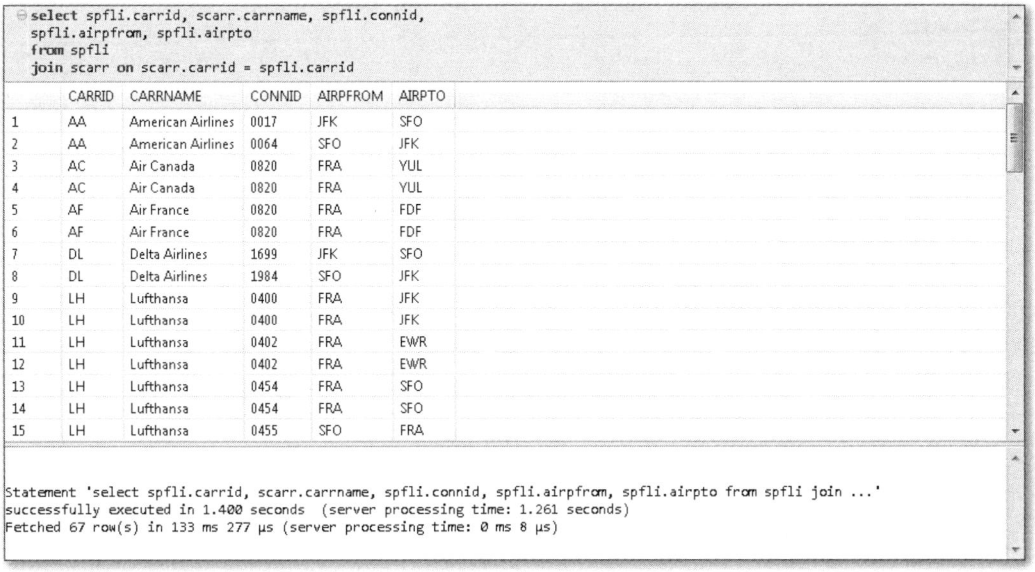

Figure 2.14 SQL Console

If you enter several SQL statements in the SQL console, each separated by a semicolon, you can execute them by choosing EXECUTE once. If you want to execute only one or some of the SQL statements, select them before you choose EXECUTE.

93

Working with the SAP HANA Repository

Development
objects

This brings us to the SAP HANA Repository, which helps to organize *development objects* (known as *content*) in a flexible and expansible manner. The development objects contained in the SAP HANA Repository are organized along a package hierarchy. In terms of their notation and significance, these packages are very similar to Java packages. Since a package defines a namespace, the identifier for development objects must only be unique within the package (unlike the global uniqueness of the identifiers for ABAP objects).

SAP delivers content below the sap root package. Parallel to this package, you can establish your own package hierarchy for your development objects. You can group multiple packages together to form a *delivery unit*, which you can then transport. We will examine the package concept and application transport in detail in Chapter 6.

Content types

In the MODELER perspective, you can create the development objects described in Table 2.2. These are also known as *content types*.

Object	Description
PACKAGE	A *package* groups development objects together. We will discuss this in detail in Chapter 6.
ATTRIBUTE VIEW	You can use *attribute views* to connect multiple database tables or to select a subset of the columns in a database table. For more information, see Chapter 4.
ANALYTIC VIEW	In particular, you use *analytic views* to quickly aggregate data. For more information, see Chapter 4.
CALCULATION VIEW	*Calculation views* are available for requirements that cannot be mapped using attribute views and analytic views. They can be modeled or implemented using SQLScript. For more information, see Chapter 4 and Chapter 5.
ANALYTIC PRIVILEGE	You can use *analytic privileges* to restrict—line by line—access to views. They are not directly relevant for access from ABAP because this is done using a technical database user.

Table 2.2 Development Objects in the SAP HANA Repository

Object	Description
PROCEDURE	You can use database *procedures* to encapsulate and reuse algorithms that are to be executed in the HANA database. For more information, see Chapter 5.
DECISION TABLE	You can use *decision tables* to store business rules in SAP HANA. We will discuss this in Chapter 11.

Table 2.2 Development Objects in the SAP HANA Repository (Cont.)

You can create additional development objects in the SAP HANA DEVEL-OPMENT perspective. This is particularly relevant for any development work based on *SAP HANA Extended Application Services*. For the moment, we will not discuss these development objects further.

We will now use a specific example to explain some key concepts associated with the SAP HANA Repository: Figure 2.15 shows the editor for the attribute view AT_FLIGHT_SCHEDULE in the package test.ah4.book. chapter02.

Example: flight schedule

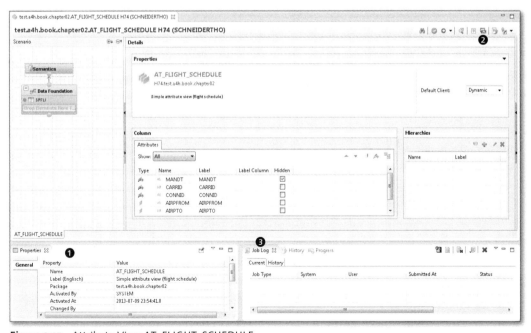

Figure 2.15 Attribute View AT_FLIGHT_SCHEDULE

Without discussing the specific features of attribute views, we wish to explain the following concepts:

► Creating development objects

► Validating development objects

► Activating development objects

► Testing development objects

► History and version management

Storage — Each development object in the SAP HANA Repository is described by different properties (❶ in Figure 2.15), some of which you can specify when creating the object and some you can also change later. Examples include the unique identifier within the package (NAME), description (LABEL), and default client (DEFAULT CLIENT). Other properties are automatically set by the system, for example, the last user who changed the object (CHANGED BY).

The system creates an XML file for each development object and ultimately stores it as *Character Large Object* (CLOB) data type in the database schema _SYS_REPO. You can choose DISPLAY XML 🖩 to display the XML file for an object ❷.

Figure 2.16 shows the XML representation of the attribute view AT_ FLIGHT_SCHEDULE. In this figure, we have highlighted some parts of the XML document, namely the identifier for the view, the description of the view, the columns in the view, and the database table underlying the view.

Similar to ABAP development objects, the development objects in the SAP HANA Repository also have a status (either inactive or active). If you create a new object or change an existing object, the system generates an inactive version first.

You can validate an object before you activate it. In addition to syntax checks (for example, correct syntax of SQLScripts within a database procedure), the validation can also consider some aspects of quality (for example, performance). This is similar to the (enhanced) syntax check in ABAP. We will discuss some of these aspects in greater detail in Chapter 14.

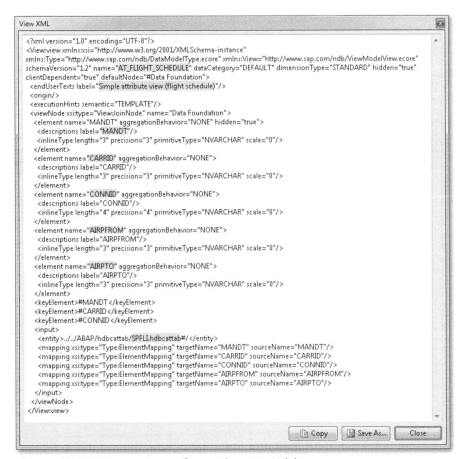

```
View XML

<?xml version="1.0" encoding="UTF-8"?>
<View:view xmlns:xsi="http://www.w3.org/2001/XMLSchema-instance"
xmlns:Type="http://www.sap.com/ndb/DataModelType.ecore" xmlns:View="http://www.sap.com/ndb/ViewModelView.ecore"
schemaVersion="1.2" name="AT_FLIGHT_SCHEDULE" dataCategory="DEFAULT" dimensionType="STANDARD" hidden="true"
clientDependent="true" defaultNode="#Data Foundation">
  <endUserTexts label="Simple attribute view (flight schedule)"/>
  <origin/>
  <executionHints semantic="TEMPLATE"/>
  <viewNode xsi:type="View:JoinNode" name="Data Foundation">
   <element name="MANDT" aggregationBehavior="NONE" hidden="true">
    <descriptions label="MANDT"/>
    <inlineType length="3" precision="3" primitiveType="NVARCHAR" scale="0"/>
   </element>
   <element name="CARRID" aggregationBehavior="NONE">
    <descriptions label="CARRID"/>
    <inlineType length="3" precision="3" primitiveType="NVARCHAR" scale="0"/>
   </element>
   <element name="CONNID" aggregationBehavior="NONE">
    <descriptions label="CONNID"/>
    <inlineType length="4" precision="4" primitiveType="NVARCHAR" scale="0"/>
   </element>
   <element name="AIRPFROM" aggregationBehavior="NONE">
    <descriptions label="AIRPFROM"/>
    <inlineType length="3" precision="3" primitiveType="NVARCHAR" scale="0"/>
   </element>
   <element name="AIRPTO" aggregationBehavior="NONE">
    <descriptions label="AIRPTO"/>
    <inlineType length="3" precision="3" primitiveType="NVARCHAR" scale="0"/>
   </element>
   <keyElement>#MANDT</keyElement>
   <keyElement>#CARRID</keyElement>
   <keyElement>#CONNID</keyElement>
   <input>
    <entity>../../ABAP/hdbcattab/SPFLI.hdbcattab#/</entity>
    <mapping xsi:type="Type:ElementMapping" targetName="MANDT" sourceName="MANDT"/>
    <mapping xsi:type="Type:ElementMapping" targetName="CARRID" sourceName="CARRID"/>
    <mapping xsi:type="Type:ElementMapping" targetName="CONNID" sourceName="CONNID"/>
    <mapping xsi:type="Type:ElementMapping" targetName="AIRPFROM" sourceName="AIRPFROM"/>
    <mapping xsi:type="Type:ElementMapping" targetName="AIRPTO" sourceName="AIRPTO"/>
   </input>
  </viewNode>
</View:view>

                                              Copy    Save As...    Close
```

Figure 2.16 XML Representation of an Attribute ViewValidate

To start validation, choose SAVE AND VALIDATE ✅. The validation result is displayed in the JOB LOG (❸ in Figure 2.15). If warnings or errors occur when validating an object, you can display them by double-clicking the corresponding row in the job log.

Job log

Figure 2.17 shows an example of what would happen if you were to validate the attribute view AT_FLIGHT_SCHEDULE without defining at least one key attribute first. This is a mandatory requirement for attribute views (see Section 4.1).

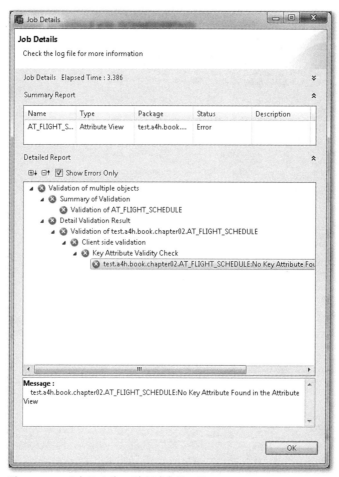

Figure 2.17 Job Details with Validation Errors

Activate When you activate an object, you generate an active (that is, executable) version of a development object. An object is automatically validated when it is activated. To start activation, choose SAVE AND ACTIVATE ●. The result is displayed in the job log.

Design time and
runtime objects Following successful activation, the system usually generates one or more database objects in the schema _SYS_BIC. The development objects in the SAP HANA Repository represent the *design time objects*, while the database objects in the database catalog represent the *runtime objects* (see Figure 2.18).

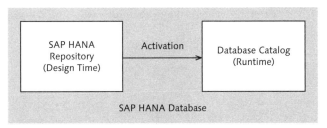

Figure 2.18 Design Time and Runtime

Authorizations for the User _SYS_REPO [«]

The internal user _SYS_REPO (the owner of the SAP HANA Repository) generates the runtime objects in the database schema _SYS_BIC. This user must have read access to the schemas used in the development objects. In other words, the user requires the SQL SELECT with GRANT authorization on the schema.

In the case of the attribute view AT_FLIGHT_SCHEDULE, the system generates (among other things) a *column view* and a public synonym for this column view in the database catalog. A column view is a special data view in SAP HANA. In our example, the name of the column view comprises the package and identifier for the attribute view (see Figure 2.19).

Column view

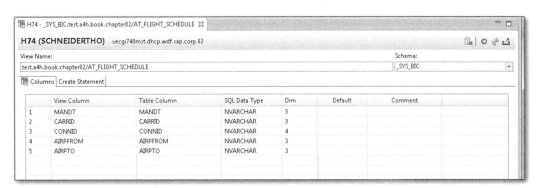

Figure 2.19 Runtime Object for an Attribute View

A *synonym* is an alias. A *public synonym* is an alias that is unique across all database schemas and can be used by all users. If, for example, you use the relevant public synonym to access the column view, you avoid having to explicitly name the schema _SYS_BIC. In our example, the name

Synonym

of the public synonym comprises the package and name of the attribute view (see Figure 2.20).

Figure 2.20 Public Synonym for a Column View

When you want to test objects in the SAP HANA Repository, it is best to use the data preview and the SQL console. You are already familiar with both of these tools, which we explained when we discussed the database catalog above.

To start the data preview for a development object, choose DATA PREVIEW ⣧. This preview is available for attribute views, analytic views, calculation views, and decision tables.

Selection log | Since we have already used the example of the database table SPFLI to explain the data preview, we will not discuss it in further detail here. However, we wish to draw your attention to the SHOW LOG button in the data preview. You can use this button to call a selection log, which helps you to very quickly find the corresponding runtime object for a design time object (see Figure 2.21).

SQL console | Alternatively, you can conduct tests directly in the SQL console. In our example, you can use the following objects here: the name of the column view generated (that is, test.a4h.book.chapter02/AT_FLIGHT_SCHEDULE in the schema _SYS_BIC) and the public synonym (test.a4h.book.chapter02:: AT_FLIGHT_SCHEDULE).

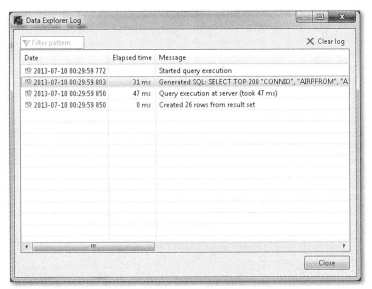

Figure 2.21 Selection Log with a Database Object

Similar to ABAP, development objects are put under version control. Each time an object is activated, the system creates a new version of the object. You can display existing versions in the version history. To access the version history, choose HISTORY . However, you see only the time when a version was created (that is, the time when an object was activated). You cannot see the actual changes made to each version.

History and version management

If there is an inactive version, you can choose SWITCH VERSION to execute the following actions:

▶ Switch between displaying active and inactive versions.

▶ Drop the version that is currently inactive and revert to the last active version.

You now know relevant tools for ABAP development on HANA and have taken your first steps towards getting started in the system. In the next chapter, we will discuss ABAP database programming. For more information on working with SAP HANA Studio, see Chapter 4 and Chapter 5.

To develop ABAP applications for SAP HANA, it's essential to have basic knowledge of the SAP NetWeaver AS ABAP architecture—and especially Open SQL—as well as the corresponding development tools. Moreover, native database access takes on greater importance when working with an SAP HANA database.

3 Database Programming Using SAP NetWeaver AS ABAP

When using ABAP in combination with SAP HANA, database accesses from ABAP programs play a decisive role: After all, they are the interface between application and data. The main difference between SAP HANA and traditional databases is the available set of queries and operations that can be executed on the existing data.

This chapter introduces database programming in ABAP, and in particular explains the specific aspects that are relevant for development on SAP HANA. While the basic ABAP database architecture for SAP HANA does not differ from other SAP-supported database systems, we will describe the options (and limitations) of classic ABAP database programming in this chapter. When reading the subsequent chapters, this will help you better understand how classic ABAP development and the new native implementations in SAP HANA can complement each other.

Simple ABAP Database Access [Ex]

Let's start by contemplating the example of a simple ABAP program in Listing 3.1:

```
DATA: wa TYPE scarr.
SELECT-OPTIONS: carrier FOR wa-carrid.

SELECT * FROM scarr INTO wa WHERE carrid IN carrier.
  WRITE: / wa-carrid , wa-carrname.
ENDSELECT.
```

Listing 3.1 Simple Database Access from ABAP via Open SQL

> Based on a selection of codes for airlines (for example, "LH"), the full names of these airlines (for example, "LH Lufthansa") are displayed.

Qualities of ABAP database access
This simple example shows some fundamental qualities of database access from ABAP that are not available in this form in most other development environments:

- Database access is integrated into the programming language.
- It is not necessary to manually open or close a database connection.
- Knowledge of the underlying database system is not required.
- You can iterate directly over a result set.
- A complex selection on the database can be derived directly from an input mask (e. g., via the SELECT-OPTIONS command and the IN clause).

In this chapter, we will first describe the technical aspects of a connection between the SAP NetWeaver AS ABAP and the database. We will then explain how ABAP developers can efficiently access the database based on a few examples. And finally, we will describe tools that can be used when developing database accesses.

Important aspects for database access
Two aspects play an important role when accessing the database from ABAP:

- ABAP tables and *views* are created and maintained in the database via the ABAP Data Dictionary. The ABAP Data Dictionary is described in Section 3.2.1.
- SQL support in ABAP makes it possible to read and modify data. There are two options for SQL access: *Open SQL* (see Section 3.2.2) and *Native SQL* (see Section 3.2.4). When reading this book, it is important to fully understand the capabilities of these two variants.

Since database access is of paramount importance in the context of SAP HANA and is enhanced by some new aspects, it is important to fully understand the interaction of ABAP and the SAP HANA database. Experienced ABAP developers may already be familiar with some of the information provided in this chapter.

For the examples throughout this book, we used a model that is available in every ABAP system—the well-known SAP NetWeaver flight data model (*SFLIGHT data model*). Appendix A introduces the technical details and business aspects of this application and describes the database tables and their relationships. This chapter only uses the tables SCARR (airlines), SFLIGHT (flights), SCUSTOM (flight customers), and SBOOK (flight bookings).

3.1 SAP NetWeaver AS ABAP Architecture

The database plays an integral role for the ABAP application server. This server cannot be operated without a running database. Ultimately, all technical and business data (except for a few configuration and log files of the server components) are database contents in SAP NetWeaver AS ABAP; even the ABAP source code and other development objects are maintained in database tables.

In this section, you will find a short description of the basic structure of an ABAP system. An ABAP system can comprise one or several application servers. Several application servers are deployed for a *scale-out* scenario to provide high availability and avoid overload situations. To coordinate several application servers, central services like the *start service*, the *message server* (load distribution), or the *enqueue server* (lock management) are available.

SAP system

Requests received on a server are forwarded to a *work process* by the dispatcher, where the request in question is processed by an ABAP program. There are different types of work processes: Examples are *dialog* (running ABAP programs in the dialog), *update* (executing *update modules* in case of a COMMIT WORK), *background* (running batch jobs), or *enqueue* (executing lock operations to synchronize database operations). The number of available work processes can be configured and depends on the hardware resources and scenario requirements (for example, the number of concurrent users).

Work processes

ABAP programs are executed by the runtime environment in the *ABAP kernel*. Within the kernel, several components are in use when executing ABAP statements; not all of those components will be explained in detail within this book. However, we would like to mention the following sample scenarios:

ABAP runtime environment

▸ When calling a function module using CALL FUNCTION <...> DESTINATION, the RFC library is used.

▶ In case of a serialization of an ABAP data structure to XML (or JSON) via `CALL TRANSFORMATION`, the kernel support for XML stylesheets is used.

▶ When accessing the database via the ABAP `SELECT` statement, the kernel's database interface is used.

Database access using the `SELECT` statement will be explained in detail in the next section. Figure 3.1 shows the basic server architecture of an ABAP system. Further details on installation and operation of the components can be found in the book *SAP NetWeaver AS ABAP—System Administration* by Frank Föse, Sigrid Hagemann, and Liane Will (4th edition, SAP PRESS 2012).

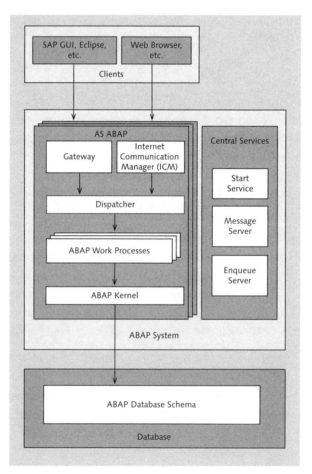

Figure 3.1 SAP NetWeaver AS ABAP Architecture

3.1.1   Database Interface

This section describes in detail how the ABAP application server accesses the database. In this context, there are three important components, which are described here:

- ▶ Database interface (DBI)
- ▶ Database-specific library (DBSL—Database Shared Library)
- ▶ Database client (driver)

Every ABAP work process is connected to the database via an active connection. If the database is accessed from an ABAP program, the DBI in the ABAP kernel is responsible for the first processing steps. The DBI is independent of the concrete database system. One of its main responsibilities is translating Open SQL (see Section 3.2.2) into Native SQL, which is then passed to the database via the DBSL (and the database driver).

Database interface (DBI)

In addition to processing SQL queries, the DBI provides the following functions:

- ▶ **Automatic client handling**
  If Open SQL is used to access client-dependent tables, the client is included automatically (for example, in the WHERE clause). This will be explained again in Section 3.2.2.

- ▶ **ABAP table buffer**
  In the ABAP Data Dictionary, you can specify if table contents should be buffered on the application server to avoid unnecessary database accesses. These buffers are maintained and synchronized by the database interface.

Database Systems Supported by SAP NetWeaver   **[«]**

The SAP NetWeaver AS ABAP currently supports the following vendors' database systems:

- ▶ SAP (SAP HANA, Sybase ASE, SAP MaxDB)
- ▶ IBM DB2
- ▶ Oracle database
- ▶ Microsoft SQL Server

Current details can be found in the Product Availability Matrix at *http://service.sap.com/pam*.

Database Shared Library (DBSL) There is a specific library for every database system supported by SAP: the *DBSL* (*Database Shared Library*). This library is dynamically linked to the ABAP kernel and integrates the respective database driver for the technical connection to the database.

Secondary database connections You can install several of those libraries on an application server. This makes it possible to establish connections to other databases besides the database of the ABAP system. This is important in the context of SAP HANA when implementing the side-by-side scenarios described in Section 3.4. The technical aspects of such *secondary* connections are described in more detail in Section 3.2.5. The prerequisites and steps for installing the SAP HANA DBSL on an existing system are described in SAP Note 1597627. Figure 3.2 shows how DBI, DBSL, and database driver interact.

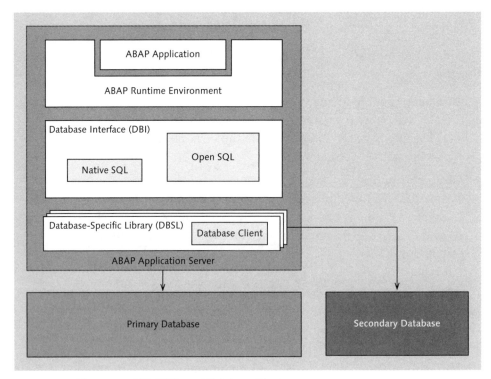

Figure 3.2 DBI, DBSL, and Database Client

3.1.2 Role of the Database for the ABAP Application Server

The SAP NetWeaver AS ABAP stores all data in exactly one specific *schema* within the database catalog. This schema is also referred to as *system schema* or *ABAP schema*. You can think of a schema as a kind of namespace within the database. In traditional ABAP development, the database schema is irrelevant. In the context of SAP HANA, however, the schema is relevant to some extent, for two reasons: First, when replicating tables to SAP HANA, the replicated data is often stored in different database schemas to separate them from the system data. Second, there are a series of technical schemas in SAP HANA that play an important role in native development in SAP HANA (see Section 2.4.3 and Chapter 4).

ABAP schema

As mentioned already, every ABAP work process is connected to the database. For the *standard database connection*, a technical database user is used.

> #### ABAP Schema and Technical Database User
>
> The name of the ABAP schema is usually composed of the *system ID* (SID) and the prefix "SAP". The default schema name of the ABAP system "NSP" would be SAPNSP, for example. ABAP tables like the SFLIGHT table can thus be addressed in the database catalog using SAPNSP.SFLIGHT.
>
> This schema also comprises a database user SAPNSP, which is used by the SAP NetWeaver AS ABAP to establish the standard database connection.

[Ex]

Every database uses a transaction concept to consider the consequences of interactions as a logic unit (*Logical Unit of Work*) and guarantee *ACID qualities* (Atomicity, Consistency, Isolation, Durability) for this unit. Database transactions are usually relatively short-lived operations and are always focused on the technical consistency of table contents (during parallel access, in error situations, etc.). Business transactions (for example, creating a new customer in the system), on the other hand, are often associated with a longer lifetime and additional requirements with regard to data consistency, since the data must also be consistent from a business perspective. The transaction concept of the database is hardly suitable to meet these additional requirements.

Transaction concept of the database

To assure consistent changes to data models in business applications, ABAP provides the *LUW concept* (Logical Unit of Work). With this concept, changes to data records are collected first and are then, at a defined point

SAP LUW concept

in time, either written to the database by a `COMMIT WORK` statement or discarded by means of a `ROLLBACK WORK`. By collecting changes, changes in transactions that comprise several dialog steps or even several application servers can be bundled (see Section 3.2.2). Since there is currently no equivalent concept in SAP HANA, only the transaction concept of the database can be used for native implementations in SAP HANA (e.g., via SQLScript). For recommendations on this topic, please read Chapter 14.

Lock concept

Physical locks are used automatically by every relational database system to synchronize parallel changes to table contents. In addition, the SAP NetWeaver AS ABAP uses a logical lock concept that is focused on business aspects. With this concept, *lock objects* can be used to indicate that a data record is unavailable for certain accesses (e.g., for changes) for a certain time period. Locks can be created or queried at runtime using special function modules that manage lock entries via the enqueue work process.

For example, when booking a flight, it isn't possible to perform another booking for the same flight to make sure it's not overbooked. Since these logical locks do not lead to physical locks on the database (so tables can technically still be changed), the effectiveness of the locks is based on conventions and guidelines for application development. These aspects must also be considered when modifying ABAP tables outside the context of an ABAP program (e.g., with SQLScript in the case of SAP HANA).

3.1.3 Data Types

As an ABAP developer, you may not have given data types a lot of thought in the past, but simply used the types that were available. In many situations, however, complex conversions and interpretations are performed in the background, and that can lead to unexpected results if they are not used properly.

Implicit type conversions

Before you learn about the different types of systems and their properties, we will shortly introduce the topic using a few examples. We start in Listing 3.2 with a simple database access using Open SQL.

```
DATA: lv_carrier TYPE string.
SELECT SINGLE carrname FROM scarr INTO lv_carrier
WHERE carrid = 'LH'.
```

Listing 3.2 Implicit Data Type Conversions

This simple ABAP program already uses different data types and conversions. The column CARRNAME of the table SCARR is based on the data element S_CARRNAME in the ABAP Data Dictionary, which is defined as type CHAR (i. e., string) with a length of 20. In the database, the data type of this column is NVARCHAR(20) (NVARCHAR is a string of variable length). A selection is made into an ABAP variable of type String; in addition, a constant (literal) LH is used in the WHERE clause, which is checked against the column CARRID of type CHAR(3). The result of this selection is the name of the airline "Lufthansa." If we now replace the filter condition in Listing 3.2 with the expression WHERE carrid = 'LH abcd', the result may not be obvious at first glance. Since the field CARRID contains only three characters, the record is found in this case as well.

In the case of character-type data types with a special semantics (for example, a date or a number as a string), there are some rather complex aspects happening in the background. Listing 3.3 for instance determines the names of all passengers who booked a flight within the last 30 days (column FLDATE of type DATS) and received a discount of more than 20 percent (column DISCOUNT of type NUMC).

Data types with semantics

```
DATA: lv_date TYPE d,
      lv_name TYPE string.

lv_date = sy-datlo - 30.
SELECT DISTINCT name FROM sbook AS b
    INNER JOIN scustom AS c ON b~customid = c~id
    INTO lv_name
    WHERE fldate > lv_date AND fldate <= sy-datlo
    AND c~discount >= '20'.

  WRITE: / lv_name.
ENDSELECT.
```

Listing 3.3 Relevance of Semantic Properties of Data Types

When calculating a time difference in days or handling the string "20" as a number for the discount, this depends on the semantics of the data types. If you execute the corresponding expression in Native SQL via the SQL console in SAP HANA Studio, for example, you will get different results.

For the *code pushdown paradigm* presented in Section 3.5.2, where certain calculations are moved to the database, it is important that the data is semantically treated and understood identically—otherwise, the calculations may lead to wrong results. This is relevant for instance for the rounding behavior and internationalization aspects. You must especially make sure that there are no unexpected effects after changing an existing program to improve performance.

[»]

SAP HANA Supports Only Unicode

Another aspect of handling text data types is the technical encoding of characters using so-called *code pages*. We would like to point out that SAP HANA only supports Unicode installations. Non-Unicode installations must be converted to Unicode before migrating them to SAP HANA. Unicode and non-Unicode systems will not be explained in more detail within the scope of this book.

We will now describe the different type systems. As an ABAP developer, you are probably already familiar with the type system of the ABAP language and the ABAP Data Dictionary, but have paid little attention to the mapping of those types to the database's type system in the past. We have to differentiate between the ABAP type system, the ABAP Data Dictionary type system, and the type system of the database.

ABAP type system

The type system of the ABAP language defines the data types that can be used in ABAP programming. It is designed in such a way that it can be mapped consistently to the supported operating systems for the application server. The following *built-in* types form the basic structure of the ABAP type system:

- **Numeric types:**
  Integers (I), floating point numbers (F), packed numbers (P), and decimal floating point numbers (decfloat16, decfloat34)

- **Character-type data types:**
  Text field (C), numeric text field (N), date (D), and time (T)

- **Hexadecimal types:**
  X

- **Types with a variable length:**
  STRING for strings and XSTRING for byte sequences

Usage of Numeric ABAP Data Types [«]

For integers, you use the I data type. If the value range of this type is not sufficient, you can use packed numbers or decimal floating point numbers without decimal places instead.

For fractional numbers with a fixed number of decimal places, packed numbers are used. This is the standard type for many business figures like monetary amounts, distances, weights, etc. This data type assures an optimal rounding behavior.

Decimal floating point numbers (decfloat) were introduced with SAP NetWeaver AS ABAP 7.02 to support scenarios where the value range of packed numbers is not sufficient or where the number of decimal places is variable.

Floating point numbers (F) should only be used for runtime-critical mathematical calculations where an exact rounding behavior is not required.

The type system of the ABAP Data Dictionary defines which data types can be used in structures, tables, etc., in the ABAP Data Dictionary. It is defined in such a way that it can be uniquely mapped to all supported database systems via SQL. This is the primary type system for database accesses from ABAP. The mapping of the ABAP Data Dictionary types to the basic types of the ABAP language is described in Table 3.1.

Type system of the ABAP Data Dictionary

The internal type system of the database defines the possible column types for tables and the corresponding operations. It is the primary type system for queries or implementations in the database (for example, by means of database procedures). Each database system uses slightly different data types or treats data types slightly differently.

Type system of the database

Table 3.1 shows the mapping of ABAP Data Dictionary types to ABAP types. The (fixed or variable) length of the corresponding ABAP type is indicated in parentheses.

Type mapping

Dictionary Type	Description	ABAP Type	Example
ACCP	Accounting period	N(6)	'201310'
CHAR	String	C(n)	'ABAP'
CLNT	Client	C(3)	'000'
CUKY	Currency key	C(5)	'EUR'

Table 3.1 Mapping of ABAP Data Dictionary Types and ABAP Types

Dictionary Type	Description	ABAP Type	Example
CURR	Currency field	P(n)	'01012000'
DATS	Date	D	'01012000'
DEC	Calculation/amount field	P(n)	100.20
DF16_RAW	Decimal floating point number (normalized; 16 digits)	decfloat16	100.20
DF16_SCL	Decimal floating point number (scaled; 16 digits)	decfloat16	100.20
DF34_RAW	Decimal floating point number (normalized; 34 digits)	decfloat34	100.20
DF34_SCL	Decimal floating point number (scaled; 34 digits)	decfloat34	100.20
FLTP	Floating point number	F(8)	ABAP Data Dictionary Type
INT1	1-byte integer	internal	ACCP
INT2	2-byte integer	internal	CHAR
INT4	4-byte integer	I	CLNT
LANG	Language	C(1)	CUKY
LCHR	Long character string	C(m)	CURR
LRAW	Long byte string	X(m)	DATS
NUMC	Numeric text	N(m)	DEC
QUAN	Quantity field	P(n)	100
RAW	Byte sequence	X(m)	F48FBFBF
RAWSTRING	Byte sequence	XSTRING	272927450108018F8F8F8F
SSTRING	String	STRING	'ABAP'
STRING	String	STRING	'ABAP is …'
TIMS	Time	T	'123000'
UNIT	Unit key	C(m)	'KG'

Table 3.1 Mapping of ABAP Data Dictionary Types and ABAP Types (Cont.)

The example in Figure 3.3 shows the mapping of the ABAP Data Dictionary types to SAP HANA data types (based on a custom technical table that uses most of the native ABAP Data Dictionary types). As described in Section 2.5.3, you can display the structure of a database table in SAP HANA Studio by double-clicking a table in the database catalog.

Mapping of ABAP Data Dictionary types to SAP HANA types

Table Name:

ZA4H_DATA_TYPES

Columns | Indexes | Further Properties | Runtime Information

	Name	SQL Data Type	Dim	Column Store Data Type	Key	Not Null	Default
1	CLNT	NVARCHAR	3	STRING	X(1)	X	000
2	ACCP	NVARCHAR	6	STRING		X	
3	CHAR10	NVARCHAR	10	STRING		X	
4	CUKY	NVARCHAR	5	STRING		X	
5	CURR	DECIMAL	10,2	FIXED		X	0
6	DATS	NVARCHAR	8	STRING		X	00000000
7	DEC10_2	DECIMAL	10,2	FIXED		X	0
8	DF16_RAW	VARBINARY	8	RAW		X	800000000000...
9	DF34_RAW	VARBINARY	16	RAW		X	800000000000...
10	DF16_DEC	DECIMAL	10,5	FIXED		X	0
11	DF34_DEC	DECIMAL	26,5	FIXED		X	0
12	DF16_SCL	VARBINARY	8	RAW		X	800000000000...
13	DF16_SCL_SCALE	SMALLINT		INT		X	0
14	DF34_SCL	VARBINARY	16	RAW		X	800000000000...
15	DF34_SCL_SCALE	SMALLINT		INT		X	0
16	INT1	SMALLINT		INT		X	0
17	INT2	SMALLINT		INT		X	0
18	INT4	INTEGER		INT		X	0
19	LANG	NVARCHAR	1	STRING		X	
20	NUMC	NVARCHAR	10	STRING		X	0000000000
21	QUAN	DECIMAL	10	FIXED		X	0
22	RAW100	VARBINARY	100	RAW			
23	RAWSTRING	BLOB		ST_MEMORY_LOB			
24	SSTRING	NVARCHAR	100	STRING		X	
25	STRING	NCLOB	21...	ST_MEMORY_LOB			
26	TIMS	NVARCHAR	6	STRING		X	000000
27	UNIT	NVARCHAR	3	STRING		X	

Figure 3.3 Mapping of ABAP Data Dictionary Types to SAP HANA Types

In addition to the SQL data type, this table also shows the specific data type used in the column store in SAP HANA. However, this type plays only a minor role for ABAP development on SAP HANA.

It is important to note that there is no representation of the NULL value from SQL in the ABAP type system. However, there is an *initial* value for every ABAP and ABAP Data Dictionary data type—for example, an empty string for string types or 0 for numeric types. This is particularly relevant for certain join variants (*outer joins*), as you will see in Section 3.2.2.

NULL value

Data types
with a binary
representation Certain data types with a binary representation can usually not be used directly in implementations in SAP HANA. These are, for example, floating point numbers of type DF16_RAW and DF16_SCL (as well as the corresponding types with a length of 34). Another example are data clusters in ABAP, a special table type allowing you to read and write any kind of data record via the ABAP commands EXPORT TO DATABASE and IMPORT FROM DATABASE. The associated data is stored in the database in a column of type LRAW in a proprietary format that can only be unpacked via the ABAP kernel. These aspects must be taken into account if you consider moving parts of the logic to the database.

3.2   ABAP Database Access

Having introduced the basic database architecture of the SAP NetWeaver AS ABAP, we will now describe the actual database access from ABAP. This includes both the definition of data models (tables, views, etc.) and write and read operations for data records.

SQL   The database is usually accessed via the *Structured Query Language* (*SQL*). The SQL database language covers three orthogonal categories, which are described in Table 3.2.

Type	Purpose	Examples
Data Definition Language (DDL)	Definition of data structures and operations	CREATE TABLE, DROP TABLE, CREATE VIEW
Data Manipulation Language (DML)	Read and write operations for data records	SELECT, INSERT, UPDATE, DELETE
Data Control Language (DCL)	Definition of access restrictions for database objects	GRANT, REVOKE

Table 3.2   Overview of SQL

In traditional ABAP application development, DML operations are implemented via Open SQL (see Section 3.2.2), while DDL is used indirectly via the ABAP Data Dictionary (see Section 3.2.1). DCL, on the other hand, is not relevant for *traditional* application development since the ABAP application server—as described in Section 3.1.2—uses a technical user to log in to the database. Also, the authorizations for the actual application user are checked using the ABAP authorization system (e.g., using the command AUTHORITY-CHECK). When using SAP HANA for implementing part of the application logic inside the database, the authorization concepts of the database must also be considered. This will be explained in more detail in Chapter 14.

3.2.1 ABAP Data Dictionary

Using the *ABAP Data Dictionary* (DDIC), you can create data models in the database. These data models can be enriched with semantic aspects such as texts, fixed values, and relationships. This metadata, which is particularly important for business scenarios, plays an important role for developments in SAP HANA since it can be used for modeling and implementation tasks in SAP HANA.

Before we describe the individual types of development objects (tables, views, etc.), we would like to introduce two very important qualities of the ABAP Data Dictionary:

Qualities of the ABAP Data Dictionary

▶ Since the ABAP Data Dictionary is fully integrated with the ABAP Lifecycle Management, you can transport the defined database artifacts and their properties into an SAP landscape.

▶ Objects in the ABAP Data Dictionary can be extended; i.e., SAP customers and partners can adjust these objects to their needs for instance by adding columns to a table.

This extensibility of ABAP Data Dictionary objects should also be particularly considered when performing modeling and programming tasks in SAP HANA.

From a development perspective, Transaction SE11 is the main tool for using the ABAP Data Dictionary. This transaction can be used to define and maintain the following object types:

Object types in the ABAP Data Dictionary

▶ **Table**
Tables define the structure for physically storing data in the database. A table consists of a number of fields (columns) and their

corresponding data types. In addition to individual fields, you can also include predefined structures.

The ABAP Data Dictionary supports different types of tables, for example, tables for application data, Customizing data, or master data, which differ in certain lifecycle management aspects. Moreover, a series of technical properties can be maintained for a table.

In addition to defining the mere field list, you can include additional metadata:

- *Foreign key relationships*
  By specifying check tables for fields, you can define specific foreign key relationships. This information is used when modeling views in SAP HANA Studio (see Chapter 4).

- *Currency and unit of measure*
  To store monetary amounts or unit of measures, the currencies or units must be defined in addition to the numeric value. This is usually done via another column, and the ABAP Data Dictionary allows you to define a relationship between the two columns.

- *Search help*
  By specifying a search help for a column, a generic input help can be provided in transactions without any programming effort.

- **View**
  Views allow you to define specific views on several Dictionary tables. The ABAP Data Dictionary supports several view types for different usage scenarios:

  - *Database views* are used to define SQL views on the database.

  - *Projection views* are used to hide fields of a table. These views do not exist physically in the database.

  - *Help views* are used as a selection method in search helps.

  - *Maintenance views* facilitate a consistent entry of data records for interlinked database tables.

As *views* plays an important role in the context of SAP HANA, the possibility to define database views via the ABAP Data Dictionary will be explained in more detail in Section 3.2.3.

▶ **Data type**
Based on the basic types, user-specific types can be defined in the ABAP Data Dictionary. These globally defined objects can be used when defining table columns and within ABAP programs.

The ABAP Data Dictionary supports three kinds of data types:

- ▶ Elementary data elements
- ▶ Composite structures
- ▶ Table types

These data types cannot be used directly for modeling and programming tasks in SAP HANA.

▶ **Domain**
Domains can be used to define value ranges. For an elementary data type, a length is specified (in the case of numeric types, the number of decimal places may also be defined). In addition, the value range can be further limited by fixed values, intervals, or check tables.

Domains cannot be used directly for modeling and programming tasks in SAP HANA.

▶ **Search help**
Search helps (also referred to as input helps or F4 helps) provide input options for fields in an SAP user interface. Using the ABAP Data Dictionary, you can define such search helps based on tables, views, or a freely programmed *Exit*.

Implementing specific search helps on SAP HANA is described in more detail in Chapter 9.

▶ **Lock object**
Lock objects can be used to define logical locks in the database. This was described in Section 3.1.2.

In addition to pure data structures, further properties can be maintained in the technical settings for a database table. These especially include the following two options:

Technical settings

▶ **ABAP table buffer**
Many tables used in application scenarios are suitable candidates for buffering on the application server, since they contain a relatively

small amount of data. Also, read operations are executed much more often for those tables than write operations. The ABAP table buffer provides an efficient option for this purpose. You can activate buffering via the technical properties in the ABAP Data Dictionary, and you can also configure if single records, ranges, or the full table should be buffered. When using SAP HANA, where table contents are usually stored in the main memory of the database, the ABAP table buffer also plays an important role (see Chapter 14).

▶ **Data class and size category**
By specifying the data class and the expected table entries, the database system can efficiently reserve the required storage space. Moreover, the size category of a table can be used to analyze ABAP program performance issues that were detected in static code analyses.

Usage of row or column store
As of SAP NetWeaver 7.4, the ABAP Data Dictionary allows you to specify if tables should be stored in the column store or in the row store in SAP HANA (see Figure 3.4). When selecting the default value UNDEFINED, the column store is used—which is recommended for basically all application cases. There are a few exceptions, which are described in Chapter 14 as well.

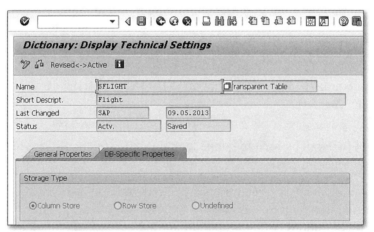

Figure 3.4 Database-Specific Settings for Tables

You can also define database indices in the ABAP Data Dictionary. When doing so, you can create indices only for certain databases (inclusion list) or exclude them by specifying an exclusion list. During a database migration to SAP HANA, the system first creates entries for existing secondary indices in the exclusion list, so that the corresponding index on SAP HANA is not created automatically. Instead, those indices should only be activated on a case-by-case basis. Technical background information and recommendations for index usage on SAP HANA can also be found in Chapter 14.

Indices

Figure 3.5 shows the index exclusion on SAP HANA for the table SBOOK. In this case, the indexes ACY and CUS are not created on SAP HANA, since HDB is on the exclusion list.

Ind	Ext. Index	Short text	Status	Unique	Author	Date	DB index name	DBSt	IE	DBS
ACY	☐	Index using travel agency number	Active	☐	DDIC	09.05.2013		D	E	HDB
CUS	☐	Index using customer number	Active	☐	DDIC	09.05.2013		D	E	HDB

Figure 3.5 Index Exclusion for SAP HANA

In the past, some database versions came with severe restrictions of the maximum number of tables in the system and provided poor compression capabilities. To avoid these problems, you can create special table types in the ABAP Data Dictionary—so-called *pool* and *cluster tables*—where several logical tables are combined into one physical database table. These logical tables can basically be accessed from ABAP like normal database tables; however, there are also a number of restrictions to consider. Since pool and cluster tables are not needed on SAP HANA, existing tables are converted into normal transparent tables when migrating to SAP HANA. The main advantage of this conversion is that the tables can also be used for modeling and programming tasks in SAP HANA, as described in Chapter 4 and Chapter 5. During migration, pool and cluster tables are compatible with existing applications. There is no need to adapt existing ABAP code. However, certain aspects must be considered with regard to the sorting behavior, which will be explained in more detail in Chapter 14.

Pool and cluster tables

3.2.2 Open SQL

Open SQL provides an option for database access that is integrated into the ABAP programming language. Both the supported syntax and the detailed semantics of Open SQL are database-independent. This makes it possible to write applications in ABAP without knowing the details of the underlying database system.

Read Access with Open SQL

SAP HANA mainly offers options to accelerate read accesses. Using Open SQL is the primary and simplest option to move data-intensive operations to SAP HANA.

In this section, we will use examples to detail some of the advanced options of Open SQL that you may not have used in the past. The syntax of the ABAP command SELECT will not be explained in detail; a comprehensive documentation of the Open SQL syntax can be found in the ABAP online help.

Expressing calculation logic in Open SQL

The examples deal with the three aspects listed below, which basically cover the advanced options for expressing calculation logic in Open SQL:

- ▶ Reading fields from several tables with foreign key relationships (use of *joins* and the FOR ALL ENTRIES clause).
- ▶ Calculating key figures based on the values of a column by using the aggregate functions (for example, determining quantities, totals, average values, etc.).
- ▶ Selecting special entries of a table based on complex criteria using subqueries (*sub-selects*) and existence checks.

Joins

In the first example, we will use a join to read values from the tables SCARR and SCURX (currencies). Depending on the table entries which should be included in the result, there are several options for creating joins in SQL. Open SQL supports *inner joins* and *left outer joins*. When describing the process for modeling views in SAP HANA Studio in Chapter 4, the different join variants will be explained in detail. Listing 3.4 uses the two variants that are supported in Open SQL and shows the differences between them.

```
REPORT zr_a4h_chapter3_open1.

TYPES: BEGIN OF result_type,
         currkey TYPE s_curr,
         currdec TYPE currdec,
         carrname TYPE s_carrname,
       END OF result_type.

DATA: wa TYPE result_type.

" Selection of all currencies and corresponding
" airlines. The inner join is used to only select
" currencies with a corresponding airline which
"uses this currency.
SELECT c~currkey c~currdec r~carrname FROM scurx AS c
    INNER JOIN scarr AS r
      ON c~currkey = r~currcode INTO wa.

  WRITE: / wa-currkey , wa-currdec , wa-carrname.
ENDSELECT.

" Selection of all currencies and corresponding
" airlines. The outer join is used to also select
" currencies without a
" corresponding airline.
" In this case, the value is initial.
SELECT c~currkey c~currdec r~carrname FROM scurx AS c
    LEFT OUTER JOIN scarr AS r
      ON c~currkey = r~currcode INTO wa.

  WRITE: / wa-currkey , wa-currdec , wa-carrname.
ENDSELECT.
```

Listing 3.4 Inner and Left Outer Joins in Open SQL

As already mentioned in Section 3.1.3, there is no representation of the NULL value in ABAP. As shown in Listing 3.4, where no corresponding data record is found in the "right-hand" table, a left outer join generates the value NULL for the corresponding columns of the result set in the database. In ABAP, this value is converted into the initial value of the column. Consequently, it cannot be determined if no value was found or if the corresponding value happens to be the initial value. When executing

NULL as the result of left outer joins

the equivalent SQL statement via the SQL console in SAP HANA Studio, NULL values are displayed as question marks (?) as shown in Figure 3.6.

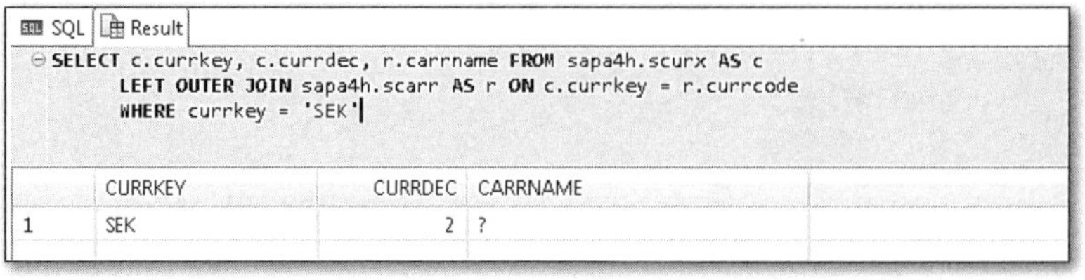

Figure 3.6 Representation of NULL Values in the SQL Console

FOR ALL ENTRIES

In addition to the described inner and left outer joins, the expression FOR ALL ENTRIES provides another option in Open SQL to leverage foreign key relationships and use internal tables to create joins. This SAP-proprietary expression is not part of the SQL standard and is a natural enhancement of the so-called *ranges* that are used in selection options. A typical example of using this expression is shown in Listing 3.5. In this example, all airlines are first read and the airlines that can be displayed by the user are then stored in an internal table. Subsequently, the FOR ALL ENTRIES clause is used for a type of inner join with the SFLIGHT table.

```
REPORT zr_a4h_chapter3_open2.

TYPES: BEGIN OF ty_carrid,
         carrid TYPE s_carrid,
       END OF ty_carrid.

DATA: ls_carrier TYPE ty_carrid,
      ls_flight TYPE sflight,
      lt_carrier TYPE TABLE OF ty_carrid.

SELECT carrid FROM scarr INTO ls_carrier.
  " Check authorization and, if
  " successful, add to internal table
  AUTHORITY-CHECK OBJECT 'S_CARRID'
      ID 'CARRID' FIELD ls_carrier-carrid
      ID 'ACTVT' FIELD '03'.

  IF sy-subrc = 0.
    APPEND ls_carrier TO lt_carrier.
  ENDIF.
```

```
ENDSELECT.

" Output of all flights of the airlines for which the user is
authorized.
IF ( lt_carrier IS NOT INITIAL ).
  SELECT * FROM sflight INTO ls_flight
      FOR ALL ENTRIES IN lt_carrier
        WHERE carrid = lt_carrier-carrid.

    WRITE: / ls_flight-carrid,
             ls_flight-connid, ls_flight-fldate.
  ENDSELECT.
ENDIF.
```

Listing 3.5 Join of a Database Table with an Internal Table

Special Properties of FOR ALL ENTRIES **[!]**

For performance reasons, changing a nested SELECT statement into a FOR ALL ENTRIES expression can be useful. However, when doing so, you should pay attention to three important properties of the expression FOR ALL ENTRIES:

▶ If the driver table (i.e., the internal table following the FOR ALL ENTRIES expression) is empty, *all* values are returned as the result. If you perhaps forget the IF check before the selection at the end in Listing 3.5, you would, under certain circumstances, select data that the user might not be allowed to access.

▶ The driver table should not contain any duplicates. This helps limiting the number of accesses to a minimum and avoids the selection of identical data from the database.

▶ Selections with FOR ALL ENTRIES are always performed with an implicit DISTINCT so that no duplicates are returned. If you only select the columns CARRID and CONNID (instead of *) for the second SELECT statement in Listing 3.5, for example, far fewer results are returned (independent of the flight date, every connection is returned only once).

▶ More information on SAP HANA can be found in Chapter 14, which also includes recommendations for optimizing ABAP programs.

In the third example, we will use the aggregate functions (COUNT, SUM, MIN, MAX, AVG). Using an SQL query, we will determine inconsistencies within the data model. To do so, we will execute a query to find out if there are more bookings for the Economy class of a flight (based on the

Aggregate functions

entries in the SBOOK table) than occupied seats (attribute SEATSOCC in the table SFLIGHT). In Listing 3.6, a join is combined directly with the calculation of a quantity (COUNT) and the limitation of the result set based on the result of the aggregation (HAVING).

```
REPORT zr_a4h_chapter3_open3.

TYPES: BEGIN OF ty_result,
         carrid TYPE sbook-carrid,
         connid TYPE sbook-connid,
         fldate  TYPE sbook-fldate,
         count_sbook TYPE i,
         count_sflight TYPE i,
       END OF ty_result.
DATA ls_result TYPE ty_result.

" Determination of all flights with more
" Economy class bookings (table SBOOK) than
" occupied seats (table SFLIGHT)
SELECT b~carrid b~connid b~fldate
       f~seatsocc AS count_sflight
       COUNT( * ) AS count_sbook
  FROM sbook AS b
  INNER JOIN sflight AS f ON b~carrid = f~carrid
                         AND b~connid = f~connid
                         AND b~fldate = f~fldate
  INTO ls_result
  WHERE b~cancelled <> 'X' AND b~class = 'Y'
  GROUP BY b~carrid b~connid b~fldate f~seatsocc
  HAVING COUNT( * ) > f~seatsocc
  ORDER BY b~fldate b~carrid b~connid.

  WRITE: / ls_result-carrid, ls_result-connid,
           ls_result-fldate, ls_result-count_sbook ,
           ls_result-count_sflight.
ENDSELECT.
```

Listing 3.6 Aggregate Functions in Open SQL

When using aggregations, it must always be noted that the GROUP BY expression lists all non-aggregated attributes; this also includes attributes that are used only in a HAVING clause.

As you can see, rather complex queries can be expressed via Open SQL. In the fourth example, we will add another element: *subqueries*—and, as a special case, *existence checks*. A subquery is a SELECT statement in parentheses which can be used as part of the WHERE clause (both in reading and writing accesses). Typical use cases are existence checks with the following structure:

Subqueries

```
SELECT ... FROM ... INTO ...
 WHERE EXISTS ( SELECT ... ).
```

If only one column is selected in a subquery, this is referred to as a *scalar subquery*. In addition to *simple comparissons* (=, >, <) for a column, these queries support other operations as well (ALL, ANY, SOME, IN). The example in Listing 3.7 shows how subqueries can be used to implement a nested filter condition.

```
REPORT zr_a4h_chapter3_open4.

DATA: ls_flight TYPE sflight.

" Output of all flights from 2013 with more
" occupied seats than the average value for the
" same route in 2012
SELECT * FROM sflight AS f INTO ls_flight
  WHERE fldate LIKE '2013%' AND seatsocc >
    ( SELECT AVG( seatsocc ) FROM sflight
            WHERE carrid = f~carrid
            AND connid = f~connid
            AND fldate LIKE '2012%' ).

  WRITE: / ls_flight-carrid,
         ls_flight-connid, ls_flight-fldate.
ENDSELECT.
```

Listing 3.7 Usage of Subqueries

The approaches described above provide a great variety of options for accessing database tables. Using joins, you can define relationships between several tables (and via FOR ALL ENTRIES, even between internal tables); the aggregate functions can be used for simple calculations; and subqueries allow nested selections. In addition to the SQL vocabulary,

Open SQL provides further techniques to flexibly and efficiently design database access, which will be described below.

Dynamic SQL   Using Open SQL, you can also specify parts of an SQL statement *dynamically* so that, for instance, the table name or the selected columns can be controlled via a variable that has to be specified in parentheses (as shown in the example in Listing 3.8).

```
DATA: lv_table   TYPE string,
      lt_fields  TYPE string_table,
      ls_carrier TYPE scarr.

" Table name as a string
lv_table = 'SCARR'.

" Dynamic output of the columns
APPEND 'CARRID' TO lt_fields.
APPEND 'CARRNAME' TO lt_fields.

SELECT (lt_fields) FROM (lv_table)
  INTO CORRESPONDING FIELDS OF ls_carrier.
    WRITE: / ls_carrier-carrid , ls_carrier-carrname.
ENDSELECT.
```

Listing 3.8   Dynamic Open SQL

When working with dynamic Open SQL, it must be noted that the separating keywords (for example, SELECT, FROM, WHERE, etc.) still have to be used statically in the code. This particularly helps preventing potential security vulnerabilities, since certain attacks by means of *SQL injection* (introduction of unwanted database operations by an attacker) are not possible. However, especially when using dynamic SQL, you should always make sure that the values of the variables are checked in order to avoid runtime errors or security issues. To do so, you can use a list of allowed values (*whitelists*) or *regular expression patterns*.

Using cursors   Using *cursors*, you can separate the definition of the selection from the data retrieval. For this purpose, you first have to open a cursor by specifying the selection, and can then retrieve the data from the database using this cursor at a later point in time or elsewhere (e.g., in a FORM routine), as shown in Listing 3.9. As the number of cursors that can be used in parallel is limited, you should always make sure to close a cursor after using it.

```
DATA: lv_cursor TYPE cursor,
      ls_flight TYPE sflight.

" Defining the cursor
OPEN CURSOR lv_cursor FOR
    SELECT * FROM sflight
              WHERE carrid = 'LH'.

" Retrieving a data record via the cursor
FETCH NEXT CURSOR lv_cursor INTO ls_flight.

" Closing the cursor
CLOSE CURSOR lv_cursor.
```
Listing 3.9 Simple Example of Using a Cursor

The data flow between the database and the application server can be controlled in Open SQL, by defining package sizes via the addition PACKAGE SIZE. When doing so, the specified number of rows is always retrieved from the database when selecting into an internal table within a loop.

Package sizes

```
DATA: lt_book TYPE TABLE OF sbook.

" Selection into packages of 1,000 rows each
SELECT * FROM sbook
        INTO TABLE lt_book
        PACKAGE SIZE 1000.

  " ...
ENDSELECT.
```
Listing 3.10 Selecting Data while Specifying a Package Size

Before dealing with writing accesses, we would like to briefly summarize the options for read access provided by Open SQL. Using the SELECT statement, you can efficiently read data records from a relational data model (tables with foreign key relationships). The aggregate function allows you to express simple calculations on a column. Data transfer from the database can be controlled using advanced techniques. However, it is not possible to use complex filter expressions, case distinctions, or business calculations directly within the database. Furthermore, interim results cannot be temporarily stored in the database, since the result of a query is always transferred to the application server.

Read operations in Open SQL

Write Accesses and Transaction Behavior

The basic principles of the ABAP transaction concept, and in particular the differences between the database LUW and the SAP LUW, were already discussed in Section 3.1.2. To change database contents, Open SQL provides the statements INSERT (creating data records), UPDATE (changing existing data records), MODIFY (changing or creating data records), and DELETE (deleting data records). In addition to changing individual entries, you can also edit several rows at the same time. For example, you can use an Open SQL statement to create or update several data records based on the contents of an internal table in one go. This usually significantly improves the performance of a program, since a lot fewer database accesses are necessary. The example in Listing 3.11 shows how these so-called *array operations* are used. Similarly, you can update all or only selected columns when changing a data record. This can also lead to an increased performance. These two techniques are particularly recommended on SAP HANA (see Chapter 14).

```
REPORT zr_a4h_chapter3_modify_array.

DATA: lt_country TYPE TABLE OF za4h_country_cls.

" Select countries and number of customers
SELECT country COUNT(*) AS class FROM scustom
  INTO CORRESPONDING FIELDS OF TABLE lt_country
  GROUP BY country.

" Change table entries in one go
MODIFY za4h_country_cls FROM TABLE lt_country.

COMMIT WORK.
```

Listing 3.11 Modifying Table Contents via Array Operations

In Open SQL, the statements COMMIT WORK or ROLLBACK WORK are used for explicit transaction control. There are also situations where an implicit Commit (for example, after completing a dialog step) or a rollback (for example, in case of a runtime error) are performed automatically. To process database changes from several dialog steps in a single database LUW, the SAP LUW concept offers several bundling techniques. This primarily includes calling update modules (CALL FUNCTION ... IN UPDATE TASK) and bundling via subroutines (PERFORM ... ON COMMIT).

If you perform direct writing operations on the database (for example, with SQLScript) the programming model differs significantly from the traditional ABAP programming model (please also refer to Section 3.1.2 and Chapter 14).

Even though Open SQL is database independent, it is possible to pass *hints* to the respective database system (or, more specifically, to the database optimizer) to specify how a statement should be executed. In practice, this variant offers tuning options for database experts and is used rather infrequently in normal ABAP development. Using hints, you can specify how the database should access the data (for example, using a specific index). Since hints must be maintained manually (e.g., when performing a release upgrade or a database migration), this option should only be used if there are no other tuning methods.

Despite the comprehensive scope of functions, Open SQL covers only a rather small part of the SQL standard. In particular, the following SQL constructs cannot be used in Open SQL at the moment:

▶ Specification of an offset for paging (for example, for a selection of 50 rows starting with row index 100)

▶ UNION, INTERSECT (creating unions or intersections for several selections)

▶ CASE (case distinctions)

▶ Expressions in the selection or WHERE clause (string operations, usage of literals and built-in functions, etc.)

These commands are not available in Open SQL partly because they were implemented differently or not at all by the different database vendors. Using the SAP HANA-specific SQL dialect beyond Open SQL will be explained in Section 3.2.4 and in Chapter 5.

Database hints

Limitations of Open SQL

Planned Extensions of Open SQL	**[«]**
SAP is currently working on significantly extending the functionality of Open SQL. In future versions, the features will include the creation of unions, case distinctions, and expressions in the selection of WHERE clause, among others.	

3.2.3 Database Views in the ABAP Data Dictionary

Database views are a standard option for looking at data based on one or several tables in the database, and thus predefining parts of a SQL query. In most database systems, views are created using SQL:

```
CREATE VIEW view_name AS SELECT ...
```

The SAP HANA-specific options for view creation, which go far beyond wrapping a simple SQL query, will be described in more detail in Chapter 4. In this section, we will focus only on what is supported by default by the ABAP Data Dictionary for all database systems.

Limitations   While you can define data views using the ABAP Data Dictionary, not all options of Open SQL are available when following this approach. Basically, you can link several tables via an inner join and add fields to the projection list. It is not possible, however, to use other join types, aggregates, or subqueries.

Example: Figure 3.7 shows the standard view SFLIGHTS which defines a join to
SFLIGHTS   add fields from the tables SCARR, SPFLI, and SFLIGHT. The corresponding CREATE VIEW statement can be displayed via the menu bar.

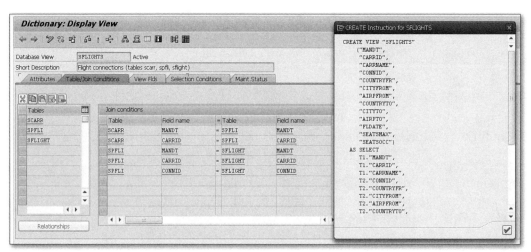

Figure 3.7 Dictionary View SFLIGHTS

These database views can be accessed like tables from ABAP coding using Open SQL and Native SQL. In this context, it must be noted that modifying operations can only be executed for views that access only one table. Similar to table access, buffering can be configured in the technical settings.

Accessing database views

> **Extending the Capabilities for View Creation in ABAP**
>
> SAP currently works on a unified view creation process in SAP HANA and the ABAP Data Dictionary (referred to as *Core Data Services*, or CDS). The goal of this approach is to significantly enhance the scope of functions for defining views in the ABAP Data Dictionary.

[«]

3.2.4   Database Access via Native SQL

In addition to Open SQL, which enables database-independent access that is integrated into the ABAP programming language, there is another method for accessing the database from ABAP. With this variant, you more or less directly specify the native database commands. For this reason, this is also referred to *Native SQL*.

Before we deal with the technical aspects of supporting Native SQL in SAP NetWeaver AS ABAP, we will explain why this variant plays a more important role in the context of SAP HANA than in the past. To fully benefit from the potential of SAP HANA, you must particularly use those functions that are not standard relational database capabilities. This particularly includes using capabilities in SAP HANA-specific SQL beyond the SQL standard, and accessing development objects in SAP HANA beyond normal tables and SQL views. This will be explained in detail in Chapter 4 and Chapter 5. At this point, we would already like to mention that using Native SQL will play an important role in this context.

Native SQL and SAP HANA

There are two options for using Native SQL in ABAP: either via the statement EXEC SQL, or via *ABAP Database Connectivity* (ADBC)—an object-oriented interface which is available as of SAP NetWeaver 2004 (release 6.40). In this context, SAP recommends using ADBC, since this approach provides greater flexibility and better options for troubleshooting. Within the scope of this book, we will therefore only describe and use the ADBC variant. With regard to some of its concepts, ADBC is similar to *Java Database Connectivity* (JDBC), a standard database interface of the Java platform.

Variants for using Native SQL

ABAP database connectivity

To use ADBC, essentially three ABAP classes are needed: CL_SQL_CON-NECTION, CL_SQL_STATEMENT, and CL_SQL_RESULT_SET. In the first step, you must use the constructor (or the static method GET_CONNECTION) of the CL_SQL_CONNECTION class to retrieve a database connection. If you do not specify any parameters, it will return the standard database connection, which is also used per default in Open SQL. However, you can also specify the name of a secondary connection (see Section 3.2.5). Using this connection, you create an object of type CL_SQL_STATEMENT via the CREATE_STATEMENT method, which can for example be used for reading database accesses via the method EXECUTE_QUERY by passing the SQL statement as a string. The result of this query is an instance of type CL_SQL_RESULT_SET. Similarly, writing accesses can be executed via EXECUTE_UPDATE, or DDL statements via EXECUTE_DDL.

Storing the query result in an internal table

To transfer the result of a query to an internal ABAP table, you will first have to pass a reference to this table via the method SET_PARAM_TABLE. Then you will be able to start the data transfer via NEXT_PACKAGE. When doing so, you can specify the package size, i.e., the number of rows.

The selected columns and corresponding data types must be compatible with the target structure for a call to be successful.

Error handling

If an error occurs when executing the SQL statement, an exception of type CX_SQL_EXCEPTION is thrown, and this can be used to obtain details like the error code and error text. Possible runtime errors are described in detail in Section 7.2.

Example

The following example shows how the named classes are used for a simple read access. In this example, the SQL statement uses expressions from the SAP HANA-specific SQL dialect, which cannot be used in the same manner in Open SQL.

```
REPORT ZR_A4H_CHAPTER3_ADBC.

" Variables for ADBC call
DATA: lv_statement  TYPE string,
      lo_conn       TYPE REF TO cl_sql_connection,
      lo_statement  TYPE REF TO cl_sql_statement,
      lo_result_set TYPE REF TO cl_sql_result_set.

" Definition of results structure
```

```abap
TYPES: BEGIN OF ty_result,
         carrid TYPE s_carr_id,
         connid TYPE s_conn_id,
         fldate TYPE s_date,
         days   type i,
       END OF ty_result.

DATA: lt_result TYPE TABLE OF ty_result,
      lr_result TYPE REF TO data.

FIELD-SYMBOLS: <l> TYPE ty_result.

" Data reference
GET REFERENCE OF lt_result INTO lr_result.

" Native SQL statement: sequence and data types
" of selected columns must match
" results structure
lv_statement =
     | SELECT carrid, connid, fldate, |
  && |   days_between(fldate, current_utcdate) as days |
  && | FROM sflight WHERE mandt = '{ sy-mandt }' and   |
  && |   days_between(fldate, current_utcdate) < 10     |.

TRY.
    " Prepare SQL connection and statement
    lo_conn = cl_sql_connection=>get_connection( ).
    lo_statement = lo_conn->create_statement( ).
    lo_result_set = lo_statement->execute_query( lv_statement
).
    lo_result_set->set_param_table( lr_result ).

    " Get result
    lo_result_set->next_package( ).
    lo_result_set->close( ).
  CATCH cx_sql_exception.
    " Error handling
ENDTRY.

LOOP AT lt_result ASSIGNING <l>.
  WRITE: / <l>-carrid , <l>-connid , <l>-fldate, <l>-days.
ENDLOOP.
```

Listing 3.12 Native SQL Access via ADBC

The function days_between in SAP HANA-specific SQL determines the number of days between the parameters, i.e., the number of days between the current date (which is obtained from the variable current_utcdate provided within SAP HANA-specific SQL) and the flight date in the example. The output of Listing 3.12 thus comprises all future flights and all flights within the last 10 days. For every flight, the system also displays the difference (in days) between the flight date and the current date. Since this query cannot be expressed via Open SQL, the only traditional option would be to load all data into the application server and calculate the dates via ABAP. Since we "pushed" a complex filter expression down to the database, this means that we implemented a so-called *code pushdown* via Native SQL.

Prepared statements and placeholders
If you want to consecutively use the same SQL statement with different parameterization, so-called *prepared statements* should be used for performance reasons. These prepared SQL statements reduce the effort for subsequent executions. To do this, you create an instance of the class CL_SQL_PREPARED_STATEMENT (a subclass of CL_SQL_STATEMENT), while passing an SQL statement with placeholders that can be bound to a variable. Listing 3.13 shows the usage of prepared statements and placeholders using some of the ABAP language elements from ABAP 7.4 (see Appendix B). Please note that placeholders can also be used independently of prepared statements. Recommendations on the use of prepared statements can be found in Chapter 14.

```
REPORT zr_a4h_chapter3_adbc2.

" Variables for the ADBC call
DATA: lv_sql    TYPE string,
      lo_result TYPE REF TO cl_sql_result_set.

DATA: lt_result TYPE TABLE OF scarr,
      lv_param  TYPE s_carrid.

" SQL statement with placeholder
lv_sql =
    | SELECT * |
&& |    FROM SCARR WHERE mandt  = '{ sy-mandt }' |
&& |                     AND carrid = ? limit 5|.
```

```
TRY.
    " Create prepared statement and set parameter
    DATA(lo_sql) =
            NEW cl_sql_prepared_statement( lv_sql ).
    lo_sql->set_param( REF #( lv_param ) ).

    " Execution with value for placeholder
    lv_param = 'LH'.
    lo_result = lo_sql->execute_query( ).
    lo_result->set_param_table( REF #( lt_result ) ).

    " Get and display result
    lo_result->next_package( ).
    lo_result->close( ).
    LOOP AT lt_result ASSIGNING FIELD-SYMBOL(<l1>).
      WRITE: / <l1>-carrid , <l1>-carrname.
    ENDLOOP.

    " Second execution with different value
    CLEAR lt_result.
    lv_param = 'UA'.
    lo_result = lo_sql->execute_query( ).
    lo_result->set_param_table( REF #( lt_result ) ).

    " Get and display result
    lo_result->next_package( ).
    lo_result->close( ).
    LOOP AT lt_result ASSIGNING FIELD-SYMBOL(<l2>).
      WRITE: / <l2>-carrid , <l2>-carrname.
    ENDLOOP.

    " Close prepared SQL statement
    lo_sql->close( ).
  CATCH cx_sql_exception INTO DATA(lo_ex).
    " Error handling
    WRITE: | Exception: { lo_ex->get_text( ) } |.
ENDTRY.
```

Listing 3.13 Prepared SELECT Statement with ADBC

In addition, when working with ABAP 7.4, you can execute mass operations via the ADBC interface—just as you can when using Open SQL. For this purpose, the method SET_PARAM_TABLE is available in the class

Mass operations

CL_SQL_STATEMENT, which can be used to pass an internal table as an input parameter. This makes it possible to, for instance, use the ADBC interface to fill a database table with the values of an internal table.

[+] **Using the SQL Console in SAP HANA Studio**

Usage of Native SQL is rather error-prone; this is especially true because syntax errors in SQL statements are only noticed at runtime. Before using a Native SQL statement in ABAP via ADBC, you should therefore first test the statement via the SQL console in SAP HANA Studio, which is introduced in Section 2.5.3.

When implementing commands that were executed successfully in the SQL console in ABAP, the following differences should be noted:

▸ To some degree, the execution of SQL statements is connected with the *session context*, i.e., the state of the database connection. This particularly includes the default schema, the client, the language, and the application user. Depending on the query, this can potentially lead to different results.

▸ A Native SQL statement in ABAP can only contain a single SQL command. It is not possible to execute several commands that are separated by semicolons.

Open SQL vs. Native SQL
In comparison to Open SQL, some capabilities are not directly integrated into Native SQL. These include the ABAP table buffer (Native SQL does not read from the buffer), automatic client handling (when using Native SQL, the client must be inserted manually in WHERE or JOIN conditions, as shown in the example from Listing 3.12), and some other useful enhancements in Open SQL (IN, FOR ALL ENTRIES, INTO CORRESPONDING FIELDS, etc.).

[+] **Pitfalls when Using Native SQL**

If you are experienced in Open SQL, there are some pitfalls with regard to the syntax when using Native SQL for the first time. To avoid unnecessary errors, the following pitfalls should be known:

Selected fields are separated by a comma:

▸ **Open SQL:** SELECT carrid connid FROM SFLIGHT

▸ **Native SQL:** SELECT carrid, connid FROM SFLIGHT

For table aliases, a period is used instead of the tilde character:

▸ **Open SQL:** SELECT f~carrid FROM SFLIGHT as f

▸ **Native SQL:** SELECT f.carrid FROM SFLIGHT as f

Moreover, the log and trace entries in different analysis tools (see Section 3.3) contain less context information for Native SQL. This means that the names of the tables or views are not visible, since the ABAP Compiler cannot obtain this information from the Native SQL statement. On the other hand, when using ADBC, this context can be set using the method SET_TABLE_NAME_FOR_TRACE of the class CL_SQL_STATEMENT.

Log and trace entries

To conclude this section, we will briefly explain some transaction-related aspects of Native SQL. If you use the standard database connection for Native SQL access, you must take into account that you share the database transaction within the ABAP session. To avoid inconsistencies, you should not run any commands for transaction control (for example, COMMIT or ROLLBACK) via Native SQL.

Transaction-related aspects

> **Comprehensive Database Knowledge Is Required to Use Native SQL** **[!]**
>
> As incorrect usage of Native SQL can impact system stability, comprehensive database knowledge is required to use this language.
>
> Using the following Native SQL statement to set a schema context for the standard database connection of the SAP NetWeaver AS ABAP leads to major problems:
>
> SET SCHEMA <name>
>
> The reason for this is that other database accesses within the same session no longer use the default schema of the SAP NetWeaver AS ABAP, but also use the set schema instead.
>
> This can easily lead to inconsistencies within the system and should be avoided at all costs. In general, Native SQL should be used with great caution and security concerns should always be taken into account (e.g., the avoidance of SQL injection).

3.2.5   Secondary Database Connections

In addition to the primary database, i.e., the database containing all tables maintained by the application server (including the actual ABAP code), the SAP NetWeaver AS ABAP can access other databases as well. These are referred to as *secondary databases* or *secondary database connections*. This section describes the technical steps to set up and use a secondary database connection.

Side-by-side scenarios Secondary connections are important in the context of SAP HANA, especially when implementing the side-by-side scenarios described in Section 3.4. In those cases, complex database queries with very long runtimes are moved to SAP HANA. Secondary connections also form the basis for *Redirected Database Access* (RDA, see Appendix D), which is offered by the SAP kernel 7.21. With this kernel release, the secondary connection cannot only be maintained in the ABAP code, but also in Customizing for specific programs and tables.

Database Shared Library (DBSL) As a prerequisite for setting up a secondary database connection, the matching Database Shared Library (DBSL) with the database driver must be installed; in the case of SAP HANA, this means that the DBSL must be installed with the SAP HANA Client. You can then create new connections in the Database Administration Cockpit (DBA Cockpit) via Transaction DBACOCKPIT (alternatively, you can also use Transaction ST04). The DBA Cockpit is the central starting point in the SAP NetWeaver AS ABAP for almost all database configuration and monitoring tasks. Within this book, we will only discuss some of these aspects in the context of Chapter 7.

Creating a connection To set up a new connection, select DB CONNECTIONS and click ADD.

For a new connection, you must then specify a unique name and the connection data (database system, host name, port, user, password, etc.) (as shown in Figure 3.8). The schema associated with the specified user will always be used as the default schema for this connection.

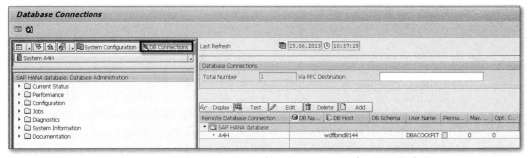

Figure 3.8 Setting Up a Secondary Connection in the DBA Cockpit

Configuring the connection Moreover, you can configure a set of parameters to define how the system should establish the created connections (see Figure 3.9):

▶ **Connection Maximum**

The parameter CONNECTION MAXIMUM defines the maximum number of concurrent connections. If this limit is reached, the system raises an error message when another connection is requested. If you do not set this parameter (initial value), the maximum number of supported connections (currently 255) is used.

▶ **Connection Optimum**

The parameter CONNECTION OPTIMUM defines an optimal number of open connections. If this number is exceeded, the system automatically closes existing connections once the transaction is completed.

▶ **Permanent Connection**

The option PERMANENT CONNECTION defines how to proceed if a connection is terminated. For permanent connections, the system tries to re-establish the connection for a running transaction—so that, at best, the transaction can continue to run. This setting should be used for critical and frequently used connections. The standard database connection of the SAP NetWeaver AS ABAP is flagged as permanent.

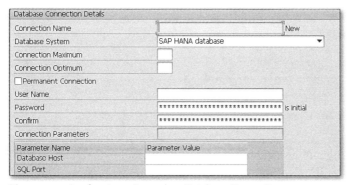

Figure 3.9 Configuring a Secondary Database Connection

After creating the connection, you can test it via the DBA Cockpit.

Secondary connections can be leveraged using both Open SQL and Native SQL. For Open SQL, the addition CONNECTION is used for this purpose (see Listing 3.14).

Secondary connections in ABAP programs

```
DATA: ls_carrier TYPE scarr.
SELECT SINGLE * FROM scarr CONNECTION ('SECONDARY') INTO
ls_carrier WHERE carrid = 'LH'.
```
Listing 3.14 Using Secondary Connections in Open SQL

To use Open SQL via a secondary connection, the tables and corresponding columns to be accessed must be known in the local ABAP Data Dictionary. This especially concerns any existing extensions.

In ADBC, the secondary connection can be specified when creating the connection (as seen in the example from Listing 3.15).

```
DATA: lo_statement  TYPE REF TO cl_sql_statement,
      lo_result_set TYPE REF TO cl_sql_result_set.

TRY.
    " Prepare SQL connection and statement
    lo_statement  = cl_sql_connection=>get_connection
( 'SECONDARY' )->create_statement( ).
    lo_result_set = lo_statement->execute_
query( |SELECT SINGLE * FROM SCARR WHERE carrid = 'LH'
AND mandt = { sy-mandt }| ).

    " ...
  CATCH cx_sql_exception.
    " Error handling
ENDTRY.
```
Listing 3.15 Using Secondary Connections in ADBC

Default schema — Both Open SQL and ADBC use the associated schema of the secondary connection—which is defined by the database user when configuring the connection—as the default schema. If the table SCARR does not exist in this schema in the examples from Listing 3.14 and Listing 3.15, the program terminates. When using Native SQL, you can manually specify the schema; however, this should be avoided in productive scenarios.

Transaction behavior — Although secondary connections are generally used to accelerate queries by means of SAP HANA, for the sake of completeness, we will briefly discuss the transaction behavior. Secondary connections form their own transaction context so that data can be committed via a secondary connection (using COMMIT CONNECTION) without affecting the actual transaction. Secondary connections are terminated, at the very latest, once the actual transaction is closed or if a change in the work process is possible in the application program.

3.3   Analyzing Database Accesses Using the SQL Trace

In this section, we will introduce some database programming tools. We will focus on tools that can be used for the database programming tasks described in this chapter. Tools for performance and error analysis are introduced in Chapter 7.

In the previous sections, we explained how the ABAP language, the data-   SQL trace
base interface in the kernel (DBI, DBSL), and the database interact. We also described how SQL access from ABAP is used via primary or secondary connections. Using the SQL trace tool, you can track and check this procedure. In the following text, we will use examples to demonstrate how you can analyze the following aspects directly within the system:

▶ Statement transformations (transformation of Open SQL into Native SQL via the database interface)

▶ Native SQL

▶ Usage of secondary connections and Native SQL (ADBC)

▶ Usage of the ABAP table buffer

3.3.1   Statement Transformations

Statement transformations of the DBI are described based on the example   Sample program
from Listing 3.16.   for DBI functions

```
" Variables for the result
DATA: ls_sflight TYPE sflight,
      lt_sflight TYPE TABLE OF sflight,
      ls_scarr TYPE scarr,
      ls_sbook TYPE sbook,
      lv_count TYPE i.
```

```
"Parameter for airlines
SELECT-OPTIONS: so_carr FOR ls_sflight-carrid,
                so_conn for ls_sflight-connid.

"Client handling and Open SQL -> Native SQL
SELECT *
  FROM sflight  UP TO 200 ROWS
  INTO ls_sflight
  WHERE carrid IN so_carr
  and connid in so_conn.

  APPEND ls_sflight TO lt_sflight.

  WRITE: / ls_sflight-mandt, ls_sflight-carrid,
           ls_sflight-connid, ls_sflight-fldate.

ENDSELECT.

"Open SQL -> Native SQL
MODIFY sflight FROM TABLE lt_sflight.
COMMIT WORK.


DELETE ADJACENT DUPLICATES FROM lt_sflight
COMPARING carrid connid.

"FOR ALL ENTRIES on SBOOK
IF lines( lt_sflight ) > 0.
SELECT *
  FROM sbook
  INTO ls_sbook
  FOR ALL ENTRIES IN lt_sflight
  WHERE carrid = lt_sflight-carrid
  AND connid = lt_sflight-connid
  AND fldate = lt_sflight-fldate.

ENDSELECT.
ENDIF.

lv_count = sy-dbcnt.
WRITE: / lv_count, 'SBOOK'.
```

```
DELETE ADJACENT DUPLICATES FROM lt_sflight
COMPARING carrid.

"FOR ALL ENTRIES on SFLIGHT
IF lines( lt_sflight ) > 0.
SELECT *
  FROM scarr
  INTO ls_scarr
  FOR ALL ENTRIES IN lt_sflight
  WHERE carrid = lt_sflight-carrid.

ENDSELECT.
ENDIF.

lv_count = sy-dbcnt.
WRITE: / lv_count, 'SCARR'.
```

Listing 3.16 Sample Program 1 for DBI Functions

Using the SQL trace in Transaction ST05, you can record the SQL state- Recording
ments that are sent to the database: SQL traces

1. Start Transaction ST05 (see Figure 3.10).

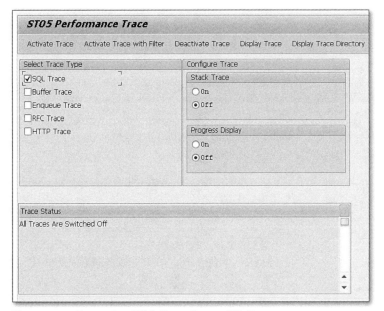

Figure 3.10 Transaction ST05: Recording an SQL Trace

2. Click ACTIVATE TRACE. Start the program and select a range of airlines. We want to display all airlines with an abbreviation from 'AA' to 'LH', but not 'DL'. Only the selection option for airlines (CARRID) is filled; the selection option for the connection numbers (CONNID) remains empty.

3. Click DEACTIVATE TRACE.

4. Click DISPLAY TRACE.

Recording result   A list with the recorded SQL statements is displayed. We will now briefly explain the most important columns; for more detailed information on SQL traces, please refer to Chapter 7.

In the result list of the recorded SQL statements (see Figure 3.11), the columns listed in Table 3.3 are important for the explanations in this section.

Figure 3.11   SQL Trace List

Column	Description
HH:MM:SS:MS	Time stamp of the execution in milliseconds
DURATION	Duration of the statement in microseconds
RECORDS	Number of records processed by the statement
PROGRAM NAME	Name of the program where the statement is executed
OBJECT NAME	Name of the object to which the statement refers
STATEMENT	The actual SQL statement
DB CONN.	Database connection used to execute the statement
USER	SAP user who executed the statement

Table 3.3   Fields of the SQL Trace Analysis

Further columns, which are not shown in Figure 3.11, are the CLIENT and WORK PROCESS TYPE where the SQL statement was executed. We will now take a closer look at the first SQL statement for the SFLIGHT table. When this statement was executed, the system read the first 200 rows (all columns) from the SFLIGHT table that are matching the selected airlines.

Double-click the first statement for the SFLIGHT table in the trace list to open the detail view shown in Figure 3.12. This view shows the SQL statement as it was sent from the DBI to the database.

Detail view

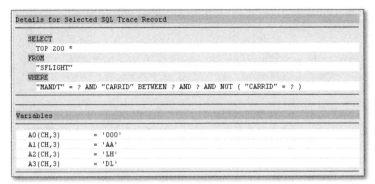

```
Details for Selected SQL Trace Record

    SELECT
        TOP 200 *
    FROM
        "SFLIGHT"
    WHERE
        "MANDT" = ? AND "CARRID" BETWEEN ? AND ? AND NOT ( "CARRID" = ? )


Variables

    A0(CH,3)      = '000'
    A1(CH,3)      = 'AA'
    A2(CH,3)      = 'LH'
    A3(CH,3)      = 'DL'
```

Figure 3.12 Detail View of the SQL Trace Record

When comparing the Native SQL statement in the SQL trace to the Open SQL statement in the ABAP program, you'll notice the following:

Client handling and selection options

▶ The client was inserted automatically in the WHERE condition of the Native SQL statement.

▶ The Open SQL addition UP TO <n> ROWS was translated into TOP 200 for the SAP HANA-specific Native SQL.

▶ The selection option IN so_carr was translated into a WHERE condition.

▶ The selection option IN so_conn was not sent to the database since it does not include any data.

Let's now take a look at the second SQL statement for the table SFLIGHT in the list from Figure 3.11. The Open SQL command MODIFY was translated into an UPSERT statement by the DBI. The command UPSERT (a combination of the terms UPdate and inSERT) first tries to update the transferred

Implementation of the MODIFY statement

records. If this is not possible because the records do not yet exist, they are inserted via an INSERT statement.

[»] **Implementation of the MODIFY Statement in the Database**

On other database platforms and older SAP releases, the MODIFY statement is split by the DBI, which can also be traced and analyzed in Transaction ST05. In the SQL trace, you will see two statements in this case: An UPDATE statement, and—if this first statement was not successful—an INSERT statement. However, an increasing number of database vendors provide native statements for this logic. The names of those statements are MERGE or UPSERT. As soon as such statements are available for a database, they will be used by SAP in the DBI. This means that the well-known UPDATE/INSERT sequence for the MODIFY statement will gradually disappear and be replaced by a Native SQL statement with the same function. This reduces the number of SQL statements sent to the database (*round trips*) and thus increases the performance.

FOR ALL ENTRIES statement

Let's now take a look at the two FOR ALL ENTRIES statements for the tables SBOOK and SCARR (Listing 3.16). When analyzing the list of SQL statements in Figure 3.11, you'll notice that even though only one FOR ALL ENTRIES statement was written in the program for the two tables, the table SBOOK is listed four times, while there is only one entry for the table SCARR. This is because the driver table of the FOR ALL ENTRIES statement is divided into packages so that several statements are created if the driver table does not fit in one package.

OR combination

When comparing the statement FOR ALL ENTRIES for the SBOOK table in the ABAP program's Open SQL versus the statement in the SQL Trace's Native SQL, you'll notice that there are several references to the internal table (driver table) in Open SQL. The fields CARRID, CONNID, and FLDATE are compared to a column from the internal table. As a consequence, for every row of the internal table, an OR expression is created. Figure 3.13 shows such a chain of OR comparisons. This way, the comparisons are appended to the statement using OR operators. When the maximum package size (a certain number of OR operators) is reached (*blocking factor*), the first statement is sent to the database. Further packages are then created until all entries of the internal table are processed.

```
Details for Selected SQL Trace Record

SELECT
  *
FROM
  "SBOOK"
WHERE
  ( "MANDT" = ? AND "CARRID" = ? AND "CONNID" = ? AND "FLDATE" = ? ) OR (
  "MANDT" = ? AND "CARRID" = ? AND "CONNID" = ? AND "FLDATE" = ? ) OR ( "MANDT" =
  ? AND "CARRID" = ? AND "CONNID" = ? AND "FLDATE" = ? ) OR ( "MANDT" = ? AND
  "CARRID" = ? AND "CONNID" = ? AND "FLDATE" = ? ) OR ( "MANDT" = ? AND "CARRID"
  = ? AND "CONNID" = ? AND "FLDATE" = ? ) OR ( "MANDT" = ? AND "CARRID" = ? AND
  "CONNID" = ? AND "FLDATE" = ? ) OR ( "MANDT" = ? AND "CARRID" = ? AND "CONNID"
  = ? AND "FLDATE" = ? ) OR ( "MANDT" = ? AND "CARRID" = ? AND "CONNID" = ? AND
  "FLDATE" = ? ) OR ( "MANDT" = ? AND "CARRID" = ? AND "CONNID" = ? AND "FLDATE"
  = ? ) OR ( "MANDT" = ? AND "CARRID" = ? AND "CONNID" = ? AND "FLDATE" = ? ) OR
  ( "MANDT" = ? AND "CARRID" = ? AND "CONNID" = ? AND "FLDATE" = ? ) OR (
  "MANDT" = ? AND "CARRID" = ? AND "CONNID" = ? AND "FLDATE" = ? ) OR ( "MANDT" =
  ? AND "CARRID" = ? AND "CONNID" = ? AND "FLDATE" = ? ) OR ( "MANDT" = ? AND
```

Figure 3.13 FOR ALL ENTRIES with OR Operators

For the second `FOR ALL ENTRIES` statement for the table `SCARR`, there is **IN list** only *one* reference to the internal table (for the field `CARRID`). This results in the statement being translated with an `IN` list. For every row of the internal table (driver table), an element is generated in the `IN` list (see Figure 3.14).

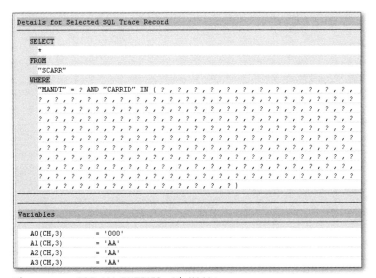

Figure 3.14 FOR ALL ENTRIES with IN List

The FOR ALL ENTRIES clause is described in more detail with regard to performance and memory consumption in Chapter 14. In this section, we mainly wanted to show you how the DBI translates Open SQL into Native SQL, and how you can trace and analyze both variants in Transaction ST05.

You learned how Open SQL statements are modified for the SAP HANA database and translated into Native SQL statements. We mentioned automatic client handling, the selection options, and the FOR ALL ENTRIES clause. In addition to those aspects, there are further transformations (for example, loading the table buffer or accessing number range buffers) that were not presented in this chapter.

3.3.2   Secondary Connections

Example of database connections

We will now use the example from Listing 3.17 to demonstrate how accesses to a secondary connection can be analyzed. In the second sample program, all unique connections of the table SFLIGHT are read once via a secondary connection (with the addition CONNECTION) and the standard connection.

```
DATA: ls_sflight TYPE sflight.

SELECT distinct connid
  FROM sflight CONNECTION ('QH3')
  INTO ls_sflight-connid
  WHERE carrid = 'LH'.
  WRITE: / ls_sflight-connid.
ENDSELECT.


ULINE.

SELECT distinct connid
  FROM sflight
  INTO ls_sflight-connid
  WHERE carrid = 'LH'.
  WRITE: / ls_sflight-connid.
ENDSELECT.
```

Listing 3.17 Sample Program 2 for Database Connections

In the SQL trace list in Transaction ST05, the name of the logical database connection is displayed in the DB CONN. column (Figure 3.15). In this list, "R/3" always stands for the standard connection. Other connections are displayed using the name that was defined upon their creation.

Standard and secondary connection

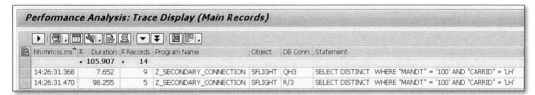

Figure 3.15 SQL Trace—Standard and Secondary Connection

Figure 3.15 shows that the statement was executed once for every connection and that the table SFLIGHT contains different flight connections in the QH3 system. Transaction STAD, which will be described in Chapter 7, provides further information (for example, the number of records read and the duration per database connection).

3.3.3 Native SQL

Moreover, Transaction ST05 can be used to check if ADBC was used. To do so, take another look at the source code from Listing 3.12. The corresponding SQL trace analysis is shown in Figure 3.16. What's interesting in this analysis is the PROGRAM NAME, which refers to the class CL_SQL_STATEMENT. This indicates that ADBC was used for access. While the SQL statement is created as a string somewhere else within the program, it is first executed in the class CL_SQL_STATEMENT in this case (after the string was passed with the statement).

Tracking the use of ADBC

Figure 3.16 Analyzing Native SQL (ADBC) in Transaction ST05

The OBJECT NAME is the name of the table, which was set using the SET_TABLE_NAME_FOR_TRACE method. If no name was specified, the system tries to translate and display the object name from the FROM clause. In general, however, a table name should always be defined, since this is very important for other tools as well.

3.3.4 Buffer

Table buffer trace Table accesses to buffered tables can also be analyzed using Transaction ST05. For this purpose, the table buffer trace (see Figure 3.10) must be activated. Otherwise, the SQL trace does not display table accesses processed via the table buffer. As an example, we will analyze the program from Figure 3.17 using the SQL and the table buffer trace.

```
" Variables for the result
DATA: ls_sflight TYPE sflight,
      ls_spfli TYPE spfli,
      lv_count TYPE i.

"Parameter for airlines
SELECT-OPTIONS: so_carr FOR ls_sflight-carrid.

" Read all flights
SELECT *
  FROM sflight
  INTO ls_sflight
  WHERE carrid IN so_carr.

" Details (buffered table)
  SELECT SINGLE *
    FROM spfli
    INTO ls_spfli
    WHERE carrid = ls_sflight-carrid
    AND connid = ls_sflight-connid.

  IF sy-subrc = 0.
  WRITE: / ls_sflight-mandt, ls_sflight-carrid,
          ls_sflight-connid,
          ls_sflight-fldate, ls_spfli-countryfr,
          ls_spfli-cityfrom, '->',
          ls_spfli-countryto, ls_spfli-cityto.
  ENDIF.

ENDSELECT.
```

Listing 3.18 Sample Program 3: Accesses to the Table Buffer

Figure 3.17 shows the common result list of the traces (for Listing 3.18). Database accesses appear in yellow (first row), while accesses to the table buffer appear in blue (second through fifth rows). In the STATEMENT column, accesses to the database can be identified by the SQL syntax, while accesses to the buffer are only displayed using the technical keys. As you can see, no SELECT statement is displayed for the buffer accesses from our example.

Trace result list

hh:mm:ss:ms Σ	Duration Σ	Records	Program Name	Object Name	Statement
15:10:20.573	3.027.843	18.265	ZR_A4H_CHAPTER3_BUFFER	SFLIGHT	SELECT WHERE "MANDT" = '000' AND "CARRID" = 'LH'
15:10:22.103	73	1	ZR_A4H_CHAPTER3_BUFFER	SPFLI	I 20 000LH 0400
	27	1	ZR_A4H_CHAPTER3_BUFFER	SPFLI	I 20 000LH 0400
	20	1	ZR_A4H_CHAPTER3_BUFFER	SPFLI	I 20 000LH 0400

Figure 3.17 Transaction ST05—SQL and Buffer Trace

PART II
Introduction to ABAP
Programming with SAP HANA

In the second part of this book, we will detail the most important new development options in SAP HANA and explain how to use them within an ABAP-based application. We will particularly focus on the innovations in ABAP 7.4, but also present possible alternatives in earlier ABAP releases. One of the main goals of this part of the book is to help you migrate or optimize existing applications on SAP HANA.

We will therefore first describe how data views are modeled, and how they provide a simple way for delegating calculations from ABAP programs to SAP HANA. Subsequently, we will introduce the programming language—SQLScript—for database procedures in SAP HANA, and show you how to call these procedures using ABAP. Using SQLScript, you can flexibly access data in SAP HANA and particularly access all of the advanced techniques described in Part III of this book. Understanding the principle of database procedures and access via SQLScript is therefore a prerequisite to understand the third part of the book.

The chapters in this part explain how native SAP HANA development objects are used in an SAP landscape and which tools are available for developers or performance experts to optimize applications for SAP HANA.

We will use the presented techniques and tools in a fictitious optimization project to analyze and incrementally optimize an existing application.

Using SAP HANA, you can perform business calculations directly on the original data in the main memory without the need to transform data. Many of these calculations can be modeled graphically as special data views in the SAP HANA Studio without having to write program code. When using ABAP 7.4, these views can then be imported to the ABAP Data Dictionary.

4   View Modeling in SAP HANA Studio

In this chapter, we'll kick off Part II of this book by looking in detail into *database views*. You may be asking yourself why exactly this topic plays such a big role in the context of SAP HANA. To answer this question, we would like to go back a little and briefly explain the underlying reasoning.

The business data of a domain are stored (usually in a normalized form) in a set of database tables that are connected via foreign key relationships (a so-called *entity-relationship model*). Using this data model, single records can be efficiently created, selected, and modified. However, if data access becomes more dynamic and complex, or if certain analyses or checks are necessary, the data must be transformed.

So far, the pattern that was most commonly used for these transformations is that the data is read from the database and used by a program for calculations before storing the result back in the database. This is referred to as *materialization* of the transformed data.

A simple example is the materialization of a totals calculation in a special column or *totals table*. In principle, the same pattern is used for data structures of a *business intelligence system*, where the original data is transformed into a form that can be used more efficiently for analyses *(star schema)*. This materialization was primarily done for performance reasons in the past, since it was not possible to perform the transformations *on the fly* at runtime when users submitted a query. However, since the different data structures had to be synchronized (which is usually done with some time offset), this performance gain also led to higher complexity and prevented a real-time experience for users. Using SAP HANA, this redundancy can now be eliminated in many scenarios. From a technical perspective, this means that the transformations are performed in real time, using the original data. As a consequence, database views are an important element, used in this context to express transformations for read accesses.

SQL views
Every relational database system provides an option for defining views. These *standard views* (also referred to as *SQL views*) are defined in the database catalog using the CREATE VIEW statement essentially as an alias for a SQL query:

```
CREATE VIEW <name> AS SELECT <SQL query>
```

Being a relation database, SAP HANA also supports SQL views; these views differ from the views of other databases only in their SAP HANA-specific SQL dialect.

Column views
In addition to these views, SAP HANA also supports so-called *column views,* which usually provide a better performance and a significantly wider scope of functions. Moreover, these views use the *engines* described in Section 1.3 when queries are executed. The currency conversion of monetary amounts is a good example for functionality that is not available directly via SQL. A prerequisite for using column views is that all involved tables are stored in the column store in SAP HANA, which should be the standard for pretty much all business data (see also Chapter 14). In SAP HANA Studio, both the existing SQL views and the column views are visible in the database catalog (Figure 4.1).

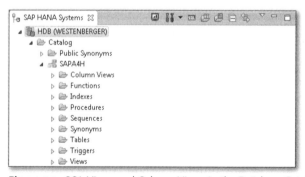

Figure 4.1 SQL Views and Column Views in the Database Catalog

In Section 3.2.2, we explained how simple operations (e.g., for summation or existence checks) can be expressed using Open SQL. However, the key figures in real business applications are usually much more complex. Units of measure and currencies, for example, play an important role and may have to be considered in mathematical operations by using conversions. Time stamps (day, time) for business processes are also very important—including the fiscally correct handling of (business) year, month, or quarter.

When dealing with these operations, standard SQL-based table access reaches its limits. And this is where one of the greatest advantages of SAP HANA comes into play: The integrated engines (see Section 1.3) provide reusable functions tailored for business processes which can be integrated in column views and then accessed using standard SQL. Column views thus enhance the scope of functions for defining database views.

In the scope of this chapter, we will create relatively simple analyses of flight bookings and the seat utilization of flights based on the SFLIGHT data model. In addition to some master data of a flight connection (airline, departure, and destination location), statistical information on seat utilization, revenues, and baggage should also be displayed per quarter. To create these analyses, we will use the different modeling options provided by SAP HANA and explain their properties and areas of use.

Reference example for this chapter

The following types of views will be discussed:

View types

▶ *Attribute views* to define master data views (see Section 4.1). We will introduce the different options available to create table joins and explain how calculated attributes can be added to a view.

▶ *Analytic views* can be used for calculations and analyses based on transaction data using a star schema (see Section 4.2). We will explain how you can define simple and calculated key figures and add dimensions. As a special case of calculated key figures, we will describe currency conversion and unit conversions.

▶ Using *calculation views*, you can flexibly combine views and basic data operations (see Section 1.3). We will describe both the modeling and the implementation of calculation views using SQLScript. Since SQLScript will be described in detail in Chapter 5, the sample implementation used in this chapter will be kept rather simple.

After demonstrating how to define and test these views in SAP HANA Studio, we will describe external access. You will first learn how to access the views from Microsoft Excel, which provides a simple option for first tests and analyses.

In the remaining sections of this chapter, we will describe how these views are accessed from ABAP. We will explain both native access via ABAP Database Connectivity (ADBC)—the only option for ABAP releases before ABAP 7.4—and the new options available as of ABAP 7.4.

4.1 Attribute Views

Overview and usage scenarios

Attribute views comprise a number of fields (columns) from database tables, which are linked through foreign key relationships. Moreover, attribute views provide a way to define calculated columns and hierarchical relationships between individual fields (e.g., parent-child relationships). They are especially relevant in the following scenarios:

▶ As components of other view types, especially as *dimensions* of analytic views (see Section 4.2) or for a more general purpose as *nodes* in calculation views (see Section 4.3).

▶ As a data provider for text searches across several tables (see Chapter 9).

Reference examples for this section

In this section, we will create a number of such views to demonstrate different functional aspects. The reason for creating several views is that it is not possible or not useful to use all functions for all tables. To give you an overview of the views used in the examples of this section, they are listed in Table 4.1 together with a description and the corresponding functionality.

Column	Description	Functionality
AT_FLIGHT_BASIC	Simple view for table SFLIGHT	First basic example
AT_FLIGHT	Flight data plus information from the flight plan and information on the airlines	Different join types and calculated fields

Table 4.1 Sample Attribute Views Used in this Section

Column	Description	Functionality
AT_MEAL	List of meals served on flights with (language-dependent) description	Text joins and filter values
AT_PASSENGER	View of passenger data and address information	Hierarchy
AT_FLIGHT_FISCAL	Flight data with assignment to accounting periods	Fiscal calendar
AT_FLIGHT_GREG	Flight data with assignment to year, quarter, calendar week	Gregorian calendar
AT_TIME_GREG	Pure time hierarchy (year, quarter, calendar week)	Attribute view of type TIME

Table 4.1 Sample Attribute Views Used in this Section (Cont.)

The views AT_FLIGHT, AT_PASSENGER, and AT_TIME_GREG will also be used in Section 4.2.

4.1.1 Basic Principles

Before describing how attribute views are modeled, let's take a quick look at the most important concepts. Since attribute views can be used to create data views based on several tables that are linked via different types of joins, they can also be referred to as *join views*. The different join types will be introduced in this section. Because joins play a major role when dealing with attribute views, accesses to attribute views are handled by the *join engine* in SAP HANA.

Join views

When modeling attribute views, we differentiate between the following concepts:

Modeling concepts

- *Attributes* refer to the columns of the attribute view. You can add columns from one or several physical tables or define additional calculated columns.

- *Key attributes* are those attributes of the view that uniquely specify an entry. These play an important role when the view is used as a dimensions of an analytic view (see Section 4.2.2).

▶ *Filters* define restrictions applied to the values of a column (similar to a WHERE condition in a SELECT statement).

▶ *Hierarchies* are relations defined for the attributes such as a parent-child relationship (*see* Section 4.1.4).

The main advantage of attribute views is the possibility to define a view based on fields from several tables. In contrast to the ABAP Data Dictionary views presented in Section 3.2.3, which can comprise only inner joins, attribute views in SAP HANA allow you to use a greater variety of join types.

Sample data

Before describing the details of join modeling, we would like to first introduce the different join types of the SQL standard. To do so, we will use the known tables SFLIGHT (flights) and SCARR (airlines) with a foreign key relationship via the CARRID field (for the sake of simplicity, the client is disregarded in the excerpt in Table 4.2). The tables have an n:1 relationship and the SCARR table may contain airlines for which no flight is entered in the SFLIGHT table (e.g., the airline "UA" in Table 4.2).

Table SFLIGHT			Table SCARR	
CARRID	**CONNID**	**FLDATE**	**CARRID**	**CARRNAME**
AA	0017	20130101	AA	American Airlines
...	...	...	...	...
LH	400	20130101	LH	Lufthansa
LH	400	20130102	...	...
...	...	...	UA	United Airways

Table 4.2 Sample Data from the Tables SFLIGHT and SCARR to Explain Join Types

Inner/outer joins

When defining joins, we differentiate between inner and outer joins. In case of an *inner join*, all combinations are included in the result if there is a matching entry in both tables. With an *outer join*, results that are present only in the left table (*left outer join*), only in the right table (*right outer join*), or in any of the tables (*full outer join*) are also included. To differentiate between left and right, the join order is used. Full outer joins are not supported for attribute views.

The differences between the join types will be explained based on the following SQL examples for selecting flights and the corresponding airline names. The first example comprises an inner join. Since the airline "UA" is not present in the sample data for the sample data for the SFLIGHT table, there is no matching entry in the result set:

SQL examples

```
select s.carrid, s.connid, c.carrname from sflight as s inner
join scarr as c on s.carrid = c.carrid
```

In case of a right outer join, where SCARR is the right-hand table, an entry for the airline "UA" is displayed in the result set, even though there is no corresponding entry in the SFLIGHT table. The columns carrid and connid thus display the value NULL:

```
select s.carrid, s.connid, c.carrname from sflight as s right
outer join scarr as c on s.carrid = c.carrid
```

Similarly, "UA" is also included in the result set in case of a left outer join with SCARR as the left-hand table. If the data model assumes that a corresponding airline exists for every entry of a flight (but not necessarily the other way around), the two outer join variants are functionally equivalent.

```
select s.carrid, s.connid, c.carrname from scarr as c left
outer join sflight as s on s.carrid = c.carrid
```

In addition to the presented standard joins, two other special join types are used when modeling attribute views in SAP HANA:

Text joins and referential joins

- ▶ *Text joins* can be used to read language-dependent texts from a different table. For this purpose, the column with the language key must be included in the text table; at runtime, a filter for the correct language is then applied based on the context. The next section shows an example for using text joins.

- ▶ *Referential joins* provide a special way of defining an inner join; with this join type, *referential integrity* is assumed implicitly (which has advantages with regard to performance). So, when using a referential join and no field from the right-hand table is queried, it is not checked if there is a matching entry. It is assumed that the data is consistent. Referential joins are often a useful standard when defining joins in attribute views.

[»] **Attribute Views Only Support Equi-Joins**

When formulating join conditions, you can use further expressions (e. g., <, >) in SQL that go beyond checking the equality of columns (*equi-join*), as shown in the following example:

`SELECT ... FROM ... [INNER|OUTER] JOIN ... ON col1 < col2 ...`

However, attribute views support only equi-joins.

4.1.2 Creating Attribute Views

Attribute views can be defined via the MODELER perspective in SAP HANA Studio, which was introduced in Section 2.4.3. To create a view, select NEW • ATTRIBUTE VIEW from the context menu of a package in the CONTENT node. You first have to specify a name and a description in the dialog shown in Figure 4.2.

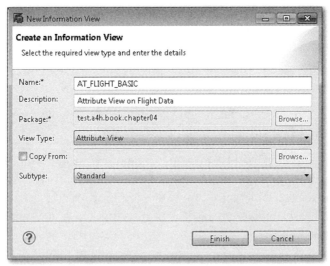

Figure 4.2 Creating an Attribute View

In this dialog, you can also copy an existing view as basis for a new attribute view. When selecting SUBTYPE, you can create special types of attribute views (e.g., for time hierarchies, which will be explained in more detail in Section 4.1.5). When clicking the FINISH button, the attribute view is created and the corresponding modeling editor opens.

The editor used to define an attribute view comprises two sections: DATA FOUNDATION and SEMANTICS. These are displayed as boxes in the SCENARIO pane on the left-hand side (see Figure 4.3). By selecting each node, you can switch between defining the data basis (DATA FOUNDATION) and the semantic configuration (SEMANTICS).

Modeling editor

The DATA FOUNDATION is used to add tables, define joins, and add attributes. Figure 4.3 shows a simple example based on the SFLIGHT table.

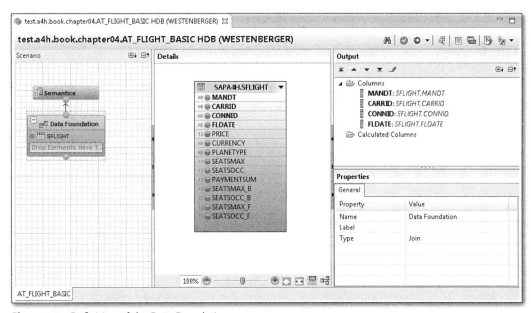

Figure 4.3 Definition of the Data Foundation

By selecting the node SEMANTICS, you can maintain further metadata for the attribute view. You can, for example, specify the following:

Defining metadata

▶ You can specify if an attribute is a key field of the view. Note that every attribute view must contain at least one key field. In addition, you can define texts (*labels*) for attributes or hide attributes, which can be useful in the context of calculated fields (see Section 4.1.3).

▶ You can specify how the client field is handled (static value or dynamically). Client handling will be discussed in detail at the end of this section.

▶ You can define hierarchies (see Section 4.1.4).

The layout of the SEMANTICS section is shown in Figure 4.4.

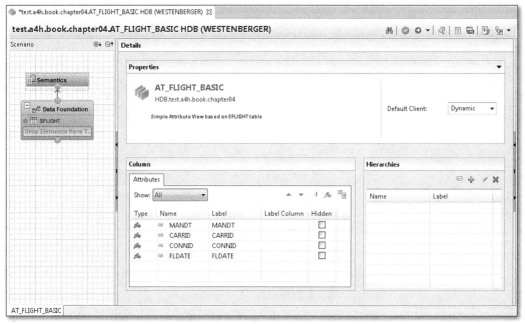

Figure 4.4 Further Semantic Configuration of the Attribute View

The selected columns from the SFLIGHT table are marked as key fields. As described in Section 2.4.3, you now have to save and activate the ATTRIBUTE view to be able to use it.

Activation errors   If the view was not modeled properly, an error will be displayed during activation. Typical errors are caused by missing key fields, invalid joins, or calculated fields that were not defined correctly. Figure 4.5 shows an example of an activation error. The cause of an error may not always be as obvious. Section 4.5.4 provides some troubleshooting tips.

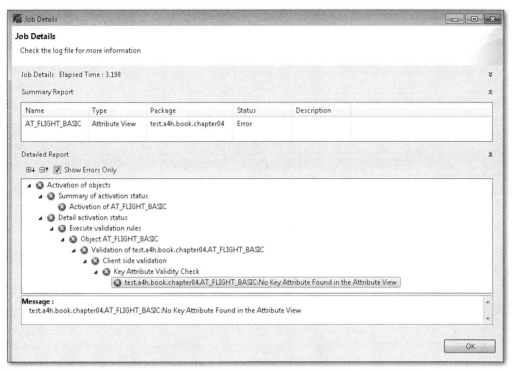

Figure 4.5 Example of an Activation Error

If the tables used are client-dependent, you can specify if the client should be automatically included in the filter condition based on the current context (DYNAMIC DEFAULT CLIENT). Alternatively, it can be defined as CROSS-CLIENT to access the data for all clients. It is also possible to specify a static value for the client. Usage tips can be found in Section 4.5.4.

Client handling

Background Information: Determining the Client **[«]**

There is a so-called *session context* for every database connection, which stores certain properties of the current connection. In particular, this information comprises the current client, which is set by the DBSL in case of a connection via the SAP NetWeaver AS ABAP. When using the Data Preview or a connection via the SQL console in SAP HANA Studio, the client is determined from the user settings. When configuring these settings, you can specify a default client for a user. If no client is specified, there is no client context; this means that all data is displayed (cross-client) when using the Data Preview. The session context is explained in more detail in Chapter 5.

Following this brief summary of the available join types, we will now define attribute views. As our first example, we want to define the SFLIGHTS view from the ABAP Data Dictionary, which you have already seen in Section 3.2.3 as an attribute view. Based on our example from Figure 4.3, we can add further tables to the DATA FOUNDATION. You can either manually select those tables or have the system propose tables based on the metadata maintained in the ABAP Data Dictionary. For the latter option, select the table and then choose PROPOSE TABLES from the context menu. The selection dialog opens the screen shown in Figure 4.6.

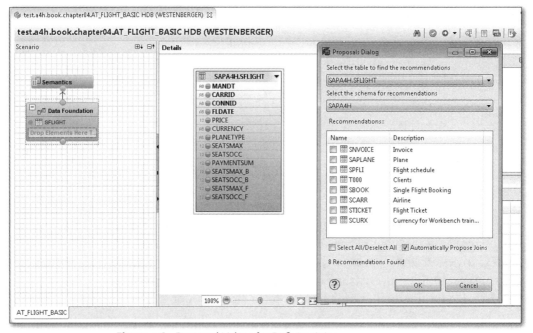

Figure 4.6 Proposed Values for Defining Joins

To reproduce the SFLIGHTS view, we will add the tables SCARR and SPFLI and define the joins as shown in Figure 4.7. If you want to define a new join, simply drag a connecting line between the corresponding attributes of two tables while holding the mouse button down. To define the properties of a join, you first have to select the join and then configure it in the PROPERTIES section (JOIN TYPE, CARDINALITY). For our example, a referential join and a cardinality of n:1 is used.

In the next step, you add the desired attributes from the tables via the context menu of the output structure of the view. The selected attributes will then be highlighted and displayed in the OUTPUT section in the right-hand pane of the editor.

Adding attributes

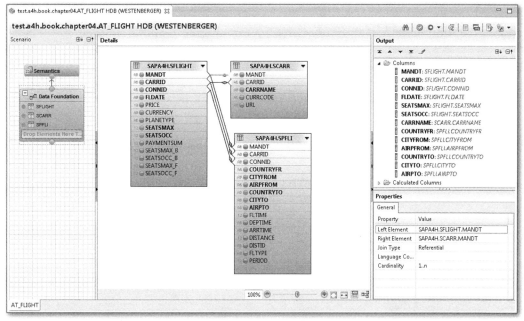

Figure 4.7 Attribute View Analogous to the DDIC View SFLIGHTS

Since we already defined the key fields, and they were not changed by adding tables, we can now activate and test the view. The result shows the name of the airline and information on the departure and destination location for every flight (see Figure 4.8).

Activate/test

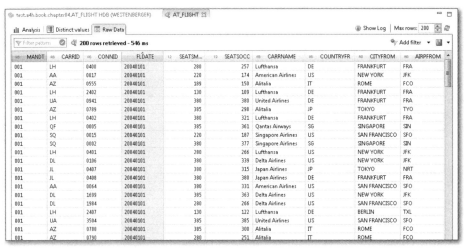

Figure 4.8 Result of the Attribute View

Using text joins To illustrate the usage of the aforementioned text join, we will create another attribute view and read the corresponding texts (table SMEALT) for the in-flight meals (table SMEAL). The required modeling is shown in Figure 4.9. Since filtering is done based on the language, the cardinality for this join is always 1:1.

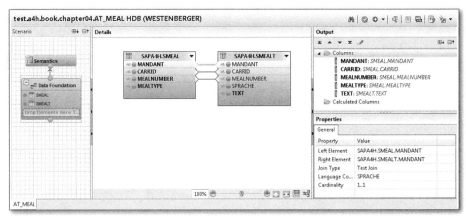

Figure 4.9 Using a Text Join

Defining filter values As in case of normal SQL views, you can also specify filter values for columns when working with attribute views. To define the filter, you open the filter dialog for an attribute via the context menu item APPLY

FILTER. Attributes with an existing filter are marked with a filter symbol (as shown in Figure 4.10).

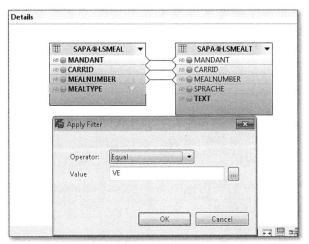

Figure 4.10 Filter for an Attribute

For the example using the meals served on the flight, we define a filter for the attribute MEAL_TYPE with an equals operator and the value "VE" (vegetarian), as shown in Figure 4.11. Alternatively, you can also try other comparison operators. The Data Preview displays all vegetarian meals with the corresponding texts in the correct language.

MANDANT	CARRID	MEALNUMBER	MEALTYPE	TEXT
001	AA	00000001	VE	SEASONAL SALAD
001	AA	00000002	VE	NICE SALAD
001	AA	00000003	VE	PARIS SALAD
001	AA	00000004	VE	HAMBURG SALAD WITH FRESH SHRIMPS
001	AA	00000023	VE	CHOCOLATE ICE CREAM
001	AA	00000024	VE	VANILLA ICE CREAM
001	AA	00000025	VE	VANILLA ICE CREAM WITH HOT CHERRIES
001	AA	00000026	VE	VANILLA ICE CREAM WITH HOT RASPBERRIES
001	AA	00000027	VE	APPLE STRUDEL
001	AA	00000028	VE	RASPBERRY SORBET
001	AA	00000029	VE	STRAWBERRY SORBET
001	AC	00000001	VE	SEASONAL SALAD
001	AC	00000002	VE	NICE SALAD
001	AC	00000003	VE	PARIS SALAD
001	AC	00000004	VE	HAMBURG SALAD WITH FRESH SHRIMPS
001	AC	00000023	VE	CHOCOLATE ICE CREAM

Analysis | Distinct values | Raw Data

Filter pattern   198 rows retrieved – 312 ms

Figure 4.11 Example of a Text Join with an Additional Filter

4.1.3 Calculated Fields

Virtual attributes

Having explained how an attribute view can be used to read data from different tables using different join types, we will now go one step further and dynamically calculate some of the view columns. Compared to classic ABAP Data Dictionary views, these *virtual attributes* (i.e., attributes that do not belong directly to a column of one of the physical tables) are a powerful new opportunity for expressing data processing logic.

As a first example, we will now add a calculated attribute to the attribute view AT_FLIGHTS from Figure 4.7, which will contain the full flight connection (departure location and airport plus destination location and airport) as its value, e.g. NEW YORK (JFK)—SAN FRANCISCO (SFO).

Defining calculated attributes

To do so, we define a calculated attribute in the DATA FOUNDATION via the node CALCULATED COLUMNS of the OUTPUT section and specify a name, a description, and a data type (see Figure 4.12).

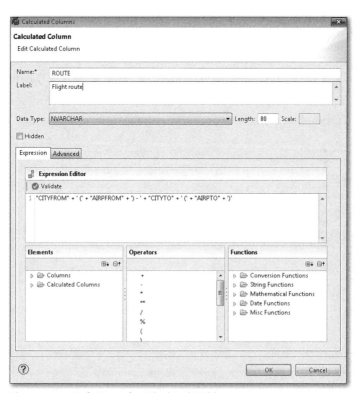

Figure 4.12 Definition of a Calculated Field

Using the EXPRESSION EDITOR, you can specify an expression that will be used to determine the value. This provides a variety of functions (conversions, mathematical operations, string operations, date calculations, and even simple case distinctions). In our example, we will only use a simple concatenation of strings for now (see Listing 4.1):

Defining expressions for calculations

```
"CITYFROM" + ' (' + "AIRPFROM" + ') - ' + "CITYTO" + ' (' +
"AIRPTO" + ')'
```

Listing 4.1 Example of an Expression for a Calculated Field

> **Attribute References and Constants in Expressions**
>
> When defining *expressions* for calculated attributes, you must make sure to use the correct type of quotation marks. For references to attributes of the view (e.g., "CITYFROM" in Listing 4.1), double quotes must be used. It is recommended to use the drag-and-drop function via the formula editor. For text constants, by contrast, simple quotes must be used (as shown in the parentheses in Listing 4.1).
>
> Using the wrong quotation marks usually leads to an activation error.

[!]

After activating the attribute view, the calculated column is displayed in the output (see Figure 4.13). Calculated columns can be queried via SQL just like normal columns, which will be demonstrated in Section 4.1.6.

Output of the calculated field

AB CARRID	AB CONNID	FLDATE	AB CARRNAME	AB ROUTE
LH	0400	20040101	Lufthansa	FRANKFURT (FRA) - NEW YORK (JFK)
AA	0017	20040101	American Airlines	NEW YORK (JFK) - SAN FRANCISCO (SFO)
AZ	0555	20040101	Alitalia	ROME (FCO) - FRANKFURT (FRA)
LH	2402	20040101	Lufthansa	FRANKFURT (FRA) - BERLIN (SXF)
UA	0941	20040101	United Airlines	FRANKFURT (FRA) - SAN FRANCISCO (SFO)
AZ	0789	20040101	Alitalia	TOKYO (TYO) - ROME (FCO)
LH	0402	20040101	Lufthansa	FRANKFURT (FRA) - NEW YORK (JFK)
QF	0005	20040101	Qantas Airways	SINGAPORE (SIN) - FRANKFURT (FRA)
SQ	0015	20040101	Singapore Airlines	SAN FRANCISCO (SFO) - SINGAPORE (SIN)
SQ	0002	20040101	Singapore Airlines	SINGAPORE (SIN) - SAN FRANCISCO (SFO)
LH	0401	20040101	Lufthansa	NEW YORK (JFK) - FRANKFURT (FRA)
DL	0106	20040101	Delta Airlines	NEW YORK (JFK) - FRANKFURT (FRA)
JL	0407	20040101	Japan Airlines	TOKYO (NRT) - FRANKFURT (FRA)

Figure 4.13 Output of the Calculated Field

Calculated fields are also supported for the other view types (see Section 4.2), where these fields are used especially for the calculations and conversions of currencies and units that we already mentioned.

4.1.4 Hierarchies

A lot of data has hierarchical relationships. The place of residence or principal office of customers is structured geographically by country, region, and city; the hierarchical structure of a creation date comprises the year, quarter, and month; a product catalog can consist of several categories, etc.

Data analysis

Hierarchies play an important role in data analyses. You can start with an aggregated view of the data and then navigate within the hierarchical structures. This is referred to as a *drilldown* (or drillup when data is aggregated). Every OLAP infrastructure (like SAP NetWeaver BW) provides built-in support for hierarchies.

Hierarchies in SAP HANA

For attribute views, hierarchies are defined in the SEMANTICS section. SAP HANA currently supports two types of hierarchies:

▶ **Parent-child relationships**
For this type, two attributes with a parent-child relationship must be defined. An example would be storing a directory structure in a table. In this context, it must be noted that this is a *full* and *consistent* self-referential relation. Each parent node must exist and (except for a special root node) must be the child node of another node. This rather limits the use of this hierarchy type, especially for ABAP tables. An example would be the ABAP hierarchy of packages, where the corresponding database table (TDEVC) comprises columns for the package name and the name of the superpackage. These columns form a parent-child relationship.

▶ **Level hierarchy**
With this hierarchy type, you define hierarchy levels based on normal or calculated attributes. If a table for example comprises columns for the country and the city, these attributes define a hierarchy of several levels (the countries at the upper level and the corresponding cities at the lower levels). However, these attributes do not have a parent-child

relationship, since this would require the city values to also appear as countries (this is not a self-referential relation as described previously).

Existing hierarchies are displayed in the SEMANTICS section, where you can also create new hierarchies. Figure 4.14 shows a level hierarchy based on the attributes of the departure location (country, city, airport) from table SPFLI. Hierarchies can also be defined for *calculation views* (see Section 4.3).

Creating hierarchies

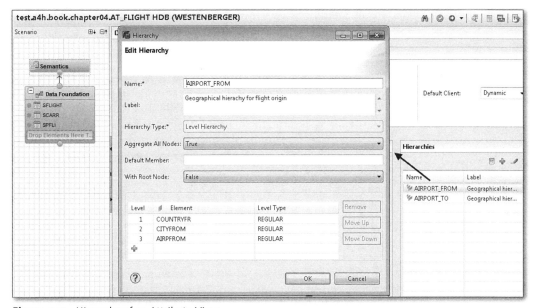

Figure 4.14 Hierarchy of an Attribute View

There are various options for using the modeled hierarchies. This information is evaluated in particular by the supported *business intelligence* clients. One particular variant (access via Microsoft Excel) will be shown in Section 4.4.

SAP HANA thus provides basic support for simple hierarchies, but compared to the comprehensive hierarchy modeling that's available in SAP NetWeaver BW (as an example), the options are rather limited. In many real-life scenarios, hierarchies are much more complex, and there are special cases like external or incomplete hierarchies. This topic is described in detail in the book *Data Modeling in SAP NetWeaver BW* by Frank K. Wolf and Stefan Yamada (SAP PRESS 2011).

Limitations of hierarchy support

4.1.5 Attribute Views for Time Values

Most business data have a time reference (e.g., a creation date or a validity period). These references are usually implemented as date fields or time stamps in the data model. The flight data model, for example, comprises the flight date in the SFLIGHT table and the booking time in the SBOOK table. For many analyses, this point in time must be mapped to a certain time interval. In the simplest case, this can be the corresponding year, month, quarter, or calendar week. However, there are also more complicated or configurable time intervals like the *fiscal year*, which is the calendar to be used for certain scenarios.

[»] **Customizing of the Fiscal Year**

Fiscal years and periods are configured via the ABAP Customizing. Using the ABAP Customizing, you can configure comprehensive settings or variants and also define special cases (e. g., a short fiscal year when a company is founded). These settings are configured via the entry MAINTAIN FISCAL YEAR VARIANT of Transaction SPRO.

The SAP standard provides several function modules to convert a normal date (e.g., of type DATS) into the corresponding fiscal year or period.

From a technical perspective, the corresponding Customizing is stored particularly in the tables T009 and T009B. These tables were previously pool/cluster tables and therefore not available directly in the database. Such tables are converted into normal database tables when performing a migration to SAP HANA (see Section 3.2.1) so that such data can also be accessed natively in the database.

Mapping of the fiscal year

In the past, when determining the corresponding fiscal year for a date in ABAP, the data first needed to be transferred to the application server in order to perform the conversion. There was therefore no way to simply create an aggregated set of records by fiscal year via Open SQL. The determination of the fiscal year had always to be done in ABAP. Using attribute views in SAP HANA, you can define these mappings to intervals of both the normal calendar (Gregorian calendar) and the fiscal calendar.

Generating calendar data

To do so, we first generate time data in special technical tables in SAP HANA. You can select the entry GENERATE TIME DATA on the initial screen of the MODELER perspective for this purpose. Subsequently, you specify the details for calendar type and time period. In our example, we specify the configuration shown in Figure 4.15 to create the fiscal calendar from 2000 to 2020.

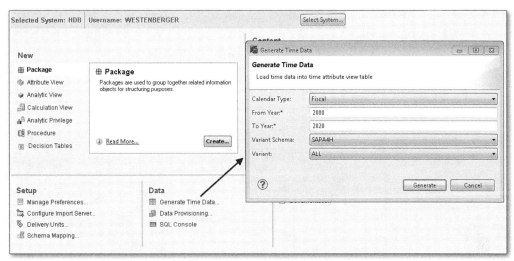

Figure 4.15 Generating the Data for the Fiscal Calendar

You can now use the underlying table M_FISCAL_CALENDAR (schema _SYS_BI) in attribute views. In the example shown in Figure 4.16, we use the attribute view to determine the fiscal year and period for every flight in the SFLIGHT table. Since we want to use only a fixed variant from the ABAP Customizing, we define a static filter for the field CALENDER_VARIANT.

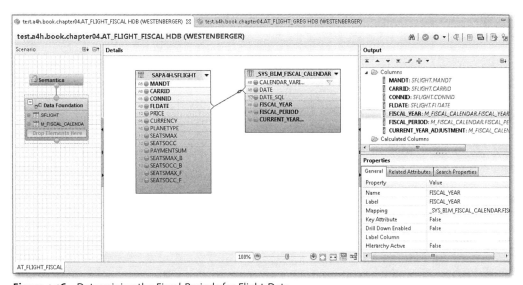

Figure 4.16 Determining the Fiscal Periods for Flight Data

Determining
the quarter or
calendar week

Another sample scenario would be to determine the quarter or the calendar week for a given date using an attribute view. For this scenario, the data from the Gregorian calendar is needed; this is stored in SAP HANA in the technical table M_TIME_DIMENSION, which is part of the _SYS_BI schema as well. This means that you will have to generate data first—as in case of the fiscal calendar. The use of table M_TIME_DIMENSION can be seen in Figure 4.17.

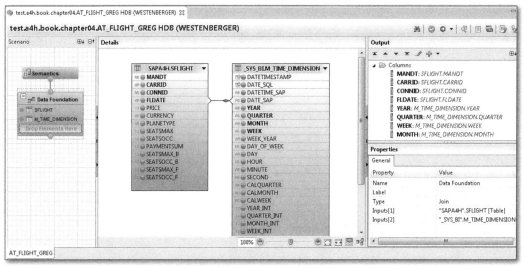

Figure 4.17 Determining the Quarter and Calendar Week

Attribute view
of type "Time"

You can also define an attribute view containing only time data. To do so, you select the type TIME and specify the desired details for the calendar when creating an attribute view. Figure 4.18 shows how the attribute view AT_TIME_GREG is created for a day-based Gregorian calendar.

Since the view contains the date as a key field, joins can be created for a date column in the business data. This means that you can use these views as time dimensions in an *analytic view* if the date is part of the fact table. This will be described in detail in Section 4.2.

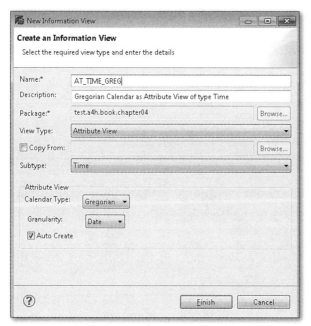

Figure 4.18   Attribute View for a Gregorian Calendar

4.1.6   Runtime Artifacts and SQL Access for Attribute Views

As described in Section 2.4.3, column views are created in the schema _SYS_BIC when activating views from the SAP HANA Repository that can be accessed via normal SQL. These column views also form the basis for ABAP access, as shown in Section 4.5. The exact *runtime artifacts* depend on the view type and the concrete modeling. Usually, there is a leading object that serves as the primary interface for data access, and further additional technical artifacts for specific aspects.

Addressing via SQL

This section describes the specifics of attribute views. Every attribute view has a corresponding column view. In addition to this view, another column view is created for every hierarchy. For our attribute view AT_FLIGHT, the column views listed in Figure 4.19 exist in the database catalog in the _SYS_BIC schema.

Column views

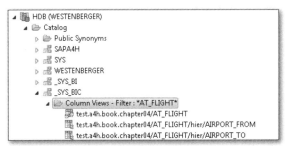

Figure 4.19 Column Views Generated for the Attribute View AT_FLIGHT

Please note that the names of the runtime artifacts always contain the package names. This is necessary because you can create objects with the same name in different packages.

Public synonym

In addition, there is a *public synonym* that can also be used to access the views:

```
"test.a4h.book.chapter04::AT_FLIGHT"
```

Attribute views can be accessed using regular SQL. However, please note that attribute views are not optimized for calculations like column aggregations, but rather for efficient join calculations. In other words, not every SQL statement should be used for every view type in SAP HANA. Recommendations can be found in Section 4.5.4.

4.2   Analytic Views

Analytic views are special views in SAP HANA that are used to calculate and analyze key figures. If you are already familiar with data warehouse or business intelligence applications, you can think of an analytic view as a *star schema*. Section 4.2.1 provides a brief introduction of the most important concepts. In the subsequent sections, we will explain how analytic views are created in SAP HANA Studio and how to define calculated key figures.

Reference examples for this section

In this section, two scenarios will be implemented as analytic views. In the first example (analytic view AN_BOOKING), we will model an analysis of the flight bookings based on attributes of the customer and the flight. In this analysis, the booking prices and the baggage weight will be examined as key figures. For both figures, conversions must be considered due to different currencies and weight units. We will also define another calculated figure based on the baggage weight, which specifies whether we are dealing with excess baggage (more than 20 kg). In the second example, we will define an analytic view AN_SEAT_UTILIZATION to analyze the seat utilization of flights.

Both analytic views use the attribute views from the previous section. In Section 4.3, the two attribute views will be combined for an analysis.

4.2.1 Basic Principles

When using analytic views, you should be familiar with the most important concepts from the OLAP environment (Online Analytical Processing), i.e., from the field of data analysis. We will therefore give you a short introduction based on an example in this section. This example will then be used again when describing the actual modeling steps. A more comprehensive description of the topic can be found in Chapter 10, where the integration of business intelligence functionality is explained.

Analyses usually focus on transaction data (purchase orders, documents, invoices, etc.). The corresponding table is referred to as the *fact table*. This data includes one or several key figures or *measures*—for example, the invoice amount—which are relevant for data analysis. Fact tables usually contain a large number of entries. Moreover, fact tables can contain data from several database tables. The key figures must be from one table, and the attributes of the other table are for instance needed as foreign keys. A typical example would be fact tables containing header data and line items.

Fact table

The transaction data includes associations with master data (e.g., via the customer number of a purchase order) and other data like time stamps (e.g., the purchase order creation date). Since this associated data can also be used to break down the fact table into data slices, it is also referred to as *dimensions* and an analysis along these dimensions as *slice and dice* operations. An example for this would be the determination of the total revenue in 2013 for customers from the US. Within the dimensions, the data is usually structured hierarchically (e.g., by geographical regions or time intervals). This makes it possible to further analyze these hierarchy

Dimensions

levels (*drilldown, drillup*); for 2013 revenue in the US, you could for instance analyze the data by state or quarter.

Example of a star schema Let's now look at a concrete example based on our flight model. We will use the table SBOOK as the fact table and the column LOCCURAM (flight price in the airline's currency) as the key figure. The customer number, the flight date, and the flight connection comprise associations which allow us to perform the analysis based on several dimensions.

When looking at a graphical representation of the data model, it resembles a typical *star schema* (see Figure 4.20).

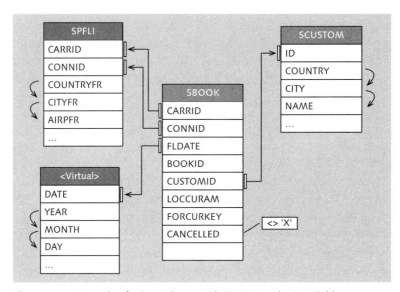

Figure 4.20 Example of a Star Schema with SBOOK as the Fact Table

Hierarchies within the dimensions The data is usually structured hierarchically within the dimensions. The geographical data of the departure location and the customers' places of residence (country, city, etc.) and the flight date (year, month, day) represent the hierarchies in this example; the hierarchical relationship is defined by the columns, as shown in Figure 4.20. Since the flight data model does not contain a database table with time data, the time hierarchy is marked as *virtual*.

A star schema provides different filter variants. On the one hand, there can be restrictions for the transaction data. When analyzing the flight bookings, for example, we only want to consider the bookings that were not cancelled. On the other hand, you can also define special key figures to directly apply restrictions within the dimensions (e.g., to consider only customers in the US). These key figures are also referred to as *restricted measures*.

Filter variants

4.2.2 Creating Analytic Views

Similar to attribute views, analytic views are created in SAP HANA Studio via the context menu of a package in the MODELER perspective. After specifying a name and a description, the corresponding editor opens (see Figure 4.21).

Figure 4.21 Editor for Analytic Views

The editor for analytic views consists of three sections:

▸ DATA FOUNDATION to define the fact table.

▸ LOGICAL JOIN to add the dimensions defined by attribute views and to define calculated attributes and restricted measures.

Editor for
analytic views

▶ SEMANTICS to semantically enrich the selected attributes and define optional input parameters for the view.

Modeling the fact table

In our first example, we will implement the star schema from Figure 4.20 as an analytic view. To do so, we add the table SBOOK as the fact table, select the required fields as we did for the attribute view, and define the filter for the column CANCELLED.

Adding dimensions

We then switch to the section LOGICAL JOIN and add the attribute views AT_FLIGHT, AT_PASSENGER, and AT_TIME_GREG from Section 4.1 as dimensions. When doing so, we draw a connecting line from the fact table to the attribute views. Figure 4.22 shows the resulting diagram.

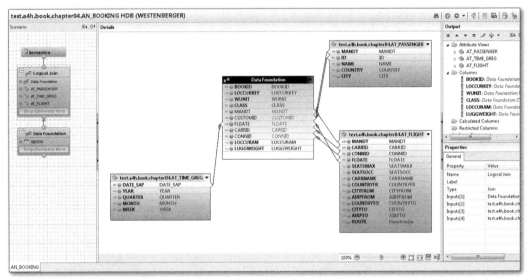

Figure 4.22 Analytic View Based on Booking Data

Assigning measures

As the final step, we select the measures in the SEMANTICS section. In our example, the flight price in the local currency of the airline (LOCCURAM) and the baggage weight (LUGGWEIGHT) are used for these measures. Once the view is activated, you can use the Data Preview for a first simple analysis of the result set. Figure 4.23 shows a sample breakdown of the revenue by year, quarter, and airline, with a filter set for the year 2013.

Figure 4.23 Data Preview with Breakdown by Year, Quarter, and Airline

Following the same procedure, we will now create a second analytic view, AN_SEAT_UTILIZATION, which uses the table SFLIGHT as the fact table instead of the flight bookings, but also uses AT_TIME_GREG as the time dimension so that the seat utilization can be analyzed by quarter. Figure 4.24 shows the resulting star schema.

Creating another analytic view

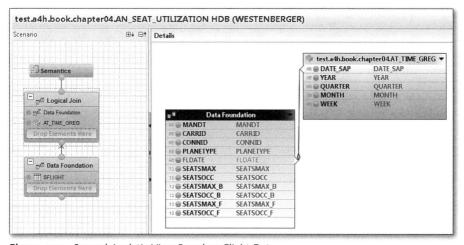

Figure 4.24 Second Analytic View Based on Flight Data

Now that you know how to create and test analytic views, we will discuss calculated key figures in the next section.

4.2.3 Calculated Key Figures

Virtual columns

As in case of attribute views, you can also define virtual columns for analytic views. The values of those columns are determined by a calculation. In case of analytic views, you usually define calculated key figures, i.e., numerical values such as amounts or units of measurement. A special case of such calculated values are conversions between different currencies and units, which will be explained in Section 4.2.4. We will calculate a key figure for each of the two analytic views from the previous section. For the view AN_BOOKING, we will use an expression to identify the bookings with excess baggage; for AN_SEAT_UTILIZATION, the relative seat utilization will be determined as percentage value based on the number of available and occupied seats.

Defining calculated key figures

Calculated key figures are basically defined following the same procedure that is used for attribute views. However, you must also flag the new column as MEASURE (via the COLUMN TYPE) and specify whether it is to be determined before or after an aggregation. In many cases, the calculation must be done using the raw data (i.e., before aggregation). Figure 4.25 shows the determination of all flight bookings with a baggage weight value of more than 20. We will ignore the fact that the weight might be specified using different weight units for now. If a summation is done on this column, the number of bookings with excess baggage is determined, since the value of the calculated column is null for all other bookings.

Calculating the seat utilization

We will now follow the same steps to define a calculated key figure UTI-LIZATION (data type DECIMAL) in the view AN_SEAT_UTILIZATION and use the following expression as the calculation formula:

```
if("SEATSMAX">0, decfloat( "SEATSOCC" + "SEATSOCC_B" +
"SEATSOCC_F" ) / decfloat( "SEATSMAX" + "SEATSMAX_B" +
"SEATSMAX_F" ),0)
```

As you can see, we divide the sum of the occupied seats by the sum of the available seats in the three booking categories. For the result to be handled as a decimal number, the type is converted using the function decfloat.

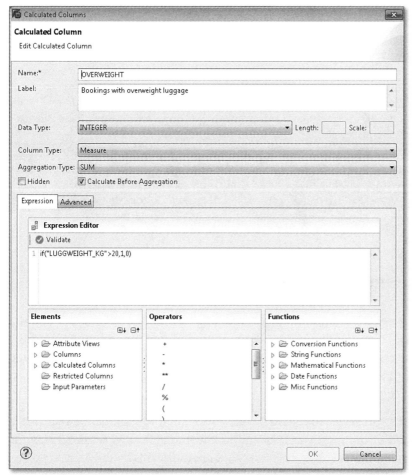

Figure 4.25 Calculated Key Figure for the Number of Flight Bookings with Excess Baggage

4.2.4 Currency Conversion and Unit Conversion

As a special case of a calculated key figure, the analytic view supports the conversion of monetary amounts and units of measure. We will show you how this is done for the sample view AN_BOOKING to indicate the flight price in Euros and the baggage weight in kilograms.

[»] **Currency Conversion and Unit Conversion in SAP NetWeaver AS ABAP**

Currency conversion and unit conversion are standard functions in SAP NetWeaver AS ABAP. The customizing of the currency conversion in SAP Basis is done via the `TCUR*` tables in the package `SFIB`. To perform a conversion in ABAP, you can for instance use the function modules in the function group `SCUN` (for example, `CONVERT_TO_LOCAL_CURRENCY`). In addition to the amount, and the source and target currency, the key date and the exchange rate type are also important parameters for the conversion.

When dealing with currency conversions, it must be noted that SAP provides different variants of conversions. In addition to the variant described in this section, which is the standard conversion used in SAP ERP (e.g., in *Financial Services*), an alternative approach with its own Customizing is also available. When modeling analytic views in SAP HANA, only the standard currency conversion from SAP ERP is supported.

Unit conversion for ISO codes can be found in the `T006*` tables of the package `SZME`. To perform a conversion in ABAP, you can use the function module `UNIT_CONVERSION_SIMPLE`.

Modeling conversions

There are two approaches for modeling currency or unit conversions: You either specify that the given conversion should be performed for every access on an existing column, or you define an additional virtual column for the conversion result. When using the second variant, you can access both the original value and the converted value.

Defining calculated fields

To use a calculated column for the conversion, you first define a calculated field of the type MEASURE and link it to the original column using the same data type. You can then configure the details on the ADVANCED tab.

You must specify whether the field contains a monetary amount or a quantity unit. Moreover, you must indicate the field where the corresponding currency or unit of measure can be found. Unfortunately, it is currently not possible to evaluate the corresponding information from the ABAP Data Dictionary, where this relationship is also defined (tab CURRENCY/ QUANTITY fields in Transaction SE11).

The example in Figure 4.26 shows a currency conversion for the column `LOCURRAM` of the `SBOOK` table into the target currency Euro with the key date January 1, 2013. Here, the standard exchange type M is being used.

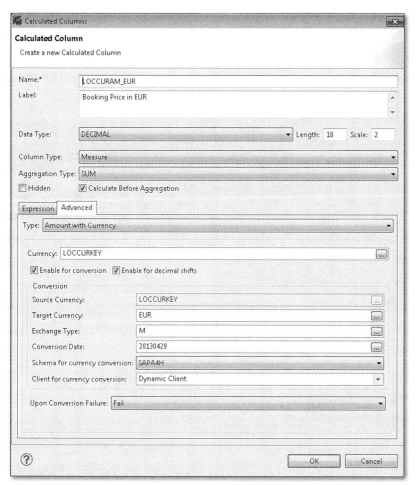

Figure 4.26 Defining the Parameters for a Currency Conversion

In many cases, it is desirable that the target currency and the key date can be parameterized for the conversion. Unfortunately, this cannot be done using the WHERE condition when accessing the view via SQL, since it is not possible to access the query parameters during modeling. For this reason, you can define *input parameters* for an analytic view, which can then be used as parameters for the conversion. Input parameters are also supported for calculation views, where they are used in the same way as when working with analytic views. This will be discussed in more detail in Section 4.3.

Parameterization for currency conversion

Defining input parameters

Input parameters can be defined via the OUTPUT section using the editor for logical joins. Figure 4.27 shows an input parameter for currency conversion. This parameter can then be used as target currency when configuring the conversion in Figure 4.26. The same procedure can be used to parameterize the key date. When subsequently calling the Data Preview, you are prompted for the input parameters' values. Accessing views via SQL using input parameters will be covered in Section 4.2.5.

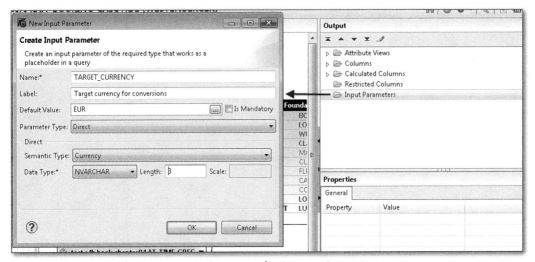

Figure 4.27 Input Parameters for Currency Conversion

Unit conversion

The same principle is used for unit conversion. In our sample view AN_ BOOKING, the baggage weight should always be considered in kilograms (KG) in order to identify bookings with excess weight. To reach this goal, unit conversion is configured as shown in Figure 4.28.

We'll contemplate another scenario in our example from Chapter 8, where the flight miles are determined based on distances specified in different units of length.

Conversions using SQLScript

Currency conversion and unit conversion can also be called in SQLScript via the built-in function CE_CONVERSION of the calculation engine. For flexible parameterization and embedding into a larger calculation, this can have advantages over the modeled variant. This will be shown in Chapter 5.

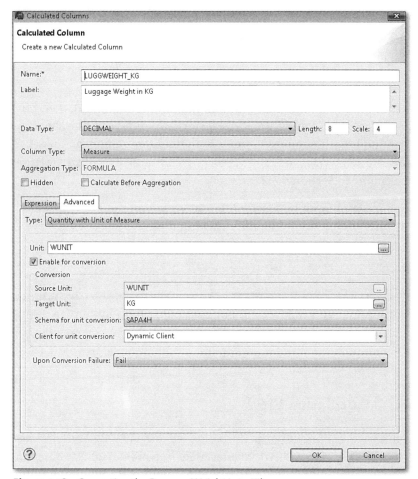

Figure 4.28 Converting the Baggage Weight into Kilograms

4.2.5 Runtime Artifacts and SQL Access for Analytic Views

As in case of the attribute views, there is a primary runtime artifact corresponding to the analytic view. In addition, several additional column views are created depending on the occurrence of hierarchies, key figures, and calculated fields. However, for application developers, these objects play only a minor role. The primary runtime artifact of the analytic view AN_BOOKING in the package test.a4h.book.chapter04 can again be addressed via a public synonym:

```
test.a4h.book.chapter04::AN_BOOKING
```

When accessing a view via SQL, remember that analytic views are not designed for single accesses, but rather for aggregated accesses. For example, reading all rows using the below statement is not supported:

```
SELECT * FROM <view name>
```

Instead, you must always use an aggregation (COUNT, SUM, etc.) and the corresponding grouping. Moreover, since grouping can only be done via columns of the analytic view, analytic views cannot be linked to other tables or views directly via SQL. This will be explained based on an example in Section 4.3.3.

If you defined input parameters for the view, you can pass them in an SQL query, as shown in the following example:

```
SELECT <columns> FROM <view> ('PLACEHOLDER' = ('$$TARGET_
CURRENCY$$', 'EUR')) WHERE ... GROUP BY ...
```

Accessing SAP HANA views from ABAP is introduced in Section 4.5. At this point, we would like to emphasize that the addition for setting input parameters is not supported via Open SQL, but requires the use of Native SQL.

4.3   Calculation Views

In this section, we will now introduce the last view type, the *calculation view*. This view is used whenever the capabilities of attribute and analytic views cannot meet your requirements. This is especially the case in scenarios where it is necessary to flexibly combine several views. Recommendations on the usage of the different view types can be found in Section 4.5.4.

There are two variants of calculation views. You can either model calculation views or implement them using SQLScript. This section describes the usage of both variants. However, we will not explain the full set of capabilities provided by SQLScript in the scope of this chapter (a comprehensive description can be found in the next chapter).

In this section, we will define two calculation views. We will combine the two analytic views from the previous section in the modeled view `CA_FLIGHT_STATISTIC` and create a combined data view on the seat utilization and number of bookings with excess baggage for a flight. In the implemented view `CA_SEAT_UTILIZATION_DELTA`, we will determine the average seat utilization and compare this result with the corresponding value from the previous year.

Reference examples for this section

4.3.1 Basic Principles

The main difference between calculation views and the other view types introduced so far is that calculation views can combine any other types of view. In case of attribute views, you can only link database tables via joins. Analytic views are always based on a star schema consisting of a fact table and dimensions. Calculation views have no such structural limitations.

A calculation view is based on a calculation model that consists of nodes and operations. These nodes can be tables or any type of view. For this reason, you can integrate views as nodes within the model.

Graphical modeling

Calculation views are modeled graphically in a tree structure, with the leaves representing tables or views. The other nodes define operations on the data. The following operations are currently supported: *join* (creating a join), *projection* (defining a field list or hiding columns), *aggregation* (performing a calculation for a column), and *union* (creating a union). The root node represents the output structure of the view and thus its external interface.

As you will learn in Section 5.2.4, SQLScript provides a built-in function for each of these operations. In other words: A graphical model, as shown in Figure 4.30, has a corresponding canonical execution plan in the calculation engine in SAP HANA. This execution plan can be displayed using the *PlanViz* tool, which will be introduced in Chapter 7.

Like attribute views or analytic views, calculation views support the definition of hierarchies and input parameters. Moreover, *counters* of different characteristics are offered exclusively for this view type.

Limitations of
graphical modeling As with almost every graphical modeling approach, there are also certain limitations to modeling calculation views. These limitations will be described briefly in this section:

- **Restrictions with regard to possible SQL types**
  It is, for example, not possible to use the entire scope of functions in SAP HANA-specific SQL. Examples would be calling the text search (see Chapter 9) or function libraries (see Chapter 12).

- **No free parameterization**
  It is not possible to flexibly parameterize modeled views. Some scenarios can be parameterized using input parameters, but there are still some limitations that must be considered when using the graphical modeling approach.

- **No options for performing calculations based on aggregates**
  There are also further scenarios that appear simple at first glance, but cannot be implemented by modeling a view in SAP HANA. Let's take a look at the example from Section 4.2. In this case, we used the view AN_SEAT_UTILIZATION to determine the seat utilization as a percentage per quarter for a flight connection. Let's assume we now also want to determine the variance from the previous year, i.e., the difference in use as a percentage. None of the presented modeling options can be used to directly perform this calculation.

Implementation
options To implement such scenarios, you can choose between different options. On the one hand, the powerful query modeling in SAP NetWeaver BW provides suitable capabilities. When using these options, however, it will no longer be possible to easily integrate the queries in a normal ABAP application. Chapter 10 describes in detail how to use the build-in BW functionality in the SAP NetWeaver AS ABAP for application development and also explains the associated advantages and disadvantages.

For specific scenarios, however, you can also use SQLScript to perform such calculations programmatically. The comprehensive options provided by SQLScript are described in Chapter 5. Since SQLScript is an extension of SQL, the seat utilization scenario described above can already be implemented using standard SQL as will be shown in this section.

4.3.2 Graphical Modeling of Calculation Views

Calculation views are created using the same procedure as attribute views and analytic views. To create a graphical calculation view, choose GRAPHICAL as the VIEW TYPE (Figure 4.29).

Creating calculation views

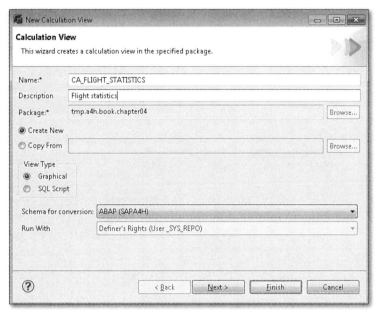

Figure 4.29 Creating a Graphical Calculation View

In the editor for calculation views, you can add tables and views as data sources and connect them using operations from the TOOLS PALETTE. These operations are PROJECTION, JOIN, AGGREGATION, and UNION. The editor displays both the data sources and the operations as nodes. The special node OUTPUT represents the output structure of the calculation view.

For our example, we will combine the data from the two analytic views. The output should include the number of bookings with excess baggage (calculated key figure OVERWEIGHT from AN_BOOKING_CALC) and the seat use (calculated key figure UTILIZATION from AN_SEAT_UTILIZATION). Since the data from AN_BOOKING_CALC is based on bookings, we have to first aggregate the key figure OVERWEIGHT and then create the union. Figure 4.30 shows the resulting graphical calculation view.

Integrating analytic views

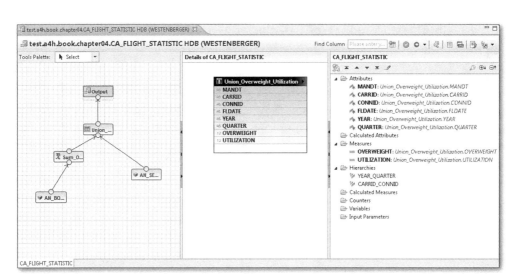

Figure 4.30 Graphical Calculation View CA_FLIGHT_STATISTIC

Connecting nodes and adding attributes To create this view, you first add the two analytic views. In the next step, you use the TOOLS PALETTE and choose AGGREGATION and UNION and connect the nodes as shown in Figure 4.30. You must select the attributes needed for each of the nodes. When creating the union, you define the mapping of the attributes in the target structure using the drag-and-drop method (see Figure 4.31).

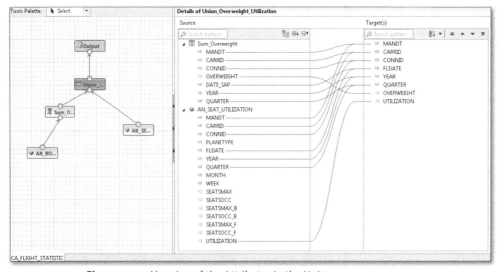

Figure 4.31 Mapping of the Attributes in the Union

Unfortunately, the hierarchies cannot be inherited from the dimensions of the analytic views, but must be defined manually (as described in Section 4.1.4).

After successful activation, the resulting calculation view CA_FLIGHT_ STATISTIC is displayed (shown in Figure 4.32).

Result

MANDT	CARRID	CONNID	FLDATE	YEAR	QUARTER	OVERWEI...	UTILIZATION
001	LH	2407	20070624	2007	02	51	0,8851
001	AA	0017	20120609	2012	02	76	0,7698
001	AA	0064	20101013	2010	04	103	0,6788
001	QF	0006	20080922	2008	03	77	0,8333
001	DL	1984	20060703	2006	03	106	0,9455
001	DL	1984	20080707	2008	03	118	0,8782
001	UA	3516	20050921	2005	03	149	0,9176
001	SQ	0988	20040604	2004	02	144	0,8764
001	DL	0106	20040204	2004	01	102	0,6674
001	AZ	0790	20071212	2007	04	83	0,7948
001	QF	0006	20090718	2009	03	80	0,7738
001	AZ	0555	20130808	2013	03	16	0,2431
001	DL	0106	20101004	2010	04	125	0,7722
001	SQ	0158	20101205	2010	04	74	0,8669
001	DL	1699	20060315	2006	01	135	0,8421

Figure 4.32 Data Preview for the Calculation View CA_FLIGHT_STATISTIC

4.3.3 Implementing Calculation Views via SQLScript

As previously mentioned, calculation views can also be implemented using SQLScript. SQLScript will be described in detail in Chapter 5. In this section, however, we will simply explain how to create implemented calculation views. We will only use very basic SQLScript for this purpose, which essentially contains a regular SQL statement with variables. Once you have learned about the further options of SQLScript in Chapter 5, you will be able to implement more complex calculation views as well.

Implemented calculation views are created following a similar procedure as used for the modeled variant; however, you choose SQLSCRIPT as the VIEW TYPE (see Figure 4.33) in this case.

Creating calculation views

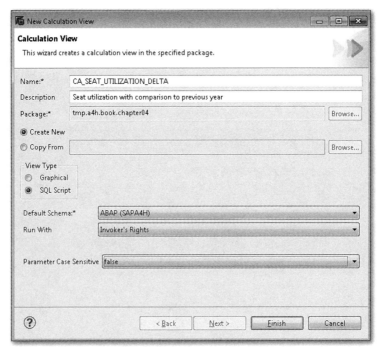

Figure 4.33 Creating an Implemented Calculation View

Settings The settings contain three selection lists that play an important role for all SQLScript implementations:

► DEFAULT SCHEMA defines the default schema so that you don't have to specify a schema name when accessing tables or views using SQL. You should usually choose the standard schema of the ABAP system for this setting.

► Via the RUN WITH setting, you can configure the user for running the SQLScript code. The INVOKER'S RIGHTS setting indicates that the invoker (e.g., the ABAP database user) must have the required SQL authorizations.

► PARAMETER CASE SENSITIVE controls whether parameters are case sensitive.

When discussing database procedures in the following chapter, we will deal with these settings and recommendations for their usage again.

After clicking the FINISH button, the system opens the editor for calculation views implemented with SQLScript (Figure 4.34).

SQLScript editor

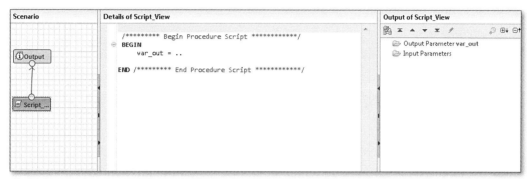

Figure 4.34 Editor for Implemented Calculation Views

The editor comprises three sections:

Editor sections

▶ The SCENARIO pane displays the model of the calculation view. In the case of a calculation view implemented with SQLScript, you use this section to switch between the column definition of the view and the SQLScript coding (i.e., the underlying database procedure).

▶ The DETAILS OF pane allows you to edit the column definition or the SQLScript coding.

▶ To define attributes, key figures, input parameters, etc., you use the OUTPUT OF section.

For our example, you first define the columns of the output parameter var_out. The result is displayed in Figure 4.35.

Defining output parameters

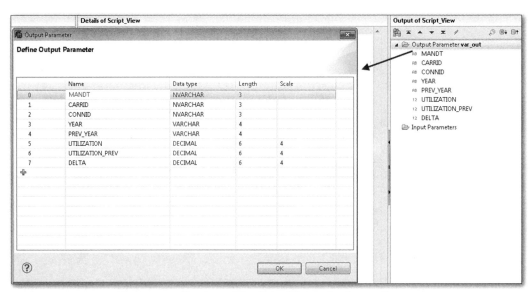

Figure 4.35 Structure of the Output Parameter "var_out"

SQLScript coding

In the next step, you can insert the SQLScript coding from Listing 4.2 as the implementation. When doing so, a complex SQL statement is used to perform a join of the view AN_SEAT_UTILIZATION with the same view (a so-called *self join*). This defines the two time slices (data of the current and the previous year) needed for determining the variance in the average utilization. In the following chapter, you will learn how to modularize such complex SQL statements using SQLScript.

```
/********* Begin Procedure Script ************/
 BEGIN

/* Self join to compare the result with the data from the
previous year
    The selection with the aggregation must be
    implemented using subqueries
*/
var_out =
  select c.mandt, c.carrid, c.connid,
         c.year, p.year as prev_year,
         c.utilization as utilization,
         p.utilization as utilization_prev,
```

```
          c.utilization - p.utilization as delta
  from (
    select mandt, carrid, connid, year,
           avg(utilization) as utilization
    from "test.a4h.book.chapter04::AN_SEAT_UTILIZATION"
    group by mandt, carrid, connid, year
  ) as c
  left outer join (
    select mandt, carrid, connid, year,
           avg(utilization) as utilization
    from "test.a4h.book.chapter04::AN_SEAT_UTILIZATION"
    group by mandt, carrid, connid, year
  ) as p
  on c.mandt = c.mandt and p.carrid = p.carrid and
     c.connid = p.connid and c.year = p.year + 1
  order by c.year desc;

END /********* End Procedure Script ************/
```

Listing 4.2 SQLScript Implementation of the Calculation View

The two time slices are called c (*current*) and p (*previous*) in the SQL statement, and the essential connection is implemented via the join condition c.year = p.year + 1.

In the next step, you define the output structure of the view via the SCENARIO section of the editor. You select the columns of the output parameter var_out of the database procedure, which will be exposed by the calculation view. In addition, you specify whether the columns are exposed as attributes or as key figures. As in case of modeled calculation views, you can also create hierarchies and variables.

Defining view columns

After successful activation, you can display the result in the Data Preview. Figure 4.36 shows the percentage increase or decrease of the seat utilization for a time period of several years for connections of the airline "LH." In this context, it must again be noted that the Data Preview only shows an excerpt of data.

Display results

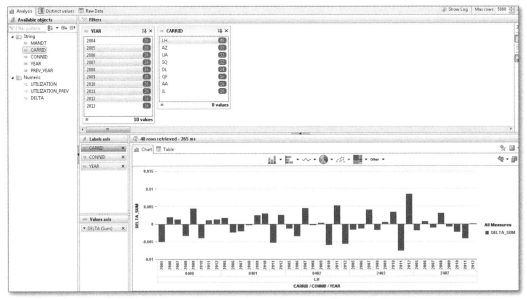

Figure 4.36 Data Preview for the Calculation View CA_SEAT_UTILIZATION_DELTA

4.3.4 Runtime Artifacts and SQL Access for Calculation Views

As in the case of attribute views and analytic views, there is a primary runtime artifact with a canonical name for calculation views as well; for our view CA_FLIGHT_STATISTIC, this is a public synonym with the name:

```
test.a4h.book.chapter04::CA_FLIGHT_STATISTIC.
```

Moreover, when dealing with calculation views, there are also special column views for the hierarchies and key figures that are irrelevant for application developers in most cases.

Database procedure

In the case of implemented calculation views, the system also creates a database procedure and a table type for the output parameter var_out of the database procedure. We'll explain how database procedures and implemented calculation views interact in more detail in the following chapter.

Similar to other view types, calculation views are accessed via SQL using the runtime artifacts. With regard to the usage of input parameters, the same rules apply as in the case of analytic views (see Section 4.2.5).

4.4 Accessing Column Views via Microsoft Excel

So far, you have only seen how the result of a view can be displayed using the Data Preview in SAP HANA Studio. While this is sufficient for first tests, the results are not complete (there is a maximum number of rows) and the Data Preview provides limited options for analysis.

SAP provides a large number of tools for accessing SAP HANA views. In particular, you can use the *SAP BusinessObjects Business Intelligence platform* for analyses, dashboards, etc., based on SAP HANA views. There is also a data modeling integration of the SAP HANA views in SAP NetWeaver BW. These advanced options will be explained in more detail in Chapter 10.

In this section, we will introduce a fairly simple method for accessing views from Microsoft Excel. To use this method, you only need the *SAP HANA Client Package for Microsoft Excel*, which is part of the SAP HANA Appliance. Installation details can be found in the corresponding documentation. After installing this package, the SAP HANA MDX Provider should be available as an OLE DB Provider (Object Linking and Embedding database interface) in the data import wizard of Microsoft Excel (see Figure 4.37).

SAP HANA Client Package for Microsoft Excel

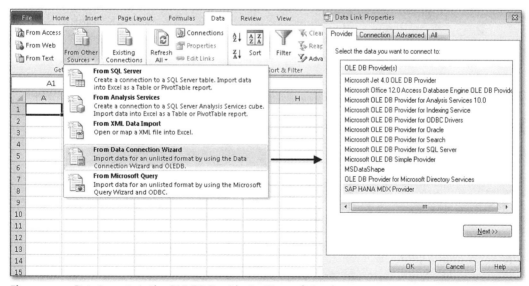

Figure 4.37 Data Import via the OLE DB Provider in Microsoft Excel

Importing data into a pivot table

Using this provider, you can import the data from an analytic view or a calculation view into a pivot table in Microsoft Excel. A prerequisite for this import, however, is that the configuration MULTI DIMENSIONAL REPORTING is activated in the properties of the view in SAP HANA Studio. Once the OLE DB driver establishes a connection, a selection dialog with the available SAP HANA views is displayed (see Figure 4.38).

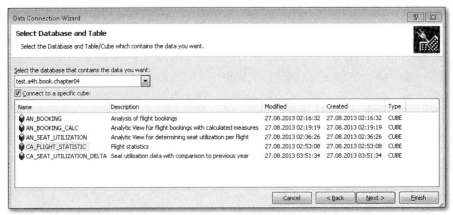

Figure 4.38   Importing SAP HANA Views into Microsoft Excel

You can then use the pivot table functions in Microsoft Excel on the data from the SAP HANA view. Figure 4.39 shows a representation of the data from the analytic view AN_BOOKING, which we created in Section 4.2.

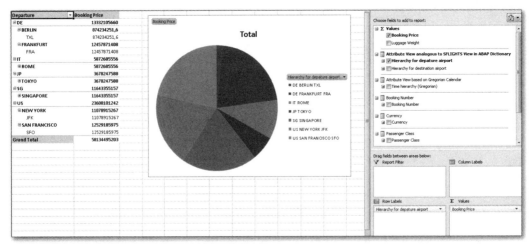

Figure 4.39   Pivot Table in Microsoft Excel Based on the Analytic View AN_BOOKING

> ### Multidimensional Expressions (MDX) [«]
>
> As the name of the OLE DB Provider *SAP HANA MDX Provider* already indicates, this driver uses an internal access mechanism based on the MDX standard (Multidimensional Expressions).
>
> MDX is a powerful database query language for OLAP scenarios which was promoted by Microsoft and has become an industry standard. In contrast to SQL, MDX is focused on multidimensional access, with the terms *measures* and *dimension* playing a decisive role for selections on a *cube* that is based on a star schema.
>
> Within the scope of this book, the MDX standard and its support in SAP HANA will not be explained in further detail. If you are familiar with MDX, however, it might be interesting to know that you can use MDX via the SQL console in SAP HANA Studio. For further information on this topic, please read the documentation at *http://help.sap.com/hana_appliance/*.

4.5   Using SAP HANA Views in ABAP

In the previous sections, you learned how to model the different view types in SAP HANA Studio and how to access the results of a view using the Data Preview or Microsoft Excel. In Section 4.3.3, we also explained how to address the generated column views via SQL.

This section describes how to access the views from ABAP. In this context, we have to differentiate between ABAP release 7.4 and earlier versions. When working with earlier releases, only Native SQL can be used for access; this will be described briefly in Section 4.5.1. As of ABAP 7.4, you can import the views from the SAP HANA Repository into the ABAP Data Dictionary and then access them using Open SQL. This will be explained in detail in Section 4.5.2 and in Section 4.5.3. In the last section, you'll find some recommendations and tips and tricks for SAP HANA view modeling.

Access with ABAP 7.4 and earlier releases

4.5.1   Access via Native SQL

When activating any of the presented view types in SAP HANA, a column view is created in the database catalog in the schema _SYS_BIC. This view is composed of the name of the package and the name of the view. Example:

```
"_SYS_BIC"."test.a4h.book.chapter04/AT_FLIGHT"
```

In addition, a *public synonym* is created with the following name:

```
"test.a4h.book.chapter04::AT_FLIGHT"
```

Using these names, the views can also be accessed from ABAP using Native SQL.

Listing 4.3 shows how the attribute view AT_FLIGHT created in Section 4.1 is accessed via ADBC. As described in Section 3.3.3, the target structure must be defined manually since the view's structure is not known in the ABAP Data Dictionary. The example in Listing 4.3 uses some ABAP language elements from release 7.4 (inline declarations and constructor expressions), which are introduced in Appendix B. These are not a prerequisite for access, but are used to shorten the ABAP code.

```
" Definition of the result structure
TYPES: BEGIN OF ty_data,
         carrid    TYPE s_carr_id,
         connid    TYPE s_conn_id,
         fldate    TYPE s_date,
         route     TYPE string,
       END OF ty_data.

CONSTANTS:  gc_view TYPE string VALUE
               'test.a4h.book.chapter04::AT_FLIGHT'.
DATA: lt_data TYPE TABLE OF ty_data.

" Access to the attribute view
DATA(lv_statement) =
   | SELECT carrid, connid, fldate, route |
&& |  FROM "{ gc_view }"|
&& |  WHERE mandt = '{ sy-mandt }' ORDER BY fldate|.

TRY.
   " Preparing the SQL connection and statement
   DATA(lo_result_set) =
      cl_sql_connection=>get_connection(
         )->create_statement(
            tab_name_for_trace = conv #( gc_view )
         )->execute_query( lv_statement ).
```

```
  " Get result
  lo_result_set->set_param_table( REF #( lt_data ) ).
  lo_result_set->next_package( ).
  lo_result_set->close( ).
CATCH cx_sql_exception INTO DATA(lo_ex).
  " Error handling
  WRITE: | { lo_ex->get_text( ) } |.
ENDTRY.

LOOP AT lt_data ASSIGNING FIELD-SYMBOL(<l>).
  WRITE: / <l>-carrid , <l>-connid, <l>-fldate,
          <l>-route .
ENDLOOP.
```

Listing 4.3 Accessing an Attribute View via ADBC

As you can see, this is a regular access using Native SQL. If an error occurs during execution, the text of the SQL exception points to the cause. In addition to SQL coding errors, which are also visible when accessing views via the SQL console, there may also be errors related to mapping the result to the ABAP data type. Recommendations regarding this topic are given in Section 4.5.4.

4.5.2 External Views in the ABAP Data Dictionary

In ABAP 7.4, *external views* are a new view type in the ABAP Data Dictionary. Using such views, you can import column views defined in the SAP HANA Repository into the ABAP Data Dictionary. These views are called external views since they are not fully defined in the ABAP Data Dictionary, but used as a kind of *proxy* allowing the corresponding column view in the schema _SYS_BIC to be accessed from ABAP.

External views can only be defined using the ABAP Development Tools in Eclipse. To do so, you create a new development object of the DICTION-ARY VIEW type. Figure 4.40 shows the creation dialog for the attribute view AT_FLIGHT.

Creating external views in Eclipse

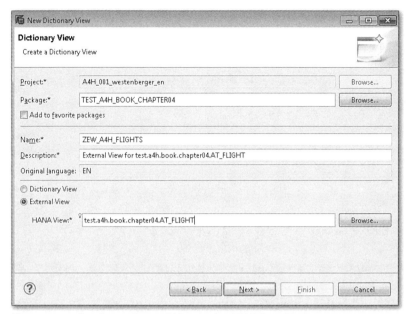

Figure 4.40 Creating an External View in the ABAP Data Dictionary

Checking whether a view can be imported

When the view is created, the system checks whether it can be imported into the ABAP Data Dictionary. It must be noted that not all SAP HANA data types are supported in ABAP. When defining calculated attributes or accessing tables from views that were not created using the ABAP Data Dictionary, such potentially unsupported data types may appear. In this case, an error occurs when creating the external view and the view cannot be imported. The supported data types are listed in Table 3.1 in Section 3.1.3.

View structure and synchronization

After successfully importing the SAP HANA view into the ABAP Data Dictionary, the editor displays the structure of the view together with the data type mapping (Figure 4.41). In addition, there is a button Syn-chronize, which can be used to synchronize the view after changing the structure of the corresponding view in SAP HANA Studio. So if you add attributes to the output structure, delete attributes, or change data types, you need to synchronize the external view in order to avoid run-time errors. Recommendations on synchronizing developments within a development team can be found in Chapter 14.

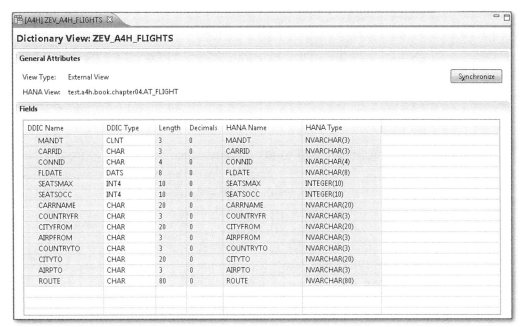

Figure 4.41 External ABAP Data Dictionary View Based on an Attribute View

As you learned in Section 3.1.3, SQL data types and ABAP Data Dictionary types cannot always be mapped uniquely. However, the data type is
decisive for the correct handling of operations (for example, the calculation of differences for a date). For this reason, the correct ABAP data type
must be mapped manually by the developer.

*Mapping
data types*

Table 4.3 shows the possible data type mappings for some columns of
the sample view AT_FLIGHT.

Column	SQL Data Type	Possible Dictionary Types
CARRID	NVARCHAR(3)	CHAR(3), NUMC(3), SSTR, CLNT, UNIT, CUKY
FLDATE	NVARCHAR(8)	CHAR(8), NUMC(8), SSTR, DATS
CARRNAME	NVARCHAR(20)	CHAR(20), NUMC(20), SSTR

Table 4.3 Example of Possible Type Mappings

For the external view in Figure 4.41, we manually mapped the column FLDATE to the ABAP data type DATS. This may appear strange at first glance, since this information is already present in the underlying Dictionary table; however, the attributes of column views in SAP HANA do not have a reference to columns of existing tables that is recognizable by the ABAP Data Dictionary. For instance, the FLDATE column could also be a calculated attribute.

Prerequisites The procedure for defining external views based on an analytic or a calculation view is identical to the procedure used for an attribute view. Note that external views in the ABAP Data Dictionary currently do not have a reference to the particular view type. By this we mean that they are just pointing to an arbitrary column view in SAP HANA. The only prerequisite is that the view is defined via the SAP HANA Repository. Column views, which solely exist in the database catalog (e.g., generated programmatically) cannot be imported into the ABAP Data Dictionary.

The transport of external views (and other SAP HANA-specific developments) is described in Chapter 6.

4.5.3   Options for Accessing External Views

Advantages The main advantage of external views is that Open SQL can be used to access SAP HANA views. This allows you to particularly benefit from the following advantages:

- ▸ Syntax checking by the ABAP Compiler and content assist during development (*code completion*)
- ▸ Automatic client handling
- ▸ Iterating through a result set within a SELECT loop
- ▸ Using the expression INTO CORRESPONDING FIELDS for a matching selection in a target structure independent of the sequence in the projection list
- ▸ Using IN for the WHERE condition to transfer selection options

Access via ADBC Listing 4.4 shows how the access to the external view from Figure 4.39 is implemented. From a functional perspective, this corresponds to the ADBC access variant from Listing 4.3. As you can see, the ABAP code required for access is significantly shorter and corresponds to the access for a standard Dictionary view.

```
REPORT ZR_A4H_CHAPTER4_VIEW_OPEN.

DATA: wa TYPE zev_a4h_flights.

" Read data from external view
SELECT carrid connid fldate route
       FROM zev_a4h_flights
       INTO CORRESPONDING FIELDS OF wa.
  WRITE: / wa-carrid , wa-connid, wa-fldate, wa-route.
ENDSELECT.
```

Listing 4.4 Accessing an External View via Open SQL

> **Possible Runtime Errors when Accessing External Views** [!]
>
> When using Open SQL to access an external view, an SQL query is executed for the corresponding column view in SAP HANA. The same rules apply as when accessing the view using Native SQL.
>
> As explained in Section 4.2.5, certain limitations must be considered when accessing analytic views via SQL. An unsupported query via Open SQL leads to a runtime error. Since these errors rarely occur when accessing ABAP tables using Open SQL, ABAP developers should use caution when following this approach. The troubleshooting tools and possible runtime errors during SQL access are explained in more detail in Section 7.1.

In addition to Open SQL, external views can also be addressed using Native SQL. This variant, which seems somewhat awkward at first glance, is useful if you want to use an SQL query to access an SAP HANA view in a way that isn't supported using Open SQL. An example would be a *fuzzy search* in an attribute view (see Section 9.4.1). Compared to accessing the generated column view in the schema _SYS_BIC via Native SQL, the external view has an advantage in that a suitable target structure for a selection via ADBC already exists in the ABAP Data Dictionary.

Native access via ADBC

4.5.4 Recommendations

To conclude this chapter, this section provides a couple of recommendations for using SAP HANA views. These are limited to functional recommendations. Tools and recommendations for performance analysis can be found in Chapter 7 and Chapter 14, where we will also deal with design aspects like naming conventions.

Using the different view types

If the scope of functions provided by standard ABAP Data Dictionary views is sufficient for your purposes and if you used these views in the past, there is no need to change your application using native SAP HANA view. However, if you want to define more complex views containing calculated fields, the described modeled views in SAP HANA provide an easy approach. The following questions can help to determine the best view type in SAP HANA for your scenario:

- Are you dealing with master data views that might be extended by calculated attributes? In this case, you should start with an attribute view.

- Are you performing an analysis of transaction data based on a star schema? In this case, you should choose an analytic view and implement the dimensions as attribute views.

- Do you have to combine or adapt the results from different tables and SAP HANA views? In this case, you should use the modeled calculation view. If the modeled variant is not sufficient for some part of your scenario, you can use a SQLScript-based implementation for that part.

Client handling   When modeling views, you should make sure that the client field is handled correctly. In particular, it is advisable to add the client field as the first field of the view and to make sure that the client is included in the join definition. In most cases, the configuration value DYNAMIC DEFAULT CLIENT is the correct setting for views that are based on ABAP tables from the same system. If tables were replicated from a different system, it may be useful to use a fixed value for the client. Cross-client access is useful only in rare cases.

You should always choose the correct default schema for analytic views and calculation views. This schema is taken into account in particular for the relevant Customizing for conversions—that is, if no special setting was configured for the attribute. The specification of the correct default schema is even more important when dealing with the implemented variant of calculation views, which will be explained in more detail when introducing SQLScript in Chapter 5.

External views should only be defined for SAP HANA views that will be used for access via ABAP, since these views have to be synchronized manually after changing the corresponding structures. Moreover, you should define a maximum of one external view for each SAP HANA view.

Defining external views

If error messages are displayed when activating an SAP HANA view, the error text usually includes information on the root cause. In some cases, however, you may need some experience to correctly interpret the error message. For this reason, we recommend following a heuristic approach to error analysis. As a first step, you should make sure that you marked at least one field of an attribute view as a key field, and that you defined at least one key figure for an analytic view. If your view contains calculated attributes, you should check if you correctly defined the corresponding expression.

Troubleshooting

Tips for Error Analysis

If you come to a dead end during error analysis, you can try to remove the corresponding attribute (e.g., in a copy of the view). If an error message or unexpected data is displayed when calling the Data Preview, this is often an indication of a problem in the join modeling. In case of currency conversions, a missing client context may result in an error.

When accessing an SAP HANA view from ABAP using Native SQL, you should pass the name of the view (via the parameter tab_name_for_trace as shown in Listing 4.3 or via the method SET_TABLE_NAME_FOR_TRACE). This facilitates the error analysis in a support scenario.

SAP HANA provides a range of programming options in addition to data modeling. In particular, ABAP developers should be familiar with the SQLScript options available in relation to mapping requirements that cannot be implemented using data modeling alone.

5   Programming Options in SAP HANA

In the last chapter, we explained how to model data views in HANA. Now, we'll provide an overview of the programming options available to you. You'll learn how to use *SQLScript* to implement database procedures and calculation views. You will also learn how to call database procedures from SAP NetWeaver AS ABAP. SQLScript error analysis will be covered in Chapter 7.

SAP HANA provides other programming options in addition to SQLScript, especially in conjunction with the *XS Engine*. However, use of the XS Engine in application development is beyond the scope of this book.

5.1   Overview of SQLScript

The HANA database supports the standard SQL92 as well as parts of the standard SQL99. It also adds some non-standardized functions to SQL. These include, for example, the option of using the ROW or COLUMN additions with the CREATE TABLE statement to specify whether a database table is stored in a *row store* or *column store* (see Section 5.2.2) as well as support for text search performed using the key word CONTAINS (see Chapter 9).

SQL92 and SQL99

SQLScript is an enhancement to the SQL standard. It is used to move data-intensive calculations to the database as easily and as completely as possible. In the following subsections, we'll discuss the qualities of SQLScript and then explain how the SAP HANA database processes SQLScript.

SQLScript

5.1.1 Qualities of SQLScript

SQLScript has several advantages over Open SQL and the SQL standard. We wish to use a specific example to illustrate the intrinsic qualities of SQLScript. We will intentionally omit some details at first (so that we can discuss them in later sections).

Example: requirements
As was the case in the previous chapters, the example we will use here is based on the SFLIGHT data model. We now wish to calculate two key performance indicators for an airline's top connections:

▶ **Total booking revenue**
This key performance indicator is calculated by totaling the field LOC-CURAM for all individual bookings that have not been canceled from the database table SBOOK (in other words, the CANCELLED field is blank).

▶ **Average number of days between the flight date and booking date**
This key performance indicator is calculated from the difference between the fields FLDATE and ORDER_DATE for all individual bookings that have not been canceled from the database table SBOOK.

We also wish to identify those travel agencies that achieve the highest sales revenue based on an airline's top connections. The sales revenue for each travel agency is determined in the same way as the total booking revenue.

Modularizing of Tasks

You can use SQLScript to implement database procedures and calculation views. Internally, calculation views implemented using SQLScript are represented as database procedures (see Section 4.3.4).

Parameters and the processing logic
A database procedure comprises input/output parameters and the processing logic. You can use database procedures to modularize complex tasks. Figure 5.1 demonstrates how different database procedures can interact with one another to determine the key performance indicators and travel agencies associated with an airline's top connections.

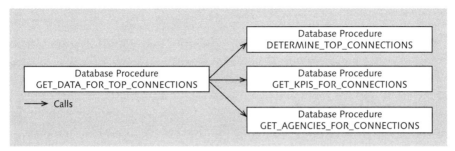

Figure 5.1 Using Multiple Database Procedures to Modularize Complex Tasks

Internally, the database procedure GET_DATA_FOR_TOP_CONNECTIONS uses:

Modularization

▶ The database procedure DETERMINE_TOP_CONNECTIONS to identify an airline's top connections.

▶ The database procedure GET_KPIS_FOR_CONNECTIONS to calculate the key performance indicators for an airline's top flight connections.

▶ The database procedure GET_AGENCIES_FOR_CONNECTIONS to identify those travel agencies with the highest sales revenue for an airline's top flight connections.

Thanks to modularization, you can simply reuse parts of the implementation for other tasks. For example, you can call the method GET_KPIS_FOR_CONNECTIONS for an airline's top connections as well as for any connections for multiple airlines.

Reuse

Splitting Up Complex Database Queries

In addition to using multiple database procedures to modularize complex tasks, SQLScript also enables you to split up complex database queries within a procedure. There you can assign the result of a SELECT statement to a *table variable* and then use this table variable for subsequent SELECT statements. We'll now demonstrate this using the example of the procedure GET_AGENCIES_FOR_CONNECTIONS.

The purpose of this procedure is to aggregate all bookings that were not canceled for a given set of flight connections, and to identify the five travel agencies with the highest sales revenue. It will then read the addresses of the five travel agencies identified. The corresponding database query can look as shown in Listing 5.1.

Procedure GET_
AGENCIES_FOR_
CONNECTIONS

```
ET_AGENCIES = SELECT A.AGENCYNUM, T.NAME, T.POSTCODE,
  T.CITY, T.COUNTRY, A.PAYMENTSUM, A.CURRENCY
  FROM ( SELECT TOP 5 B.AGENCYNUM, SUM(B.LOCCURAM) AS
    PAYMENTSUM, B.LOCCURKEY AS CURRENCY
    FROM :IT_CONNECTIONS AS C INNER JOIN SBOOK AS B ON
    B.CARRID = C.CARRID AND B.CONNID = C.CONNID
    WHERE B.MANDT = :IV_MANDT AND B.CANCELLED <> 'X'
    GROUP BY B.AGENCYNUM, B.LOCCURKEY
    ORDER BY SUM(B.LOCCURAM) DESC ) AS A
  INNER JOIN STRAVELAG AS T ON
  T.AGENCYNUM = A.AGENCYNUM WHERE T.MANDT = :IV_MANDT;
```

Listing 5.1 Example of a Complex Database Query

Splitting up complex database queries

Alternatively, with SQLScript, you can use one table variable to combine two database queries (see Listing 5.2):

```
LT_AGENCIES = SELECT TOP 5 B.AGENCYNUM,
  SUM(B.LOCCURAM) AS PAYMENTSUM, B.LOCCURKEY AS
  CURRENCY FROM :IT_CONNECTIONS AS C
  INNER JOIN SBOOK AS B ON B.CARRID = C.CARRID AND
  B.CONNID = C.CONNID
  WHERE B.MANDT = :IV_MANDT AND B.CANCELLED <> 'X'
  GROUP BY B.AGENCYNUM, B.LOCCURKEY
  ORDER BY SUM(B.LOCCURAM) DESC;

ET_AGENCIES = SELECT A.AGENCYNUM, T.NAME, T.POSTCODE,
  T.CITY, T.COUNTRY, A.PAYMENTSUM, A.CURRENCY
  FROM :LT_AGENCIES AS A INNER JOIN STRAVELAG AS T
  ON T.AGENCYNUM = A.AGENCYNUM
  WHERE T.MANDT = :IV_MANDT;
```

Listing 5.2 Splitting Up a Complex Database Query

Advantages of splitting up complex database queries

The following advantages are associated with using SQLScript to split up complex database queries:

► Several relatively simple SELECT statements are frequently easier to read and therefore easier to maintain than one relatively complex database query.

▶ Interim results in the form of a table variable can easily be reused (for example, to calculate key performance indicators and to identify travel agencies).

▶ Splitting up complex database queries may make it easier for the HANA database optimizer to detect redundant subqueries and to prevent their repeated calculation.

The database optimizer decides how to execute multiple database queries (both within and across database procedures). Internally, it can combine multiple SELECT statements into one database query. Under certain conditions, it is able to process multiple SELECT statements in parallel (see also the next section).

Parallel Processing

Another advantage of SQLScript is that SAP HANA can process independent database queries in parallel. We will also demonstrate this using the same example. The following four steps must be undertaken to solve the task at hand:

▶ Identify an airline's top connections.

▶ Calculate the two key performance indicators.

▶ Identify those travel agencies with the highest sales revenue.

▶ Read the addresses of the travel agencies identified.

Calculating the key performance indicators and identifying the travel agencies with the highest sales revenue (including reading their addresses) are dependent on identifying an airline's top connections but are fully independent of each other. Consequently, the HANA database can process these database queries in parallel, as shown in Figure 5.2.

Parallelization

Parallel processing of database queries in SQLScript is a fundamental difference from Open SQL. If you use Open SQL to send multiple SELECT statements to the HANA database (and use, for example, the FOR ALL ENTRIES clause to connect them), they are processed in succession.

Difference to Open SQL

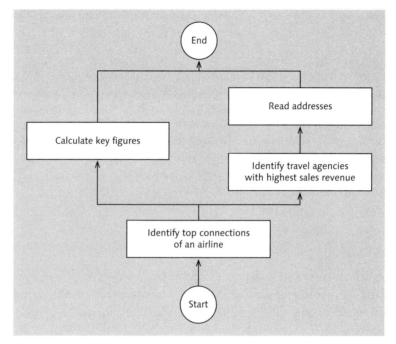

Figure 5.2 Parallel Processing

As a result of processing database queries in parallel, tasks can be accelerated considerably. However, this is only one form of parallelization in SAP HANA. The system can also use multiple threads to process individual database queries (for example, calculating key performance indicators) in parallel (see also Section 5.2.2). Open SQL also benefits from this form of parallelization.

Orchestrating the Processing Logic

Imperative programming

SQL is a declarative programming language. Declarative programming focuses on the problem description (in other words, the "what"). SQLScript adds elements of imperative programming to the SQL standard. Imperative programming focuses on the problem solution (in other words, the "how").

The imperative language elements in SQLScript enable you to work, for example, with case distinctions (IF ... THEN ... ELSEIF ... ELSE ... END IF) and loops (WHILE ... ENDWHILE) in database procedures and calculation views, thus enabling you to orchestrate the (declarative) processing logic. Here, you also have options that extend far beyond the SQL standard.

Let's imagine that an airline's top connections are to be identified on the basis of the sales revenue or percentage utilization. In this case, you can assign an input parameter to the DETERMINE_TOP_CONNECTIONS database procedure and, depending on its value, you can execute different database queries (see Listing 5.3):

Orchestration

```
IF IV_ALGORITHM = 'P' THEN
  ET_CONNECTIONS = SELECT TOP 5 CARRID, CONNID
    FROM SFLIGHT
    WHERE MANDT = :IV_MANDT AND CARRID = :IV_CARRID
    GROUP BY CARRID, CONNID
    ORDER BY SUM(PAYMENTSUM) DESC;
ELSE
  ET_CONNECTIONS = SELECT TOP 5 CARRID, CONNID
    FROM SFLIGHT
    WHERE MANDT = :IV_MANDT AND CARRID = :IV_CARRID
    GROUP BY CARRID, CONNID
    ORDER BY AVG(TO_DECIMAL(SEATSOCC + SEATSOCC_B +
    SEATSOCC_F) / TO_DECIMAL(SEATSMAX + SEATSMAX_B +
    SEATSMAX_F)) DESC;
END IF;
```

Listing 5.3 Imperative Language Elements

Note that the use of imperative programming may prevent paralleliza-tion of database queries. In particular, we recommend that you avoid loop processing combined with the use of cursors as much as possible (see Section 3.2.2).

Disadvantages of imperative language elements

Accessing Business Logic

It's often a challenge to access business logic in the event of a code pushdown from the application layer to the database layer. In ABAP application development, a large part of the business logic previously lay in the application layer and therefore was only available for data records transferred from the database to the application server. Currency conver-sion is a good example here.

SQLScript makes crucial business logic functions available in the database layer. In addition to currency conversion, SQLScript also supports the conversion of units of measure in accordance with Customizing for SAP NetWeaver AS ABAP. You can also access the HANA function libraries in database procedures and calculation views (see Chapter 12), which gives you considerably more options in terms of moving data-intensive calculations to the database than those available with Open SQL or Native SQL.

5.1.2 Processing SQLScript

Now that we have discussed the advantages of SQLScript, we'll explain how the HANA database processes SQLScript. Here, we distinguish between processing when activating SQLScript and processing when invoking SQLScript.

Activating SQLScript

When activating SQLScript, the HANA database first checks the syntax of the database procedure.

Semantic check The system then checks the semantic correctness. It derives, among other things, the table variable types because these are implicitly typed in SQLScript. The system checks whether the variables are being used consistently and whether all of the output parameters associated with the database procedure have been filled.

Optimizing the database procedure The system then optimizes the database procedures and creates a (possibly multilevel) *calculation model* that resembles a graphical calculation view. In this model, imperative language elements are generated as *L nodes*. *L* is a programming language that makes some language elements of C++ available and supports HANA's system of data types. Internally, the HANA database uses L as an intermediate language when compiling a database procedure to C++.

Finally, the system stores the database procedure in the database catalog and, if necessary, in the SAP HANA Repository.

Invoking SQLScript

Two phases are associated with invoking a database procedure—namely, *compilation* and *execution*.

When compiling a database procedure, the HANA database rewrites the database procedure call so that it can be executed by the *calculation engine*. Then, when executing the database procedure, the system binds the *actual parameters* associated with the call to the calculation model created when the procedure was activated. This process is known as *instantiating* the calculation model. During instantiation, the system possibly optimizes the calculation model further. Lastly, the system uses the *engines* available (see Section 5.3) to execute the calculation model.

Compilation and execution

5.2 Implementing Database Procedures

In this section, we will explain how to implement database procedures.

5.2.1 Basic Principles of Database Procedures

As already described in the previous section, a database procedure comprises input parameters, output parameters, and the processing logic.

The main difference between database procedures and views is the fact that database procedures can return more than one result set. In other words, they can have multiple output parameters. Furthermore, database procedures and views are called differently from ABAP. We will describe this in detail.

Multiple output parameters

From a technical perspective, SQL is used to generate, call, change, and delete database procedures. The HANA database provides the following statements for this purpose:

SQL statements

▶ You can use the `CREATE PROCEDURE` statement to create a new database procedure.

▶ You can use the `CREATE TYPE` command to create a table type for use in the database procedure interface.

▶ You can use the `ALTER PROCEDURE` statement to recompile the calculation model for a database procedure.

▶ You can use the `CALL` statement to call a database procedure.

▶ You can use the `DROP PROCEDURE` statement to delete a database procedure.

SQL console

Even though you can execute these commands directly via the SQL console, we do not recommend this (with the exception of simple tests) because procedures created via the SQL console are not stored in the SAP HANA Repository. You therefore lose version management and transport management, among other things.

Editors

Instead, we recommend that you use the editors in the MODELER and SAP HANA DEVELOPMENT perspectives in the SAP HANA Studio to create database procedures in the SAP HANA Repository. We will discuss both options in this section. We anticipate that, in future, it will only be possible to create database procedures for the SAP HANA Repository in the SAP HANA DEVELOPMENT perspective.

Types of database procedures

SAP HANA distinguishes between two types of database procedures:

▶ Database procedures that only read data (known as *read-only procedures*).

▶ Database procedures that can read and write data (known as *read/write procedures*).

The use of INSERT, UPDATE, DELETE, and DDL statements (Data Definition Language statements) are prohibited in read-only procedures. Whereas read/write procedures can call any database procedure, read-only procedures can only call read-only procedures (see Figure 5.3).

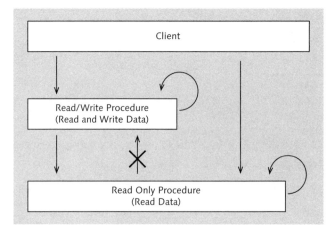

Figure 5.3 Read-Only and Read/Write Procedures

In general, SQLScript is used to implement database procedures. The HANA database also supports two additional programming languages, namely L and R:

SQLScript, L, and R

▶ The programming language L is based on C++. The use of L to implement database procedures is currently reserved for SAP itself.

▶ R is a free programming language for resolving statistical problems (*http://www.r-project.org/*). Implementing a database procedure in R enables you to use the R functionality in SAP HANA and, if necessary, embed it into a more extensive calculation model. The programming language R is beyond the scope of this book.

User-Defined Functions

[«]

We do not wish to overlook the fact that *user-defined functions* (UDF) are also available in addition to database procedures. User-defined functions are also implemented in SQLScript and are created or deleted using the CRE-ATE FUNCTION and DROP FUNCTION statements. The user-defined function DETERMINE_TOP_CONNECTIONS is created in the following example:

```
CREATE FUNCTION DETERMINE_TOP_CONNECTIONS(IV_MANDT
  NVARCHAR(3), IV_CARRID NVARCHAR(3), IV_ALGORITHM
  NVARCHAR(1)) RETURNS TABLE(CARRID NVARCHAR(3), CONNID
  NVARCHAR(4)) LANGUAGE SQLSCRIPT SQL SECURITY INVOKER AS
BEGIN
...
END;
```

In contrast to database procedures, you can use user-defined functions directly in SQL statements. This can look as follows:

```
SELECT C.CARRID, C.CONNID, S.CARRNAME
  FROM DETERMINE_TOP_CONNECTIONS('000', 'LH', 'P') AS C
  INNER JOIN SCARR AS S ON S.CARRID = C.CARRID
  WHERE S.MANDT = '000';
```

At present, you can only create user-defined functions in the SQL console.

5.2.2 Creating Database Procedures

We now wish to provide a detailed description of how to create a database procedure. We will use the MODELER and SAP HANA DEVELOPMENT perspectives in SAP HANA Studio for this purpose. Before we describe the steps for creating a database procedure, we wish to discuss the relevant SQL statements in more detail.

Statement for Creating a Database Procedure

CREATE PROCEDURE

You use the CREATE PROCEDURE statement to create a database procedure. The complete syntax is shown in Listing 5.4.

```
CREATE PROCEDURE <proc_name> [(<parameter_clause>)]
[LANGUAGE <lang>] [SQL SECURITY <mode>]
[READS SQL DATA [WITH RESULT VIEW <view_name>]] AS
[<local_scalar_variables>]
BEGIN
  <procedure_code>
END
```

Listing 5.4 Syntax for the CREATE PROCEDURE Statement

Additions to CREATE PROCEDURE

The CREATE PROCEDURE statement is followed by the name <proc_name> of the database procedure, a series of optional additions, and finally, enclosed between BEGIN and END, the actual implementation in the form of source code <procedure_code> (in other words, the processing logic). The optional additions have the following meaning:

▶ After the name of the database procedure, you can define input and output parameters in the parameter list <parameter_clause>. Here, you can use *scalar parameters* based on *simple data types* (such as INTE-GER, DECIMAL, or NVARCHAR) and *table parameters* based on database tables or *table types*. You will learn more about the system of data types deployed by the HANA database in Section 3.1.3. In the next section, we will discuss table types in greater detail.

▶ After the parameter list, you can specify the programming language LANGUAGE used to implement the database procedure. SQLSCRIPT and RLANG are permitted for <lang>.

▶ You can use the SQL SECURITY addition to specify the user against which the system checks authorizations at runtime. DEFINER (creator of the procedure) and INVOKER (caller of the procedure) are permitted for <mode>.

▶ You use READS SQL DATA to indicate that a database procedure only reads data. If the read-only procedure returns exactly one table parameter, you can use WITH RESULT VIEW <view_name> to create a view. In this case, you can later use a SELECT statement to query the result of the database procedure.

▶ Within database procedures, you can work with local variables. You define scalar variables under <local_scalar_variables>. We will discuss table variables in Section 5.2.3.

Statement for Creating a Table Type

If you want to use table parameters in a database procedure interface, you can define them with reference to database tables or table types. Table types are an enhancement to the SQL standard and are part of the data type system supported by the HANA database. Conceptually, table types are similar to the *structures* within the ABAP Data Dictionary. The relevant command here is CREATE TYPE. The complete syntax is shown in Listing 5.5.

CREATE TYPE

```
CREATE TYPE <type_name> AS TABLE (<column_definition>
[{,<column_definition>}...])
```
Listing 5.5 Syntax for the CREATE TYPE Statement

The CREATE TYPE command is followed by the name of the table type <type_name> and individual columns. Each table type has at least one column, and each column definition <column_definition> comprises the name of the column and its (simple) data type.

Creating a Database Procedure in the "Modeler" Perspective

We will now explain how to create a database procedure in the MODELER perspective. To do this, we will implement a DETERMINE_CONNECTION_UTILIZATION read-only procedure that determines the percentage utilization for each flight connection:

Creating a read-only procedure

1. Open the MODELER perspective, navigate to the package in which you want to create the database procedure, and open the context menu. In the context menu, choose NEW • PROCEDURE...

2. In the next window (see Figure 5.4), enter the technical name and a description of the database procedure. In this example, the package

cannot be changed because you used the context menu of a package to create the procedure.

3. If you want to use an existing database procedure as a copy template, select the COPY FROM radio button.

4. Once you have activated the database procedure, the schema _SYS_BIC contains the relevant runtime objects. We will explain this in greater detail at the end of this section.

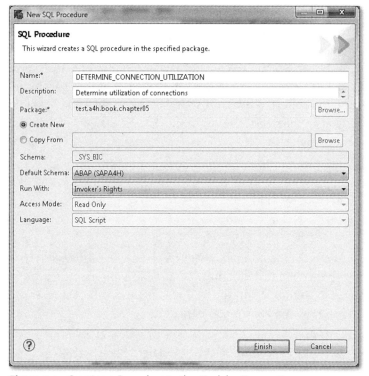

Figure 5.4 Creating a Procedure in the Modeler Perspective

Default schema It is important to specify the DEFAULT SCHEMA, as this determines which database schema the system will search to find database tables or data views if, within the database procedure, the database is accessed without a schema being specified.

Additions when creating a database procedure The remaining selection lists correspond to the additions previously explained for the CREATE PROCEDURE statement (see the section entitled "Statement for Creating a Database Procedure"):

▶ Use Run With to control the authorization check at runtime. We generally recommend that you perform authorization checks on the basis of the caller of the procedure.

▶ Use Access Mode to specify that the database procedure only reads data.

▶ In the Language selection list, specify the programming language used.

After you choose Finish, the system opens the editor (in the Modeler perspective) for database procedures (see Figure 5.5). This is partly source code-based, partly form-based.

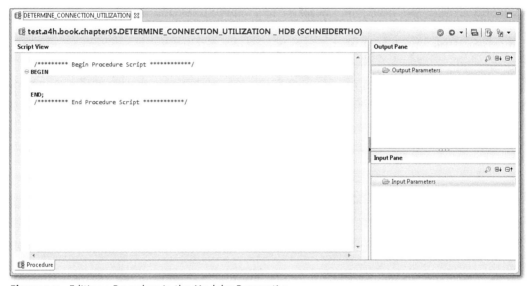

Figure 5.5 Editing a Procedure in the Modeler Perspective

The editor comprises the following three areas:

Areas within the editor

▶ In the Input Pane area, you define input parameters for the database procedure. You use the context menu of the Input Parameters node for this purpose.

▶ In the Output Pane area (and also in the context menu), you define output parameters for the database procedure. At present, only table

229

parameters are permitted here, even though in principle the CREATE PROCEDURE statement also permits scalar output parameters.

▶ You use the SCRIPT VIEW area to implement the processing logic. In other words, you create the actual SQLScript source code here.

If you want to display and—if necessary—change the entries made in Figure 5.4, open the PROPERTIES view.

Input and output parameters

When you define the input and output parameters, you must specify which SQL data types are to be used. The DETERMINE_CONNECTION_UTILIZATION procedure has three parameters:

▶ The input parameter IV_MANDT (client) of the SQL data type NVARCHAR(3)

▶ The input parameter IV_CARRID (airline) of the SQL data type NVAR-CHAR(3)

▶ The output parameter ET_UTILIZATION

The output parameter ET_UTILIZATION is a table parameter that comprises the following columns (see Figure 5.6):

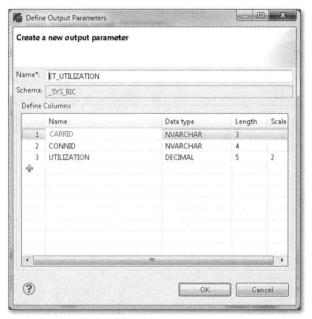

Figure 5.6 Table-Based Output Parameter ET_UTILIZATION

▶ CARRID (airline) of the SQL data type NVARCHAR(3)

▶ CONNID (flight connection) of the SQL data type NVARCHAR(4)

▶ UTILIZATION (utilization) of the SQL data type DECIMAL(5, 2)

[+]

> **Where to Find the SQL Data Types for Parameters**
>
> As an ABAP developer, you are familiar with the data elements, dictionary types, and/or ABAP types associated with an application domain, but not the underlying SQL data types (see also Section 3.1.3).
>
> If, when defining input and output parameters, you are unsure about which SQL data types you must use, you can generally determine this by displaying the table definition in the database catalog (see Section 2.5.3).

Once you have defined the input and output parameters, you can implement the processing logic. Our sample procedure contains (between BEGIN and END) the source code from Listing 5.6:

Processing logic

```
ET_UTILIZATION = SELECT CARRID, CONNID,
AVG(TO_DECIMAL(SEATSOCC + SEATSOCC_B + SEATSOCC_F) /
TO_DECIMAL(SEATSMAX + SEATSMAX_B + SEATSMAX_F) * 100)
AS UTILIZATION FROM SFLIGHT
WHERE MANDT = :IV_MANDT
  AND CARRID = :IV_CARRID
GROUP BY CARRID, CONNID;
```

Listing 5.6 Source Code for Sample Procedure

The database procedure accesses the database table SFLIGHT. It determines the percentage utilization for each flight and uses the aggregate function AVG to determine the average value for each flight connection (described by CARRID and CONNID). It assigns the result to the output parameter ET_UTILIZATION.

In the case of the database table SFLIGHT, we intentionally chose not to specify the database schema. Instead, we defined a default schema when we created the procedure (see above). We recommend that you always work with a default schema and never hard code a database schema in SQLScript. Otherwise, it is highly likely that your source code will no longer run after a transport. Imagine that you want to transport the database procedure DETERMINE_CONNECTION_UTILIZATION from the development system ABD (with the schema SAPABD) to the test system ABQ (with the

Accessing database schemas

schema `SAPABQ`). If you work with a default schema, you can use *schema mapping* (see Section 6.1.2) to ensure that the database procedure in the test system accesses the table `SAPABQ.SFLIGHT` instead of the table `SAPABD.SFLIGHT`. This will not work if you have hard coded the database schema `SAPABD` in the source code.

[+] **Accessing Runtime Objects and Database Tables from Different Database Schemas in a Procedure**

If, within a database procedure, you want to access the runtime objects associated with attribute views, analytic views, and/or calculation views, you can use the public synonym of the objects for this purpose (see Section 2.5.3).

If, within a database procedure, you want to access database tables from different database schemas (which may very well be the case if you are working with data replicated from multiple systems), use views to wrap these accesses. Therefore, for example, create an attribute view for each database table and then work with the public synonyms of the attribute views.

Client handling

We have transferred the client as the input parameter `IV_MANDT`. We are using the input parameter in the `WHERE` clause to ensure that the database procedure returns client data only. This is necessary because SQLScript does not have automatic client handling. Section 5.2.6 discusses appropriate alternatives to using an input parameter.

Case sensitivity

We wish to say a few words about case sensitivity. If, for example, you use identifiers for tables or table columns without double quotation marks, the system automatically converts your entry into upper case. If you work with double quotation marks, you must bear case sensitivity in mind. Since the ABAP Data Dictionary only recognizes upper case, we recommend that you do not use upper and lower case in SQLScript in the context of ABAP development. Refer to the information provided in Section 5.3.

Validation and activation

When you want to check the database procedure, choose SAVE AND VALIDATE ✅. When you want to activate the procedure, choose SAVE AND ACTIVATE (⭕; see Figure 5.5). In both cases, you can check the JOB LOG for any problems that have occurred.

Runtime objects

When you activate a database procedure, the system creates the following runtime objects in the database catalog:

▶ The database procedure itself.

▶ One table type for each tabular input/output parameter. Consequently, each procedure created in the MODELER perspective has its local table types.

▶ A public synonym for accessing the procedure.

Figure 5.7 shows the procedure created in the database catalog in the schema _SYS_BIC, as well as the table type for our example.

Figure 5.7 Runtime Objects for a Database Procedure

When you want to test the database procedure, you can call it in the SQL console. You use the CALL statement to call a database procedure. The complete syntax is as follows:

Testing a database procedure

```
CALL <proc_name> (<param_list>) [WITH OVERVIEW] [IN DEBUG MODE]
```

The CALL statement is followed by the name <proc_name> of the database procedure. You then transfer the current parameters as a parameter list <param_list>.

You can use the WITH OVERVIEW addition to write the result of the database procedure to one or more physical database tables. The IN DEBUG MODE addition is used for error analysis. Figure 5.8 shows an example of a call for the database procedure DETERMINE_CONNECTION_UTILIZATION in the SQL console.

Creating a Database Procedure in the "SAP HANA Development" Perspective

Now that you have created your first database procedure in the MOD-ELER perspective, we wish to explain the alternative option of using the

SAP HANA DEVELOPMENT perspective (see Figure 5.9) to create database procedures.

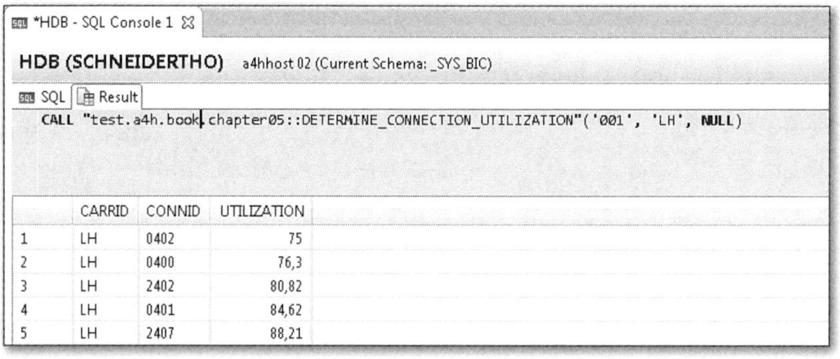

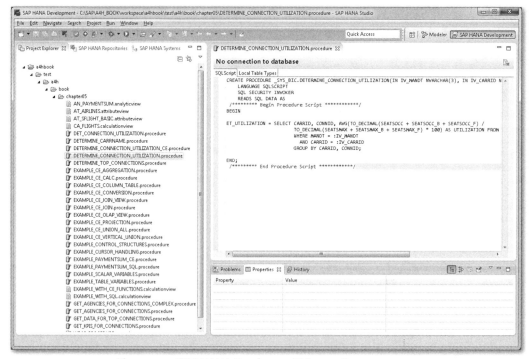

Figure 5.8 Testing a Database Procedure in the SQL Console

Figure 5.9 "SAP HANA Development" Perspective

Why are there two options?

You may be asking yourself the following question: Why are there two options for creating procedures? Historically, the SAP HANA DEVELOPMENT perspective exists as of SAP HANA 1.0, Support Package Stack 5. In other words, up to and including Support Package Stack 4, database procedures could only be created in the MODELER perspective.

As of Support Package Stack 5, you can build applications on the basis of SAP HANA Extended Application Services without the need for an additional application server. In order to provide the best possible support to developers in this regard and when programming in SAP HANA, SAP made the new SAP HANA DEVELOPMENT perspective available for Eclipse as of Support Package Stack 5.

If you create a database procedure in the SAP HANA DEVELOPMENT perspective, the system stores it as content in the SAP HANA Repository (which is also the case when you use the MODELER perspective) and, when you activate the database procedure, it generates the relevant runtime objects for the procedure in the database catalog.

When compared with the MODELER perspective, the following two major advantages are associated with using the SAP HANA DEVELOPMENT perspective to create a database procedure:

Advantages

▶ In the SAP HANA DEVELOPMENT perspective, you can define input and output parameters with reference to local table types or with reference to database tables and global table types. When you use the MODELER perspective, separate table types are (as you have already seen) generated for each database procedure.

▶ When you use the SAP HANA DEVELOPMENT perspective, you can debug database procedures. This function is not available to you when you work with the MODELER perspective. We will discuss this in more detail in Chapter 7.

However, some preparatory tasks need to be undertaken before you can use the SAP HANA DEVELOPMENT perspective. We will provide an overview of these tasks next (further detailed information is available in the *SAP HANA Developer Guide*):

Preparatory tasks

▶ **SAP HANA Repository Client**
The SAP HANA DEVELOPMENT perspective works with a *check-in/check-out mechanism*. This uses the SAP HANA Repository Client (see Section 2.4.1) to communicate with the SAP HANA Repository. In technical

terms, the SAP HANA Repository Client is the program `regi`. If you want to work with the SAP HANA DEVELOPMENT perspective, you must define the path for this program in SAP HANA Studio under the following menu option: WINDOW • PREFERENCES • SAP HANA DEVELOPMENT • REPOSITORY ACCESS.

▶ **System connection**
You require a system connection to the HANA database. We described the procedure for setting up a system connection in Section 2.5.3.

▶ **SAP HANA Repository Workspace**
You require an *SAP HANA Repository Workspace*. This directory is located on your PC's or laptop's hard drive. Generally, it lies within the Eclipse workspace (see Section 2.5.1).

To create an SAP HANA Repository Workspace, choose NEW REPOSITORY WORKSPACE in the context menu for the SAP HANA REPOSITORIES view.

▶ **Project**
You have to create a project and link this to the SAP HANA Repository Workspace. To create a project, choose NEW • PROJECT in the context menu for the PROJECT EXPLORER view.

To link the project with the SAP HANA Repository Workspace, choose TEAM • SHARE PROJECT... in the context menu for your project.

Creating a database procedure

Now that you have completed your preparatory work, you can create a database procedure in the SAP HANA DEVELOPMENT perspective. To do this, choose FILE • NEW • FILE. For the file name, use the name of the database procedure followed by the file extension .procedure. You can then use the CREATE PROCEDURE statement to define the database procedure in a purely source code-based editor.

Additional functions

If you want to use tabular input and output parameters, you can refer to database tables and global table types, or you can use CREATE TYPE to define suitable local table types. The context menu for the project respectively for the file created for the database procedure contains functions for saving (COMMIT), checking (CHECK), and activating (ACTIVATE) the database procedure in SAP HANA Repository.

As already mentioned in Section 5.2.1, we are assuming that, in the future, it will only be possible to create database procedures in the SAP HANA DEVELOPMENT perspective.

5.2.3 Using Variables

Now that you know how to create a database procedure, we wish to explain how to use variables. SQLScript distinguishes between table variables and scalar variables.

Table Variables

Table variables can be input/output parameters or local variables. They are based, either explicitly or implicitly, on a table type and can be linked to the result of an SQL statement or CE Plan Operator (see Section 5.2.4) by means of the equals sign "=". The contents of the table variables are accessed using the relevant variable name supplemented by the prefix ":". This occurs in the same way in which database tables are accessed. We will explain this further below by means of an example.

If you want to define a tabular input or output parameter, you must type this explicitly. When you create a database procedure in the MODELER perspective, the system automatically creates the necessary table types for each procedure. If, on the other hand, you create a database procedure in the SAP HANA DEVELOPMENT perspective, you can also reference existing database tables or table types during the typing process.

Explicit typing

When you assign the result of an SQL statement or CE Plan Operator to a tabular output parameter, the system checks whether both are type-compatible.

You *must not* (or rather *cannot*) explicitly type a local table variable. Instead, the system automatically derives the required table type from the SQL statement or CE Plan Operator that has been assigned.

Implicit typing

We now wish to use the example in Listing 5.7 to explain how to use table variables. We have intentionally omitted some details from the source code (for example, restricting the selection to one client):

Example of table variables

```
CREATE PROCEDURE EXAMPLE_TABLE_VARIABLES (OUT
ET_FLIGHTS TT_FLIGHTS) LANGUAGE SQLSCRIPT SQL SECURITY
```

```
INVOKER READ SQL DATA AS
BEGIN
  LT_FLIGHTS = SELECT CARRID, CONNID, FLDATE
                     FROM SFLIGHT;
  ET_FLIGHTS = SELECT * FROM :LT_FLIGHTS;
END;
```

Listing 5.7 Using Table Variables

In this example, a SELECT statement is used to assign the columns CAR-RID, CONNID, and FLDATE in the database table SFLIGHT to the local table variable LT_FLIGHTS, which is implicitly typed by the system.

Then, a second SELECT statement is used to assign the contents of the table variable LT_FLIGHTS to the table variable ET_FLIGHTS, which is an output parameter and is explicitly typed. It uses the table type TT_FLIGHTS.

Scalar Variables

Similar to table variables, scalar variables can be input/output parameters or local variables (note the restriction associated with output parameters in the MODELER perspective). They are based on a simple data type. Values are assigned using the assignment operator ":=". Similar to table variables, the value of scalar variables is accessed using the variable name supplemented by the prefix ":".

Typing You must always explicitly type a scalar variable. During the typing process, you can refer to the SQL data types supported by SAP HANA.

Example of scalar variables We now wish to use a simple example to explain how to use scalar variables. Once again, we have intentionally omitted some details from the source code in Listing 5.8.

```
CREATE PROCEDURE EXAMPLE_SCALAR_VARIABLES (IN
IV_CUSTOMID NVARCHAR(8) , IN IV_ADDITIONAL_DISCOUNT
INTEGER) LANGUAGE SQLSCRIPT SQL SECURITY INVOKER
READS SQL DATA AS
  LV_DISCOUNT INTEGER;
  LV_NEW_DISCOUNT INTEGER;
BEGIN
  SELECT TO_INT(DISCOUNT) INTO LV_DISCOUNT
         FROM SCUSTOM WHERE ID = :IV_CUSTOMID;
```

```
     LV_NEW_DISCOUNT := :LV_DISCOUNT +
                        :IV_ADDITIONAL_DISCOUNT;
END;
```

Listing 5.8 Using Scalar Variables

The database procedure used in this example increases the customer discount by a specific percentage. It uses multiple scalar variables for this purpose. The variables IV_CUSTOMID and IV_ADDITIONAL_DISCOUNT are input parameters, while the variables LV_DISCOUNT and LV_NEW_DISCOUNT are local variables.

5.2.4 Calculation Engine Plan Operator

In this section, we will discuss *CE Plan Operators*, which you can use in database procedures as an alternative to SQL statements.

Introductory Example

To help you understand the concept of CE Plan Operators, we will consider a very simple database procedure for determining the sales revenue of all flight connections associated with an airline. When an SQL statement is implemented, this database procedure looks as shown in Listing 5.9:

Implementation using an SQL statement

```
ET_PAYMENTSUM = SELECT CARRID, CONNID, CURRENCY,
   SUM(PAYMENTSUM) AS PAYMENTSUM
   FROM SFLIGHT
   WHERE MANDT = :IV_MANDT AND CARRID = :IV_CARRID
   GROUP BY CARRID, CONNID, CURRENCY;
```

Listing 5.9 Implementation Using an SQL Statement

The SQL statement selects data from the table SFLIGHT. This statement uses a WHERE clause to restrict the selection to the specified airline. It also uses the aggregate function SUM combined with a GROUP BY expression to add the sales revenue for each airline, connection, and currency.

When CE Plan Operators are used, the same database procedure looks like the one shown in Listing 5.10:

Implementation using CE Plan Operators

```
LT_SFLIGHT = CE_COLUMN_TABLE("SFLIGHT");
LT_SFLIGHT_PROJECTION = CE_PROJECTION(:LT_SFLIGHT,
   ["MANDT", "CARRID", "CONNID", "CURRENCY",
```

```
 "PAYMENTSUM"], '"MANDT" = '':IV_MANDT'' AND
 "CARRID" = '':IV_CARRID'' ');
LT_SFLIGHT_AGGREGATION = CE_AGGREGATION(
 :LT_SFLIGHT_PROJECTION, [SUM("PAYMENTSUM") AS
 "PAYMENTSUM"], ["CARRID", "CONNID", "CURRENCY"]);
ET_PAYMENTSUM = CE_PROJECTION(:LT_SFLIGHT_AGGREGATION,
 ["CARRID", "CONNID", "CURRENCY", "PAYMENTSUM"]);
```

Listing 5.10 Implementation Using CE Plan Operators

The database procedure uses different CE Plan Operators, which are linked to one another by means of table variables:

1. First, the database procedure uses the CE Plan Operator CE_COLUMN_ TABLE to bind the table variable LT_SFLIGHT to the database table SFLIGHT.

2. It then uses the CE Plan Operator CE_PROJECTION to restrict the selection to the columns MANDT, CARRID, CONNID, and CURRENCY, as well as to restrict the selection to the connections associated with the specified airline. The table variable LT_SFLIGHT, which was bound in the first step, is used as the input, while the table variable LT_SFLIGHT_PROJEC-TION is used as the output.

3. The CE Plan Operator CE_AGGREGATION adds the sales revenue for each airline, connection, and currency. Here, the table variable LT_SFLIGHT_ PROJECTION is used as the input and the table variable LT_SFLIGHT_ AGGREGATION is used as the output.

4. In a final step, the database procedure uses the CE Plan Operator CE_PROJECTION to perform a projection again. This projection is necessary because (due to the way the CE Plan Operator CE_AGGREGATION works) the sequence of the columns in the table variable LT_SFLIGHT_ AGGREGATION does not correspond to the sequence of the columns in the output parameter ET_PAYMENTSUM.

SQL versus CE Plan Operators

At first glance, the use of CE Plan Operators to implement the database procedure looks much more complicated than using SQL statements (or, in our example, exactly one SQL statement). However, CE Plan Operators provide functions that are not available with SQL statements. In some cases, executing database procedures that use CE Plan Operators is more efficient than executing equivalent database procedures that use SQL statements. We will return to this at the end of this section.

CE Plan Operators are implemented directly in the calculation engine. They are divided into *data source* access operators, *relational operators*, and *special operators*. We now wish to use specific examples to describe the CE Plan Operators currently available. To this end, we will compare equivalent implementations that use SQL statements and CE Plan Operators. We will omit some details initially (in particular, we will not restrict the selection in many of our examples to just one client, because this generally requires an additional call involving the CE Plan Operator CE_PROJECTION).

Available CE Plan Operators

For a detailed description of CE Plan Operators (including their complete syntax), see the *SAP HANA SQLScript Reference*.

Data Source Access Operators

You can use data source access operators to bind table variables to a database table or view. You are already familiar with the CE Plan Operator CE_COLUMN_TABLE, which you use to link a table variable to a database table (see Listing 5.11). You also have the option to perform a projection. The database table must be located in the column store.

CE_COLUMN_TABLE

```
/* Implementation using SQL */
ET_AIRLINES = SELECT CARRID, CARRNAME, CURRCODE
                     FROM SCARR;

/* Implementation using CE Plan Operators */
ET_AIRLINES = CE_COLUMN_TABLE("SCARR", ["CARRID",
              "CARRNAME", "CURRCODE"]);
```

Listing 5.11 Using the CE Plan Operator CE_COLUMN_TABLE

You can use the CE Plan Operator CE_JOIN_VIEW to link a table variable to an attribute view (see Listing 5.12). You also have the option to perform a projection.

CE_JOIN_VIEW

```
/* Implementation using SQL */
ET_AIRLINES = SELECT CARRID, CARRNAME, CURRCODE FROM
  "test.a4h.book.chapter05::AT_AIRLINES";
```

```
/* Implementation using CE Plan Operators */
ET_AIRLINES = CE_JOIN_VIEW
  ("_SYS_BIC"."test.a4h.book.chapter05/AT_AIRLINES",
  ["CARRID", "CARRNAME", "CURRCODE"]);
```
Listing 5.12 Using the CE Plan Operator CE_JOIN_VIEW

CE_OLAP_VIEW You can use the CE Plan Operator CE_OLAP_VIEW to link a table variable to an analytic view (see Listing 5.13). Note that you have to use at least one aggregate function here. (At present, the following aggregate functions are supported: COUNT, SUM, MIN, and MAX. The aggregate function AVG is *not* supported at present.)

```
/* Implementation using SQL */
ET_PAYMENTSUM = SELECT CARRID, CONNID, CURRENCY,
  SUM(PAYMENTSUM) AS PAYMENTSUM FROM
  "test.a4h.book.chapter05::AN_PAYMENTSUM"
  GROUP BY CARRID, CONNID, CURRENCY;

/* Implementation using CE Plan Operators */
ET_PAYMENTSUM = CE_OLAP_VIEW
  ("_SYS_BIC"."test.a4h.book.chapter05/AN_PAYMENTSUM",
  ["CARRID", "CONNID", "CURRENCY",
  SUM("PAYMENTSUM")]);
```
Listing 5.13 Using the CE Plan Operator CE_OLAP_VIEW

CE_CALC_VIEW You can use the CE Plan Operator CE_CALC_VIEW to access calculation views. Since this is similar to the CE Plan Operator CE_JOIN_VIEW, we will not provide an example here.

Relational operators

Relational operators make the operations typically associated with relational algebra available to you. They work on the table variables that you previously bound using the data source access operators, for example.

CE_JOIN You use the CE Plan Operator CE_JOIN to join two table variables (see Listing 5.14). This result is an *inner join*. Note that the columns used in the join condition (MANDT and CARRID in the example) must have the same name in both table variables. You also have the option to perform a projection. If you do this, the projection list must contain the columns used for the join.

```
/* Implementation using SQL */
ET_CONNECTIONS = SELECT C.MANDT, C.CARRID, A.CARRNAME,
  C.AIRPFROM, C.AIRPTO
  FROM SPFLI AS C INNER JOIN SCARR AS A
  ON A.MANDT = C.MANDT AND A.CARRID = C.CARRID;

/* Implementation using CE Plan Operators */
LT_SPFLI = CE_COLUMN_TABLE("SPFLI");
LT_SCARR = CE_COLUMN_TABLE("SCARR");
ET_CONNECTIONS = CE_JOIN(:LT_SPFLI, :LT_SCARR,
  ["MANDT", "CARRID"], ["MANDT", "CARRID", "CARRNAME",
  "AIRPFROM", "AIRPTO"]);
```
Listing 5.14 Using the CE Plan Operator CE_JOIN

If you want to execute a *left outer join* or a *right outer join* instead of an inner join, the CE Plan Operators `CE_LEFT_OUTER_JOIN` and `CE_RIGHT_OUTER_JOIN` are available for this purpose. The syntax corresponds to the CE Plan Operator `CE_JOIN`. At present, a *full outer join* is not available as a CE Plan Operator.

You can use the CE Plan Operator `CE_PROJECTION` to perform a projection on a table variable and, optionally, to filter the records (see Listing 5.15). If necessary, you can rename the columns and use the CE Plan Operator `CE_CALC` to insert expressions (both of which we will describe in more detail).

CE_PROJECTION

```
/* Implementation using SQL */
ET_CONNECTIONS = SELECT MANDT, CARRID, CONNID,
  AIRPFROM, AIRPTO FROM SPFLI
  WHERE MANDT = :IV_MANDT AND CARRID = :IV_CARRID;

/* Implementation using CE Plan Operators */
LT_SPFLI = CE_COLUMN_TABLE("SPFLI");
ET_CONNECTIONS = CE_PROJECTION(:LT_SPFLI, ["MANDT",
  "CARRID", "CONNID", "AIRPFROM", "AIRPTO"],
  '"MANDT" = '':IV_MANDT'' AND "CARRID" =
  '':IV_CARRID''');
```
Listing 5.15 Using the CE Plan Operator CE_PROJECTION

CE_AGGREGATION

You can use the CE Plan Operator CE_AGGREGATION to calculate aggregates on a table variable (see Listing 5.16). The aggregate functions available to you when you use the CE Plan Operator CE_OLAP_VIEW are also available to you here. You also have the option to specify columns to group the result correspondingly. If necessary, you can rename the columns.

Note that the CE Plan Operator CE_AGGREGATION implicitly performs a projection. Columns that are not used for aggregation or grouping purposes do not form part of the result.

```
/* Implementation using SQL */
ET_PAYMENTSUM = SELECT SUM(PAYMENTSUM) AS PAYMENTSUM,
  CARRID, CONNID, CURRENCY
  FROM SFLIGHT GROUP BY CARRID, CONNID, CURRENCY;

/* Implementation using CE Plan Operators */
LT_SFLIGHT = CE_COLUMN_TABLE("SFLIGHT");
ET_PAYMENTSUM = CE_AGGREGATION(:LT_SFLIGHT,
  [SUM("PAYMENTSUM") AS "PAYMENTSUM"],
  ["CARRID", "CONNID", "CURRENCY"]);
```

Listing 5.16 Using the CE Plan Operator CE_AGGREGATION

CE_UNION_ALL

The CE Plan Operator CE_UNION_ALL is equivalent to the UNION ALL SQL statement and enables you to unite two table variables (see Listing 5.17).

```
/* Implementation using SQL */
ET_AIRLINES = SELECT * FROM SCARR
                UNION ALL
                SELECT * FROM SCARR;

/* Implementation using CE Plan Operators */
LT_SCARR1 = CE_COLUMN_TABLE("SCARR");
LT_SCARR2 = CE_COLUMN_TABLE("SCARR");
ET_AIRLINES = CE_UNION_ALL(:LT_SCARR1, :LT_SCARR2);
```

Listing 5.17 Using the CE Plan Operator CE_UNION_ALL

CE_CALC

You can use the CE Plan Operator CE_CALC within other relational operators in order to analyze expressions (see Listing 5.18). Functions associated with date processing, mathematics, and character string processing, among others, are available here. (A complete list of supported functions is available in the *SAP HANA SQLScript Reference*.) Typically, the result of CE_CALC is an additional column in the result set.

```
/* Implementation using SQL */
ET_CONNECTIONS = SELECT CARRID, CONNID, FLTYPE,
  ( CASE FLTYPE WHEN 'X' THEN 'Charter' ELSE
  'Scheduled' END ) AS TEXT_FLTYPE FROM SPFLI;


/* Implementation using CE Plan Operators */
LT_SPFLI = CE_COLUMN_TABLE("SPFLI");
ET_CONNECTIONS = CE_PROJECTION(:LT_SPFLI, ["CARRID",
  "CONNID", "FLTYPE", CE_CALC('if("FLTYPE"=''X'',
  ''Charter'', ''Scheduled'')', NVARCHAR(10)) AS
  "TEXT_FLTYPE"]);
```

Listing 5.18   Using the CE Plan Operator CE_CALC

Other Functions

In addition to data source access operators and relational operators, the calculation engine currently makes the following three additional functions available: CE_VERTICAL_UNION, CE_CONVERSION, and TRACE. We will now discuss the first two CE Plan Operators in greater detail. We will discuss the third function, the CE Plan Operator TRACE, in Chapter 7.

You can use the CE Plan Operator CE_VERTICAL_UNION to connect columns in multiple table variables to each other (for example, if this cannot be done using a *join*, see Listing 5.19). If necessary, you can rename the columns.

CE_VERTICAL_ UNION

It is important to note the sort order of the table variables used. Otherwise, you may receive some unexpected results.

```
LT_SCUSIOM = CE_COLUMN_TABLE("SCUSTOM");
LT_NAME = CE_PROJECTION(:LT_SCUSTOM, ["NAME"]);
LT_ADDRESS = CE_PROJECTION(:LT_SCUSTOM, ["POSTCODE",
  "CITY", "COUNTRY"]);
ET_CUSTOMERS = CE_VERTICAL_UNION(:LT_NAME, ["NAME"],
  :LT_ADDRESS, [ "POSTCODE", "CITY", "COUNTRY"]);
```

Listing 5.19   Using the CE Plan Operator CE_VERTICAL_UNION

[+]

> **Tip**
>
> You could also implement the example in Listing 5.19 without using `CE_VERTICAL_UNION`.

CE_CONVERSION

The CE Plan Operator `CE_CONVERSION` enables you to perform quantity and currency conversions. The example shown in Listing 5.20 uses the CE Plan Operator `CE_CONVERSION` to convert the sales revenue associated with flight connections into any currency (passed to the database procedure).

```
LT_SFLIGHT = CE_COLUMN_TABLE("SFLIGHT");
LT_SFLIGHT_PROJECTION = CE_PROJECTION(:LT_SFLIGHT,
  ["MANDT", "CARRID", "CONNID", "CURRENCY",
  "PAYMENTSUM"], '"MANDT" = '':IV_MANDT'' AND
  "CARRID" = '':IV_CARRID''');
LT_PAYMENTSUM = CE_AGGREGATION(:LT_SFLIGHT_PROJECTION,
  [SUM("PAYMENTSUM") AS "PAYMENTSUM"],
  ["CARRID", "CONNID", "CURRENCY"]);
LT_PAYMENTSUM_CONVERTED =
  CE_CONVERSION(:LT_PAYMENTSUM,
  [FAMILY = 'currency',
  METHOD = 'ERP',
  OUTPUT = 'passed_through, source_unit, unconverted,
            output_unit, converted',
  TARGET_UNIT = :IV_TARGET_UNIT,
  REFERENCE_DATE = :IV_REFERENCE_DATE,
  SOURCE_UNIT_COLUMN = "CURRENCY",
  OUTPUT_UNIT_COLUMN = "CURRENCY_CONVERTED",
  CLIENT = :IV_MANDT,
  CONVERSION_TYPE = :IV_CONVERSION_TYPE],
  ["PAYMENTSUM" AS "PAYMENTSUM_CONVERTED"]);
ET_PAYMENTSUM =
  CE_PROJECTION(:LT_PAYMENTSUM_CONVERTED, ["CARRID",
  "CONNID", "CURRENCY", "PAYMENTSUM",
  "CURRENCY_CONVERTED", "PAYMENTSUM_CONVERTED"]);
```

Listing 5.20 Using the CE Plan Operator CE_CONVERSION

SQL Versus CE Plan Operators

Now that you have learned which CE Plan Operators are available and how their use differs from using SQL statements, you may be asking yourself which is better, SQL or CE Plan Operators?

The answer to this question (as is often the case) is, "It depends." We now wish to give you some background information that will help you to choose whether SQL statements or CE Plan Operators are, at any given time, best suited to your requirements.

Since SQL statements and CE Plan Operators differ in terms of their functional scope, you may not always have a choice. Some functions are only available with SQL statements. Examples include the union involving *duplicate elimination* (UNION), the join across more than two tables (which can, however, be reproduced by multiple calls of the CE Plan Operator CE_JOIN, which are linked with table variables) or the full outer join. Conversely, other functions are only available with CE Plan Operators. The CE Plan Operators CE_VERTICAL_UNION, CE_CONVERSION, and TRACE do not have an equivalent in SQL. Consequently, you must use SQL statements to meet some of your requirements, and CE Plan Operators to meet others.

Functional scope

As already described at the start of this section, CE Plan Operators are, to some extent, more efficient than equivalent SQL statements because the system performs other optimizations for CE Plan Operators. However, particular care is required here because the semantics may change in comparison to SQL (and CE Plan Operators and SQL statements are then no longer semantically equivalent). We also wish to illustrate this using a simple example.

Optimizations

The example compares two implemented calculation views that aggregate booking revenue. Internally, calculation views use database procedures (see Section 4.3.4). First, we will take a look at the source code for both calculation views.

The calculation view EXAMPLE_WITH_SQL in Listing 5.21 simply uses a SELECT statement:

Implementation using SQL

```
var_out = SELECT CARRID, CONNID, SUM(PAYMENTSUM) AS
  PAYMENTSUM FROM SFLIGHT GROUP BY CARRID, CONNID;
```

Listing 5.21 Implementation Using SQL

On the other hand, the calculation view EXAMPLE_WITH_CE_FUNCTIONS in Listing 5.22 is implemented using CE Plan Operators. It uses the

Implementation using CE Plan Operators

following three CE Plan Operators: CE_COLUMN_TABLE, CE_PROJECTION, and CE_AGGREGATION.

```
LT_SFLIGHT = CE_COLUMN_TABLE("SFLIGHT");
LT_SFLIGHT_PROJECTION = CE_PROJECTION(:LT_SFLIGHT,
  ["MANDT", "CARRID", "CONNID", "PAYMENTSUM"]);
LT_SFLIGHT_AGGREGATED =
  CE_AGGREGATION(:LT_SFLIGHT_PROJECTION,
  [SUM("PAYMENTSUM") AS "PAYMENTSUM"], ["CARRID",
  "CONNID"]);
var_out = CE_PROJECTION(:LT_SFLIGHT_AGGREGATED,
  ["CARRID", "CONNID", "PAYMENTSUM"]);
```

Listing 5.22 Implementation Using CE Plan Operators

Comparing both implementations

At first glance, it seems that both calculation views have the same function. Is that the case?

We will call both calculation views twice. The first time, we will select the fields CARRID, CONNID, and PAYMENTSUM. The second time, we will select only the fields CARRID and PAYMENTSUM:

▶ First SQL statement
  SELECT CARRID, CONNID, PAYMENTSUM FROM <view_name>

▶ Second SQL statement
  SELECT, CARRID, PAYMENTSUM from <view_name>

Figure 5.10 compares the various calls. Clearly, the two calculation views behave differently in the second call. While the system performs only a projection (on the fields CARRID and PAYMENTSUM) for the calculation view implemented using a SELECT statement, it also removes the grouping according to flight connection for the calculation view implemented using CE Plan Operators. Therefore, when a call is made using SELECT, CARRID, PAYMENTSUM from <view_name>, the second calculation view groups according to the airline instead of according to the airline and connection. This is more efficient. However, it also changes the semantics. You should keep the effects of optimization in mind if you are choosing between using SQL or CE Plan Operators to implement a given requirement.

SELECT CARRID, CONNID, PAYMENTSUM FROM <view_name>		SELECT CARRID, PAYMENTSUM FROM <view_name>

SQL

CARRID	CONNID	PAYMENTSUM
AA	17	794.831,60
AZ	555	254.920,75
AZ	789	1.220.900,20
DL	106	1.212.190,50
JL	407	2.161.776,52
JL	408	2.049.856,12
LH	400	1.433.638,26
LH	401	1.124.640,90
LH	402	1.935.196,20
LH	2402	744.362,96
QF	5	1.594.441,50
SQ	2	3.745.404,62
SQ	15	2.918.843,11
UA	941	2.693.925,33

CARRID	PAYMENTSUM
AA	794.831,60
AZ	254.920,75
AZ	1.220.900,20
DL	1.212.190,50
JL	2.161.776,52
JL	2.049.856,12
LH	1.433.638,26
LH	1.124.640,90
LH	1.935.196,20
LH	744.362,96
QF	1.594.441,50
SQ	3.745.404,62
SQ	2.918.843,11
UA	2.693.925,33

CE-Funktionen

CARRID	CONNID	PAYMENTSUM
AA	17	794.831,60
AZ	555	254.920,75
AZ	789	1.220.900,20
DL	106	1.212.190,50
JL	407	2.161.776,52
JL	408	2.049.856,12
LH	400	1.433.638,26
LH	401	1.124.640,90
LH	402	1.935.196,20
LH	2402	744.362,96
QF	5	1.594.441,50
SQ	2	3.745.404,62
SQ	15	2.918.843,11
UA	941	2.693.925,33

CARRID	PAYMENTSUM
AA	794.831,60
AZ	1.475.820,95
DL	1.212.190,50
JL	4.211.632,64
LH	5.237.838,32
QF	1.594.441,50
SQ	6.664.247,73
UA	2.693.925,33

Figure 5.10 SQL Versus CE Plan Operators

SQL and CE Plan Operators are optimized independently, so you should avoid using a mixture of SQL statements and CE Plan Operators as far as possible for performance reasons. This recommendation applies both within a database procedure and across database procedures that call one another (because, in this case, the system generates a multilevel calculation model across the database procedures).

Performance and using a mixture of SQL and CE Plan Operators

To determine whether implementing a database procedure is more suitable than another implementation for performance reasons, we recommend using the tools described in Chapter 7.

5.2.5 Imperative Enhancements

If necessary, you can also work with imperative language elements in SQLScript, which we will briefly discuss here for the sake of completeness. In general, however, you should observe the following rule for imperative enhancements: "As much as necessary, but as little as possible."

In particular, SQLScript is used to move data-intensive calculations to the database. SAP HANA should process data-intensive calculations in parallel as much as possible. If you work with imperative enhancements, this may prevent parallelization.

Control Structures

You can use control structures to control (orchestrate) a database procedure's process flow. SQLScript supports loops and case distinctions.

Loops   The statements WHILE... DO... END WHILE and FOR... IN... DO... END FOR are available for loop processing. If you want to end the current loop pass during loop processing, you can use the CONTINUE statement for this purpose. If you want to fully exit a loop, you can use the BREAK statement for this purpose.

Case distinctions   You can use the statement IF... THEN... ELSEIF... ELSE... END IF to implement case distinctions.

Example of control structures   We now wish to use the sample database procedure in Listing 5.23 to illustrate the use of control structures.

```
LT_SPFLI = SELECT MANDT, CARRID, CONNID FROM SPFLI
              WHERE MANDT = :IV_MANDT
                AND AIRPFROM = :IV_AIRPFROM
                AND AIRPTO = :IV_AIRPTO;
LV_DAYS := 0;
WHILE LV_DAYS <= IV_MAX_DAYS DO
  ET_FLIGHTS = SELECT P.CARRID, P.CONNID, F.FLDATE
    FROM :LT_SPFLI AS P
    INNER JOIN SFLIGHT AS F ON F.MANDT = P.MANDT AND
    F.CARRID = P.CARRID AND F.CONNID = P.CONNID
    WHERE TO_DATE(F.FLDATE) >=
      ADD_DAYS (TO_DATE(:IV_FLDATE), -1 * :LV_DAYS)
      AND TO_DATE(F.FLDATE) <=
      ADD_DAYS (TO_DATE(:IV_FLDATE), :LV_DAYS);
```

```
SELECT COUNT(*) INTO LV_CONNECTION_FOUND
  FROM :ET_FLIGHTS;
IF :LV_CONNECTION_FOUND > 0 THEN
  BREAK;
ELSE
  LV_DAYS := :LV_DAYS + 1;
END IF;
END WHILE;
```

Listing 5.23   Control Structures in SQLScript

The database procedure determines the flights available between two given airports (IV_AIRPFROM and IV_AIRPTO) for a given flight date (IV_FLDATE). If (and only if) no flight is available for the given flight date, the database procedure tries to find flights one day before and one day after. If (and only if) no flights are available for this date, the database procedure tries to find flights two days before and two days after. The input parameter IV_MAX_DAYS controls the maximum number of days searched before or after a given flight date. The database procedure uses a WHILE... DO... END WHILE loop combined with an IF... THEN... ELSE... END IF case distinction. It uses the BREAK statements to exit the loop prematurely, if necessary.

Cursor Processing

Similarly, as described in Section 3.2.2, you can also work with *cursors* in SQLScript.

The example in Listing 5.24 shows how to define a cursor in SQLScript and then use it to read data.

Example of cursor processing

```
CURSOR LT_CONNECTIONS (LV_MANDT NVARCHAR(3),
  LV_CARRID NVARCHAR(3)) FOR
  SELECT CARRID, CONNID FROM SPFLI
  WHERE MANDT = :LV_MANDT AND CARRID = :LV_CARRID;
BEGIN
  FOR LS_CONNECTIONS AS LT_CONNECTIONS(:IV_MANDT,
    :IV_CARRID) DO
    /* DO SOMETHING */
    ...
  END FOR;
END;
```

Listing 5.24   Cursor Processing with SQLScript

Only use cursors if there is no other way to implement the required processing logic. The HANA database cannot easily optimize database procedures that contain cursors.

Dynamic SQL

You can use dynamic SQL to construct SQL statements at runtime. The EXEC and EXECUTE IMMEDIATE statements are available for this purpose.

Example of dynamic SQL

The example in Listing 5.25 shows how you can construct a SELECT statement at runtime in order to determine an airline's flight connections. In this example, it would not be absolutely necessary to use dynamic SQL.

```
EXECUTE IMMEDIATE 'SELECT * FROM SPFLI
  WHERE MANDT = ''' || :IV_MANDT || ''' AND CARRID =
  ''' || :IV_CARRID || ''''';
```

Listing 5.25 Dynamic SQL

We advise you to refrain, as much as possible, from using dynamic SQL because it has limited optimization options. A database procedure that contains dynamic SQL may need to be recompiled for each call. With dynamic SQL, there is also a risk of *SQL injections*.

5.2.6 Accessing System Fields

In Section 5.2.2, we used an input parameter to transfer the client to the database procedure for data selection purposes. In this section, we wish to explain which system fields are available to you in database procedures and how you can use them, for example, to implement client handling.

Overview of system fields

As an ABAP programmer, you are no doubt familiar with the structure SYST and the option of using the variable SY to query different system fields while a program is running. Table 5.1 provides an overview of some important system fields or functions for accessing the relevant information. In the HANA database, you do not use system fields to access the relevant information (which is the case in SAP NetWeaver AS ABAP). Instead, you use special functions.

Description	The System Field or Function to Be Accessed
Application user	`SELECT SESSION_CONTEXT` `( 'APPLICATIONUSER' ) FROM DUMMY` In **ABAP**: `SY-UNAME`
User of the current statement	`SELECT CURRENT_USER FROM DUMMY` In **ABAP**: `SY-UNAME` Comment: Has the value `_SYS_REPO` if the authorization check is performed on the basis of the creator of the procedure.
User of the current connection	`SELECT CURRENT_USER FROM DUMMY` In **ABAP**: The user `<SAP>SID` is used to establish the connection to the database.
Client	`SELECT SESSION_CONTEXT( 'CLIENT' ) FROM DUMMY` In **ABAP**: `SY-MANDT`
Language	`SELECT SESSION_CONTEXT( 'LOCALE' ) FROM DUMMY` In **ABAP**: No direct equivalent
Language (SAP format)	`SELECT SESSION_CONTEXT( 'LOCALE_SAP' ) FROM DUMMY` In **ABAP**: `SY-LANGU`
System date	`SELECT CURRENT_DATE FROM DUMMY` In **ABAP**: `SY-DATUM` (based on the current application server)
System time	`SELECT CURRENT_TIME FROM DUMMY` In **ABAP**: `SY-UZEIT` (based on the current application server)
Connection ID	`SELECT SESSION_CONTEXT( 'CONN_ID' ) FROM DUMMY` In **ABAP**: No direct equivalent

Table 5.1 Accessing System Fields or Functions

In conjunction with Table 5.1, and in particular when using `CURRENT_USER` and `SESSION_USER`, note that SAP NetWeaver AS ABAP uses a technical database user to communicate with the database (see Section 3.1.2). If

APPLICATION USER

you need to access the user logged on to the application server, you must use APPLICATIONUSER for this purpose.

5.2.7 Error Handling

We now wish to discuss error handling in the context of database procedures. We will explain both how to catch standard exceptions and how to trigger custom exceptions.

Catching Standard Exceptions

Exception handler

The DECLARE... HANDLER FOR... statement enables you to define an exception handler for a particular situation, which you can describe generically as SQLEXCEPTION or using an SQL error code (see also *http://help.sap.com/hana/html/_jsql_error_codes.html*) or a user-defined condition. Listing 5.26 shows an example of this:

```
DECLARE SOME_ERROR CONDITION
  FOR SQL_ERROR_CODE 1299;
DECLARE EXIT HANDLER FOR SOME_ERROR RESIGNAL
  SET MESSAGE_TEXT = 'Carrier not found';
SELECT CARRID INTO LV_CARRID FROM "SCARR"
        WHERE MANDT = :IV_MANDT
          AND CARRID = :IV_CARRID;
```

Listing 5.26 Exception Handler in SQLScript

First, this example declares a user-defined condition SOME_ERROR, which references SQL error code 1299 (No data found). If the SELECT statement does not find a data record in the table SCARR, the system starts the subsequently declared exception handler, which uses the RESIGNAL command supplemented by the message text 'Carrier not found' to pass the exception to the caller of the database procedure.

User-specific error codes

Triggering Custom Exceptions

SQLScript also gives you the option to trigger custom exceptions with user-specific SQL error codes. User-specific error codes lie within the following range: 10000 to 19999. An example is shown in Listing 5.27.

```
DECLARE CARRIER_1_NOT_FOUND CONDITION
  FOR SQL_ERROR_CODE 10001;
```

```
DECLARE CARRIER_2_NOT_FOUND CONDITION
  FOR SQL_ERROR_CODE 10002;
SELECT COUNT(CARRID) INTO LV_COUNTER1 FROM "SCARR"
      WHERE MANDT = :IV_MANDT
        AND CARRID = :IV_CARRID1;
IF :LV_COUNTER1 = 0 THEN
  SIGNAL CARRIER_1_NOT_FOUND;
END IF;
SELECT COUNT(CARRID) INTO LV_COUNTER2 FROM "SCARR"
      WHERE MANDT = :IV_MANDT
        AND CARRID = :IV_CARRID2;
IF :LV_COUNTER2 = 0 THEN
  SIGNAL CARRIER_2_NOT_FOUND;
END IF;
```

Listing 5.27 User-Specific Error Codes in SQLScript

In this example, the system triggers error code 10001 if the airline `IV_CAR-RID1` does not exist and error code 10002 if the airline `IV_CARRID2` does not exist.

Parallelization

In error handling, keep in mind that database queries are not necessarily executed in the sequence in which they occur in the source code. Parallelization is also possible. Therefore, in this example, it is entirely conceivable that the second `SELECT` statement is executed even though `IV_CARRID1` does not exist.

5.3   Using Procedures in ABAP

Now that you know what SQLScript is and how you can use it to implement database procedures and calculation views, we wish to explain how to call database procedures from ABAP. Here, we distinguish between the following two options:

Call options

▶ Access using *Native SQL* and *ABAP Database Connectivity* (*ADBC*, see also Chapter 3)

▶ Use of *database procedure proxies*

As of ABAP release 7.0 and SAP Kernel 7.20, it is possible to use ADBC to call database procedures in SAP HANA. Database procedure proxies

Prerequisites

255

are available as of release 7.4. The following two prerequisites exist here: You must use SAP HANA as the primary database, and you must have created the called database procedures in the SAP HANA Repository (the latter should be a rule.).

5.3.1 Access Using Native SQL

As already described in Section 5.2.2, the system generates different runtime objects in the schema _SYS_BIC when activating a database procedure. It also generates a public synonym. Here, you can use Native SQL to access the database procedure from ABAP.

Disadvantages of Native SQL

However, the use of Native SQL to call a database procedure is relatively time-consuming and prone to errors. Later on in this section, you will see how you can only use temporary tables to exchange tabular input and output parameters with the database procedure. Furthermore, SAP NetWeaver AS ABAP does not detect syntax errors in Native SQL statements until runtime. For more information, refer to the explanations provided in Chapter 3.

Examples

We will now use several examples to provide a detailed description of how to use Native SQL to access database procedures. First, we will consider a database procedure that determines the name of an airline on the basis of the ID. For the remaining examples, we will revert to the database procedures from Section 5.1.1.

Example 1: Calling a Database Procedure

If you use ADBC to call a database procedure, the class CL_SQL_STATEMENT makes the method EXECUTE_PROCEDURE available. You can use this as long as a database procedure does not have a tabular input/output parameter.

Sample call

The program ZR_A4H_CHAPTER5_CARRNAME_ADBC shows an example of the EXECUTE_PROCEDURE method (see Listing 5.28). It calls the database procedure DETERMINE_CARRNAME, which has the following input and output parameters:

- IV_MANDT (client)
- IV_CARRID (ID of an airline)
- EV_CARRNAME (name of an airline)

```
PARAMETERS: p_carrid TYPE s_carr_id.

DATA: lo_sql_statement  TYPE REF TO cl_sql_statement,
      lv_carrname TYPE s_carrname.

TRY.
    " Generate SQL statement object
    lo_sql_statement =
      cl_sql_connection=>get_connection(
      )->create_statement( ).

    " Set parameter
    lo_sql_statement->set_param( data_ref =
      REF #( sy-mandt )
      inout = cl_sql_statement=>c_param_in ).
    lo_sql_statement->set_param( data_ref =
      REF #( p_carrid )
      inout = cl_sql_statement=>c_param_in ).
    lo_sql_statement->set_param( data_ref =
      REF #( lv_carrname )
      inout = cl_sql_statement=>c_param_out ).

    " Execute database procedure
    lo_sql_statement->execute_procedure(
  '"test.a4h.book.chapter05::DETERMINE_CARRNAME"' ).

  CATCH cx_sql_exception INTO DATA(lo_ex).
    " Error handling
    WRITE: | { lo_ex->get_text( ) } |.
ENDTRY.

WRITE: / lv_carrname.
```

Listing 5.28 Using Native SQL to Call a Database Procedure

First, the program generates an instance of the class CL_SQL_STATEMENT. Then, it calls the method SET_PARAM to bind the input and output parameters of the database procedures to the actual parameters. It then calls the method EXECUTE_PROCEDURE.

Explanation of the program

Example 2: Tabular Output Parameters

Alternatively, you can use the method EXECUTE_QUERY (together with the WITH OVERVIEW addition) to execute a database procedure. This also works for database procedures that have tabular input and output parameters.

Example of output parameters

The program ZR_A4H_CHAPTER5_TOP_ADBC in Listing 5.29 shows an example of the method EXECUTE_QUERY, in which the database procedure DETER-MINE_TOP_CONNECTIONS is called. This database procedure determines an airline's top connections and has the following input and output parameters:

▶ IV_MANDT (client)

▶ IV_CARRID (ID of an airline)

▶ IV_ALGORITHM (controls how the top connections are to be determined)

▶ ET_CONNECTIONS (a table parameter that contains the airline's ID CAR-RID and connection code CONNID)

```
PARAMETERS: p_carrid TYPE s_carr_id.

" Definition of the result structure
TYPES: BEGIN OF ty_connections,
         carrid TYPE s_carr_id,
         connid TYPE s_conn_id,
       END OF ty_connections.

DATA: lt_connections TYPE TABLE OF ty_connections,
      lv_statement TYPE string,
      lo_result_set TYPE REF TO cl_sql_result_set,
      lo_connections TYPE REF TO data.

TRY.
    " Delete local temporary table
    lv_statement = | DROP TABLE #ET_CONNECTIONS |.
    cl_sql_connection=>get_connection(
  )->create_statement( )->execute_ddl( lv_statement ).
  CATCH cx_sql_exception.
    " The local temporary table may not exist,
    " we ignore this error
ENDTRY.

TRY.
```

```
    " Create local temporary table
    lv_statement = | CREATE LOCAL TEMPORARY ROW|
    && | TABLE #ET_CONNECTIONS LIKE "_SYS_BIC".|
    && |"test.a4h.book.chapter05/DETERMINE_TOP_|
    && |CONNECTIONS/tabletype/ET_CONNECTIONS" |.
    cl_sql_connection=>get_connection(
  )->create_statement( )->execute_ddl( lv_statement ).

    " Call database procedure
    lv_statement = | CALL "test.a4h.bo|
    && |ok.chapter05::DETERMINE_TOP_CONNECTIONS|
    && |"( '{ sy-mandt }' , '{ p_carrid }', 'P'|
    && |, #ET_CONNECTIONS ) WITH OVERVIEW |.
    lo_result_set = cl_sql_connection=>get_connection(
      )->create_statement( )->execute_query(
      lv_statement ).
    lo_result_set->close( ).

    " Read local temporary table
    lv_statement = | SELECT * FROM #ET_CONNECTIONS |.
    lo_result_set = cl_sql_connection=>get_connection(
      )->create_statement( )->execute_query(
      lv_statement ).

    " Read result
    GET REFERENCE OF lt_connections INTO
      lo_connections.
    lo_result_set->set_param_table( lo_connections ).
    lo_result_set->next_package( ).
    lo_result_set->close( ).
  CATCH cx_sql_exception INTO DATA(lo_ex).
    " Error handling
    WRITE: | { lo_ex->get_text( ) } |.
ENDTRY.

LOOP AT lt_connections ASSIGNING
  FIELD-SYMBOL(<ls_connections>).
  WRITE: / <ls_connections>-carrid ,
          <ls_connections>-connid.
ENDLOOP.
```

Listing 5.29 Handling Table-Based Output Parameters

Temporary tables

We now wish to use the program to explain, in particular, how tabular input and output parameters are exchanged with a database procedure. The program `ZR_A4H_CHAPTER5_TOP_ADBC` uses the *temporary table* `#ET_CON-NECTIONS` to transfer the table parameter `ET_CONNECTIONS`.

[»]

> ### Temporary Tables
>
> Many databases, including the HANA database, enable you to *temporarily* save the interim and final results of calculations in *temporary tables*. For this use case, temporary tables have many different advantages over conventional tables:
>
> ▸ The table definition and table contents are automatically deleted from the database if they are no longer required.
>
> ▸ The database automatically isolates data in parallel *sessions* from one another. It is neither necessary nor possible to place locks on temporary tables.
>
> ▸ The database does not write a transaction log for temporary tables.
>
> ▸ Generally, it is more efficient to use temporary tables than conventional tables.
>
> SAP HANA supports global and local temporary tables:
>
> ▸ The table definition of *global* temporary tables can be used in different sessions. The table contents can only be displayed for the current session. At the end of the session, the table contents are automatically deleted from the database.
>
> ▸ In the case of *local temporary tables*, both the table definition and the table contents are only valid for the current session. In other words, both are automatically deleted from the database at the end of the session.

Using temporary tables in AS ABAP

When using temporary tables to transfer data between SAP NetWeaver AS ABAP and a database procedure, you should note the following:

▸ If you work with global temporary tables, you can create these once (because they can be used in different sessions). Organizationally, however, you must ensure that the table name is not used for different use cases (that require a different table structure).

▸ You can create global temporary tables at *design time*. Then you must ensure that the tables are also available in the test and production systems after a transport.

▸ If you decide to create global temporary tables at *runtime*, you must ensure that, before you call a database procedure, the table structure is suitable for the interface of the database procedure called (because this may have changed in the meantime).

▶ You must create local temporary tables at least once for each session (also note the explanations below in relation to the ABAP *work process* and database connection). Consequently, you can only create local temporary tables when an ABAP program is running.

▶ Since each ABAP work process has only one connection with the database, multiple ABAP programs processed by the same work process subsequently, are one session for the database. Therefore, after an ABAP program ends, neither the definition nor the contents of local (and global) temporary tables are deleted automatically.

▶ In the case of global and local temporary tables, you should delete the contents (of the current session) before you call the database procedure.

The program `ZR_A4H_CHAPTER5_TOP_ADBC` in Listing 5.29 works with a local temporary table. First, it uses `DROP TABLE` #ET_CONNECTIONS to delete the local temporary table #ET_CONNECTIONS if it exists. It then uses the `CREATE LOCAL TEMPORARY ROW TABLE` statement to create a (new) local temporary table with the name #ET_CONNECTIONS. Here, the program makes reference to the table type that the system automatically created for the output parameter ET_CONNECTIONS when the database procedure was activated. This approach enables the program to ensure that, before the database procedure is called, the temporary table is empty and suitable for the current structure of the output parameter ET_CONNECTIONS.

Explanation of the program

The program now uses the method EXECUTE_QUERY to call the database procedure. It transfers SY-MANDT, P_CARRID, and 'P' to the input parameters, and it transfers the temporary table #ET_CONNECTIONS to the output parameter for the database procedure.

After the database procedure has been called, the program reads the contents of the temporary table #ET_CONNECTIONS, which correspond to the transferred airline's top connections.

Example 3: Tabular Input Parameters

If a database procedure has tabular input parameters, you can proceed in the same way as you do for tabular output parameters. The program ZR_A4H_CHAPTER5_KPIS_ADBC in Listing 5.30 shows how to call the database procedure GET_KPIS_FOR_CONNECTIONS for a set of flight connections. The database procedure determines some key performance indicators for each connection transferred.

Example of an input parameter

It has the following input and output parameters:

▶ IV_MANDT (client)

▶ IT_CONNECTIONS (a table parameter that contains the airline's ID CAR-RID and connection code CONNID)

▶ ET_KPIS (a table parameter that contains key performance indicators for connections)

```
...
LOOP AT lt_connections INTO ls_connections.
  lv_statement = | INSERT INTO #IT_CONNECTIONS VALUES
    ( '{ ls_connections-carrid }', '{ ls_connections-
    connid }' )|.
  cl_sql_connection=>get_connection(
    )->create_statement(
      )->execute_update( lv_statement ).
ENDLOOP.

" Call database procedure
lv_statement = | CALL "test.a4h.bo|
&& |ok.chapter05::GET_KPIS_FOR_CONNECTIONS|
&& |"( '{ sy-mandt }' , #IT_CONNECTIONS, #ET_KPIS )
  WITH OVERVIEW |.
lo_result_set = cl_sql_connection=>get_connection(
)->create_statement( )->execute_query( lv_statement ).
lo_result_set->close( ).
...
```

Listing 5.30 Handling Table-Based Input Parameters

Explanation of the program

Before the database procedure is called, the program fills the local temporary table #IT_CONNECTIONS with the relevant flight connections. EXE-CUTE_QUERY is used to call the database procedure.

5.3.2 Defining Database Procedure Proxies

As of ABAP release 7.4, you can define a *database procedure proxy* in order to access database procedures from ABAP. Such procedures were defined in the SAP HANA Repository within the primary database. A database procedure proxy is (as the name suggests) a *proxy object*. It represents a database procedure in the ABAP Data Dictionary.

[!]

Multiple Proxy Objects for One Database Procedure

Technically, it is possible to create multiple database procedure proxies for one database procedure. However, we do *not* recommend this. In the ABAP Data Dictionary, you should never create more than one proxy object for a database procedure.

The system also automatically creates an interface for each database procedure proxy. You can use this interface to influence the parameter names and data types used when calling the database procedure with ABAP:

Interface of the proxy object

▶ You can change the names of the input and output parameters as soon as they exceed 30 characters. In this case, the system initially abbreviates the parameter names. You can then overwrite these abbreviated names, if necessary.

▶ You can always overwrite the component names of table parameters.

▶ You can assign the relevant data type to each parameter. This is important because SQL data types are not uniquely mapped to ABAP data types and dictionary data types. Consequently, when creating a proxy object, the system cannot (always) derive the correct ABAP data type and/or dictionary data type.

We will now explain how to create a proxy object for the database procedure DETERMINE_TOP_CONNECTIONS. To do this, open the ABAP perspective in the ABAP Development Tools in Eclipse, and choose the menu option FILE • NEW • OTHER.... Then, choose DATABASE PROCEDURE PROXY and NEXT. Figure 5.11 shows the window that opens.

Creating a database procedure proxy

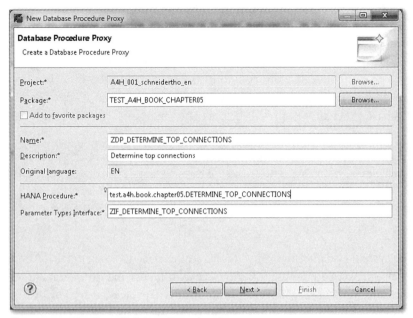

Figure 5.11 Creating a Database Procedure Proxy

Creation
parameters

In this window, enter the following data for the database procedure proxy:

- NAME: You can use the name of the database procedure proxy to (later) call the database procedure in ABAP.

- DESCRIPTION: The description is a piece of explanatory text.

- HANA PROCEDURE: Name of the (existing) database procedure in the SAP HANA Repository.

- PARAMETER TYPES INTERFACE: Name of the interface that is automatically created when you create the proxy object (see Listing 5.31).

After you choose NEXT and FINISH, the system creates the database procedure proxy and the corresponding interface.

The PROJECT EXPLORER contains the database procedure proxy in the corresponding package below the DICTIONARY • DB PROCEDURE PROXIES node. Just like the other interfaces, the parameter types interface is located in the corresponding package below the SOURCE LIBRARY node.

Figure 5.12 shows the database procedure proxy for the database procedure DETERMINE_TOP_CONNECTIONS. If you wish to adjust parameter names
or data types, you can do this in the ABAP NAME, ABAP TYPE, and DDIC
TYPE OVERRIDE columns. For example, you can map the column CONNID
in the table-based output parameter ET_CONNECTIONS to the data element
S_CONN_ID (and therefore to the ABAP data type N length 4).

Adjusting the
interface

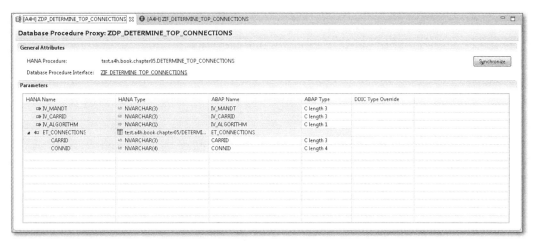

Figure 5.12 Database Procedure Proxy and Interface

Listing 5.31 shows the interface that the system automatically creates
after the data types have been adjusted.

```
interface ZIF_DETERMINE_TOP_CONNECTIONS public.
types: iv_mandt type mandt.
types: iv_carrid type s_carr_id.
types: iv_algorithm type c length 1.
types: begin of et_connections,
         carrid type s_carr_id,
         connid type s_conn_id,
       end of et_connections.
endinterface.
```

Listing 5.31 Interface of the Proxy Object

5.3.3 Calling Database Procedure Proxies

Now that you have activated the database procedure proxy, you can
use the proxy object to call the database procedure. The program

ZR_A4H_CHAPTER5_TOP_PROXY in Listing 5.32 shows an example of this usage.

```
PARAMETERS: p_carrid TYPE s_carr_id.

DATA: lt_connections TYPE TABLE OF
      zif_determine_top_connections=>et_connections.

TRY.
    CALL DATABASE PROCEDURE
      zdp_determine_top_connections
      EXPORTING
        iv_mandt = sy-mandt
        iv_carrid = p_carrid
        iv_algorithm = 'P'
      IMPORTING
        et_connections = lt_connections.

  CATCH cx_sy_db_procedure_sql_error
    cx_sy_db_procedure_call INTO DATA(lo_ex).
    " Error handling
    WRITE: | { lo_ex->get_text( ) } |.
ENDTRY.

LOOP AT lt_connections ASSIGNING
  FIELD-SYMBOL(<ls_connections>).
  WRITE: / <ls_connections>-carrid ,
           <ls_connections>-connid.
ENDLOOP.
```

Listing 5.32 Calling a Database Procedure Proxy

The program uses the CALL DATABASE PROCEDURE statement to call the database procedure DETERMINE_TOP_CONNECTIONS via the proxy ZDP_DETER-MINE_TOP_CONNECTIONS. When defining the internal table LT_CONNECTIONS, the program refers to the interface ZIF_DETERMINE_TOP_CONNECTIONS.

The program catches any problems that may occur when calling the database procedure (exceptions of the type CX_SY_DB_PROCEDURE_SQL_ERROR and CX_SY_DB_PROCEDURE_CALL).

5.3.4   Adjusting Database Procedure Proxies

If you change a database procedure (or more accurately, the interface of   Synchronization
a database procedure) in SAP HANA Studio, you must synchronize the
proxy object with the SAP HANA Repository. The SYNCHRONIZE button
(see Figure 5.12) is available for this purpose.

During the synchronization process, you can decide whether you want to   Additional
retain or overwrite the adjustments made to the proxy object (component   information
names or data types).

Finally, we again wish to explicitly point out that the use of SQLScript in
calculation views does not differ in principle from the use of SQLScript
in database procedures. For more information about calculation views,
see Section 4.3, and for more information about error analysis in relation
to SQLScript, see Chapter 7.

ABAP-Managed Database Procedures
SAP is currently working on facilitating the creation of database procedures from ABAP for future releases (so-called ABAP-managed database procedures). The idea is to flag a method of an ABAP class as database procedure and then use SQLScript code directly in the method body.

ABAP developers are accustomed to an efficient transport system. In the context of developing ABAP on SAP HANA, consistent transport is made more difficult if some development objects are created directly in SAP HANA. Nevertheless, consistent transport is possible using the Change and Transport System.

6   Application Transport

In this chapter, we'll explain how you can consistently transport ABAP applications in your system landscape for developing objects directly in SAP HANA Studio, even if you use the options described in Chapter 4 and Chapter 5.

As long as you create and manage *all* of an applications' required development objects with the SAP NetWeaver Application Server (AS) ABAP, you can very easily ensure that the application is consistently transported by the automatic change recording. Otherwise, you cannot rely solely on the automatic change recording.

Figure 6.1 illustrates the problem by means of a database table that was created using the ABAP Data Dictionary and a column view. This view, after its creation via SAP HANA Studio, was exposed in ABAP as an *external view* (see Section 4.5.2).

There are no problems with the transport of the database table because the system, if configured accordingly, automatically records the creation of the table and any changes to it in a change request. We will explain how this works in Section 6.1.1.

The external view is a proxy object that refers to a column view. The column view is not subject to the automatic change recording of SAP NetWeaver AS ABAP. Thus, it is missing from the transport target system if you rely solely on the change recording in AS ABAP. This can lead to a runtime error when you access the external view.

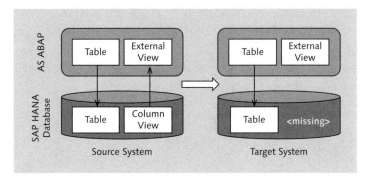

Figure 6.1 Transport Problems with Non-ABAP Objects

System landscape example In this chapter, we will explain which transport mechanisms are provided by the ABAP application server and by SAP HANA. In doing so, we will also discuss some aspects of development organization. The three-level system landscape outlined in Figure 6.2 serves as an example of our descriptions.

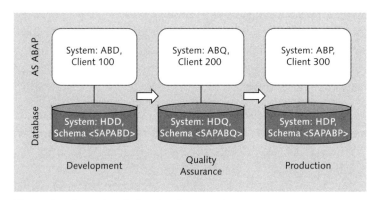

Figure 6.2 Exemplary System Landscape

For some of the following explanations, it is irrelevant whether an SAP HANA database is involved. In other cases, we assume that the application server uses the HANA database as the primary database and will indicate this prerequisite.

We will then show you how to transport applications, which consist in part of ABAP objects and in part of SAP HANA Repository objects, via the *HANA transport container* and the *enhanced Change and Transport System* (*CTS+*).

6.1 Basic Principles of the Transport System

In this section, we will explain the basic principles of the transport system of SAP NetWeaver AS ABAP, as well as the HANA database.

6.1.1 Transport in SAP NetWeaver AS ABAP

We assume that you have already worked with the transport system of SAP NetWeaver AS ABAP in the past. Nevertheless, we'll discuss some key aspects of development organization and the transport system, because this will help you understand the following sections.

Development Organization

The development objects of SAP NetWeaver AS ABAP are organized hierarchically in packages.

Package hierarchy

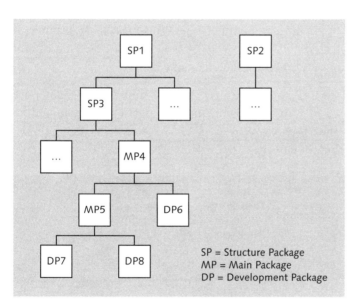

Figure 6.3 Package Types in SAP NetWeaver AS ABAP

When you create a package in SAP NetWeaver AS ABAP, you can use three different package types (see Figure 6.3):

Package types in AS ABAP

▶ **Structure packages**
Structure packages form the top level of a package hierarchy and define the basic architecture of applications. They very often correspond to *software components* (which we will discuss more fully). Structure packages can contain additional structure packages and main packages. However, structure packages do not directly contain development objects.

▶ **Main packages**
Main packages form the middle level of a package hierarchy and, in simple terms, group functions. Main packages can contain additional main packages as well as development packages. However, they also do not directly contain development objects.

▶ **Development packages**
Development packages form the lower level of a package hierarchy and contain development objects. They can also contain additional development packages. The names of the development objects must be unique across development packages. This means, for example, if you have created a program ZR_REPORT1 in package EP6, you cannot create another report with the same name in EP7.

Software components Each package in SAP NetWeaver AS ABAP is assigned to a software component. A software component includes packages that should be delivered together. SAP NetWeaver AS ABAP 7.4 contains, for example, the software components listed in Table 6.1.

Software Component	Description
HOME	Customer developments
LOCAL	Local objects
PI_BASIS	Basis plug-in
SAP_ABA	Application basis
SAP_BASIS	Basis
SAP_BW	SAP NetWeaver Business Warehouse
SAP_GWFND	Gateway Foundation
SAP_UI	User interface technology

Table 6.1 Software Components of SAP NetWeaver AS ABAP 7.4

The software components HOME and LOCAL are of special significance. The software component HOME is intended for customer developments. You use the software component LOCAL for testing or, in general, for development objects that should not be transported.

As an ABAP developer, you usually do not create *any* of your own software components for customer developments, but assign these to the software component HOME. An exception to this is formed by add-ons that you package using the *Add-on Assembly Kit*. SAP Partners in particular (as well as SAP itself) avail themselves of this option. We do not deal with the Add-on Assembly Kit within this book.

Add-on Assembly Kit

A package in SAP NetWeaver AS ABAP allows you to control the use of the development objects that it contains and to define their transport properties.

To control the use of the development objects in a package, you can mark a package as *encapsulated*. From other packages, you can thus access only the objects of the package that were exposed via a *package interface* (in addition you must also define a *use access*).

Package encapsulation

The *transport properties* of a package determine whether changes to a development object are automatically recorded, and whether the recording takes place on a local or a transportable change request. The transport properties result from three attributes of a package:

Transport properties of a package

▶ The assignment of the package to a software component.

▶ The transport layer of the package; we will discuss this in more detail in the next section.

▶ The value of the checkbox RECORD OBJECT CHANGES IN TRANSPORT REQUESTS, which can be maintained only for *test packages*.

Table 6.2 shows which combinations of the three attributes are possible, and how the attributes affect the change recording.

Package Name Starts With	Software Component	Transport Layer	Record Changes	Recording
T (test package)	LOCAL	No	No	No recording
T (test package)	LOCAL	No	Yes	Local change request
$ (local package)	LOCAL	No	No	No recording
Z*, Y*, and prefix namespace	HOME	No	Yes	Local change request
Z*, Y*, and prefix namespace	HOME	Yes	Yes	Transportable change request

Table 6.2 Change Recording in SAP NetWeaver AS ABAP

Automatic change recording

Automatic change recording guarantees that development objects cannot undergo uncontrolled changes by multiple developers. It also ensures version management, and allows transport to subsequent systems (for example, quality assurance system or production system) in the case of a transportable change request. We will explain this by means of an example in the following section.

Transport System

In this section, we will take a look at the development of a report ZR_A4H_CHAPTER6_LIST_CUSTOMER as an example. This uses a *projection view* ZPV_A4H_CUSTOMER, which was defined in the ABAP Data Dictionary, to read customer data from the database table SCUSTOM. The report is assigned via its package to the software component HOME and a transport layer.

The transport layer controls which of subsequent systems receive a development object. In the example, the transport takes place from the development system to the quality assurance system and then to the production system (as shown in Figure 6.2).

Entering the transport request

When you create the report, you must enter a change request (due to the transport properties of the package). The system adds the report to the object list of the change request. At the same time, it also sets a *lock indicator*. As long as the change request has not been released, the lock indicator ensures that only you and other designated developers who are also assigned to the change request can edit the report.

When you have completed the development, you can release the change request for transport. The transport consists, in simple terms, of exporting from the source system and importing into the target system (or target systems).

Transport

The transport is controlled by the *Transport Domain Controller* of the *Change and Transport System* (*CTS*). This is the system in which all configuration settings relevant for transport are centrally maintained and distributed to all other systems. In the example, the production system (ABP) could assume the role of the Transport Domain Controller. Figure 6.4 illustrates the transport process schematically.

Change and Transport System

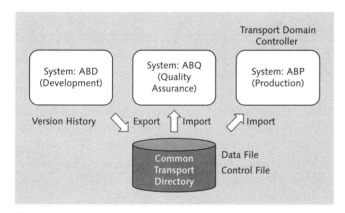

Figure 6.4 Transport in SAP NetWeaver AS ABAP via CTS

When releasing a transport request, the system first checks whether all development objects contained in the object list are active (and thus without syntax errors). You can also perform an enhanced check of the development objects with the infrastructure of the *ABAP Test Cockpit*. After a successful check, the system generates a version of all objects contained in the transport request to historically record all changes. Finally, the system exports the objects and writes two files in the common *transport directory*:

Releasing and exporting

▶ The *data file* contains the exported objects in a platform-independent format. It describes a delta, as it does not contain a complete package—it only contains the changed development objects that are documented in the object list.

▶ The *control file* contains metadata for the transport and describes the necessary steps for the import.

Importing When importing into the target system (ABQ in our example), the system creates a copy of the objects in the transport request in several steps, using the metadata in the control file and the objects in the data file. Postprocessing is performed after the actual import by *after-import methods*. After importing successfully, for example, you can use the program ZR_A4H_CHAPTER6_LIST_CUSTOMER immediately.

For problems with exporting or importing, see the transport log.

[»]   **Relocations and Transports of Copies**

For the sake of completeness, we would like to mention that you can also transport development objects—for which there is no automatic change recording or a recording by means of local change requests—with a *transport of copies* or *relocation*. Only objects of local packages form an exception here.

Original system You cannot simply make changes to the imported objects in the target system. Each development object has an *original system,* and that's the only place where you can make unrestricted changes. In all other systems, you must make the changes via the *Modification Assistant*. When you do so, the changed objects are given a repair flag. This is to prevent changes from being accidentally overwritten during the next import.

6.1.2   Transport in SAP HANA

Next, we will explain the transport system—and also, in some aspects, the development organization—of the HANA database. It is especially important that you understand its main differences from SAP NetWeaver AS ABAP. In Section 6.2, we will then discuss the *combined transport* in SAP NetWeaver AS ABAP and SAP HANA.

Development Organization

The development organization in SAP HANA is similar in many ways to SAP NetWeaver AS ABAP. However, it also differs in some essential aspects. As described in Chapter 2, the SAP HANA Repository is the central storage of the HANA database development objects.

Like SAP NetWeaver AS ABAP, the SAP HANA Repository structures development objects in a package hierarchy. However, it only knows two package types (see Figure 6.5):

Package types in SAP HANA

▶ **Structural packages**
Structural packages group functions. They can contain additional structural packages and non-structural packages. However, structural packages do not contain any development objects.

▶ **Non-structural packages**
Non-structural packages directly contain development objects. They can also contain additional non-structural packages. The names of the development objects must be unique per package. In other words, the same name can be used in two packages; the corresponding development artifacts are uniquely identified in combination with the package name.

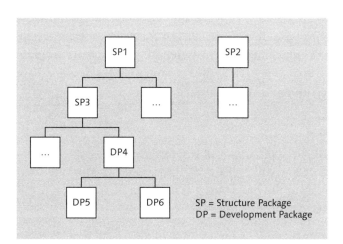

Figure 6.5 Package Types in SAP HANA

SAP provides content under the root package `sap`. Thus, no customer developments may be created under this package, because they could be accidentally overwritten. Build a parallel package hierarchy for customer

Namespace for customers

developments instead. As a root package, for example, use your domain name.

Local developments
The package system-local represents a special case. It is similar to the concept of local packages of SAP NetWeaver AS ABAP. Use it for development objects that are not to be transported.

Delivery units
Each package in SAP HANA is—for transport, at the latest—assigned to a *delivery unit*. A delivery unit combines packages that are to be transported or delivered together. Conceptually, it broadly corresponds to a software component in the sense of AS ABAP. While you usually work in AS ABAP with the software component HOME, you must always create your own delivery units for customer developments in SAP HANA. To do so, you or an administrator are required to have maintained, in advance, the system parameter content_vendor in the file *indexserver.ini* using the *Administration Console* of SAP HANA Studio.

Package encapsulation
Unlike in AS ABAP, a package in SAP HANA currently does not allow you to restrict the use of the development objects that it contains.

Transport properties of a package
Apart from the assignment of a delivery unit, a package has *no* transport properties that control whether a development object will be transported, and (if applicable) to which subsequent systems it would go. In addition, automatic change recording—as AS ABAP knows it—does not take place in SAP HANA. Versioning is still supported.

Transport System

A transport usually takes place in SAP HANA on the basis of a delivery unit. In this section, we will explain the process using attribute view AT_CUSTOMER. Similar to the report used as an example in Section 6.1.1, this reads customer data from table SCUSTOM.

Package assignment
When you create an attribute view, you assign a package to it. You can maintain a delivery unit in the package properties. To do so, use the context menu entry *Edit* of the package. You see all existing delivery units in the system in the *Quick Launch* view using the menu entry *Delivery Units...* You can also create new delivery units there. Figure 6.6 illustrates the relationship between the development object, package, and delivery unit using the example of the attribute view AT_CUSTOMER (the delivery unit ZA4H_BOOK_CHAPTER06 is *not* part of the examples provided with this book).

A change recording in terms of the ABAP system does not take place. Thus, all other developers can also change the attribute view. When editing an object, SAP HANA Studio indicates if another developer's inactive version of the object exists, and it prevents simultaneous editing of a development object by multiple developers with an *optimistic lock*. Each time an object is activated, the system creates a version of the object—which is permanently stored to record changes, as in the ABAP system.

Multiuser editing

Figure 6.6 Development Object, Package, and Delivery Unit

279

When you have completed the development, you can transport the attribute view. Similar to ABAP, the transport consists of exporting from the source system and importing into the target system or systems.

In SAP HANA Studio, you can import and export development artifacts in two ways:

- Exporting/importing a delivery unit (optionally coupled with CTS+)
- Exporting/importing individual objects (the *developer mode*)

For a consistent transport of HANA content (which is not closely coupled with an ABAP development) in a production system landscape, we always recommend exporting/importing based on delivery units and the CTS+. We will discuss a combined ABAP/SAP HANA transport in Section 6.2 and will also give you recommendations there.

Enhanced Change and Transport System

CTS+ enhances the Change and Transport System of the ABAP application server with the option of also transporting non-ABAP objects.

[»]   **Availability of the Enhanced Change and Transport System**

The enhanced Change and Transport System (CTS+) has been available since SAP NetWeaver 7.0 Support Package Stack 12. However, SAP recommends that you use at least Support Package Stack 14 when using CTS+, as this has simplified the configuration significantly.

For more information on the enhanced Change and Transport System, see *http://scn.sap.com/docs/DOC-8576*.

A possible system landscape for the transport of HANA content via CTS+ is shown in Figure 6.7.

Prerequisites for CTS +

The Transport Domain Controller consists of an ABAP stack and a Java stack in the case of CTS+. For the transport of HANA content, the following prerequisites must be fulfilled (also see Note 1665940):

- The Transport Domain Controller is based at least on SAP NetWeaver 7.31 or 7.4 (alternatively, SAP Solution Manager 7.1 or 7.01).
- The *CTS plug-in 2.0* is installed (on the TCA system in the example from Figure 6.7).

▶ The CTS Deploy Web Service is installed (on the TCJ system in the example from Figure 6.7). It establishes the connection from the ABAP transport tools to the non-ABAP applications.

▶ The HANA system corresponds to the Support Package Stack 4 or higher.

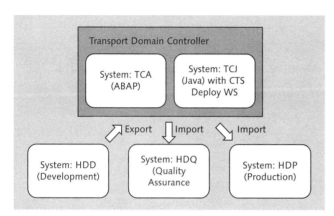

Figure 6.7 Transport in SAP HANA via CTS+

You start exporting HANA content directly in SAP HANA Studio. To do so, navigate to the QUICK LAUNCH view. There, choose EXPORT... and then SAP HANA CONTENT • DELIVERY UNIT.

Exporting

Figure 6.8 shows the window in which you then maintain the details for the export.

To attach the content of the delivery unit to a transport request of CTS+, you must select ATTACH TO TRANSPORT REQUEST. When exporting, the system then writes the content of the delivery unit as a packed file in the transport directory. The system always exports the complete delivery unit. The checkbox FILTER BY TIME alternatively allows you to export only the content of the selected delivery unit that was changed in a specific time interval. However, use this option cautiously because you may create dependencies between transports under certain circumstances.

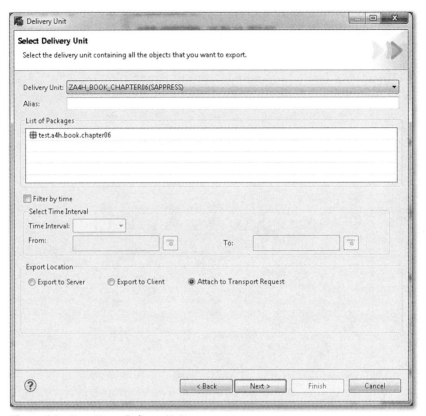

Figure 6.8 Exporting a Delivery Unit

Releasing and importing

The transport request is released and imported via the user interface of CTS+. When importing, CTS+ transfers the content of the packed file to the SAP HANA Repository of the target system and triggers the activation of the changed development objects (thus the activation of the attribute view AT_CUSTOMER in the example).

Original system

Similar to SAP NetWeaver AS ABAP, the SAP HANA Repository is also familiar with the concept of the original system. You can make changes in the non-original system only if you have a special authorization (the package authorization REPO.EDIT_IMPORTED_OBJECTS).

The HANA system does not set a repair flag here as in the ABAP system. Changes in the non-original system will thus be overwritten during the next import of the corresponding delivery unit.

Schema Mapping

Schema mapping is a special feature in transporting SAP HANA content. Schema mapping is necessary when the database schemas differ in the source system and target system of a transport. This involves mapping an *authoring schema* to a *physical schema*.

You maintain a schema mapping in the *Quick Launch* view via the menu option Schema Mapping… (see Figure 6.9). Before we discuss more precisely when and how the system evaluates it, we would first like to explain the need for schema mapping using the attribute view AT_CUSTOMER and the system landscape from Figure 6.2.

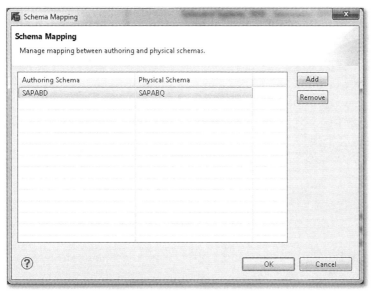

Figure 6.9 Maintaining a Schema Mapping

Remember that the attribute view AT_CUSTOMER reads customer data from the database table SCUSTOM. This table is part of the flight data model of AS ABAP, and therefore is located in the development system in the database schema SAPABD (because the system ID of the ABAP system is ABD). As a result, the attribute view refers to SAPABD.SCUSTOM.

Schema mapping example

The table SAPABD.SCUSTOM does not exist in the quality assurance system or production system. Due to the different system IDs, the database table resides in the schema SAPABQ in the quality assurance system and in the schema SAPABP in the production system.

Schema mapping enables you to map the schema SAPABD to SAPABQ in the quality assurance system and to SAPABP in the production system. This is illustrated in Figure 6.10.

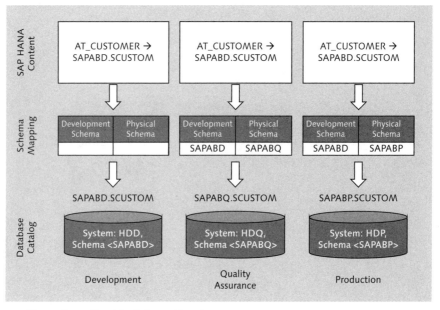

Figure 6.10 Need for Schema Mapping

Schema mapping
maintenance When maintaining schema mapping, you must consider some aspects:

- Schema mapping ultimately controls where—that is, in which database schema—an SAP HANA Repository development object searches for a database catalog object.

- If no schema mapping is maintained, the authoring schema and physical schema are identical.

- You can map multiple authoring schemas to the same physical schema.

- You *cannot* assign multiple physical schemas to an authoring schema.

- The SAP HANA content stores references to database objects with the authoring schema. If this cannot be clearly determined (due to a multiple assignment), the system stores the reference with the physical schema.

> **Schema Mapping When Installing SAP NetWeaver AS ABAP 7.4** [«]
>
> If you install SAP NetWeaver AS ABAP 7.4 on a HANA database, the installation program creates the ABAP schema SAP<SID>. Furthermore, the installation program also creates (at least) one schema mapping—that is, from the authoring schema ABAP to the physical schema SAP<SID>.

By means of this section, you have refreshed your knowledge with regard to transport in AS ABAP, and have learned how to perform transports of SAP HANA content. Next, we will deal with the combined ABAP/HANA transport.

6.2 Combined ABAP/SAP HANA Transport

How do you transport applications that consist of part ABAP objects and part SAP HANA Repository objects? This question is relevant, for example, if you want the report ZR_A4H_CHAPTER6_LIST_CUSTOMER (see example in Section 6.1.1), to use the external view ZEV_A4H_CUSTOMER of the ABAP Data Dictionary to access the attribute view AT_CUSTOMER of the SAP HANA Repository, which you know from the example in Section 6.1.2 (see Listing 6.1).

Sample report

```
REPORT zr_a4h_chapter6_list_customer.

DATA: lt_customer TYPE STANDARD TABLE OF
      zpv_a4h_customer,
      ls_customer TYPE zpv_a4h_customer.

IF cl_db_sys=>dbsys_type = 'HDB'.
  SELECT * FROM zev_a4h_customer
    INTO TABLE lt_customer.
ELSE.
  SELECT * FROM zpv_a4h_customer
    INTO TABLE lt_customer.
ENDIF.

LOOP AT lt_customer INTO ls_customer.
```

```
      WRITE: / ls_customer-id, ls_customer-name.
ENDLOOP.
Listing 6.1 shows the source code of the report.
REPORT zr_a4h_chapter6_list_customer.

DATA: lt_customer TYPE STANDARD TABLE OF
      zpv_a4h_customer,
      ls_customer TYPE zpv_a4h_customer.

IF cl_db_sys=>dbsys_type = 'HDB'.
  SELECT * FROM zev_a4h_customer
    INTO TABLE lt_customer.
  ELSE.
  SELECT * FROM zpv_a4h_customer
    INTO TABLE lt_customer.
   ENDIF.

LOOP AT lt_customer INTO ls_customer.
  WRITE: / ls_customer-id, ls_customer-name.
ENDLOOP.
```

Listing 6.1 Sample Report to be Transported

Options for combined transport For a combined ABAP/HANA transport, you basically have two options:

▶ The HANA transport container (which closely couples the parts of the development from the ABAP and HANA system).

▶ The enhanced Change and Transport System (which provides for only a loose coupling of objects from the ABAP and HANA system).

We will explain both options in the next sections. We will focus here on the HANA transport container.

6.2.1 HANA Transport Container

The HANA transport container is available in SAP NetWeaver 7.31 as of Support Package 5 and as of release 7.4. It can be used if SAP HANA is the primary database.

The HANA transport container allows you to transport development objects created via SAP HANA Studio using the mechanisms of the Change and Transport System of the ABAP application server (and in particular, without the need for a Java stack, as would be required for CTS+).

Basic Functions

From a technical perspective, the HANA transport container is a logical transport object that acts as a proxy object for exactly one delivery unit. Figure 6.11 illustrates how the HANA transport container works.

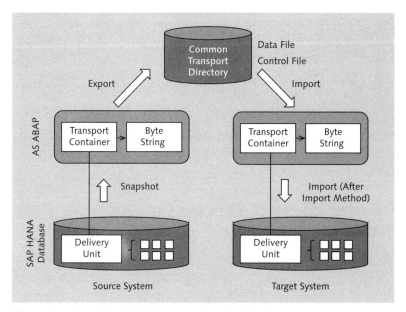

Figure 6.11 How the HANA Transport Container Works

You can create a HANA transport container using the ABAP Development Tools (and there only). In the *ABAP* perspective, for example, choose the menu path FILE • NEW • OTHER… • ABAP • HANA TRANSPORT CONTAINER. Then enter the name of the delivery unit for which you want to create the transport container. The system automatically derives the name of the transport container (see Figure 6.12; the HANA transport container ZA4H_BOOK_CHAPTER06 is *not* part of the examples provided with this book).

Creating the transport container

If you would like to use a prefix namespace in ABAP, you must assign the desired prefix name to the name of the content_vendor (see Section 6.1.2) before creating the transport container. To do so, you can fill the database table SNHI_VENDOR_MAPP using the Table View Maintenance.

Using a prefix namespace

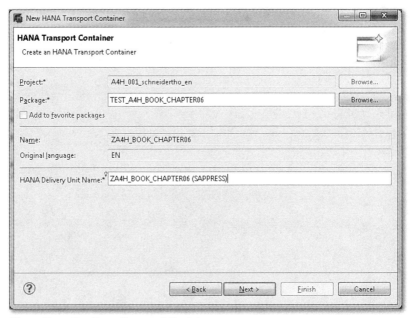

Figure 6.12 Creating a Transport Container

Change Recording   If the transport properties of the package that is used — in the example
TEST_A4H_BOOK_CHAPTER06 — are maintained accordingly (see Section
6.1.1), the system records the creation of the transport container in a
transportable change request.

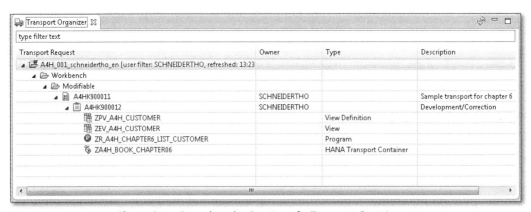

Figure 6.13 Recording the Creation of a Transport Container

The change request in Figure 6.13 contains all development objects used in this chapter:

- The report `ZR_A4H_CHAPTER6_LIST_CUSTOMER`
- The projection view `ZPV_A4H_CUSTOMER`
- The external view `ZEV_A4H_CUSTOMER`
- The attribute view `AT_CUSTOMER` via the delivery unit `ZA4H_BOOK_CHAPTER06`

When you create a transport container, the system automatically synchronizes the content of this container (once) with the content of the delivery unit. This means that all objects of the delivery unit are loaded as a packed file on the ABAP application server and are stored there as a *byte string* in a database table (that is, the table `SNHI_DU_PROXY`). Strictly speaking, the content of the delivery unit then appears twice in the HANA database:

Synchronization

- In the SAP HANA Repository
- Via the database table `SNHI_DU_PROXY`

If, after creating it, you would like to synchronize the transport container with the delivery unit—because you have made changes to the attribute view `AT_CUSTOMER`, for example—you must do so manually. Use the link *Take Snapshot and Save* in this case. You can view the current content of the transport container using the CONTENTS tab (both are shown in Figure 6.14).

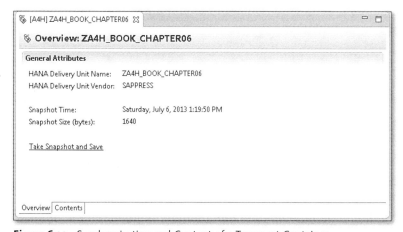

Figure 6.14 Synchronization and Content of a Transport Container

Exporting and importing
The transport from the development system to the quality assurance and production systems takes place via the CTS mechanisms:

▶ When exporting (more precisely, during *export release preprocessing*), the system writes the content of the transport container in the data file to the common transport directory of the systems involved in the transport.

▶ When importing (more precisely, in an *after-import method*), the system reads the transport container's content from the data file and imports the delivery unit in the HANA database of the target system. Activation of content occurs only if you have activated this for the software component of the transport container in the table SNHI_DUP_PREWORK (in the target system).

Transport log
You can reproduce the two steps at any time using the transport log. Figure 6.15 shows the transport log when you import the transport container ZA4H_BOOK_CHAPTER06.

```
Post-import method SNHI_DELIVERY_UNIT_IMPORT started for NHDU L, date and time: 20130706132952
Import of HANA Delivery Unit ZA4H_BOOK_CHAPTER06
Import does not include activation
Number of imported objects: 1
Number of reverted objects: 0
Number of activated objects: 0
Number of deleted objects: 0
A complete HANA delivery unit was imported.
Content snapshot was uploaded in source system HDB at 2013-07-06 11:22:47.3770000.
Details: Vendor SAPPRESS, Version 0, Support Package 0, Patch 0
Object AT_CUSTOMER (Attribute View), package test.a4h.book.chapter06, was processed successfully
No error
Import of HANA Delivery Unit ZA4H_BOOK_CHAPTER06 successful
No error
Post-import method SNHI_DELIVERY_UNIT_IMPORT completed for NHDU L, date and time: 20130706132953
Post-import methods of change/transport request A4HK900013 completed
    Start of subsequent processing ... 20130706132952
    End of subsequent processing... 20130706132953
```

Figure 6.15 Transport Log Entries of the Transport Container

Mixed System Landscapes

Mixed system landscapes represent a special case of the ABAP development on SAP HANA. Imagine that you, as an ABAP developer, want to optimize a program for SAP HANA and make use thereby of specific options of the HANA database. At the same time, however, this program should also be able to run on traditional databases—for example, because your employer uses SAP HANA as a database only in certain areas of the company. A system landscape could look in this case (simplified) as in Figure 6.16.

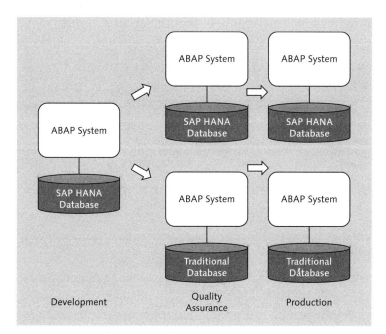

Figure 6.16 Mixed System Landscape

Using a case distinction, you can—to stick with the example of the program ZR_A4H_CHAPTER6_LIST_CUSTOMER—call the projection view ZPV_A4H_CUS-TOMER once and the external view ZEV_A4H_CUSTOMER once (see Listing 6.1). As a result, you ensure that no errors occur at runtime.

The implementation of the transport container ensures that no errors occur *during the transport* and the SAP HANA content is only imported if the target system of the import is a HANA-based system.

Systems without a HANA database

Recommendations for Using the Transport Container

When using the transport container, you should note some restrictions:

Restrictions

▶ When using the transport container, you always transport the complete delivery unit. You cannot transport only the content of a delivery unit that was changed in a specific time interval.

▸ Unlike development objects that are managed in SAP NetWeaver AS ABAP, the system does not automatically record changes to the content of a delivery unit, and the objects of a delivery unit are not locked exclusively for a transport request. It is thus your responsibility to manually synchronize the transport container with the delivery unit.

▸ When exporting the development objects from the source system, the transport considers only the active objects.

▸ The transport system does not recognize any dependencies between multiple transport containers that are transported simultaneously.

Within the restrictions, the transport container allows you to consistently transport applications that consist partly of ABAP objects and partly of SAP HANA content. We recommend its use if the prerequisites that are described at the start of Section 6.2.1 are fulfilled.

6.2.2 Enhanced Transport System

If your system landscape does not fulfill the prerequisites described in Section 6.2.1 for using the SAP HANA transport container, or if you do not want to use it for any other reason, you can resort to a combined ABAP/HANA transport in CTS+, which we have already addressed in Section 6.1.2, in connection with the transport of SAP HANA content (which is not related to ABAP objects).

Independent transport requests

When using CTS+ for a combined ABAP/HANA transport of an application, use two change requests:

▸ A change request for the ABAP objects (in the exemplary system landscape of Figure 6.2, this would have the number ABDKxxxxxx).

▸ And a change request for the SAP HANA content (in the exemplary system landscape of Figure 6.2, this would be a request with the number HDDKxxxxxx).

The two change requests are initially independent of each other. When using SAP Solution Manager, however, you can release the change requests centrally to ensure that there is always a consistent state of your application in the quality assurance and production system. For more information, see SAP Solution Manager documentation.

The ABAP application server is home to a collection of powerful runtime and error analysis tools that can assist you in accelerating ABAP programs on SAP HANA. When used correctly, they make it easier to identify potential areas of optimization, implement changes, and test such changes.

7   Runtime and Error Analysis with SAP HANA

In the previous chapters, you learned about the various ABAP options available to you in relation to accessing the HANA database. In addition to the already-familiar process of using SQL (Open SQL and Native SQL) to access tables in the database, you learned various new ways to model and implement views and database procedures, and also know how to use ABAP to access these objects.

If you intend to develop a new application or to optimize an existing application for use with SAP HANA, you may be asking yourself: What is the best approach to adopt, and which tools can support this undertaking? In this chapter, we wish to provide you with an overview of the runtime and error analysis tools available. In particular, we will focus on correct usage of these tools within the context of optimizing database accesses. As a result, we will not discuss any other usage scenarios (for example, system administration) or configuration options in detail here. As an ABAP developer, you are already familiar with some of the tools that can be used for this purpose: For example, the SQL trace (Transaction ST05), ABAP runtime analysis (Transaction SAT), and the SAP Code Inspector. Therefore, we will not describe their use in any great detail. Basic information about these tools is available in the book *ABAP Performance Tuning* by Hermann Gahm (SAP PRESS 2009). Ultimately, this chapter will focus on the new SAP HANA-specific analysis options that are available within these tools.

In this chapter, we will use very simple examples to demonstrate the capabilities of (and differences between) each tool. Then, building upon this, we will demonstrate correct use of these tools (either individually or in combination) within the context of a fictitious optimization project for an overall scenario, which we will discuss in the next chapter.

7.1 Overview of the Tools Available

Before we introduce you to each tool, we'll provide you with an overview of all tools available and classify them according to their usage scenario and primary user role. This overview also contains the release requirements for ABAP. We have classified the tools under the categories listed in Table 7.1.

Category	Purpose	Roles
Error analysis (Section 7.2)	To identify and resolve functional problems	▶ Developers ▶ Support
ABAP code analysis (Section 7.3)	To identify those parts of the ABAP program with potential for optimization	▶ Developers ▶ Quality managers
Runtime statistics and traces (Section 7.4)	To perform a detailed analysis of the runtime associated with an individual request (for example, the runtime associated with a dialog step)	▶ Developers ▶ Performance experts
System-wide SQL analyses (Section 7.5)	To determine the SQL profile of an application or system	▶ Administrators ▶ Performance experts
SQL performance optimization (Section 7.6)	To plan and perform an optimization	▶ Developers ▶ Performance experts

Table 7.1 Categorizing Runtime and Error Analysis Tools

Error analysis   If you optimize implementations on SAP HANA by transferring calculations to the database, this may lead to new sources of error. Within error analysis, our primary goal is to introduce you to the options available in relation to analyzing (and avoiding) program terminations associated with database accesses. In particular, we will discuss testing, analyzing, and debugging SQL statements and SQLScript procedures from ABAP programs.

A static *code analysis* provides clues about which parts of the ABAP program have potential for optimization. This is known as a *static* analysis because no runtime data is incorporated into it (for example, the frequency with which a program or function is called within a particular period) and no dynamic calls are analyzed (for example, SQL statements that are first generated at runtime). For the code analysis, SAP NetWeaver AS ABAP has a *Code Inspector* (Transaction SCI), which provides a set of checks that can be grouped into check variants. You can use the ABAP Test Cockpit (Transaction ATC) or the Code Inspector to perform these checks in the development environment. To ensure efficient ABAP programming, some new or improved checks have been added to ABAP 7.4.

Code analysis

SAP NetWeaver AS ABAP contains a number of runtime analysis tools for a database request (or a sequence of requests). The *statistic records* (Transaction STAD) provide a simple overview of database times and are a useful starting point. The *ABAP trace* (Transaction SAT) provides detailed analysis options for individual statements. The new *ABAP profiler* in the ABAP development environment in Eclipse, which provides additional functions such as graphical representations, is also based on this infrastructure. In Chapter 3, we introduced you to the *SQL trace* (Transaction ST05), which also provides other useful runtime analysis functions. *Single transaction analysis* (Transaction ST12) is a special tool that combines transactions STAD, SAT, and ST05 into one interface.

Runtime analysis

In SAP HANA, special tools are available for analyzing an individual SQL statement or a more complex SQLScript implementation. The *explain plan* provides information about the execution plan for an SQL statement, while SAP HANA Plan Visualizer (*PlanViz*) visualizes the execution plans for SQL statements and combines them with additional runtime information.

In Section 3.2.5, we introduced you to the database administration cockpit (DBA cockpit, Transaction DBACOCKPIT). In addition to managing and configuring the database, the DBA cockpit also provides some SQL performance analysis functions through, for example, the *SQL cache* and *expensive SQL statement trace*.

System analysis and optimization

New tools In order to determine a detailed SQL profile for applications within an SAP system, a new tool, the *SQL Monitor* (Transaction SQLM), is available as of SAP NetWeaver AS ABAP 7.4. This tool monitors the production system and provides valuable performance optimization data. You can use the new *SQL performance tuning worklist* tool (Transaction SWLT) to combine the data from the SQL Monitor with the results of a code analysis, and therefore make plans towards achieving a promising optimization. In the following sections, we will explain how to use each of these tools.

7.2   Error Analysis

Before we discuss performance optimization tools, we wish to introduce you to some important error analysis tools. As the saying goes, "You can't make an omelet without breaking eggs," so functional problems may occur when making changes to a program or a new development, especially if the previous program code is very old and the author is no longer available.

Testing, analyzing, tracing, and debugging Therefore, in this section, we will discuss some aforementioned elements, namely testing, analyzing program terminations, tracing, and debugging. Here, we will focus on error analyses within the context of database accesses and the use of native implementations in SAP HANA.

We will explain some approaches in relation to writing *unit tests* for SAP HANA views and procedures in ABAP, discuss the analysis of program terminations in the context of database accesses in Transaction ST22, and introduce you to the concept of tracing and debugging SQLScript.

7.2.1   Unit Tests

When making changes to program code (a concept known as *refactoring*), it is very helpful to have a set of (preferably automatic) tests that can be performed both before and after making the changes; this helps to identify errors as soon as possible. In this context, the approach of testing single objects (*units*), either individually or in combination, is known as *unit testing*. *ABAP Unit* is integrated into the ABAP language and development infrastructure, and it can be used to write unit tests. This tool is also integrated into the ABAP Test Cockpit, which we will discuss in Section 7.3. You can also use unit tests as a basis for a performance analysis involving the ABAP profiler. Such an analysis can determine the effect of code changes on runtimes (see Section 7.4.2). In addition to the ABAP Unit tool, SAP NetWeaver AS ABAP also provides support for further testing approaches, such as integration tests or simulated user interactions. However, these are beyond the scope of this book.

You should also conduct tests in order to safeguard complex implementations in SAP HANA (in SQL and SQLScript, in particular). The sophisticated test infrastructure in the ABAP application server provides a good framework here. We wish to use the database procedure DETERMINE_TOP_CONNECTIONS, which we introduced in Section 5.1, as an example. This procedure determines the top five connections for an airline. For this purpose, two variants that use different sorting criteria are implemented here, and they can be selected by means of an input parameter. We will also use the database procedure proxy ZDP_DETERMINE_TOP_CONNECTIONS, which was created in Section 5.3.3, to access the database procedure. A simple unit test for the database procedure is shown in Listing 7.1.

Testing complex SQL/SQLScript operations

This test validates that the procedure invocation works properly for a set of input parameters. In particular, the test class contains an example of a *negative test*, which checks the return value when passing an airline carrier that doesn't exist as input data.

```
CLASS ltcl_test_db_procedure DEFINITION FINAL FOR TESTING
   INHERITING FROM cl_aunit_assert
   DURATION MEDIUM
   RISK LEVEL HARMLESS.

   PRIVATE SECTION.
     DATA: lt_conn TYPE TABLE OF
                 zif_determine_top_connections=>et_connections.
     METHODS:
       test_determine_top_conn FOR TESTING,
       test_determine_top_conn_neg FOR TESTING.
ENDCLASS.

CLASS ltcl_test_db_procedure IMPLEMENTATION.

METHOD test_determine_top_conn.
```

```
DATA: lv_cnt TYPE i,
      lv_carrid TYPE s_carrid VALUE 'LH'.
 " Determine # connections for 'LH' (max. 5).
 SELECT COUNT( DISTINCT connid ) FROM sflight
        INTO lv_cnt WHERE carrid = lv_carrid.
IF ( lv_cnt > 5 ).
  lv_cnt = 5.
ENDIF.

CALL DATABASE PROCEDURE zdp_determine_top_connections
  EXPORTING
    iv_mandt      = sy-mandt iv_carrid = lv_carrid
    iv_algorithm = 'P'
  IMPORTING
    et_connections = lt_conn.

" Procedure should contain correct number of lines
" and correct airline
assert_equals( exp = lv_cnt act = lines( lt_conn ) ).
LOOP AT lt_conn ASSIGNING FIELD-SYMBOL(<l>).
  assert_equals( exp = lv_carrid act = <l>-carrid ).
ENDLOOP.

ENDMETHOD.

METHOD test_determine_top_conn_neg.
 " Negative test
  CALL DATABASE PROCEDURE zdp_determine_top_connections
    EXPORTING
      iv_mandt = sy-mandt iv_carrid = 'XXX'
      iv_algorithm = ''
    IMPORTING
      et_connections = lt_conn.
  assert_equals( exp = 0 act = lines( lt_conn ) ).
ENDMETHOD.

ENDCLASS.
```

Listing 7.1 Unit Test for a Database Procedure

Test data To gauge whether the calculation within the procedure is correct, the exact output data must be known. In general, it pays to have different sets of stable, consistent test data, which can be used in different systems

298

for different purposes (e.g., mass data for conducting performance tests). You can also use the ABAP client concept to generate suitable test data constellations in special clients.

Design Patterns Make it Easier to Write Tests
The use of suitable *design patterns* makes it easier to write unit tests. These include modularization and decoupling as a result of well-defined interfaces, as well as avoiding dependencies in relation to specific system statuses.
For example, when testing database procedures, it makes sense to avoid reading directly from a Customizing table or application context within the procedure, but to transfer the required values as parameters. Such (generic) implementations are easier to test and also increase the potential for re-use in other contexts.
Furthermore, it is generally recommended to use a suitable interface to abstract a calculation in the ABAP application and therefore encapsulate a HANA-specific implementation.

7.2.2   Dump Analysis

If a program terminates during a transaction (known as a *dump*), Transaction ST22 provides valuable troubleshooting information. In this section, we will explain the information you obtain when an error occurs with a database access.

In the case of SQL statements, different types of runtime errors can occur and trigger a dump. Many of these errors can be caught within the application by means of a class-based exception. Table 7.2 groups together the most important exceptions. Here, special runtime error types exist for each category.

Runtime errors and exceptions

Category	Exception	Example
Error during Open SQL access	CX_SY_OPEN_SQL_DB	Use of an invalid cursor (see also Section 3.2.2)
Syntactical error in dynamic Open SQL	CX_SY_DYNAMIC_OSQL_ SYNTAX	Invalid, dynamically generated WHERE condition (see also Section 3.2.2)
Semantic error in dynamic Open SQL	CX_SY_DYNAMIC_OSQL_ SEMANTICS	Aggregation by means of a non-numerical, dynamically specified column (see also Section 3.2.2)

Table 7.2   Error Categories for SQL Accesses

Category	Exception	Example
Error during ABDC access (ABAP Database Connectivity)	CX_SQL_EXCEPTION	Syntactical error in a Native SQL statement (see also Section 3.2.4)
Error while calling a database procedure	CX_SY_DB_PROCEDURE	Runtime error in SQLScript (see Chapter 5)
Non-catchable errors	None	Internal error during a database access

Table 7.2 Error Categories for SQL Accesses (Cont.)

SQL error number and error text in the database

In Transaction ST22, the short text is the initial starting point for an analysis, in addition to the exception that occurred and the runtime error type (for example, DBIF_RSQL_SQL_ERROR). The short text contains, for example, information such as "SQL error <number> occurred while accessing table <table>". Figure 7.1 shows an example of an error that occurred while accessing an SAP HANA view that does not exist. In most cases, this error text contains enough information to enable you to localize and resolve the problem.

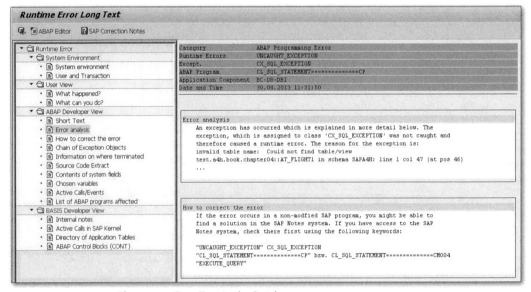

Figure 7.1 Error Text in the Database

Further contextual information in relation to an ABAP program is available in the following sections in Transaction ST22:

▶ Information on which statement caused the dump

▶ Source code extract

▶ Contents of system fields

▶ Chosen variables

▶ Active calls/events

> **Error When Accessing SAP HANA Views and Database Procedures**
>
> When you use external views (see Section 4.5) and database procedure proxies (see Section 5.3), development errors can occur as a result of inconsistencies (for example, if the view or the procedure was changed without updating the proxy). In most cases, this situation causes an exception of the type CX_SY_OPEN_SQL_DB (with the error text "Invalidated view …", for example). In this case, you need to synchronize the objects across the development environment as described in Section 4.5 and Section 5.3.

[+]

If you require further information from the database, the analysis must continue there. The information in Transaction ST22 is no longer sufficient, particularly in the case of more extensive implementations within the database (for example, a database procedure that calls an additional procedure). In such cases, however, you can use the information available to reconstruct the call that triggered the error and then use tracing and debugging to continue the analysis.

Restrictions associated with dump analysis

7.2.3 Tracing in SQLScript

If you analyze an error within an implementation in SQLScript, you may want to view certain interim results. For this purpose, SQLScript contains the CE Plan Operator TRACE, which enables you to log the contents of a local table variable (which ultimately displays an interim result for a database procedure) in a local temporary table, thus enabling you to reproduce individual steps within a database procedure.

CE Plan Operator
TRACE

For the database procedure GET_AGENCIES_FOR_CONNECTIONS, which we used as an example in Section 5.1.1, the use of the TRACE Plan Operator can look as follows:

```
LT_AGENCIES = SELECT...
LT_AGENCIES = TRACE(:LT_AGENCIES);
ET_AGENCIES = SELECT...
```

The system automatically creates the local temporary table when it calls the database procedure. This table has the same structure as the table variable. To determine its name, you can read the monitoring view SQLSCRIPT_TRACE after you call the database procedure. Since this is a local temporary table, it can only be viewed within the same database connection. Note that the system does not undertake some optimizations when the CE Plan Operator TRACE is used. Furthermore, logging the contents of the table has a negative impact on runtime. Therefore, do not use the TRACE statement in productive code.

[»]

Additional Tracing Options

In addition to the TRACE statement, two additional mechanisms can support you in analyzing an SQLScript procedure. We will mention both options in compact form here, and refer to the SQLScript documentation available at *http://help.sap.com/hana_appliance/* for further information.

You can use the debug trace to log the execution of a database procedure. To do this, use the IN DEBUG MODE addition when you call a database procedure. You can then use the database table SYS.M_CE_DEBUG_NODE_MAPPING to reproduce the instantiation of the costing model. You can also use the WITH PLAN addition to compile a database procedure and then use the tables SYS. PROCEDURE_DATAFLOWS and SYS.PROCEDURE_MAPPING to analyze the data flow associated with the procedure, among other things.

Just like the CE Plan Operator TRACE, these two variants also have a negative effect on runtime and therefore should not be used in a productive environment.

7.2.4 Debugging SQLScript

The SQLScript debugger is the last option we will discuss in relation to SQLScript error analysis. This is a powerful tool for finding errors in database procedures. It makes use of the DEBUG perspective from Eclipse and its use requires you to work with the SAP HANA DEVELOPMENT perspective in SAP HANA Studio.

At present (that is, for Support Package Stack 5), the SQLScript debugger still has some restrictions. In particular, it cannot debug any database procedures that contain input parameters. However, the database procedure that you want to debug can be wrapped in a procedure that does not contain any input parameters. For the procedure DETERMINE_TOP_CONNECTIONS, which we implemented in Section 5.1, such a wrapper can look as shown in Listing 7.2:

Using the SQLScript debugger

```
CREATE PROCEDURE WRAP_PROCEDURE( ) LANGUAGE SQLSCRIPT
  SQL SECURITY INVOKER READS SQL DATA AS
BEGIN
CALL "_SYS_BIC"."test.a4h.book.chapter05/
  DETERMINE_TOP_CONNECTIONS"('000', 'LH',
  LT_UTILIZATION);
END;
```

Listing 7.2 Wrapping a Database Procedure

You can then set one or more breakpoints in the database procedure that you want to debug.

In the next step, switch to the DEBUG perspective in SAP HANA Studio and ensure that the wrapper procedure is opened in the editor (that is, the database procedure WRAP_PROCEDURE in our example) is called. Then, choose RUN • DEBUG CONFIGURATIONS… and create a configuration for debugging SQLScript (even though this configuration is completely empty, it is required for technical reasons.). You can then choose DEBUG in the DEBUG CONFIGURATIONS window to start the debugger.

Figure 7.2 shows the DEBUG perspective after starting the debugger for the database procedure WRAP_PROCEDURE. In the call hierarchy ❶, you can see that the procedure WRAP_PROCEDURE called the procedure DETERMINE_TOP_CONNECTIONS. The import parameters IV_MANDT, IV_CARRID, and IV_ALGORITHM are filled. At present, the output parameter ET_CONNECTIONS is still empty (VARIABLES ❷).

Debug perspective

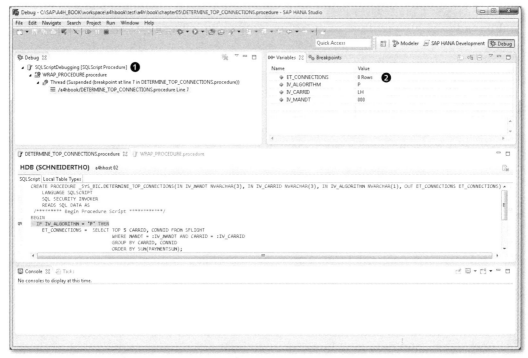

Figure 7.2 SQLScript Debugger

You can choose RUN • RESUME to navigate to the next breakpoint. You can then choose RUN • TERMINATE to exit the debugger. Currently, the SQLScript debugger does not support other standard debugger functions (for example, STEP INTO or STEP OVER). However, SAP is currently working on a number of improvements to the SQLScript debugger.

[»] **Outlook: SQLScript Debugger in Support Package Stack 6**

Support Package Stack 6 for the HANA database contains various improvements to the SQLScript debugger. For example, it supports debugging of database procedures that contain input parameters.

7.3 ABAP Code Analysis

The Code Inspector can support you in identifying those parts of the program that have potential for improvement. With this in mind, the Code Inspector has a series of checks that you can perform on your development objects. You then receive a prioritized list of messages, each assigned to the relevant check. Since "false alarms" can occur with these checks (in other words, there is no real problem), you can insert special comments in the code to prevent a message from being issued. In the case of a code analysis, you must bear in mind that SAP does not allow standard SAP code to be scanned.

Since the Code Inspector has very extensive functions, they cannot be considered in detail here. If you are interested in learning more about the Code Inspector, we recommend the book *Managing Custom Code in SAP* by Alisdair Templeton and Tony de Thomasis (SAP PRESS 2013). Here, we will introduce you, in particular, to those new and revised Code Inspector checks that are relevant for SAP HANA. You will learn how to perform checks in the development environment and how to check the entire system.

Extensive check options

7.3.1 Checks and Check Variants

When the Code Inspector performs a code analysis, it executes a checklist that comprises a defined set of development objects. Here, you can use *check variants* to configure the list of checks to be performed and their settings.

Checklist

In this section, we will introduce you to those checks that can support you in migrating to or optimizing SAP HANA. These checks primarily relate to the following areas: Robust Programming, Security Checks, and Performance Checks. The Code Inspector also contains a large number of additional checks that we will not discuss here in detail. Accurate technical documentation on all checks is available in Transaction SCI, which is used to configure the check variants that you will learn about in this section.

Relevant Checks when Migrating to SAP HANA

During migration, the main priority is to ensure that you do not experience any functional setbacks, including program terminations and unwanted changes to the behavior of an application. In general, thanks to the compatibility and portability of ABAP code, no adjustments are required.

Native SQL/
database hints

An exception here is any part of a program where you used database-dependent implementations in the past. These include the use of Native SQL and database hints. The following two checks can help you to locate such parts within a program: Use of ADBC Interface and Critical Statements.

Depooling/
declustering

A further example involves pool/cluster tables, which, when migrated to SAP HANA, are converted into transparent tables (we previously covered this in Section 3.2.1). This does not require any change to the application. However, you must consider the following: When data is selected in Open SQL without any specified sorting, the documentation states that the user cannot rely on sorting (for example, according to the primary key). In the case of pool/cluster tables, however, the database interface always supplements the ORDER BY PRIMARY KEY addition internally. If you have relied on this behavior (that is, you chose not to specify a particular sorting), you may have to add an ORDER BY statement after the migration. In the Robust Programming category, a check is available to help you find the relevant parts within the program. SAP recommends that you adjust these parts of the program irrespective of a migration to SAP HANA, because this is a programming error. In Chapter 14, we will give further recommendations for existing ABAP code when migrating to SAP HANA.

Relevant Checks During Optimization for SAP HANA

A range of checks are available to identify optimization potential in the context of database accesses. These checks essentially reflect the performance recommendations for Open SQL, which are explained in detail in Chapter 14. In the next section, we will introduce you to some important checks. In particular, we will discuss some key enhancements and improvements in SAP NetWeaver AS ABAP 7.4.

Unsecure Use of FOR ALL ENTRIES

The following performance optimization is frequently successful: Converting a nested SELECT statement into a FOR ALL ENTRIES statement or a join. In the case of a FOR ALL ENTRIES expression, the *driver table* must never be empty. Otherwise, all the data records are read from the database, which is generally not desired. Therefore, a check to determine whether the driver table is empty must always be performed before a FOR ALL ENTRIES statement is executed. The check to detect unsecure use of FOR ALL ENTRIES searches for parts of the program in which the driver table does not appear to be checked.

Empty driver table

Searching FOR ALL ENTRIES Clauses to Be Transformed

In many situations, a join offers additional performance advantages over a FOR ALL ENTRIES clause. For this reason, the system performs a check on those FOR ALL ENTRIES clauses to be transformed, and finds clauses that could be converted to joins. This is only ever the case if a database access was used to determine the driver table for the FOR ALL ENTRIES expression.

SELECT Statements that Bypass the Table Buffer

The ABAP table buffer still plays an important role when using SAP HANA as a database. In order to avoid an increased database load, you should not bypass this buffer if buffering has been switched on for a table. To this end, a check is performed on SELECT statements that ignore the buffer. Note that this check cannot support you in finding the right buffer setting for a table.

Problematic SELECT* Statements

You should avoid reading database columns that you do not require. To this end, a check is available to find SELECT statements for which too many fields are selected. Frequently, this concerns pure *existence checks*—where all fields are selected, even though the return code for the SELECT statement would be sufficient. However, there are also scenarios in which only a small part of the fields is actually used. With SAP NetWeaver AS ABAP 7.4, these checks are also able to identify usage in another *modularization*

Reading volumes of data that are too large

unit (for example, in another ABAP class or another function module). Therefore, the entire call sequence is analyzed whereby you can set the depth of search when configuring this check.

Searching SELECTs in Loops in Modularization Units

Usually, performance problems are not caused by a single database access, but rather a large number of accesses in succession. For example, problems can occur with accesses that are executed in loops. Consequently, there is a range of checks that can find such loops. In particular, they include a check that finds SELECT statements that are executed in loops. As of SAP NetWeaver AS ABAP 7.4, searches can also extend beyond modularization units. Consequently, the triggering part of the program for a SELECT statement can also be determined for complex implementations.

Change Database Accesses in Loops

In the case of change operations, you should also favor array processing (see also Section 3.2.2) over individual operations at all times, if possible. To this end, a check is available to find individual INSERT, UPDATE, or DELETE statements that are executed in loops.

EXIT/CHECK in SELECT… ENDSELECT Loop

If you use EXIT to exit a SELECT… ENDSELECT loop, a large number of data records may be read unnecessarily because the data is transferred in blocks. A CHECK statement that immediately follows a SELECT statement indicates that a filter is not used until the data has been read. Frequently, these two expressions can be converted into a suitable WHERE condition.

Configuring Check Variants

Default variants   You can configure check variants in Transaction SCI or in the ABAP Test Cockpit. SAP provides a range of default variants. Figure 7.3 shows the check variant PERFORMANCE_DB, which is available in SAP NetWeaver AS ABAP 7.4. It provides a useful default configuration, and contains the checks introduced in this section.

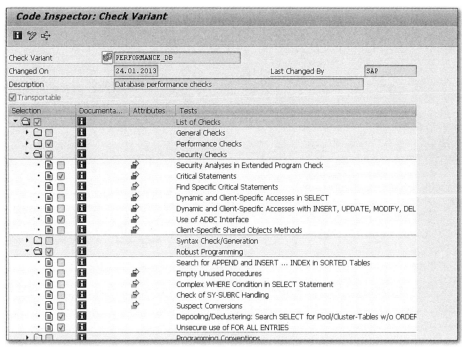

Figure 7.3 Code Inspector—Check Variant "Performance_DB"

However, you can also define custom check variants by selecting and configuring suitable checks from the tree. Furthermore, you can define check variants specifically for one system user, or globally for all system users.

Configuring custom variants

7.3.2 Checks in the Development Infrastructure

In this section, we will explain how you, as the developer, can check individual objects. This enables you to perform a static code analysis before you release a new development or change, so errors are found before they are transported to a test system.

In the ABAP Workbench (Transaction SE80), you can use the context menu option CHECK • ABAP TEST COCKPIT to perform a check on a development object or package. The results are displayed in form of a list. From here, you can navigate to the relevant parts of the program (see Figure 7.4).

Code check in Transaction SE80

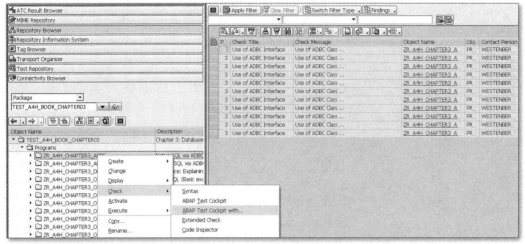

Figure 7.4 Code Check in Transaction SE80

Code check in Eclipse The checks are also natively integrated into the ABAP Development Tools in Eclipse. This offers some advantages. Here, you use the context menu option RUN AS • ABAP TEST COCKPIT to start the check. Figure 7.5 shows the result of a check performed using the example from Listing 3.10 in Section 3.2.2. The relevant parts of the program are clearly highlighted and it is easy to navigate via the found locations.

```
REPORT ZR_A4H_CHAPTER3_OPEN7.

DATA: lt_book TYPE TABLE OF sbook.

" Fetch result data in packages of 1000 rows
SELECT * FROM sbook
        INTO TABLE lt_book
        PACKAGE SIZE 1000.

Empty SELECT...ENDSELECT Loop: EXIT or no statement in SELECT...ENDSELECT loop
ENDSELECT.
```

Description	Resource	Path	Location	Type
▲ ⊗ Errors (2 items)				
⊗ Existence check. No fields used: Search problematic SELECT * statements	zr_a4h_chapt...	/A4H_001_westenb...	line 14	ATC Problem
⊗ Large table ...: No WHERE condition: Analysis of WHERE Condition for SELECT	zr_a4h_chapt...	/A4H_001_westenb...	line 14	ATC Problem
▲ ⚠ Warnings (1 item)				
⚠ DB Operation SELECT for ... found.: Search DB Operations	zr_a4h_chapt...	/A4H_001_westenb...	line 14	ATC Problem
▲ ⓘ Infos (1 item)				
ⓘ Empty SELECT...ENDSELECT Loop: EXIT or no statement in SELECT...ENDSELECT loop	zr_a4h_chapt...	/A4H_001_westenb...	line 18	ATC Problem

Ⓞ Task Repositories   ▤ Task List   ▥ Problems ⊠   ▭ Properties   ▤ Templates   ▥ Feed Reader   ▭ Transport Organizer

2 errors, 1 warning, 1 other

Figure 7.5 Code Check in Eclipse

The system default check variant is used first. However, you can use the project setting in Eclipse to replace the default variant with a custom variant, as shown in Figure 7.6.

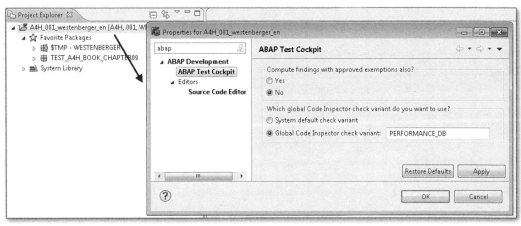

Figure 7.6 Selecting a Check Variant in Eclipse

7.3.3 Global Check Runs in the System

In the last section, you learned how to check individual development objects or an entire development package. To ensure systematic use of such checks within a quality management process, it makes sense to automatically perform the checks at certain times for all developments (or selected parts) and to analyze the results.

In this section, we will show you how to perform code checks in the *ABAP Test Cockpit* (ATC), which offers considerable advantages over the Code Inspector. You can manage the results of check runs, replicate them to other systems, manage exceptions, and automatically send results by email. Furthermore, the ATC is integrated into the ABAP Workbench (by means of a special browser) and SAP Solution Manager.

Using the ABAP Test Cockpit

To start the ABAP Test Cockpit, call Transaction ATC. Here, you can configure the cockpit, schedule check runs, and analyze the results. Figure 7.7 shows the initial screen for the transaction.

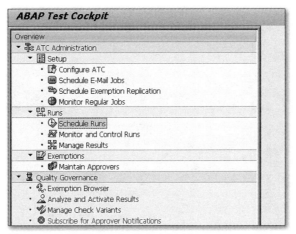

Figure 7.7 ABAP Test Cockpit: Initial Screen

You can use the SCHEDULE RUNS option to configure a check run. To do this, select a Code Inspector check variant and a set of objects. Figure 7.8 shows a configuration for the variant PERFORMANCE_DB (introduced in Section 7.1) checking the packages TEST_A4H_BOOK*, which contain examples from this book.

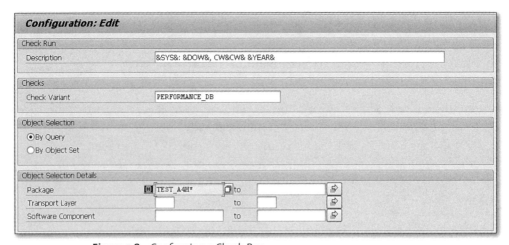

Figure 7.8 Configuring a Check Run

You can now schedule such a check run (either once or at specific times), which is then executed asynchronously in the background. You can then view the result under ANALYZE AND ACTIVATE RESULTS in the ATC or in the ATC RESULT BROWSER in the ABAP Workbench (see Figure 7.9). To do this, you may first have to activate this browser in the workbench settings for your user.

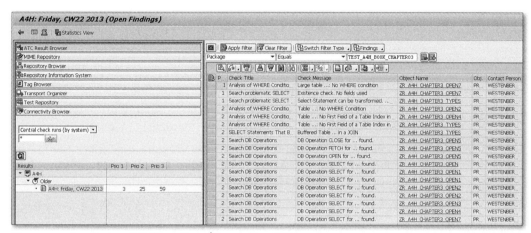

Figure 7.9 Result of an ATC Check Run in Transaction SE80

In Section 7.6, we'll show you how to merge the results of an ATC run with runtime data from the SQL Monitor for performance optimization.

7.4   Runtime Statistics and Traces

Runtime statistics and traces are used if a long-running program is already known and you want to analyze its runtime behavior more closely. Runtime statistics provide you with an initial overview of where the time was consumed—that is, whether this time was consumed on the database or in the application server. The traces record the ABAP or SQL execution in detail and help you identify expensive statements, while the explain plan and SAP HANA PlanViz show in detail how a certain SQL statement was executed.

7.4.1 Runtime Statistics

In the SAP system, statistical data is collected and persisted for each *request*. Examples of a request include the execution of a program, dialog step, or RFC call. This data is collected from the application server where the request is executed, and then written to the local file system. By default, the files are available for 48 hours before they are overwritten. These statistics include data about the overall runtime, CPU time, database time, and time associated with SAP locks, as well as other values (for memory usage, for example).

Selection

Once the program to be analyzed has been executed, you can select the statistical records in Transaction STAD. On the initial screen, you specify the required time frame. Note, however, that the statistic record is not written until the request has been fully executed. You can also specify other filters here. Examples include the user name, program or transaction, task type (dialog, RFC, background, and so on), and different thresholds (for example, minimum response time or minimum database time).

Analysis

The basic list (see Figure 7.10) contains some key performance indicators (KPIs) such as RESPONSE TIME, CPU TIME, and DB REQUEST time.

SAP Workload: Single Statistical Records - Overview

Download 　　　　　　　Disp. mode 　　Sel. fields 　Server ID

System:　　A4H　　　　　Number of RFCs which responded (without errors):　1 (　1)
Analysed time:　28.06.2013 / 00:00:00　-　28.06.2013 / 23:50:00
Display mode:　All statistic records, sorted by time

Started	Server	Transaction	Program	T Scr. Wp	User	Response time (ms)	Time in WPs (ms)	Wait time (ms)	CPU time (ms)	DB req. time (ms)
		*	*		*	1.000		0	0	0
19:00:34	a4hhost_A4H_00	SE38	ZR_A4H_CHAPTER8_TOP_CUST_2	D 0120 7	SCHNEIDERTHO	23.030	23.030	0	10	2
19:31:17	a4hhost_A4H_00		RSAL_BATCH_TOOL_DISPATCHING	B　　11	DDIC	30.293	30.293	0	230	50
19:35:17	a4hhost_A4H_00		RFC	R 3004 8	DDIC	1.192	1.192	0	890	344
19:35:17	a4hhost_A4H_00		SWNC_TCOLL_STARTER	B　　12	DDIC	2.060	2.060	0	20	10
19:37:13	a4hhost_A4H_00	SE38	ZR_A4H_CHAPTER8_TOP_CUST_2	D 0120 2	SCHNEIDERTHO	23.468	23.468	0	0	1
19:39:19	a4hhost_A4H_00	SE38	ZR_A4H_CHAPTER8_TOP_CUST_1	D 0120 7	SCHNEIDERTHO	76.257	76.257	0	55.040	25.353
20:00:25	a4hhost_A4H_00	SE38	ZR_A4H_CHAPTER8_TOP_CUST_2	D 0120 9	SCHNEIDERTHO	22.930	22.930	0	0	2
20:24:01	a4hhost_A4H_00	SE38	ZR_A4H_CHAPTER8_TOP_CUST_2	D 0120 0	SCHNEIDERTHO	23.062	23.062	0	20	2
20:31:17	a4hhost_A4H_00		RSAL_BATCH_TOOL_DISPATCHING	B　　12	DDIC	30.314	30.314	0	230	55
20:32:23	a4hhost_A4H_00	SE16	/1BCDWB/DBSPFLI	D 1000 1	SCHNEIDERTHO	1.163	33	0	30	8
20:35:17	a4hhost_A4H_00		SWNC_TCOLL_STARTER	B　　12	DDIC	2.065	2.064	1	20	10
21:31:17	a4hhost_A4H_00		RSAL_BATCH_TOOL_DISPATCHING	B　　11	DDIC	30.315	30.314	1	230	57
21:35:17	a4hhost_A4H_00		SWNC_TCOLL_STARTER	B　　12	DDIC	2.058	2.057	1	20	11
21:38:21	a4hhost_A4H_00	SE24	SEO_STARTUP	D 0200 1	SCHNEIDERTHO	1.387	70	1	50	21
21:54:47	a4hhost_A4H_00	SE16	/1BCDWB/DBSBOOK	D 1000 3	GAHM	637.030	637.030	0	401.800	40.290
22:04:43	a4hhost_A4H_00	STAD	RSSTAT26	D 0120 4	GAHM	2.105	2.105	0	2.090	3
22:05:14	a4hhost_A4H_00	STAD	RSSTAT26	D 0120 9	GAHM	2.187	2.187	0	2.190	0
22:05:33	a4hhost_A4H_00	STAD	RSSTAT26	D 0120 4	GAHM	2.088	2.088	0	2.080	0

Figure 7.10 Basic List in Transaction STAD

When you double-click a statistical record in the basic list, further information appears in the detail display (see Figure 7.11). Here, we wish to draw your attention to database-relevant topics such as response time (TIME), database time (DB), and database procedures and tables (DB PROCEDURES and TABLES).

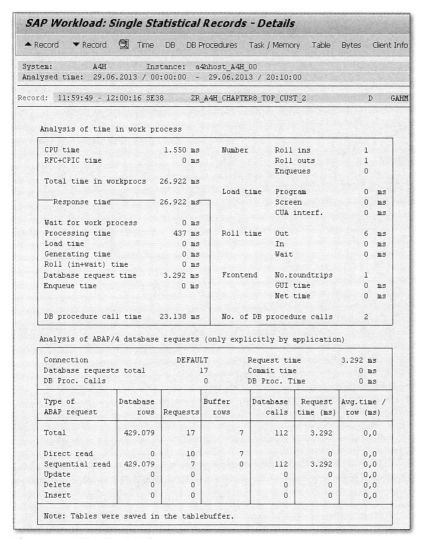

Figure 7.11 STAD DB: Details

Times

Time overview Table 7.3 lists the components of the RESPONSE TIME. For SAP HANA, the database time and the time for database procedures are of particular interest.

Time	Explanation
WAIT FOR WORK PROCESS	Time spent waiting for a work process to become available (in the dispatcher queue).
PROCESSING TIME	Uses the response time as the basis for calculating all other times named here. Generally contains the time associated with ABAP processing and CPU consumption, but also wait times (for example, RFC time, update time, and roll wait time) if the work process is not rolled out.
LOAD TIME	Time taken to load programs.
GENERATING TIME	Time taken to generate programs.
ROLL (IN+WAIT) TIME	Times when the work process was rolled out and the time for the subsequent roll-in (loading of the user context).
DATABASE REQUEST TIME	Time consumed for database accesses (Open SQL and Native SQL).
ENQUEUE TIME	Time for lock requests in relation to the SAP enqueue service.
DB PROCEDURE CALL TIME	Time taken to call database procedures (CALL DATABASE PROCEDURE, see Section 5.3.3).

Table 7.3 Time Components in Transaction STAD

For the most part, the CPU time is generally consumed during the processing time. However, it also occurs in all of the other time components listed in Table 7.3. RFC+CPIC TIME is the time associated with *remote function calls* (RFC). It is consumed during the *processing time* or the *roll-in* and *roll wait time*, depending on whether or not the work process was rolled out. The upper half of the screen shown in Figure 7.11 contains a detailed analysis of the individual times.

Database Times

In the DB view, the DATABASE REQUEST TIME is broken down further. **Access times**
Here, you see how the database time is divided into different access types
SELECT, INSERT, UPDATE, and DELETE). For each access type, you see how
many rows were processed and how much time was needed to process
them. The lower half of Figure 7.11 contains detailed information about
the database.

Database Procedures and Tables

In the DB PROCEDURES and TABLE views, you see those database procedures
and tables that required the most time. The maximum number of procedures and tables displayed here is configured in the profile parameters
stat/dbprocrec and stat/tabrec. The following information is displayed
for each procedure: the name of the procedure, the database connection,
the number of calls, and the time (see Figure 7.12). For tables or views,
you see the name of the table (or view), the number of data records processed, and the time required (see Figure 7.13).

DB procedures (list might be incomplete!)				
DB procedure	Log. DB connection	No. of exec.	Exec. time (ms)	Time / exec. (ms)
"_SYS_BIC"."test.a4h.book.chap	R/3	1	23.137	23.137,0
GET_OBJECT_VERSION	R/3	1	1	1,0

Figure 7.12 STAD: Database Procedures

Table accesses (list might be incomplete!)		Number of rows accessed			
Table name	Total	Dir. reads	Seq. reads	Changes	Time (ms)
TOTAL	429.079	0	429.079	0	3.292
SBOOK	429.079	0	429.079	0	3.292
AAB_ID_ACT	0	0	0	0	0
VARID	0	0	0	0	0

Figure 7.13 STAD: Table Details

Useful Parameters for Transaction STAD

You can use the parameter `stat/max_files` to extend the default analysis time frame of 48 hours up to 99 hours. The detailed data introduced here at table and database procedure level is displayed only if the two parameters `stat/tabrec` and `stat/dbprocrec` are set to values greater than zero. You can use the following path in Transaction ST03 to dynamically change these parameters for a specific time frame: COLLECTOR & PERFORMANCE DB • STATISTIC RECORDS AND FILE • ONLINE PARAMETERS • DIALOG STEP STATISTICS.

7.4.2 ABAP Trace and ABAP Profiler

The *ABAP trace* (Transaction SAT) is a powerful runtime analysis tool for ABAP applications and, as of SAP NetWeaver release 7.02, it is the successor to Transaction SE30. Based on this infrastructure, its new interface (the *ABAP profiler*) forms part of the ABAP development environment in Eclipse. The interface provides developers with a clear results overview, including a graphical representation. In this section, we will introduce you to both variants.

ABAP Trace

Configuration and recording

In order to record the ABAP trace, a measurement variant is configured first and then the trace is recorded. In a measurement variant, you define the following:

▸ What type of recording will take place and for how long (DURATION AND TYPE tab page)?

▸ What will be recorded (STATEMENTS tab page, see Figure 7.14)?

You then use the configured measurement variant to execute the program that will perform the recording.

Analysis

To perform an analysis, double-click a trace on the ANALYZE tab page. Four or six views are available for analysis, depending on whether the trace was created with or without aggregation. All of the views are linked to each other. In other words, you can open the context menu for an event in one view and display this event in another view.

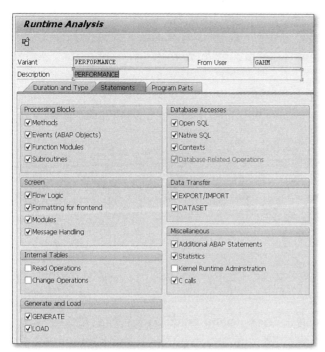

Figure 7.14 Measurement Variant in the ABAP Trace

The following views are available:

▶ HIT LIST
Displays all trace events with details about the number of calls, gross time, and net time. The gross time roughly corresponds to the TOTAL TIME, while the net time corresponds to the OWN TIME associated with the ABAP profiler (see Figure 7.18).

▶ DB TABLES
Displays all accesses to database tables and corresponds to the DATABASE ACCESSES view in the ABAP profiler (see Figure 7.21).

▶ PROFILE
Displays the events according to different profiles. The following views are available for selection: EVENTS, PACKAGES, COMPONENTS, and PROGRAMS.

▶ PROCESSING BLOCKS
Displays an interactive, hierarchical representation of events with details about the gross and net times. The various levels of the call

319

hierarchy can be analyzed arbitrarily. An automatic analysis that displays critical processing blocks is also available here. For example, all modularization units that occupy more than 5 percent of the net time are highlighted.

▶ CALL HIERARCHY
Displays a list of events with details about the call level, gross time, and net time.

▶ TIMES
Displays a detailed list of events whereby the time is further subdivided into components such as database time, database interface time, time for internal tables, and so on.

ABAP Profiler

In this section, we will show you how you can use the ABAP profiler in Eclipse to create an ABAP runtime analysis.

Recording options If you want to use the ABAP profiler to create a trace, choose the PROFILE icon (see Figure 7.15), which starts a trace with default settings. In the dropdown menu for the profile icon, you can use the PROFILE CONFIGURATIONS... menu option to select some recording options. To do this, make the necessary settings on the TRACING tab page and choose PROFILE to confirm your entries (see Figure 7.16).

Figure 7.15 ABAP Profiler with Default Settings

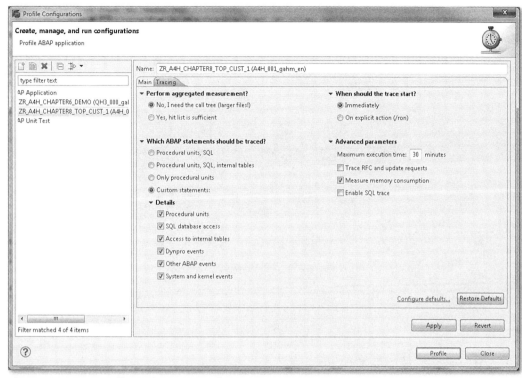

Figure 7.16 ABAP Profiler with a Trace Configuration

The basic settings are summarized in Table 7.4.

Category	Setting	Explanation
How?	PERFORM AGGREGATED MEASUREMENT (YES/NO)?	Defines the level of detail for the recording. This setting has a major impact on the trace scope. The call hierarchy is not available for an aggregated measurement (see Figure 7.19).
When?	WHEN SHOULD THE TRACE START (IMMEDIATELY/ RON)?	Defines whether the trace is to be started immediately or only when an explicit action is performed.

Table 7.4 Settings for the ABAP Profiler

Category	Setting	Explanation
What?	WHICH ABAP STATEMENT SHOULD BE TRACED?	Here, you can configure which calls are to be traced: ▶ Modularization units only ▶ Modularization units and SQL calls ▶ Modularization units, SQL calls, and table accesses
Additional parameters	ADVANCED PARAMETERS	Here, you can make the following additional settings: ▶ Recording duration ▶ Trace RFCs and updates ▶ Record memory consumption ▶ Enable an SQL trace

Table 7.4 Settings for the ABAP Profiler (Cont.)

Trace analysis
If you want to analyze a trace you have created, switch to the ABAP PROFILING perspective. In the lower screen area, update the list on the ABAP TRACES tab page. The system then displays a list of trace files. Double-click to open your trace.

An overview screen is displayed. In the GENERAL INFORMATION area of the screen, you can see what was recorded, and when, where, and how it was recorded. The ANALYSIS TOOLS area contains different detail views, each of which we will explain in greater detail next. Finally, the RUNTIME DISTRIBUTION area provides an initial overview of the runtime. A graphical representation of the amount of time consumed for ABAP statements is shown (for example, processing of internal tables, the database [Open SQL, and so on], and the system [for example, loading processes]). Figure 7.17 shows a representation of a trace in the ABAP profiler.

The overview area shows you the overall runtime and how it's distributed between the database and application server. We'll now explain the various detail views associated with the ABAP profiler.

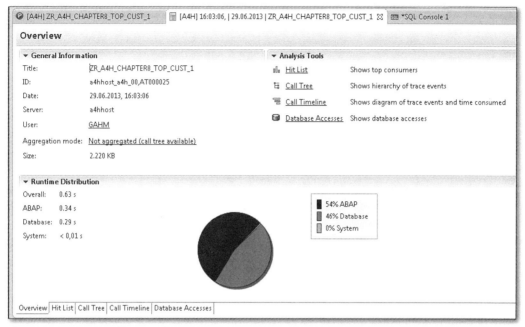

Figure 7.17 ABAP Profiler: Initial Screen

All recorded trace events are displayed in the HIT LIST (see Figure 7.18), which is sorted in descending order according to OWN TIME; that is, the time consumed by the relevant event itself. This time excludes calls that were called within the event and subsequently measured. The TOTAL TIME, on the other hand, includes all calls and specifies the total amount of time consumed by the event itself and the calls executed by the event. The hit list also shows you the frequency with which an event was executed, and the program in which it was called. In the case of calls concerning modularization units, you see which program was called. If you sort this list according to the OWN TIME column, you see the most expensive executions associated with the statements recorded. If you sort this list according to the TOTAL TIME, you see the most expensive modularization units in the program.

Hit list

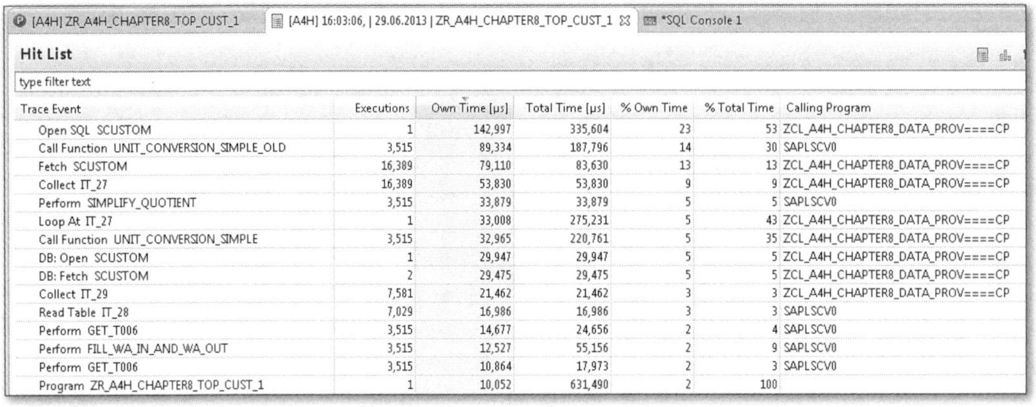

Trace Event	Executions	Own Time [µs]	Total Time [µs]	% Own Time	% Total Time	Calling Program
Open SQL SCUSTOM	1	142,997	335,604	23	53	ZCL_A4H_CHAPTER8_DATA_PROV====CP
Call Function UNIT_CONVERSION_SIMPLE_OLD	3,515	89,334	187,796	14	30	SAPLSCV0
Fetch SCUSTOM	16,389	79,110	83,630	13	13	ZCL_A4H_CHAPTER8_DATA_PROV====CP
Collect IT_27	16,389	53,830	53,830	9	9	ZCL_A4H_CHAPTER8_DATA_PROV====CP
Perform SIMPLIFY_QUOTIENT	3,515	33,879	33,879	5	5	SAPLSCV0
Loop At IT_27	1	33,008	275,231	5	43	ZCL_A4H_CHAPTER8_DATA_PROV====CP
Call Function UNIT_CONVERSION_SIMPLE	3,515	32,965	220,761	5	35	ZCL_A4H_CHAPTER8_DATA_PROV====CP
DB: Open SCUSTOM	1	29,947	29,947	5	5	ZCL_A4H_CHAPTER8_DATA_PROV====CP
DB: Fetch SCUSTOM	2	29,475	29,475	5	5	ZCL_A4H_CHAPTER8_DATA_PROV====CP
Collect IT_29	7,581	21,462	21,462	3	3	ZCL_A4H_CHAPTER8_DATA_PROV====CP
Read Table IT_28	7,029	16,986	16,986	3	3	SAPLSCV0
Perform GET_T006	3,515	14,677	24,656	2	4	SAPLSCV0
Perform FILL_WA_IN_AND_WA_OUT	3,515	12,527	55,156	2	9	SAPLSCV0
Perform GET_T006	3,515	10,864	17,973	2	3	SAPLSCV0
Program ZR_A4H_CHAPTER8_TOP_CUST_1	1	10,052	631,490	2	100	

Figure 7.18 ABAP Profiler: Hit List

Call hierarchy

The *call hierarchy* (also known as the CALL TREE; see Figure 7.19) displays statements in a hierarchy. In other words, you see which statements were called at which level in the call hierarchy. Statements that occur directly within a modularization unit are hidden initially. However, you can choose SHOW to display them. The row ALL STATEMENTS WITHIN PROGRAM... specifies the duration of those statements that were not recorded separately. These times are included in OWN TIME for the modularization unit selected.

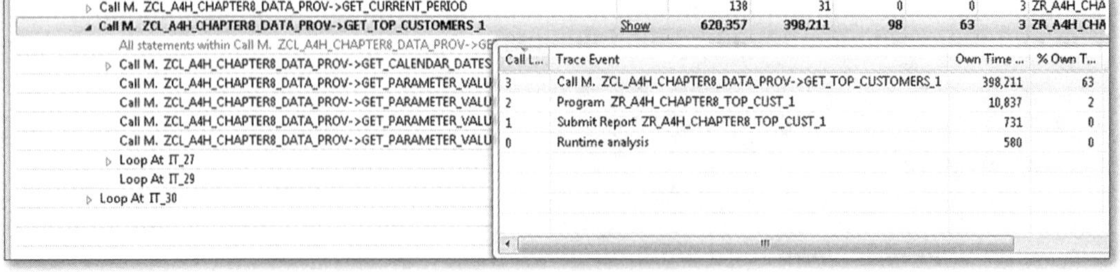

Figure 7.19 ABAP Profiler: Call Hierarchy

The CALL TIMELINE displays the call hierarchy in the form of a timeline (see Figure 7.20). Each call is displayed as a horizontal bar whose length corresponds to the call duration. Calls made within a call are displayed below this bar. The depth of the call hierarchy (known as the *call stack*) is shown from top to bottom. These bars are color-coded according to the call type, thus making it possible for you to identify (for example, database calls) immediately. You can use the black square in the lower area of the graphic to maximize or minimize the area shown. If you move the mouse over a bar, a dialog box displays information about the event, TOTAL TIME, and OWN TIME. When you right-click a bar, you can execute the following actions:

Call timeline

▶ Navigate to the same event in the hit list.

▶ Display the call stack for this event.

▶ Display the event in the database accesses.

▶ Navigate to the call point in the ABAP program.

You can also adjust the color coding used in the diagram.

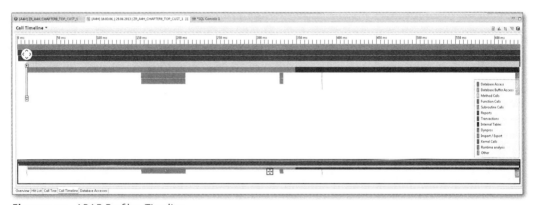

Figure 7.20 ABAP Profiler: Timeline

The DATABASE ACCESSES view shows you which tables were accessed using which statements (see Figure 7.21). Here, you see the number of executions (divided into database accesses and table buffer accesses) and the time required. You also obtain information about the table type, a short description, and the package to which the table is assigned.

Database accesses

| | [A4H] ZR_A4H_CHAPTER8_TOP_CUST_1 | | [A4H] 16:03:06, | 29.06.2013 | ZR_A4H_CHAPTER8_TOP_CUST_1 | | *SQL Console 1 |

Database Accesses [Total Time: 632 ms, Database Time: 290.134 µs (46%)]

type filter text

Table Name	SQL Statement	Access Type	Executions	Buffered Acce...	Positions	Total Time [µs]	% Tota...	Buffer Settings	Table T...	Short Text	Package
SCUSTOM	select	OpenSQL	1	0	1	281,774	44	Single Entries bu	TRANSP	Flight customers	SAPBC_DATAMODEL
SCUSTOM	select single	OpenSQL	10	10	1	5,390	1	Single Entries bu	TRANSP	Flight customers	SAPBC_DATAMODEL
<DB Time of S			0	0	0	2,464	0				
<DB Access fr			2	0	0	134	0				
ZA4H_C8_PAR	select single	OpenSQL	4	4	1	105	0	Entirely buffered	TRANSP	Parameters for miles calcula	TEST_A4H_BOOK_CHAPTER8
T006	select single	OpenSQL	2	2	1	84	0	Generically buff	TRANSP	Units of Measurement	SZME
T009Y	select	OpenSQL	1	1	1	79	0	Generically buff	TRANSP	Shortened fiscal years in Ass	SFBX
T006D	select	OpenSQL	1	1	1	44	0	Entirely buffered	TRANSP	Dimensions	SZME
T009	select single	OpenSQL	1	1	1	34	0	Entirely buffered	TRANSP	Fiscal Year Variants	SFBX
T006A	select single	OpenSQL	1	1	1	26	0	Generically buff	TRANSP	Assign Internal to Language	SZME

Figure 7.21 ABAP Profiler: Database Accesses

7.4.3 SQL Trace

Transaction ST05 contains various functions, one of which—the SQL trace—we wish to examine in greater detail. In Chapter 3, we used the SQL trace to explain how Open SQL is translated to Native SQL statements. In this section, we will explain how to use the SQL trace as a runtime analysis tool.

Recording

On the main screen, select SQL TRACE as the TRACE TYPE. On the right-hand side of the screen, you can also activate a stack trace recording, which enables you to record not only the SQL statement itself, but also information about the call stack. To record an SQL trace, choose ACTIVATE TRACE or ACTIVATE TRACE WITH FILTER. With the first option, the trace is activated for your user. With the second option, you can activate the trace with different filters. Figure 7.22 shows the trace recording with filter options. Execute the program upon activating the trace recording. Choose DEACTIVATE TRACE as soon as the program ends.

Analysis

To display the trace, choose DISPLAY TRACE. In the next dialog box, the filters are predefined in accordance with the settings for the recording. In other words, you generally do not have to change anything here if you want to display the trace immediately after the recording. However, if you want to display the trace at a later time or you want to display a trace associated with another user, you must ensure the following:

► You are logged on to the server on which the trace was saved.

► The filters for the user and time frame correspond to those for the trace recording.

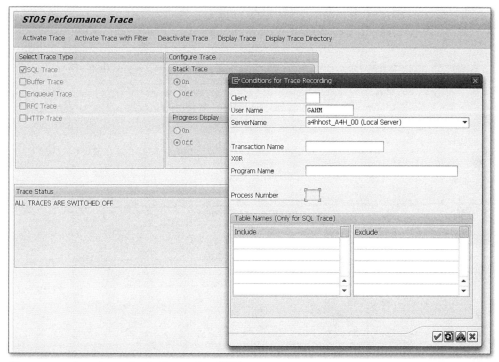

Figure 7.22 Trace Recording in Transaction ST05

You can choose between different views by clicking the relevant icon on the upper screen border (see Figure 7.23).

The following views are available, which you can select using the icons located on the upper screen border:

► SUMMARIZED STATEMENTS
Here, an SQL statement corresponds to a row in the trace. In other words, detailed information such as OPEN, FETCH, and CLOSE are aggregated into one row.

From this list, you can navigate to a list of detailed statements, a list of identical statements, or an aggregated view for each table.

▶ DETAILED STATEMENTS

Here, you see all of the calls that were sent to the database. An SQL statement is displayed, for example, in an OPEN statement, one or more FETCH statements, or a CLOSE statement.

▶ STRUCTURE-IDENTICAL SUMMARY

All SQL statements with an identical structure are summarized here. Therefore, if there are similar SQL statements at different call points within a program, these are displayed in aggregated form.

▶ TRACE OVERVIEW

A summary of the entire SQL trace is shown here.

▶ SAVE

In addition, a function is available for saving the SQL trace in the database.

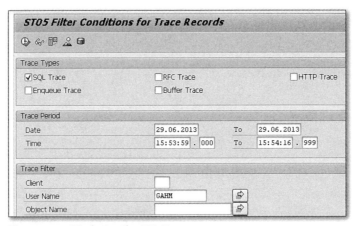

Figure 7.23 Displaying the SQL Trace

Next, we will show you the structure-identical summary and an analysis of the call hierarchy (*stack trace*).

Structure-identical statements

First, display the structure-identical statements (see Figure 7.24). We recommend that you start your analysis with this list because it provides you with the best overview of the most expensive SQL statements. You see which statement had the longest duration overall, the frequency with which it was executed, and whether there were redundant accesses (known as *identical selects*). This information is made available to you both in absolute figures and as a percentage. You also see all execution times (for each execution and data record), and the number of data records—both in total and for each execution. Finally, you obtain buffering information from the ABAP Data Dictionary.

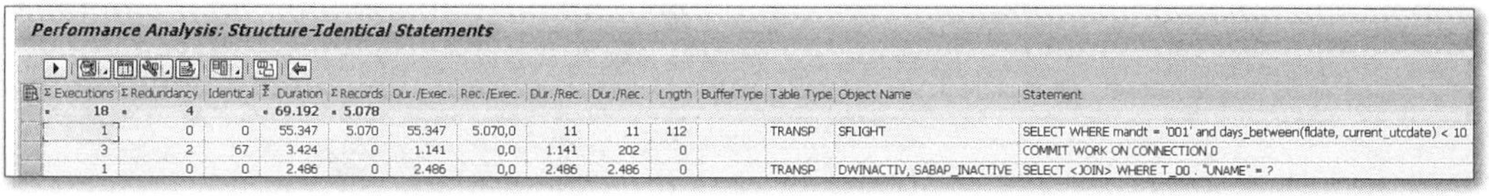

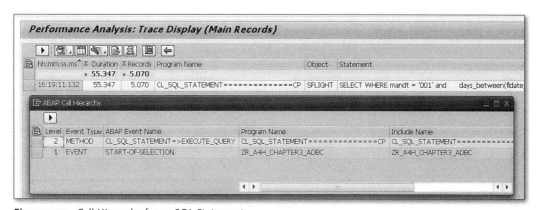

Figure 7.24 Structure-Identical Statements

If you double-click the number of executions, you branch to a list of sum-marized STATEMENTS. Here, one row corresponds to one execution. You can display the call hierarchy for this execution. The ABAP call stack for this statement is then displayed in a dialog box (see Figure 7.25). This function is very helpful in the case of ADBC calls, for example. The SQL statement is first executed in the ADBC classes, while the actual execu-tion occurs at a higher level in the call stack. The stack trace enables you to navigate to any level within the call stack. To do this, double-click the relevant row.

Stack trace

Figure 7.25 Call Hierarchy for an SQL Statement

If you want to display identical selects from within the list of summarized statements, select the menu option TRACE • VALUE-IDENTICAL STATEMENTS.

Identical selects

Here, you see those statements that are executed repeatedly in the WHERE condition with exactly the same values. You also see their duration and the number of data records that were read.

Statement details If you double-click the text for a SQL statement contained in the list of summarized statements, you see the entire statement as well as the parameters used to execute the statement.

[!] **Overwriting Trace Data**

The SQL trace is a part of the database interface and is therefore specific to a particular application server. The trace itself is written to files on the relevant application server. These files have a size restriction. Therefore, if all of the files are full, the first file is overwritten again. If traces are very large, data may be overwritten in this way. If this situation arises, you are notified (in Transaction ST05) that some files may have been overwritten. To avoid this, you can also save the contents of the files to the database before they are overwritten.

7.4.4 Single Transaction Analysis

Transaction ST12 combines Transactions SAT, ST05, and STAD into one interface and, thanks to this combination, offers some advantages in terms of recording and analyzing traces during a performance analysis.

Requirements Transaction ST12 is an additional development within the context of service tools for applications (ST-A/PI). SAP Active Global Support makes this software available as an add-on, and SAP Note 69455 explains how to obtain and import this software. This software package does not form part of the standard SAP delivery. It is not formally documented and is only available in English. SAP Active Global Support originally developed Transaction ST12 for their own use within the context of the services they offer. Essentially, however, all SAP customers can use this transaction.

Advantages The following advantages are associated with combining the various transactions into one interface:

▶ During an analysis, the ABAP trace and SQL trace can be activated together and then deactivated. If you do not know which application server is associated with a particular request, you can start the recording on all application servers simultaneously.

▶ The trace data and the data from Transaction STAD are collected and stored in the database, thus making subsequent analyses easier because all the data is stored in one central location and is no longer overwritten.

▶ The trace data can be combined with other data. For example, in the ABAP trace for a SELECT statement, you can display related data from Transaction ST05. For data from Transaction ST05, you can specify which percentage of the overall runtime can be attributed to a SELECT statement. You can also call the Code Inspector for individual results.

▶ In the case of ABAP traces, additional functions (which are not possible in Transaction SAT) are available for analyzing aggregated traces. For example, it is possible to draw conclusions about call hierarchies.

If you perform a large number of performance analyses, single transaction analysis can offer some advantages over the standard delivery. Further information is available in SAP Note 7559777 and in the SCN: *http://wiki. sdn.sap.com/wiki/display/ABAP/Single+Transaction+Analysis.*

7.4.5   Explain Plan

The EXPLAIN PLAN is a database function that can be used to display an execution plan, which is a textual or graphical description of how an SQL statement was executed. The database optimizer always creates this description when the function is executed. The decision made by the optimizer is based on the system status at the time when the plan was created.

You can call the EXPLAIN PLAN from various locations (for example, in the SQL trace in Transaction ST05 or in the EXPENSIVE STATEMENTS or SQL CACHE areas in Transaction DBACOCKPIT). This function is also available in SAP HANA Studio. Here, for example, the EXPLAIN PLAN is available in the SQL console.

To call the execution plan in SAP HANA Studio, proceed as follows: Enter an SQL statement in the SQL console and right-click to select the EXPLAIN PLAN function in the context menu for the statement.

From an analysis perspective, the following columns are of interest:

▶ OPERATOR NAME
Name of the operation executed (for example, access to a column table, row table, or join).

▶ OPERATOR DETAILS
Additional information about the operation (for example, filter or join conditions).

▶ TABLE NAME
Name of the database object referenced by the operator.

▶ EXECUTION_ENGINE
The engine that executes the operator.

▶ SCHEMA_NAME
Name of the database schema.

▶ TABLE_TYPE
The type of table used (for example, a column table, row table, OLAP view, calculation view, and so on).

▶ TABLE_SIZE
Estimated size of the table for this step (the number of rows in the case of column tables, or the number of pages in the case of row tables).

▶ OUTPUT_SIZE
Estimated number of rows for the result set associated with this step.

A sample execution plan output is shown in Figure 7.26. A graphical variant of the execution plan is also available, which we'll discuss in Section 7.4.6. In the execution plan, you can see how an SQL statement is executed (in particular, which engine is responsible for which parts of the execution). If you require a more in-depth look at the execution details, you can use SAP HANA PlanViz (see the next section).

Figure 7.26 Explain Plan in SAP HANA Studio

7.4.6 SAP HANA Plan Visualizer

SAP HANA Plan Visualizer (PlanViz) provides a graphical representation of an SQL statement or database procedure execution. You can also execute the statement and collect runtime data here, provided that you have the required permissions.

If you want to use PlanViz to analyze an SQL statement or procedure, open the SQL console and insert the statement (or procedure) that you want to analyze. Choose VISUALIZE PLAN in the context menu for the SQL console. The anticipated execution plan is then displayed on the VISUALIZED PLAN tab page. Here, you see nodes (known as *plan operators* in technical terms), which are connected to each other by means of arrows and provide information about the estimated number of data records for the call. The parentheses around these numbers indicate that they are estimates. In the context menu, choose EXECUTE to execute the query. If the SQL statement contains parameters, the PREPARED SQL tab page is displayed after you choose EXECUTE. Specify the necessary input parameters here. The return parameter fields are left blank. Then, choose the EXECUTE icon ⊙ on the upper right screen border. Runtime data is collected internally and presented in a graphic on the EXECUTION tab page as soon as the query has ended.

The execution view contains various execution nodes, which are connected to each other by means of arrows. These, in turn, represent the flow of data from one node to another. The volume of data actually transferred is displayed at the arrow itself, followed by the estimated

Recording

Analysis

333

volume of data transferred in parentheses. Here, you can see the extent to which the estimated volume of data corresponds to the volume of data actually transferred. The nodes also contain additional information about tables, columns, filters, execution times, and CPU times. You can use the icon displayed on the upper right border of a node ▸ to open the relevant node.

Timeline

The *timeline* is a very helpful tool. To display it, proceed as follows: In the menu WINDOW • SHOW VIEW • OTHER..., select TIMELINE under PLAN VISUALIZER and choose OK to confirm your entry.

In the timeline, each node is displayed as a bar, and the length of the bar corresponds to the runtime for that particular node. You therefore easily see the start time, runtime, and end time associated with executing the node. You also see which nodes were processed parallel to one other.

If you move the mouse over a node in the main screen, a dialog box opens to reveal detailed information that has been recorded for the node. Depending on the node, this box contains different values, such as the execution time and CPU time, information about tables, columns, and filters, as well as the degree of parallelization for a node.

Analyzing a database procedure

Finally, we will show you how to analyze a database procedure. We will do this using the sample procedure GET_DATA_FOR_TOP_CONNECTIONS, which you learned about in Section 5.1.1. Three additional procedures, namely DETERMINE_TOP_CONNECTIONS, GET_KPIS_FOR_CONNECTIONS, and GET_AGENCIES_FOR_CONNECTIONS, will be called within this procedure.

To analyze the main procedure, enter the following call in the SQL console (please note that '001' stands for the client; if you use a different client, please change this entry accordingly):

```
call "test.a4h.book.chapter05::GET_DATA_FOR_TOP_
CONNECTIONS"('001', 'LH', ?, ?)
```

Call VISUALIZE PLAN in the context menu for the SQL console. On the VISUALIZED PLAN tab page, choose EXECUTE in the context menu (see Figure 7.27).

Figure 7.27 PlanViz: Recording

The PREPARED SQL tab page is displayed here because the return parameter variables for the procedure are specified in the call. However, since they are return parameters, no data is specified here. Choose EXECUTE or press F8 to start the analysis (see Figure 7.28).

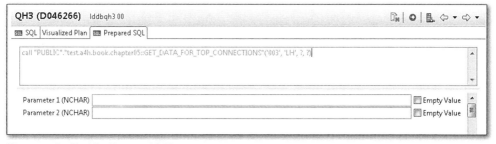

Figure 7.28 PlanViz: Prepared SQL

The execution is displayed on the next tab page. Here, expand the first node by choosing the icon ⬛ in the upper right corner of the node.

In Figure 7.29, you see that the first node is a CELJIT POP, which calls a sub-execution node. In the detail view for this node, you ascertain that it concerns the procedure DETERMINE_TOP_CONNECTIONS, whose runtime is 65.587 milliseconds.

Runtime for individual procedures

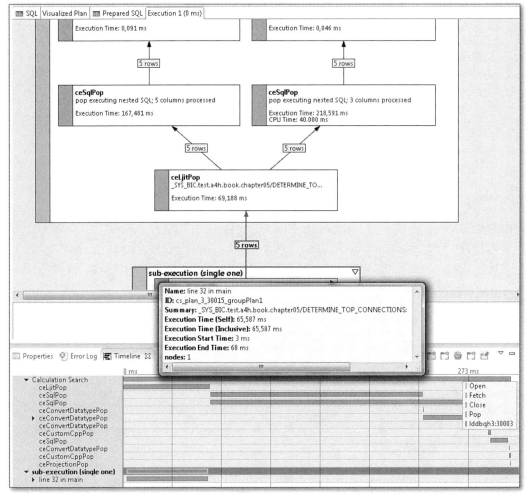

Figure 7.29 PlanViz: Analysis

Once you have completed this procedure, the results are transferred to two additional nodes that run parallel to one other. This becomes apparent if you select both nodes and take a look at their bars in the timeline. The two blue bars start at the same time and run for approximately the same length of time (see Figure 7.30).

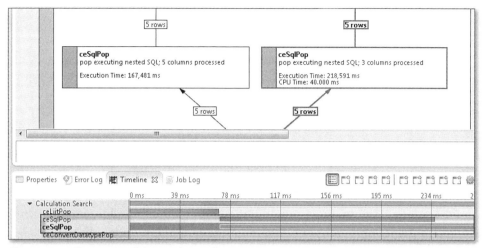

Figure 7.30 PlanViz: Parallel Procedure Calls

In the detailed information for each node, you see that it concerns two procedures, namely GET_KPIS_FOR_CONNECTIONS and GET_AGENCIES_FOR_ CONNECTIONS. You also see the duration of each execution. All of the above enables you to analyze a procedure execution in more detail.

The node name enables you to draw conclusions in relation to the engine or process in which the node is executed. For example, CE stands for calculation engine, BW for the OLAP engine, and JE for the join engine. You also see which type of operation it concerns (for example, aggregation, sorting, and so on).

Processing engines

7.5 System-Wide SQL Analyses

System-wide SQL analyses help you to identify expensive SQL statements in the entire system. At first, you do not require any information about the application. During the optimization process, however, you may find such information helpful or even necessary. In this section, we will show you how to conduct such analyses in the DBA cockpit. You will also learn about two new transactions for system-wide SQL analyses, which are available as of SAP NetWeaver AS ABAP 7.4.

7.5.1 DBA Cockpit

The DBA cockpit contains all the functions needed for database moni-toring and database administration. Here, you find an overview of the current database status as well as error messages and warnings. Functions are also available for the following: performance analysis, configuration, database jobs, diagnostics, and system information. These are a subset of the functions available in SAP HANA Studio for analyzing the HANA database. In some cases, however, the DBA cockpit contains advanced functions that are not available in SAP HANA Studio (for example, direct navigation to the ABAP source code).

Overview and alerts

The OVERVIEW screen provides information about the current database status. Here, you see, for example, the current CPU and memory consump-tion in the database. Current warnings are displayed on the ALERTS screen.

Performance

In the PERFORMANCE area, various views containing different database statistics are displayed under STATISTICS SERVER. Under THREADS, you see those threads that are currently active on the database. The EXPENSIVE STATEMENTS view contains a list of SQL statements if this particular trace is activated, while the SQL CACHE area displays aggregated information about the SQL statements that have been executed. This information is taken from the SQL cache in the database. All executed SQL statements are stored in the SQL cache and the runtime data associated with these statements is entered there. If, however, some data is displaced due to a lack of space or because new SQL statements are created, the data may be incomplete. In other words, only some of the execution data created since the database started is available. We will take a closer look at these two functions.

Configuration

The CONFIGURATION area contains information about the LANDSCAPE and SERVICES available. It also contains information about trace configurations, configuration files, and database files.

Diagnostics

The DIAGNOSTICS area contains a range of expert functions, some of which we wish to describe here. The SQL EDITOR can be used to execute read-only SQL statements. Queries in relation to monitoring views and application tables can be executed in this way if the relevant authorization exists. The TABLES/VIEWS area contains the definition and runtime information for database objects. Here, you can use the PROCEDURES function to also view the database procedures available. The DIAGNOSIS FILES and MERGED DIAGNOSIS FILES areas enable you to view important trace and diagnosis files in the database, and to merge them together to arrange information from different files in chronological order. You can use the BACKUP CATALOG function to view information about database backups. Here, you also find various pieces of information about locks and other different trace CE Plan Operators, which we will not describe in greater detail here.

In the SYSTEM INFORMATION area, you can query different monitoring views. Information about connections, transactions, caches, large tables, memory, and the SQL workload is available here.

System information

Now we will show you how you can use the overview, threads, SQL cache, and the expensive statement trace in the DBA cockpit to analyze the load on the HANA database.

In the upper area of the overview (GENERAL SYSTEM INFORMATION), you see whether all of the database services are active and when they were started. You also see whether it concerns a distributed system. Furthermore, you obtain information about the database version and operating system. In the upper right area, you see whether there are current alerts. If there are, you can click the information displayed here to navigate directly to the alerts.

ST04—overview

The middle and lower areas of the overview contain information about the current load on the main memory and CPU (on the basis of the database and the host on which the database is running). These areas also contain information about the hard drive or data, log, and trace areas. All of this information is based on the time when you called the overview or chose UPDATE. This information is shown in Figure 7.31.

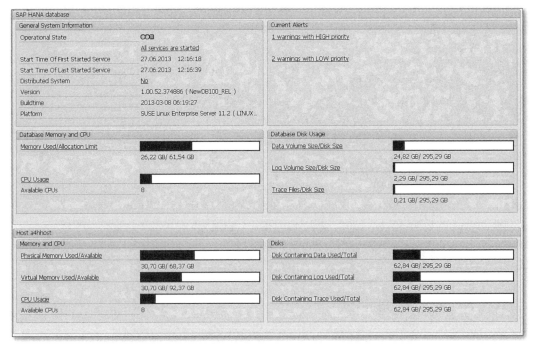

Figure 7.31 ST04: Overview

Threads In the THREADS area, you see which threads are active in the database. This area also contains information about the service, type, and method executed. The recently executed SQL statement, previous runtime, caller, and the name of the user who executed the statement are displayed. An example of a thread is shown in Figure 7.32.

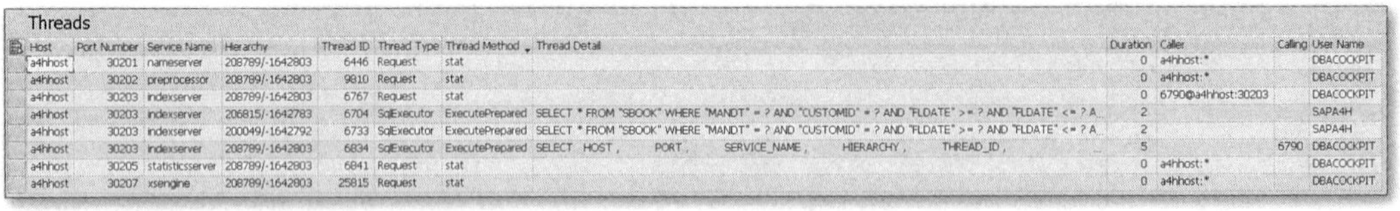

Figure 7.32 ST04: Threads

SQL cache In the upper area of the SQL cache, you can specify filters for the SQL statements to be displayed (see Figure 7.33).

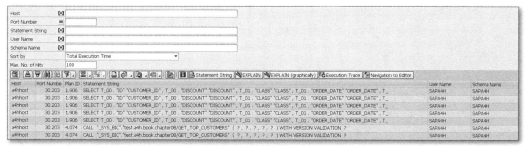

Figure 7.33 SQL Cache

You can execute the following functions for each SQL statement:

Functions

▸ STATEMENT STRING: Displays the entire SQL statement.

▸ EXPLAIN: Displays the execution plan as a piece of text.

▸ EXPLAIN (GRAPHICALLY): Displays the execution plan graphically.

▸ EXECUTION TRACE: Generates a file that can be analyzed further using PlanViz (see Section 7.4.6) in SAP HANA Studio. This works for `SELECT` statements only, which the trace executes in the background if the relevant authorizations exist.

▸ NAVIGATION TO EDITOR: Displays the call point of the ABAP program within the program.

The SQL cache contains an entry for each unique SQL string. Therefore, different call points within ABAP programs can be aggregated into one entry if they concern exactly the same SQL statement. A large amount of information can be retrieved for each entry (for example, the number of executions, the execution times, the number of data records transferred, the time when the last execution was performed, and the times relating to database locks).

Information in the SQL cache

The EXPENSIVE STATEMENTS view contains similar functions to the SQL cache, but works according to the trace principle. In other words, you must configure which SQL statements you want to record (for example, all SQL statements that take longer than three seconds to execute). Such statements are written to a restricted memory area within the database. Whenever this area is full, old entries are simply overwritten, so space is always available. This particular function has the advantage over the SQL cache in that individual statements that satisfy the configuration criteria are

Expensive statements

341

recorded without needing to be aggregated. Therefore, information about the application user (the user in the SAP system) is also available here.

7.5.2 SQL Monitor

The SQL Monitor (Transaction SQLM) is a new development that is available as of SAP NetWeaver AS ABAP 7.4 and will be made available for release 7.00 and above (see SAP Note 1885926). The basic idea of the SQL Monitor is to collect, aggregate, and persist runtime information about SQL statements in the database interface (DBI).

The SQL cache in the database provides database-specific information about the SQL statement (for example, the number of pages read or the I/O and CPU times required), but information about the ABAP program and the call context in which the statement was executed is available in the SQL Monitor. Consequently, these two data sources complement each other and provide specific additional information about SQL statements. In this section, we will show you how to activate the SQL Monitor and explain which data is collected.

Recording To launch the SQL Monitor, call Transaction SQLM. Here, you can activate the SQL Monitor on every application server or on specific application servers only. You can also define the period in which the recording will take place (default setting: one week). Figure 7.34 shows the initial screen of the SQL Monitor after it has been activated.

Once activated, data is collected and aggregated for each SQL statement executed. The data is collected in the main memory and written asynchronously to a database table. It is then made available for analysis in Transaction SQLM approximately one hour after the recording. In order to minimize the effects that these measurements have on the runtime, the data is made available in a background job.

Analysis To analyze the data, choose DISPLAY DATA. The selection screen shown in Figure 7.35 is displayed. Here, you can filter data according to the following information:

▶ PACKAGE (software package)

▶ OBJECT TYPE (program, function module, and so on)

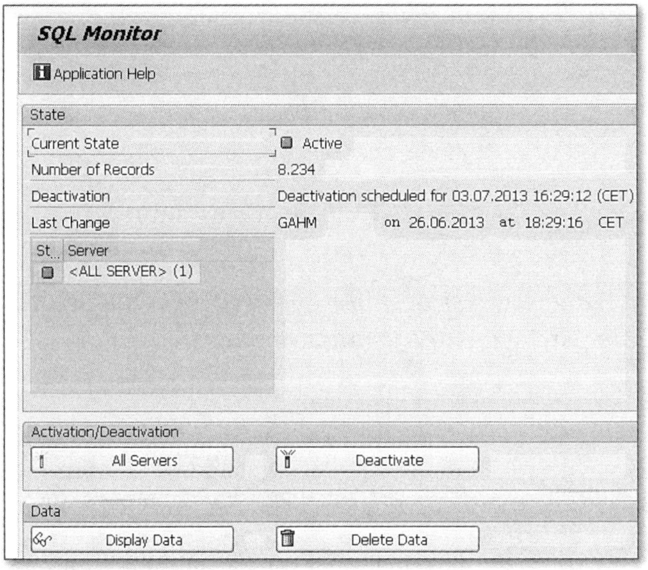

Figure 7.34 SQL Monitor: Activation

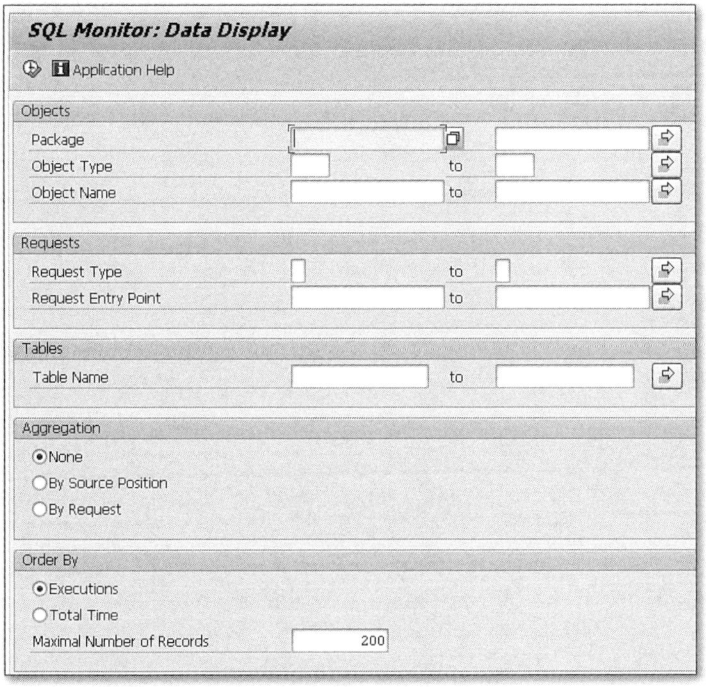

Figure 7.35 SQL Monitor Analysis

▶ OBJECT NAME (name of the object)

▶ REQUEST TYPE (type of entry point)

▶ REQUEST ENTRY POINT (name of the entry point)

▶ TABLE NAME (name of the table)

You can display and sort the analysis list in aggregated form, as well as restrict the number of data records displayed.

Entry point The entry point is the first entry in the ABAP call hierarchy that is deemed to be of semantic importance. Entry points can include transactions, RFC modules, URLs, or ABAP reports.

Example: A program ZR_A4H_CHAPTER8_TOP_CUST calls a method of the class ZCL_A4H_CHAPTER8_DATA_PROV in which a SELECT statement is executed. The object name for this statement is ZCL_A4H_CHAPTER8_DATA_PROV, while the program ZR_A4H_CHAPTER8_TOP_CUST is the entry point. Without this entry point, it may not be possible to establish a reference to the ABAP report, nor to assign the SQL statement to a business process. If a function module now calls this method via a remote function call (RFC), a new entry is created and receives the object name ZCL_A4H_CHAPTER8_DATA_PROV. Furthermore, its entry point bears the name of the RFC function module. Consequently, SELECT statements can easily be assigned to a business process—even if they are called in modularization units, which do not recognize such an assignment.

Result list The result list contains the following information:

▶ Number of executions

▶ Time consumed (total, average, maximum, minimum, and standard deviation)

▶ Data records (total, average, maximum, minimum, and standard deviation)

▶ Table name (in the case of joins, the tables are stored in a list, separated by commas)

▶ Information about the object (type, name, and include)

▶ Main program (type and name)

- Number of sessions and executions per session
- Information about the program, package, and modularization unit

The fields Int. Sess. and Exe./Se... enable you to analyze the number of executions in greater detail. Here, you see whether the total number equates to one program run (session) in which the same statement is executed several times (sessions = 1, number of executions per session = 1,000) or to a large number of sessions in which the statement is executed once in each session (sessions = 1,000, number of executions per session = 1). Figure 7.36 shows a sample result list in the SQL Monitor.

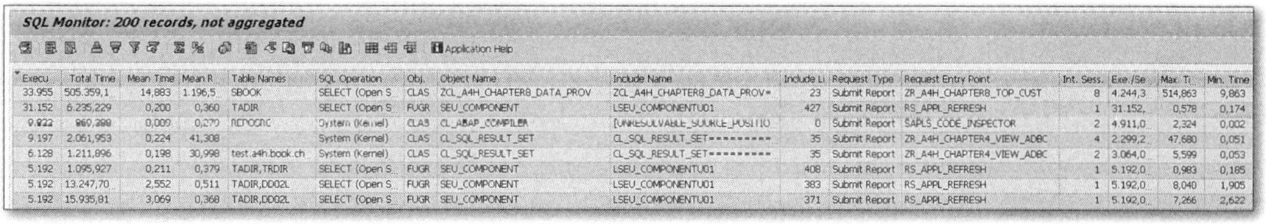
SQL Monitor: 200 records, not aggregated

Execu	Total Time	Mean Time	Mean R	Table Names	SQL Operation	Obj.	Object Name	Include Name	Include Li	Request Type	Request Entry Point	Int. Sess.	Exe./Se	Max. Ti	Min. Time
33.955	505.359,1	14,883	1.196,5	SBOOK	SELECT (Open S	CLAS	ZCL_A4H_CHAPTER8_DATA_PROV	ZCL_A4H_CHAPTER8_DATA_PROV=	23	Submit Report	ZR_A4H_CHAPTER8_TOP_CUST	8	4.244,3	514,863	9,863
31.152	6.235,229	0,200	0,360	TADIR	SELECT (Open S	FUGR	SEU_COMPONENT	LSEU_COMPONENTU01	427	Submit Report	RS_APPL_REFRESH	1	31.152,	0,578	0,174
9.822	860,288	0,009	0,279	REPOSRC	System (Kernel)	CLAS	CL_ABAP_COMPILER	[UNRESOLVABLE_SOURCE_POSITIO	0	Submit Report	SAPLS_CODE_INSPECTOR	2	4.911,0	2,324	0,002
9.197	2.061,953	0,224	41,308		System (Kernel)	CLAS	CL_SQL_RESULT_SET	CL_SQL_RESULT_SET=========	35	Submit Report	ZR_A4H_CHAPTER4_VIEW_ADBC	4	2.299,2	47,680	0,051
6.128	1.211,896	0,198	30,998	test.a4h.book.ch	System (Kernel)	CLAS	CL_SQL_RESULT_SET	CL_SQL_RESULT_SET=========	35	Submit Report	ZR_A4H_CHAPTER4_VIEW_ADBC	2	3.064,0	5,599	0,053
5.192	1.095,927	0,211	0,379	TADIR,TRDIR	SELECT (Open S	FUGR	SEU_COMPONENT	LSEU_COMPONENTU01	408	Submit Report	RS_APPL_REFRESH	1	5.192,0	0,983	0,185
5.192	13.247,70	2,552	0,511	TADIR,DD02L	SELECT (Open S	FUGR	SEU_COMPONENT	LSEU_COMPONENTU01	383	Submit Report	RS_APPL_REFRESH	1	5.192,0	8,040	1,905
5.192	15.935,81	3,069	0,368	TADIR,DD02L	SELECT (Open S	FUGR	SEU_COMPONENT	LSEU_COMPONENTU01	371	Submit Report	RS_APPL_REFRESH	1	5.192,0	7,266	2,622

Figure 7.36 SQLM: Result List

Points of reference for analyses

You can use this information to conduct some interesting analyses. The following examples serve to give you some points of reference:

- Which statements took the longest to execute (sorted according to time)?
- Which statements were executed most often (a large number of sessions or a large number of executions per session)?
- Which statements were executed directly within a specific function module (for example, `ZFUNC2`) (selection according to the object name `ZFUNC2`)?
- Which statements were called directly within and below a specific function module (for example, `ZFUNC2`) and by other function modules, methods or programs called by the function module (selection according to the main program = `ZFUNC2`)?
- Which statements relating to customer tables were called within and below a specific transaction (for example, `VA01`) (selection according to the main program = `VA01` and table name = `Z*`)?

▶ Which programs accessed a specific table (for example, ZTAB1) (selection according to the table name ZTAB1)?

Advantages of the SQL Monitor Since the data in the SQL Monitor is periodically stored in a database table, no data is displaced here (which is the case with the SQL cache). You can link the data in the SQL Monitor to the results of a static code analysis, thus providing runtime information for the static check results. Consequently, it quickly becomes apparent where an optimization would be most beneficial. We will show you how to do this in Section 7.6.

The SQL Monitor is a very powerful tool for determining an SQL profile for an application or an entire system. For each call point, an entry is created for each table and main program. Since the data is written asynchronously to the database tables, performance is not negatively affected. Furthermore, no information is lost and the additional information makes it possible to draw more accurate conclusions in relation to the ABAP program and the context in which it was executed.

7.6 SQL Performance Optimization

The SQL performance optimization tool (known as the *SQL Performance Tuning Worklist*, Transaction SWLT) is a new development that is available as of SAP NetWeaver AS ABAP 7.4. It can be used to combine data from a static code analysis (for example, the data associated with a check run in the ABAP Test Cockpit) with runtime measurements from the SQL Monitor. This enables you to quickly identify where an optimization would be most promising for SAP HANA.

Linking data from SQLM and SCI In Section 7.3, you learned how to perform static code analyses and, in Section 7.5.2, we explained how to use Transaction SQLM to collect data. These two pools of data are now linked to each other in Transaction SWLT.

To do this, choose MANAGE SNAPSHOTS in Transaction SWLT to generate a snapshot of the SQL Monitor. The following options are available:

▶ Online snapshot of the SQL Monitor from the local system or a system connected via an RFC.

▶ Reading a snapshot from a file that was created using the SQL Monitor and the DOWNLOAD DATA function.

You can make additional data settings here. For example, you can choose whether you want to use results from the Code Inspector or the ABAP Test Cockpit. To do this, choose SELECT INSPECTION (see Figure 7.37).

Selecting source tools

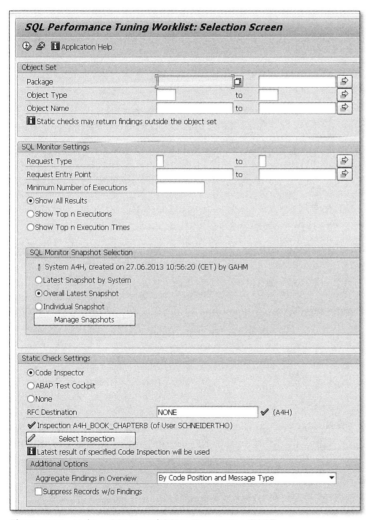

Figure 7.37 Linking SQLM and SCI in Transaction SWLT

Here, you can also access the local system directly, or access a remote system by means of an RFC. You should select a check variant that contains all the necessary performance checks. Choose SUPPRESS RECORDS W/O FINDINGS, so it only displays data records that originate in the SQL Monitor and for which there is also a message in the Code Inspector. If you wish, you can make additional restrictions in the upper screen area. These functions correspond to those associated with the SQL Monitor. Choose EXECUTE to start the analysis. Make sure the snapshot of the SQL Monitor covers a relevant period in the production system so that it contains all key processes.

The SQL Performance Tuning Worklist can also be used to link the data from the SQL Monitor with data from the *Coverage Analyzer,* which records ABAP program usage. You can also display the data from the SQL Monitor without linking it to any other data. During the selection, the data from both data sources are linked to one another by means of a join that is based on the call point (object, include, or row).

Analysis The result list comprises a screen that is divided into three sections (see Figure 7.38). The upper area contains the data from the SQL Monitor. As soon as you double-click a data record in the upper area, the data is filled in the lower screen areas. If you select an entry in the INCLUDE NAME column, you navigate directly to the call point in the ABAP program.

▶ In the list on the lower left-hand side of the screen, you see the relevant caller for the SQL statement (REQUEST ENTRY POINT, first program in the ABAP call hierarchy) and the most important measurement readings for this from the SQL Monitor. When you select the table name, you call Transaction SE12 (ABAP Data Dictionary) for this table.

▶ In the list on the lower right-hand side of the screen, you see the consolidated results from the Code Inspector and the ABAP Test Cockpit. From here, you can call the documentation for the check, or you can select the entry in the ADDITIONAL INFORMATION column to navigate directly to detailed information about the results in the Code Inspector or the ABAP Test Cockpit.

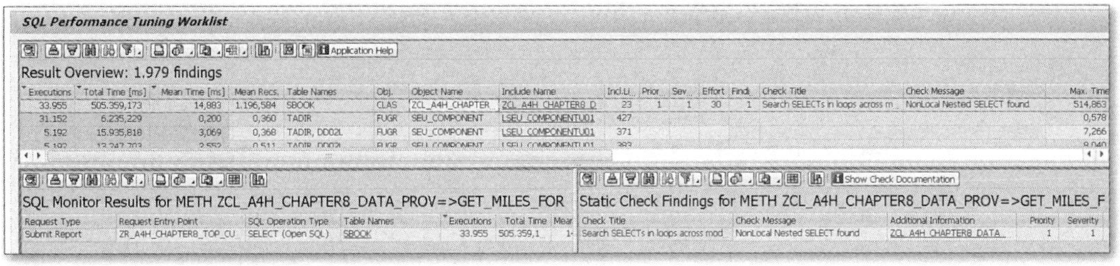

Figure 7.38 Analysis in Transaction SWLT

Compared to the SQL Monitor, the main result list contains some additional columns. From the ABAP Data Dictionary, you obtain the following information for the database tables:

Data from the ABAP Data Dictionary

▶ BUFFERING TYPE: Buffering type associated with the table

▶ COLUMNS: Number of columns in the table

▶ KEY COLUMNS: Number of key columns

▶ WIDTH IN BYTES: Row length in bytes

▶ STORAGE TYPE: Table type (COLUMN STORE and ROW STORE)

▶ SIZE CATEGORY: Size category for the table

▶ TABLE CLASS: Table type (TRANSPARENT, POOL, and CLUSTER)

You also obtain information about the Code Inspector checks:

Information from the Code Inspector

▶ PRIORITY: The priority of the message as configured in the Code Inspector.

▶ SEVERITY: This value depends on the relevant check. (For more information, refer to the documentation for the Code Inspector.) It specifies the severity of the result. In the case of the SELECT * check, this column specifies how many superfluous columns were read. In general, the following applies: The higher this value, the greater the negative impact on performance.

▶ EFFORT: This value depends on the relevant check (see the documentation for the Code Inspector) and is an estimate of the effort associated with the correction. In general, the following applies: The higher this value, the greater the effort.

▶ FINDINGS: Number of Code Inspector results for this SQL statement.

You can use these columns to compare the results and prioritize where an optimization would be most beneficial.

The SQL Performance Tuning Worklist is a very powerful tool and can be used to plan optimization projects for SAP HANA very efficiently. If SQL statements are assigned to main programs, they can also be assigned to business processes. Runtime measurements show which SQL statements require a large amount of time or run very frequently. The static analysis shows where there is potential for optimization and how time-consuming such an optimization would be. Combining this data into one transaction is extremely useful for detecting the source code with the best cost-benefit ratio for applying optimizations.

By optimizing existing ABAP programs, significant performance gains may be achieved. ABAP developers should be able to identify programs that are suitable candidates for optimization and then modify them in such a way that they benefit from the SAP HANA architecture.

8 Sample Scenario: Optimizing an Existing Application

In the previous chapters, we described the basic principles of the in-memory technology and ABAP development on SAP HANA. You now know how portions of the application logic (especially complex calculations with large amounts of data) can be moved to the database layer. In addition, you learned which tools the SAP NetWeaver AS ABAP provides to identify optimization potentials in programs.

This chapter now deals with combining and using the individual techniques and tools in a first sample scenario. In this example, a given application is to be optimized for SAP HANA.

This chapter is divided into three parts. We'll start with a description of the necessary steps to optimize systems and applications. In the second part, the sample scenario and optimization requirements are introduced. To conclude the chapter, you'll learn how to optimize the sample program. In this part, we won't explain every step in detail, but focus on the most important excerpts that are relevant for optimization. You can download the application and its source code in the download area for this book at *www.sap-press.com* (see Appendix E).

8.1 Optimization Procedure

This section describes the general procedure in optimization projects. We differentiate between the following scenarios:

► Migration to SAP HANA

► System optimization

► Application optimization

Every scenario has a different focus and different roles of responsibility. For every scenario, the most important tools are listed and described. Some tools are used in several scenarios, with a different focus in each case.

8.1.1 Migrating to SAP HANA

When performing a migration to SAP HANA, you want to make sure that all programs continue to run as before. Moreover, you might want to identify optimization potential with regard to database access before or during the migration, and implement the necessary adjustments. These tasks are mainly the responsibility of ABAP developers and quality managers for ABAP programs. In addition, it may be necessary that process owners work with these employees to prioritize possible performance optimizations based on the importance of the respective business process.

Steps for analyzing and optimizing ABAP code

When migrating to SAP HANA, the following steps are necessary to analyze and possibly modify or optimize ABAP code:

► Collect respective data information

► Analyze ABAP code (in combination with the collected data)

► Prioritize the applications identified as relevant for optimization

► Adjust the programs accordingly

Data collection

You should examine the coding statically and combine the analysis results with runtime data to facilitate prioritization, so the first step is to schedule a data collection. To do this, activate the SQL Monitor in the production system for a period of time where all important business processes are run (see Section 7.5.2). For the month-end closing processes to be considered, this time period should contain at least one period end. We recommend a time period of at least six weeks.

Running the checks

While collecting the data, you can simultaneously use the SAP Code Inspector and the ABAP Test Cockpit to analyze ABAP code. When doing so, a distinction is made between functional checks and performance checks (see Section 7.3.1). Run the tests on a development system that has developments and coding that are comparable to the production system.

We recommend that you prioritize the results of the performance checks based on their importance in the business process, the impact on the system, and the required effort for the optimizations. For prioritization, combine the results of the ABAP code analysis with the runtime data in the SQL performance optimization tool:

Prioritization

▶ The Code Inspector provides information on the SQL statements that have optimization potential, on the impact on performance, and on the effort for modifying these statements.

▶ The SQL Monitor indicates whether or not an SQL statement was executed, the number of executions, and the time needed for execution. Moreover, information on the entry point is provided so that you can identify the business process affected. This makes it possible to consider the business-process relevance when prioritizing the results of the performance tests, and to discuss the weighting with the respective process owners.

While adjusting programs, suitable measures can be derived from the results of the functional checks and the performance checks:

Adjusting programs

▶ To make sure that all programs continue to run in the same way after the migration, we recommend that you consider the results of functional checks in all cases—i.e., independent of runtime measurements—and implement the necessary corrections. Since these adjustments are independent of the runtime analysis, you can start implementation at the same time as data collection.

▶ If the performance checks indicate optimization potential, you should optimize the affected programs, in order, according to their prioritization. We describe how to identify the exact modifications that are necessary for each program in Section 8.1.3.

8.1.2 System Optimization

System optimization considers the system as a whole. Its focus is highly technical and the required steps are usually performed by SAP system and database administrators. When dealing with applications that system and database administrators cannot optimize directly, ABAP developers will also be involved in the optimization measures. System optimization has priority if a large number of system processes are too slow and the runtime problems cannot be narrowed down to one or a few applications.

Approaches

There are two possible approaches for system optimization: Analysis of system settings and hardware resources on the one hand, and application and SQL analysis on the other. In this context, it must be noted that the two subject areas are inter-dependent. This means that non-optimal system settings or resource bottlenecks can lead to slow applications. Slow applications (e.g., with high resource consumption), in turn, can lead to resource bottlenecks.

System settings and hardware resources

When analyzing the system settings and hardware resources, the system settings are checked using different configuration parameters (for memory size, number of processes, CPU, etc.). Moreover, it is verified if the available hardware resources are sufficient for the workload or if the system is overloaded and needs more hardware. Tools used for these analyses are typically the SAP memory settings in Transaction ST02, the database performance monitor (Transaction ST04 or DBACOCKPIT), and the Operating System Monitor (Transaction ST06). In addition to this, the system load can be analyzed in SAP HANA Studio.

Application and SQL analysis

Another approach would be to analyze which applications or SQL statements are resource-intensive enough to have a negative impact on the entire system. For this task, you can use the Workload Monitor (Transaction ST03), the SQL Monitor, the SQL cache of the database, and the Expensive Statement Trace.

If necessary, resource-intensive applications can be further analyzed using the tools described in Section 8.1.3. In case of resource-intensive SQL statements, the following cases in particular are possible:

▸ SQL statements used to transfer a large number of records from the database to the application server.

▸ SQL statements that have fast execution times when contemplated individually, but which still take up a lot of time in total since they are executed frequently.

354

▶ SQL statements that are executed rarely and transfer only a few records from the database to the application server, but which have a long runtime.

In the first and second case, the applications must often be optimized to solve the problem. In the third case, the access path to the database must be analyzed. In some cases, SAP system or database administrators can optimize the runtime of those statements (e.g., with an index).

With system optimization, you can identify configuration problems, resource bottlenecks, and expensive ABAP programs or SQL statements. This type of optimization is described in detail in the book *SAP Performance Optimization Guide: Analyzing and Tuning SAP Systems* by Thomas Schneider (7th edition, SAP PRESS 2013) and included in the learning content of the SAP course ADM315 on workload analysis.

8.1.3 Application Optimization

The goal of application optimization is to optimize the performance of an existing application or of individual programs of that application. Concrete complaints by end-users often motivate an organization's move to optimize an application.

Applications are usually optimized by ABAP developers. In some cases, SAP system or database experts give consulting guidance on technical aspects. It may also be necessary to work with business-process specialists to discuss design changes or questions regarding a given business process.

Application optimization is an iterative process. It mainly consists of three phases:

Phases

▶ Analysis
▶ Adjustment
▶ Comparison

Analysis

During the analysis, you try to identify reasons for performance problems and determine possible performance optimizations.

Runtime statistics — We recommend starting the analysis of a program by first evaluating the runtime statistics, i.e., by using Transaction STAD (see Section 7.4.1). This will provide early hints on the areas that constitute large portions of the runtime and on the tools that are best suited for a more comprehensive analysis. Three distinct types of cases emerge:

- CPU time constitutes the largest portion of the runtime.
- Database time constitutes the largest portion of the runtime.
- Wait times constitute the largest portion of the runtime.

CPU time — If the largest portion of the runtime is CPU time, we recommend continuing the analysis with an ABAP trace (Transaction SAT or ABAP Profiler).

Database time — If the database time is the problem, Transaction STAD already provides further information on the database accesses (e.g., with regard to the affected database tables). If this information is not sufficient, you can run an SQL trace in the next step. This delivers detailed information on the number of executions of an SQL statement on the database and the number of records processed. In addition to that, you can use the SQL Monitor and the SQL Performance Tuning Worklist to create an SQL profile of the application and combine this profile with the data from a static code analysis. If necessary, you can then run further analyses using the execution plan and/or the SAP HANA Plan Visualizer (PlanViz). However, both tools require very good knowledge of the SAP HANA database.

Wait time — If the largest portion of the runtime is neither CPU time nor database time, there are usually long wait times. These can be caused by synchronous RFC calls, the ABAP statement WAIT, or synchronous updates. In this case, you should analyze the causes of the wait times. When dealing with RFC or update modules, this can mean that you should first evaluate the runtime statistics of the function that was called and then examine the CPU and database time based on those results.

Adjustment

The analysis results are used to adjust the program. You have very distinct options for program adjustments. You might, for example, be able to increase the performance by changing the table type of an internal table or by a few simple changes to a data selection. In other cases, fundamental modifications might be necessary to accelerate the program.

For every modification, you should consider possible side effects. After adjusting a program, you should therefore make sure to run functional tests. By executing unit tests, you can make sure that a given adjustment will not lead to regression.

Functional testing

Comparison

After or during adjustments, you compare the runtime of the optimized program with the runtime from when you performed the analysis. If the performance did not increase at all or not to the extent expected, you can run another analysis with subsequent adjustments before comparing the programs again. Figure 8.1 shows the sequence of application optimization.

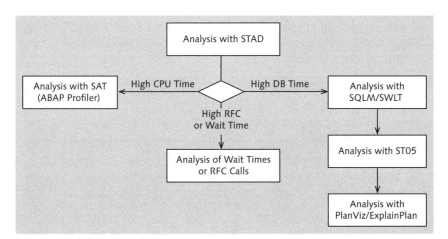

Figure 8.1 Application Analysis

8.2 Scenario and Requirements

Now that you have an overview of the required steps for system and application optimization, we'll introduce the sample application that will be optimized for SAP HANA in this chapter.

8.2.1 Initial Situation

Initial situation

The focus of our sample scenario is a network of airlines that provides a variety of services for the connected airlines based on a central database. This includes regularly generating reports on flight occupancy, sales figures, and the booking behavior of customers. Moreover, the network provides a bonus system that allows customers of the connected airlines to earn and spend miles.

Reporting

Available reports

The following reports are provided via the network:

▶ Utilization per flight connection for a fiscal year or a fiscal year period

▶ Miles earned per customer within a fiscal year or a fiscal year period

▶ List of premium customers (customers with the highest numbers of earned miles within a period of 24 months)

▶ Average use, total turnover, booking behavior for each flight connection per fiscal year period and in comparison to the previous period

Calculation of Miles

Calculation of miles

Miles are calculated based on a set of rules that was agreed upon by the connected airlines. The following formula is used to determine the miles earned for a flight booking:

$$Miles = \begin{aligned}&(\textit{distance of flight connection} \times \textit{booking class factor} \\ &+ \textit{distance of flight connection} \times \textit{early booking factor}) \\ &\times (100 - \textit{customer-specific discount rate}) / 100\end{aligned}$$

Booking class factor

Using the *booking class factor*, customers earn more miles when booking business or first class than when booking an economy class flight. The following factors are currently used:

▶ Business class factor: 1.2

▶ First class factor: 1.5

Early booking factor

The *early booking factor* is an incentive for customers to book their flights early. For flights that are booked at least 100 days before the flight date, this factor is 0.1. In all other cases, the factor is 0.

Some customers receive *customer-specific discounts* when booking a flight. In this case, the miles earned are reduced by the same percentage as the airfare. If a customer receives a 30% discount so that he or she only pays 70% of the regular airfare, he or she only earns 70% of the miles that are earned by a customer who pays the full price.

Customer-specific discount

To illustrate and explain these rules, we'll now contemplate a flight booking by customer Tom Peterson (customer number 178, the customer-specific discount is 20%) from Frankfurt to New York flying business class. The distance of this connection is 6,162 kilometers. This corresponds to 3,829 miles. The flight took place on 8/20/2012 and was booked on 7/24/2012. Mr. Peterson earns the following miles for this flight:

Example for mile calculation

Miles = (3,829 × 1.2 + 3,829 × 0) × (100 − 20) / 100 = 3,676

8.2.2 Technical Implementation

The airline network uses an ABAP-based IT system. The tables and data within this system are based on the SFLIGHT data model.

Database Tables

The airlines connected to the system transfer all relevant data to a central system in real time. The relevant database tables of the SFLIGHT data model are listed in Table 8.1.

SFLIGHT data model

Table	Description
SCARR	Airlines
SPFLI	Flight schedule
SCUSTOM	Customer data
SFLIGHT	Flights
SBOOK	Flight bookings

Table 8.1 Relevant Database Tables of the SFLIGHT Data Model

Moreover, there are two extensions of the SFLIGHT data model, as shown in Table 8.2.

Other database tables

Table	Description
ZA4H_C8_PARAMS	Parameters for mile calculation
ZA4H_C8_STATIST	Storage of static data regarding the flight connections

Table 8.2 Other Database Tables

Reports

ABAP program

All reports needed are executable ABAP programs and transaction codes exists for each of these programs (see Table 8.3).

ABAP Program	Transaction	Description
ZR_A4H_CHAPTER8_UTILIZATION	ZR_A4H_C8_UTIL	Use per flight connection
ZR_A4H_CHAPTER8_MILES	ZR_A4H_C8_MILES	Miles earned per customer
ZR_A4H_CHAPTER8_TOP_CUST	ZR_A4H_C8_TOP_CUST	List of premium customers
ZR_A4H_CHAPTER8_FILL_STATISTIC	ZR_A4H_C8_FILL_STAT	This report fills database table ZA4H_C8_STATIST
ZR_A4H_CHAPTER8_READ_STATISTIC	ZR_A4H_C8_READ_STAT	This report analyzes database table ZA4H_C8_STATIST

Table 8.3 ABAP Program Needed

For visualization, the ABAP programs use classic ABAP lists. Figure 8.2 shows a sample output of the program ZR_A4H_CHAPTER8_TOP_CUST.

```
00001487 Guenther Leisert              3.036.866  MI
00000732 Irene Prinz                   3.001.776  MI
00004610 Thilo Detemple                2.995.032  MI
00000162 Schwarz Konstruktionen Gm     2.983.372  MI
00000419 Astrid Leisert                2.973.894  MI
00000244 Reserv.f.Kreditprozess        2.973.888  MI
00000387 Allen Detemple                2.965.883  MI
00002940 Salvador Fischmann            2.962.162  MI
00004405 Johannes Gueldenpfennig       2.950.499  MI
00003574 Holm Gueldenpfennig           2.937.021  MI
```

Figure 8.2 Output of Program ZR_A4H_CHAPTER8_TOP_CUST

Customizing

The parameters for mile calculation are stored in the customizing table ZA4H_C8_PARAMS. The system stores the following values in this database table:

▶ FACTOR_C: factor for business-class flights

▶ FACTOR_F: factor for first-class flights

▶ EARLYB_D: minimum time difference between booking date and flight date to earn additional miles

▶ EARLYB_F: factor for early bookings

The customer-specific discount is derived from the field DISCOUNT in the database table SCUSTOM.

Parameters for mile calculation

Miscellaneous

In addition to the executable ABAP programs, the application comprises a Web Dynpro ABAP application and an RFC interface:

▶ The Web Dynpro application ZWD_A4H_CHAPTER8_APP can be used to evaluate the miles earned per customer via the browser (Figure 8.3).

▶ The remote-enabled function module ZA4H_CHAPTER8_GET_UTILIZATION can be used by all airlines connected to the network to query the utilization of flight connections.

Web Dynpro, RFC

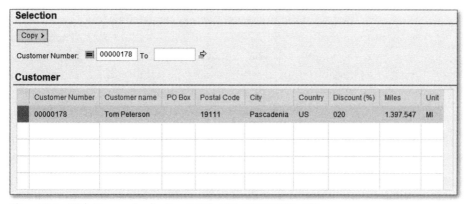

Figure 8.3 Web Dynpro Application ZWD_A4H_CHAPTER8_APP

Central class   Internally, the ABAP programs, the Web Dynpro application, and the function module use methods of the ZCL_A4H_CHAPTER8_DATA_PROV class.

8.2.3   Current Problems

Bad performance   The connected airlines have been complaining about the network service for some time. The necessary reports typically have long delays, and end-users are not satisfied with the response time.

Migrating to   Due to these complaints, the system was migrated to SAP HANA. Although
SAP HANA   the migration was performed without any issues and some of the reports are now generated faster (for example, the program ZR_A4H_CHAPTER8_ TOP_CUST had a runtime of 1,491 seconds before the migration; with SAP HANA, it now runs within 567 seconds), not all problems could be solved by merely migrating the system.

To determine how the response-time behavior of the system can be improved, you should follow the application and process-optimization procedure now. Due to time constraints, you will limit this analysis to the program ZR_A4H_CHAPTER8_TOP_CUST to determine the premium customers. You should suggest and implement possible modifications as fast as possible while avoiding any unnecessary risks.

8.3   Meeting the Requirements

As you've learned in the previous chapters, an existing ABAP application can only benefit from SAP HANA if it uses the *code-to-data paradigm*. To avoid any risks, however, you should modify as few parts of the existing system as possible. Moreover, to ensure portability of the system, you only want to use SAP HANA views and SQLScript if it's necessary or if it leads to significant performance gains in comparison with Open SQL.

In the following sections, you will learn how to determine the extent to which the program ZR_A4H_CHAPTER8_TOP_CUST uses the SAP HANA database and which modifications can be implemented to accelerate the program.

8.3.1 Narrowing Down the Problem Using the Runtime Statistics

When analyzing the program `ZR_A4H_CHAPTER8_TOP_CUST`, you start by using Transaction STAD. Within this transaction, you call the runtime statistics for a program execution to analyze the program's runtime and determine the amount of data that was processed by the program.

The runtime statistics in Figure 8.4 show that the program `ZR_A4H_CHAP-TER8_TOP_CUST` was executed in 567 seconds (RESPONSE TIME). This runtime is made up of 499 seconds PROCESSING TIME and 68 seconds DATABASE REQUEST TIME. This means that the largest portion of the runtime is attributed to the ABAP program itself and not the time needed for database access. However, database access also takes too long for a dialog program.

Time distribution

```
Analysis of time in work process

CPU time                 515.430 ms    Number      Roll ins          1
RFC+CPIC time                  0 ms                Roll outs         1
                                                   Enqueues          0
Total time in workprocs  567.417 ms
                                        Load time   Program          0 ms
  Response time          567.417 ms                 Screen           0 ms
                                                    CUA interf.      0 ms
Wait for work process          0 ms
Processing time          499.140 ms    Roll time   Out               0 ms
Load time                      0 ms                In                0 ms
Generating time                0 ms                Wait              0 ms
Roll (in+wait) time            0 ms
Database request time     68.277 ms    Frontend    No.roundtrips     1
Enqueue time                   0 ms                GUI time          0 ms
                                                   Net time          0 ms


Analysis of ABAP/4 database requests (only explicitly by application)

Connection                  DEFAULT        Request time       68.277 ms
Database requests total   19.364.803       Commit time            0 ms
DB Proc. Calls                    0        DB Proc. Time          0 ms
```

Type of ABAP request	Database rows	Requests	Buffer rows	Database calls	Request time (ms)	Avg.time / row (ms)
Total	5553.485	*64803	19360163	4.641	68.277	0,0
Direct read	0	*60162	19360162		0	0,0
Sequential read	5553.485	4.641	1	4.641	68.277	0,0
Update	0	0		0	0	0,0
Delete	0	0		0	0	0,0
Insert	0	0		0	0	0,0

```
Note: Tables were saved in the tablebuffer.
```

Figure 8.4 Runtime Statistics from Transaction STAD

Details on database access times

The lower part of Figure 8.4 shows detailed information on the database accesses. As you can see, a little over 5.5 million records were read within the database request time of 68 seconds.

Table access statistics

Since the table access statistics (see Section 7.4.1) was activated during the selected execution of the program, you also examine the five tables where the program took the longest time for read accesses (see Figure 8.5). The access time of 68 seconds was almost exclusively used for accesses to the table SBOOK (with 5,548,847 records read from this table). Accesses to the table SCUSTOM only took 0.02 seconds (with a total of 4,637 records read from this table).

```
Table accesses    (list might be incomplete!)

                              ──────── Number of rows accessed ────────
 Table name                   Total Dir. reads Seq. reads    Changes  Time (ms)

 TOTAL                     5.553.496        10  5.553.486          0    68.277
 SBOOK                     5.548.847         0  5.548.847          0    68.251
 SCUSTOM                       4.637         0      4.637          0        26
 TRDIR                             1         0          1          0         0
 TRDIRT                           10        10          0          0         0
 T006D                             1         0          1          0         0
```

Figure 8.5 Table Access Statistics

The above analysis results have shown that most of the execution time of the ABAP program was not used within database accesses. Only 12% (68 seconds) of the runtime was used within the database to read about 5.5 million records. In the next steps, you must therefore analyze the ABAP processing and further analyze the database accesses.

8.3.2 Detailed Analysis of the ABAP Program Using Transaction SAT

To learn more about the ABAP processing, you now analyze the program ZR_A4H_CHAPTER8_TOP_CUST in more detail using the ABAP runtime analysis in Transaction SAT. Figure 8.6 shows the result of the program execution using Transaction SAT. The program was executed in 656 seconds, so it took a little longer than before. This can be attributed partly to a higher system load when running the detailed analysis and partly to the load for the actual runtime measurement.

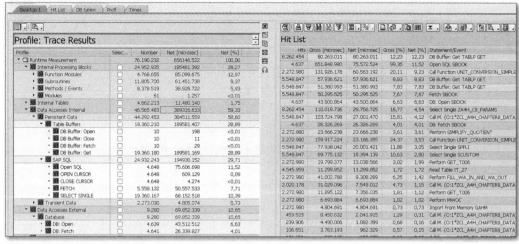

Figure 8.6 ABAP Trace in Transaction SAT

The results of the runtime measurement can be evaluated as follows:

Evaluation of the runtime measurement

▶ **Function modules for conversions**
About 28% (185 seconds) was needed for internal processing blocks, particularly for calling function modules and subprograms. You will immediately notice that the function module UNIT_CONVERSION_SIMPLE, which is used for unit conversions, was called more than two million times. This function module thus accounts for 20% (131 seconds) of the total runtime.

▶ **Database interface and table buffer**
Transaction SAT differentiates between internal (INTERNAL DATABASE ACCESSES) and external database time (EXTERNAL DATABASE ACCESSES). Internal database time refers to the time needed by SQL statements within the ABAP work process and accesses to the table buffer. In our example, about 60% (389 seconds) of the total runtime can be attributed to the internal database time. About 50% of this time is needed for SQL statements within the ABAP work process (195 seconds), with the other half being used for accesses to the table buffer (189 seconds).

You will immediately notice the high number of accesses to the database and the table buffer. The analysis results show 25 million executions of SQL statements and 19 million accesses to the table buffer. When double-clicking a row within the hit list for a buffer access, the source code is displayed (not shown in Figure 8.6). From this source code, you can see that the accesses to the table buffer were mainly done for the tables ZA4H_C8_PARAMS, SCUSTOM, and SPFLI.

The external database time refers to the time needed for SQL statements outside the ABAP work process. In our example, the external database time accounts for about 10% (70 seconds) of the total runtime.

8.3.3 Detailed Analysis of Database Accesses

Before further analyzing the program using the SQL trace, we should check the SQL profile of our application and compare this with static code analyses.

Code Analysis Using Transaction SCI, SQLM, and SWLT

SQL profile and Code Inspector

You first use the SAP Code Inspector to examine the performance of the package TEST_A4H_BOOK_CHAPTER08. The results are then linked to the existing data from the SQL Monitor in Transaction SWLT. In this transaction, runtime data for the entire system is displayed for our access to the table SBOOK. Figure 8.7 shows that the SELECT statement was executed 33,000 times with an average execution time of 14.8 milliseconds and 1,196 records read. If you scroll to the right of the screen, the columns TYPE and NAME OF PROCESSING BLOCK (not displayed in Figure 8.7) show that the SELECT statement is run in the method GET_MILES_FOR_CUSTOMER.

The columns CHECK TITLE and CHECK MESSAGE also display a Code Inspector check for this method, which indicates that this is a SELECT statement within a loop (with the loop not being present within the same modularization unit as the database access).

When clicking the column ADDITIONAL INFORMATION, the system displays the different levels of the call hierarchy (not shown in this screen). This allows you to easily navigate to the different levels of the call hierarchy where you will find the loop in the GET_TOP_CUSTOMERS method. When clicking the SHOW CHECK DOCUMENTATION button (shown in Figure 8.7), a document with optimization tips is displayed. This documentation contains a description of the problem together with possible optimization measures.

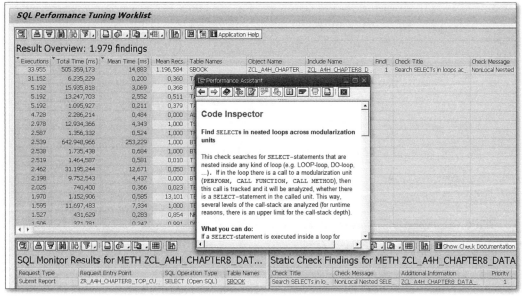

Figure 8.7 Performance Analyses in Transaction SWLT

You know now that accesses to the table SBOOK are caused by a very frequently executed SQL statement and also know where this statement is executed and where to find the loop responsible for its execution. Since you also want to know if the SQL statement is executed with identical values each time, we'll record an SQL trace.

SQL Trace with Transaction ST05

You run the program ZR_A4H_CHAPTER8_TOP_CUST again while creating an SQL trace. This will show you how often each statement was executed, if there were identical executions, the execution times, the number of data records read, and the text of the SQL statement that was transferred to the database.

Figure 8.8 and Figure 8.9 show you the list of structure-identical SQL statements and the call hierarchy (call stack) for the SQL statement used to access the table SBOOK. The columns REDUNDANCY and IDENTICAL show that the statements were not executed with identical values and that all bookings within a certain time period that were not cancelled are read for a customer. Using the stack trace from the main records, you can display how the statement for the table SBOOK was used via the ABAP stack. By double-clicking an entry, you can easily navigate between the levels of the call hierarchy.

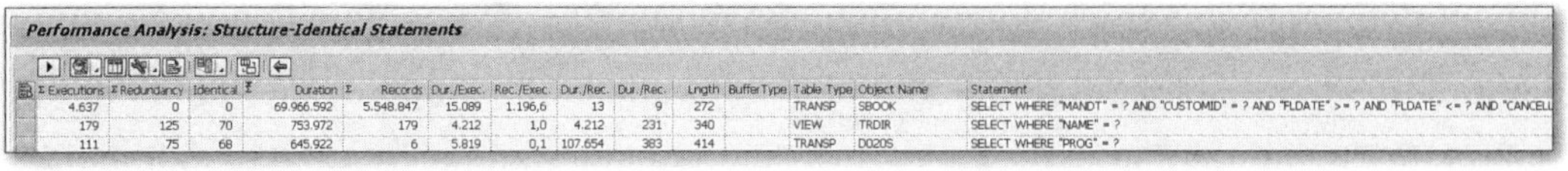

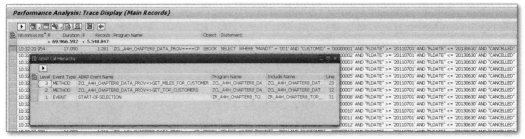

Figure 8.8 SQL Trace: SQL Statements with the Same Structure

Figure 8.9 SQL Trace: Call Hierarchy

8.3.4 Analysis Result

The analysis of the ZR_A4H_CHAPTER8_TOP_CUST program described in the previous sections has shown that the long runtime can be attributed mainly to a large number of SQL statement and function module executions (particularly for unit conversion). The reason for this is the large number of records that are transferred from the database to the application.

Separate processing of flight bookings

When analyzing the source code, you'll notice that by using the method GET_TOP_CUSTOMERS, the flight bookings are read and processed separately for each customer. Due to the large number of flight bookings (in our example, 5 million bookings were read), the database and table buffer are accessed frequently and there are many function module calls.

Records are often processed individually if function modules and methods are (re-)used that are not suitable for mass data. In our example, each customer's miles are determined using the GET_MILES_FOR_CUSTOMER method to identify the premium customers.

8.3.5 Optimization Using Open SQL

In the first step, we will try to accelerate the identification of premium customers without using SAP HANA views and SQLScript. For this purpose, we will create a new program ZR_A4H_CHAPTER8_TOP_CUST_1 and call the method GET_TOP_CUSTOMERS_1 within this program.

The new implementation differs from the originally used program in the following:

Code optimizations

▶ Nested SELECT statements are avoided (since these are disadvantageous both in general and especially for SAP HANA).

▶ Structures are used instead of the SELECT * statement.

▶ The number of buffer accesses is minimized (in particular by reading the customizing table ZA4H_C8_PARAMS only once).

▶ The number of function module calls is minimized; the new implementation converts units only at the end of the algorithm, after the bookings are already aggregated (wherever possible).

Listing 8.1 shows the original implementation of the code for identification of premium customers as pseudo code.

Coding before optimization

```
"Selecting customers
SELECT * FROM scustom ...
  ...
  "Determining miles per customer by re-
  "using the method GET_MILES_FOR_CUSTOMER
  CALL METHOD GET_MILES_FOR_CUSTOMER(...)
    ...
    "Selecting the bookings for the customer
    SELECT * FROM sbook...
      ...
      "Selecting the connection master data for the
      "bookings
      SELECT SINGLE * FROM spfli...
      ...
      "Unit conversion per booking
      CALL FUNCTION 'UNIT_CONVERSION_SIMPLE'...
      ...
      "Reading the Customizings per booking
      CALL METHOD GET_PARAMETER_VALUE(...)
```

```
      ...
      "Selecting the master data for the customer
      SELECT SINGLE * FROM scustom...
        ...
    ENDSELECT.
    ...
  ...
ENDSELECT.
```

Listing 8.1 Original Implementation

Coding after
optimization

Listing 8.2 shows the optimized coding for determining the premium
customers.

```
"Single reading operation for the Customizing
CALL METHOD GET_PARAMETER_VALUE(...)

"Reading all customers, bookings, and master data of the
"connections using a JOIN and a
"field string
SELECT... FROM scustom
  INNER JOIN sbook...
  INNER JOIN spfli...
  WHERE...
  ...
  "Calculating the miles in accordance with the
  "Customizing read
  IF class = 'C'.
    lv_miles = ...
  ELSEIF class = 'F'.
    lv_miles = ...
  ELSE.
    ...
  ENDIF.
  ...
  COLLECT ls_miles INTO lt_miles.
ENDSELECT.

"One-time unit conversion per customer and
"for the unit used for this customer
LOOP AT lt_miles INTO ls_miles.
  ...
  CALL FUNCTION 'UNIT_CONVERSION_SIMPLE'...
```

```
    . . .
ENDLOOP.
```

Listing 8.2 Coding Optimized with Open SQL

Despite the optimization, premium customers are still identified in ABAP since the logic described in Section 8.2.1 cannot be expressed using Open SQL.

8.3.6 Analysis of the First Optimization

You now run the program ZR_A4H_CHAPTER8_TOP_CUST_1. It runs much faster. A runtime analysis using Transaction STAD confirms the positive impact of the modifications (see Figure 8.10). The program is now executed within only 76 seconds. The database portion was reduced to about 25 seconds. However, a large amount of records (more than 5.5 million records) are still read from the database.

```
Analysis of time in work process

CPU time              55.380 ms   Number    Roll ins        1
RFC+CPIC time             0 ms              Roll outs       1
                                            Enqueues        0
Total time in workprocs  76.233 ms
                                    Load time Program       0  ms
  Response time           76.233 ms           Screen        0  ms
                                              CUA interf.   0  ms
Wait for work process       0 ms
Processing time         51.245 ms   Roll time Out           0  ms
Load time                   0 ms              In            0  ms
Generating time             0 ms              Wait          0  ms
Roll (in+wait) time         0 ms
Database request time   24.988 ms   Frontend  No.roundtrips  1
Enqueue time                0 ms              GUI time      0  ms
                                              Net time      0  ms


Analysis of ABAP/4 database requests (only explicitly by application)

Connection             DEFAULT         Request time     24.988 ms
Database requests total      39         Commit time          0 ms
DB Proc. Calls                0         DB Proc. Time        0 ms

Type of        Database           Buffer  Database  Request  Avg.time /
ABAP request       rows  Requests  rows     calls   time (ms) row (ms)

Total          5548.848     39       36      383    24.988     0,0

Direct read          0     35       35               0         0,0
Sequential read 5548.848    4        1      383    24.988     0,0
Update               0      0                 0       0         0,0
Delete               0      0                 0       0         0,0
Insert               0      0                 0       0         0,0

Note: Tables were saved in the tablebuffer.
```

Figure 8.10 Runtime Statistics after the First Optimization

Function
module calls

The ABAP trace (Transaction SAT) clearly shows these improvements. From Figure 8.11, you can see that the function module UNIT_CONVERSION_SIMPLE was called only once per customer (4,637 times) and that the table buffers were not accessed as frequently. However, the same amount of records was read from the database so that the related load of the database interface remained unchanged.

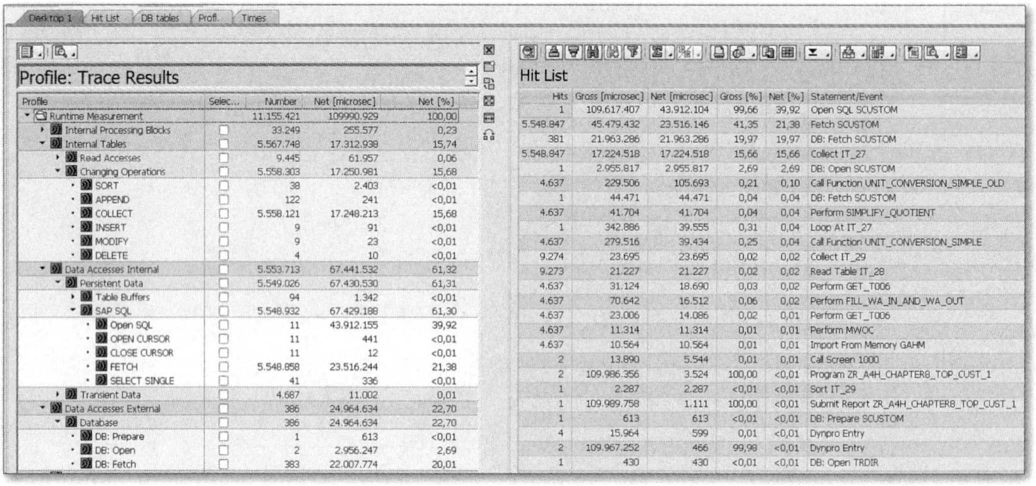

Figure 8.11 ABAP Trace after the First Optimization

Join to transfer
data records

The SQL trace in Transaction ST05 shows the improvement as well. A join is now executed only once to transfer all records (over 5.5 million) to the program in one operation (see Figure 8.12).

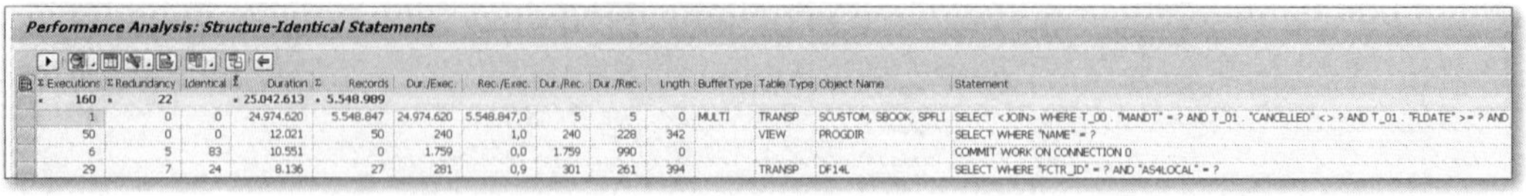

Figure 8.12 SQL Trace after the First Optimization

8.3.7 Analysis Result

The analysis using Transaction STAD, SAT, and ST05 shows that despite the adjustment, over 5.5 million records are still transferred from the database server to the application server. The reason for this is primarily that some of the calculations are done for individual bookings. These are:

- Application of the booking-class factor
- Application of the early-booking factor
- Application of the customer-specific discount

In particular, the application of the early-booking factor can only be done for individual bookings, since it depends on the time difference between booking date and flight date.

To further optimize the program, we have to avoid transferring every individual booking from the database to the application server. Basically, there are two options to reach this goal:

- Implementing a database procedure with SQLScript (or CE functions).
- Modeling a view in SAP HANA Studio.

8.3.8 Optimization Using an Analytic View

We will optimize the program using an SAP HANA view, specifically an analytic view. To do this, you will create a new program ZR_A4H_CHAP-TER8_TOP_CUST_2. This program calls the GET_TOP_CUSTOMERS_2 method. This method uses the calculation view CA_MILES in the test.a4h.book. chapter08 package, which is wrapped via an external view. This view again uses the analytic view AN_MILES.

The analytic view has four input parameters. These parameters correspond to the parameters for mile calculation listed in Section 8.2.2. Due to the input parameters, the call from the ABAP program is done via Native SQL (see Listing 8.3):

Input parameters and program call

```
TRY.
  lo_sql_statement = NEW cl_sql_statement(
  tab_name_for_trace = 'ZEV_A4H_MILES' ).
  lo_sql_result_set = lo_sql_statement->execute_query(
  | select top 10 customer_id, name, sum(miles), miles_unit |
&& | from zev_a4h_miles | &&
```

```
| where fldate between '{ lv_date_from }' and '{ lv_date_to
}' and mandt = '{ sy-mandt }' | &&
| group by customer_id, name, miles_unit | &&
| order by sum(miles) desc | &&
| WITH PARAMETERS ('PLACEHOLDER' = ( '$$IV_FACTOR_C$$', '{
lv_factor_c }' ), | &&
| 'PLACEHOLDER' = ( '$$IV_FACTOR_F$$', '{ lv_factor_f }' ),
| &&
| 'PLACEHOLDER' = ( '$$IV_EARLYB_D$$', '{ lv_earlyb_d }' ),
| &&
| 'PLACEHOLDER' = ( '$$IV_EARLYB_F$$', '{ lv_earlyb_f }' ) )
| ).

lo_sql_result_set->set_param_table( itab_ref = REF #( et_top_
customer ) ).
lo_sql_result_set->next_package( ).

CATCH cx_sql_exception INTO DATA(lo_sql_exception).
  " error handling
ENDTRY.
```

Listing 8.3 Calling the Analytic View

As you can see, the miles are now calculated in the SAP HANA database. When calling the analytic view, the customer number, the name, and the miles earned by the premium customers are transferred to the ABAP report.

8.3.9 Analysis of the Second Optimization

The second optimization is once again analyzed using Transaction STAD. Figure 8.13 shows that the database time was reduced to a little less than three seconds and that only 10 records are transferred.

Aggregated records   Regarding the table accesses in Figure 8.14, you can see that only ten records are now read from the view ZEV_A4H_MILES. This is the aggregated final result.

```
Analysis of time in work process

CPU time                     0 ms    Number      Roll ins           1
RFC+CPIC time                0 ms                Roll outs          1
                                                 Enqueues           0
Total time in workprocs   2.955 ms
                                     Load time   Program          1 ms
 ─Response time─          2.955 ms               Screen           0 ms
                                                 CUA interf.      0 ms
Wait for work process        0 ms
Processing time              6 ms    Roll time   Out              0 ms
Load time                    1 ms                In               0 ms
Generating time              0 ms                Wait             0 ms
Roll (in+wait) time          0 ms
Database request time     2.948 ms   Frontend    No.roundtrips      1
Enqueue time                 0 ms                GUI time         0 ms
                                                 Net time         0 ms


Analysis of ABAP/4 database requests (only explicitly by application)

Connection                DEFAULT      Request time      2.948 ms
Database requests total        20      Commit time          0 ms
DB Proc. Calls                  0      DB Proc. Time        0 ms

Type of      Database           Buffer   Database  Request  Avg.time /
ABAP request rows   Requests    rows     calls     time (ms) row (ms)

Total            12     20        16        3       2.948     245,7

Direct read       0     16        16                   0       0,0
Sequential read  12      4         0        3       2.948     245,7
Update            0      0                   0          0       0,0
Delete            0      0                   0          0       0,0
Insert            0      0                   0          0       0,0

Note: Tables were saved in the tablebuffer.
```

Figure 8.13 Runtime Statistics after the Second Optimization

```
Table accesses    (list might be incomplete!)

                        ─── Number of rows accessed ───
Table name            Total Dir. reads Seq. reads  Changes Time (ms)

TOTAL                   22     10        12           0     2.948
ZEV_A4H_MILES           10      0        10           0     2.947
D345T                    1      0         1           0         1
TRDIR                    1      0         1           0         0
TMSACTDAT               10     10         0           0         0
T009Y                    0      0         0           0         0
```

Figure 8.14 Runtime Statistics: Table Accesses

Due to the smaller result set, the number of calls of the internal database statements in the ABAP program could be dramatically reduced. As you can see from the ABAP trace (Figure 8.15), the program is now executed almost entirely in the database (99%).

Program execution moved to the database layer

375

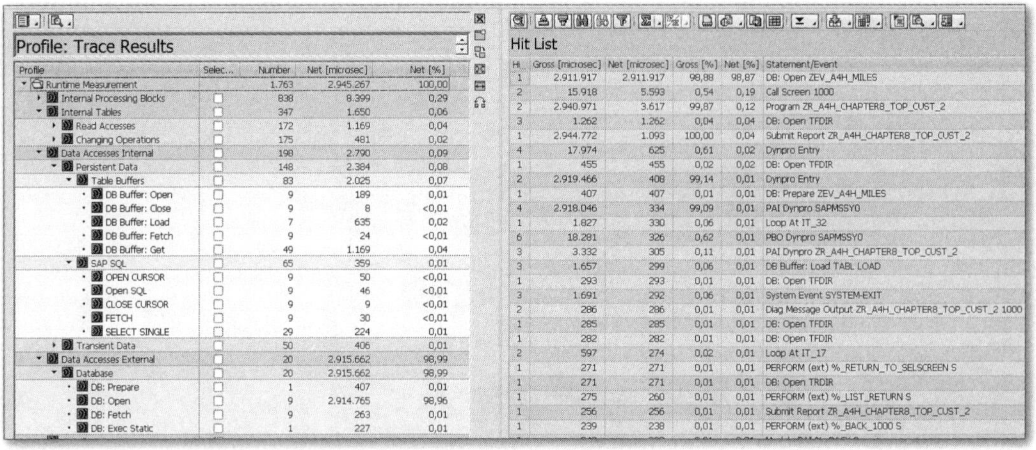

Figure 8.15 ABAP Trace after the Second Optimization

Single access

The SQL trace in Transaction ST05 (see Figure 8.16) also confirms the good result. This trace also shows that the ZEV_A4H_MILES view is accessed only once. As mentioned before, only ten records are transferred during this access.

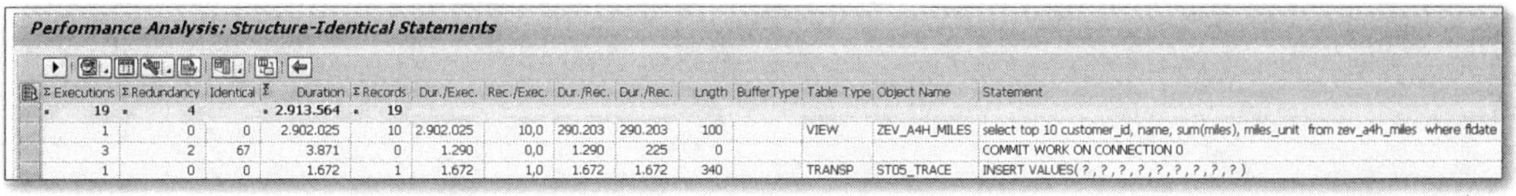

Figure 8.16 SQL Trace after the Second Optimization

Displaying the SQL statement

For a detailed analysis of the SQL statement using PlanViz, you can now double-click the SQL statement in Transaction ST05 to display the entire SQL statement. You then run the statement in the SQL Console in SAP HANA Studio (see Listing 8.4).

```
SELECT
    top 10 customer_id, name, sum(miles), miles_unit
FROM
    <schema>.zev_a4h_miles
WHERE
    fldate between '20110701' and '20130630'
    and mandt = '001'
```

```
GROUP BY
  customer_id, name, miles_unit
ORDER BY
  sum(miles) desc  WITH PARAMETERS
 ('PLACEHOLDER' = ( '$$IV_FACTOR_C$$', '1.2' ),
  'PLACEHOLDER' = ( '$$IV_FACTOR_F$$', '1.5' ),
  'PLACEHOLDER' = ( '$$IV_EARLYB_D$$', '100' ),
  'PLACEHOLDER' = ( '$$IV_EARLYB_F$$', '0.10' ) ) )
```

Listing 8.4 Calling the External Database View

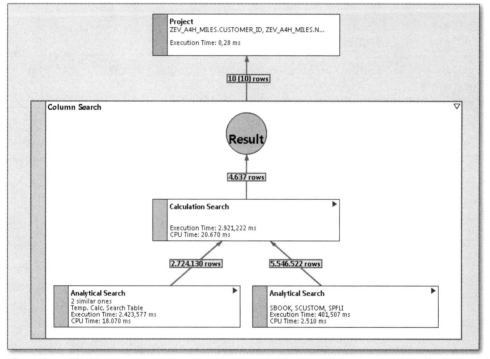

Figure 8.17 PlanViz

The analysis result of PlanViz is displayed in Figure 8.17. As you can see, a so-called *analytical search* was performed. This means that the OLAP engine was used. You can see the execution time and the CPU time in microseconds for each node. The fact that the value for CPU time is higher

Analytical search and CPU time

377

than the value for execution time shows that the respective nodes were run in parallel. This means that several threads were started and run on several CPUs so that about 20 seconds of CPU time were used within the runtime of 2.9 seconds.

[»] **Sample Execution Times**

Please note that our sample program and the optimized versions were run on a small system in the cloud and did not use very powerful hardware. If these sample programs were run on a more powerful system with more CPUs, runtimes of about one second would be possible for this procedure.

8.3.10 Analysis Result

Runtime improvement

The identification of premium customers was optimized in two steps:

▸ By optimizing the program using Open SQL, the runtime could be reduced from 567 seconds to 76 seconds. This is a factor of about 7.5.

▸ In the subsequent optimization steps using an analytical view, the runtime was reduced to three seconds. In comparison to the original runtime, this corresponds to a factor of about 190.

By optimizing both the program and the database access, premium customers can now be identified at much higher speeds. Figure 8.18 shows a graphical representation of the runtimes.

Summary

Due to this improvement, the code can now be used in dialog programs and you benefit from a range of new possibilities and options. You can, for example, use the analytical view for planning and simulation purposes to analyze the impact of changed parameters for mile calculation.

With this sample scenario, we were able to illustrate the following:

▸ How to use the optimization tools presented in Chapter 7.

▸ How you can write fast programs using Open SQL and good ABAP programming techniques.

▸ In some cases, performance gains are only possible when using native functions from SAP HANA.

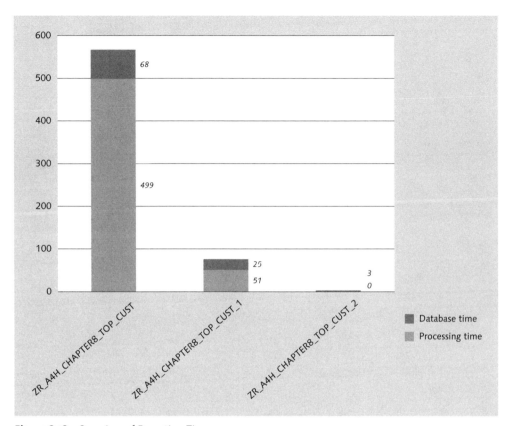

Figure 8.18 Overview of Execution Times

You can now also further analyze the other programs from the TEST_A4H_ BOOK_CHAPTER08 package and try to accelerate them using your technical options.

PART III
Advanced Techniques for ABAP Programming for SAP HANA

Now that you know how to optimize existing ABAP applications for SAP HANA, Part III of this book introduces you to additional options provided by the HANA platform to develop new, innovative applications. In this context, you'll learn about some advanced techniques that allow you to gain new insight from existing datasets that can support companies and users in complex planning and decision-making processes.

Because the chapters in this part do not build on each other, you can read them in a different sequence, depending on what subject interests you most. Some of the topics in this part are based on existing components (for example, of data modeling in SAP NetWeaver BW) or concepts (such as the mathematical concepts of *predictive analysis*) which cannot be treated exhaustively in the scope of this book. It was our intention to provide examples that allow for an easily understandable entry into the respective topics—but, depending on your previous knowledge, some of the chapters might contain a lot of new terminology.

After the introduction of the various options available for developing applications in SAP HANA, you will be guided in a step-by-step process through the creation of a new application that uses a combination of these new techniques. You will also be provided with recommendations for optimizing and developing new applications.

SAP HANA offers powerful means for analyzing and searching in unstructured data. By leveraging these built-in capabilities, you can improve search scenarios within business applications. In addition, patterns in existing datasets can be recognized for gaining further insight.

9 Text Search and Analysis of Unstructured Data

Hardly any other functionality has experienced as great a boost from the Internet in recent years as the search within large datasets—irrespective of whether you search through a product catalog, the telephone book, or the entire Internet. This chapter introduces options provided by SAP HANA to search and analyze texts and documents. These options open up many ways to employ the HANA platform, particularly in business applications, which have not been extensively equipped with these kinds of functions until now.

Input helps represent a simple usage scenario for text searches in SAP HANA. SAP applications contain input helps in many different places. When using input helps, users sometimes search for an entry in a large dataset without knowing the details of the entry, or at least without having these details at hand. For example, you may be searching for a specific customer in Argentina who is based in Buenos Aires and works in the telecommunications industry. Because his customer number is not available to you, you enter information such as the company name, country, location, and industry into a complex input template, and it often happens that you have to enter this data several times and use *wild cards* such as the asterisk (*). In addition, if you mistype an entry or the data is stored in a different way in the database (for example, if the name of the location was entered using the country-specific spelling), you usually won't obtain any results.

Input help use scenario

The text search function in SAP HANA allows you to develop search helps that work similarly to modern Internet searches. They provide a certain error tolerance and are able to process multilingual terms and synonyms. In the above example, such a search help could consist of an input field that *correctly* interprets a user request such as "buenes eires tele", despite the incorrect spelling and the search via multiple columns. However, users cannot always easily determine whether the returned result is the expected one in this type of error-tolerant search, also referred to as *fuzzy search*. Have you ever asked yourself why you sometimes obtain unexpected results when performing a search on the Internet?

Pattern recognition usage scenario
The recognition of patterns in texts and documents represents an entirely different kind text-analysis function. This feature can be employed in many different scenarios, some of which will be presented in the following sections. For example, in order to avoid having duplicate business partners in your master data, you may want to check in the system whether a *similar* client already exists in the dataset prior to creating a new client, and if so, notify the application user about it. In this context, being "similar" could mean that the last name and address of an existing and new client are (almost) identical. As it often happens that names and addresses in particular are entered with different kinds of spellings, a simple check for identical entries rarely returns satisfactory results.

The text analysis function in SAP HANA not only allows you to run searches within texts, but also to extract additional information from the texts. For example, you can recognize relationships and even intentions or emotions within texts. Let's suppose you run a web store that enables clients to order products online as well as to post comments about the products and the vendor. The *Sentiment Analysis* is part of the text engine functionality in SAP HANA and enables you to recognize patterns in these types of unstructured data. In the context of the online store, for instance, it would allow you to analyze whether a specific product evokes more positive or negative comments.

Chapter overview
This chapter begins with an introduction of some of the basic technical principles and prerequisites for using the text search in SAP HANA. This is followed by a description of how to call the function using SQL and to use it in ABAP, with a special focus on embedding the text search function in input helps. In addition to using the text search function directly, you

will learn about several existing SAP components that support the implementation of complex searches. Moreover, the chapter contains practical examples of pattern recognition within texts. And finally, you'll become acquainted with non-functional aspects such as resource consumption, performance, and error analysis.

The practical examples will be used to implement search runs across airline names (table `SCARR`), flight schedule data (airports and locations from tables `SPFLI` and `SAIRPORT`), and the flight passenger address data (name, address, town, and country from table `SCUSTOM`).

Reference example for this chapter

9.1   Basic Principles of the Text Search in SAP HANA

The main purpose of the text search function in SAP HANA is to provide users with an optimized usability of search interfaces. In addition to various features common in Internet search engines, this includes functions with special significance for business applications, such as industry-specific lists of synonyms.

This involves the following characteristics:

Characteristics of the HANA text search

▶ **Freestyle search**
The user does not need to know the exact database columns in which the search is supposed to be carried out. For example, you can implement an address search across a single input field and include all technical characteristics such as street name, ZIP code, town, country, and so on.

▶ **Error-tolerant search (fuzzy search)**
The user may vary the spelling slightly in his search requests.

▶ **Linguistic search and synonym search**
Linguistic variants and synonymous terms are included.

▶ **Value suggestions**
The system can already efficiently identify probable search results while the user is typing and present these to the user in real time.

▶ **Results ranking**
The sequence of the search results is optimized in such a way that

results with the highest probability rate are presented at the top of the list.

▶ **Search facets**
The search results can be counted and grouped according to specific criteria. For example, when searching for airlines, you can view the distribution of the airlines per country.

▶ **Text analysis (particularly sentiment analysis)**
You can extract additional information from texts, which allows you to gain insights on semantical aspects.

9.1.1 Technical Architecture

The following sections describe how you can use the text search and text analysis functions. In order to provide you with an idea of which components are involved in SAP HANA, Figure 9.1 shows the architecture of the text search functionality. The column store supports the data types and operations that are required for the search and which are described in further detail in Section 9.2 and Section 9.3. For complex text analyses and to extract information, the column store draws on the *preprocessor server*. In this context, the system uses the so-called *Document Analysis Toolkit*.

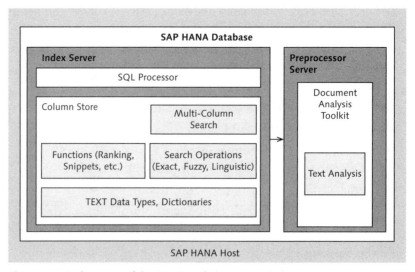

Figure 9.1 Architecture of the Text Search Function in SAP HANA

Section 9.2 provides further details on other text search components.

In Section 9.1.3, we'll explain additional usage scenarios for text search.

> **Heritage of the Fuzzy Search Component in SAP HANA** [«]
>
> The fuzzy search function in SAP HANA represents the advanced development of a data-quality analysis solution initially developed by the German company Fuzzy Informatik AG. This solution was adopted by SAP indirectly, through the acquisition of BusinessObjects. In addition to the genuine fuzzy search, this solution is particularly useful for recognizing *duplicates*, especially in sets of address data.

9.1.2 Error-Tolerant Search

The error-tolerant or *fuzzy* search involves the search for character strings (i.e., the search request) in text-based data, where the data does not have to exactly correspond to the search request; this way, sufficiently similar entries will also be included into the result set. This section provides an overview of the techniques used for the fuzzy search in SAP HANA. — *Fuzzy search*

The degree to which a data record must correspond to the search request is generally determined by mathematical algorithms that form the basis of the fuzzy search. The result of the calculation is often a numerical value that is used to decide whether a data record is sufficiently similar to the search request. With regard to texts, the simplest type of such an algorithm consists of determining the minimum number of operations (such as replacing and moving characters) that are required to generate a section of the actual data record from the search request. In practice, it is very complicated to determine the degree of similarity between texts, and it involves using variants and heuristics that all have their pros and cons depending on the scenario in which they are used. The text search function in SAP HANA determines a value between 0 and 1 that marks the degree of similarity. As a programmer, you must define a threshold value (for example, 0.8) from which a value of the dataset that has been searched is categorized as matching the search request. — *Algorithms*

In addition, the functionality of the fuzzy search can be adapted for specific (semantic) data types. For example, the fuzzy search for a date can include date values that are several days before or after the specific date — *Semantic fuzzy search*

387

being searched. In this case, the similarity criterion is the period rather than the similarity of the character string (so, according to this criterion, the date 01/01/1909 is not similar to 01/01/1990, although the position of only one character has been changed). Another example involves the search for a town on the basis of a ZIP code. In most countries, ZIP codes are structured in such a way that a similarity of the code's first digits tells more about geographical proximity than a similarity of the last digits.

Expressions used in searches

When running a fuzzy search, you can use a set of simple *expressions* that enable an expert to formulate more precise search requests. For example, this includes the option to enforce an exact search for a specific portion of the search request or to use logical expressions. Table 9.1 contains some sample expressions of the HANA text search based on the example of an airline search.

Search Request	Description
lufthansa OR united	Results that are similar either to "Lufthansa" or to "United".
airline—united	Results that are similar to "airline," but not to "united".
"south air"	Results that are similar to the entire expression, "south air", and not only to its components, "south" and "air". In this example, "South African Airways" would not be returned as a result.

Table 9.1 Using Expressions in the HANA Text Search

Linguistic search

To determine the degree of similarity, it is also useful to include grammatical and other linguistic aspects. In this context, terms are reverted to their word stem so that word variants such as "house," "houses," "housing," and so on, can be recognized. In addition, the linguistic search provides opportunities for handling multilingual texts and search requests.

Lists of synonyms

The fuzzy search can also be extended by *lists of synonyms*. In this context, you can store a list of terms that are equivalent to a specific term; this list can then be drawn upon in your search request. For example, "notebook" could be regarded as a synonym of "laptop," or "monitor" as a synonym of "screen." This feature is particularly useful for industry-specific abbreviations and concepts.

Another option to implement a more intelligent search is to familiarize the system with semantic characteristics of specific terms. In this context, it is important to know that not every term in a search request has the same *selectivity*. For example, terms such as "Inc." or "LLC" are not as selective as the actual company name when you search for a specific company. It is therefore usually more important to enter a company name similar to the one you are searching for than to enter that the search result is an "Inc.," for example. Likewise, in longer texts such as product descriptions, similarities in certain parts of speech such as articles or pronouns are less important than similarities in names within the text (for example, in brand names). When you run a search request in SAP HANA, you can enter a list of so-called *stop words* (also referred to as *noise words*) that are considered less important than other words.

Stop words

Because the text search function is based on a number of rather complex algorithms, it may be necessary to create specific *fuzzy search indexes* in order to accelerate the search runs and thus optimize the system performance, particularly if large amounts of data are involved. However, these indexes require additional memory. Section 9.6 contains some recommendations on how to use them.

Fuzzy search index

9.1.3 SAP Components and Products for Search

In Section 9.3, you will learn in detail how to directly access the search features of SAP HANA through SQL. In addition, SAP provides specific components and frameworks that support you in the creation of search runs, but since these are not the focus of this book, they are mentioned only briefly in the following paragraphs.

Since release 7.0, SAP NetWeaver AS ABAP contains the so-called *Embedded Search*. This component allows users to extract data for indexing via the *TREX Search and Classification Engine*, which represents an SAP NetWeaver component that can be installed separately (*standalone engine*). Embedded Search provides interfaces that enable a more efficient search within the extracted data of an application.

Embedded Search

However, Embedded Search is limited to searches within an SAP system. In order to run searches across different systems (in an application portal, for example), you can use the *SAP NetWeaver Enterprise Search* solution.

SAP NetWeaver Enterprise Search

This is based on the capabilities of the local Embedded Search functionality in integrated systems.

TREX

Because SAP HANA supports most of the functions of the TREX engine, you can use these functions directly in SAP HANA without a separate TREX installation. This means you can use existing Embedded Search models in SAP HANA, while, by default, the data continues to be extracted and replicated within SAP HANA. SAP currently plans to enable direct searches in tables via Embedded Search in SAP HANA without the data having to be replicated.

UI Toolkit for Information Access (InA)

Since SPS 5, SAP HANA additionally provides the *UI Toolkit for Information Access*, which allows you to create simple HTML5-based search interfaces. Based on attribute views, you can use HTML, JavaScript, and reusable *UI templates* to build a simple search application according to the modular design principle. This application employs SAP HANA Extended Application Services (XS) described in Section 9.3.

9.2 Types of Text Data and Full Text Indexes in SAP HANA

The fuzzy search in SAP HANA is based on the data types in the column store. Here, TEXT and SHORTTEXT represent two specific data types that are dedicated for text searches (and text analyses). The SHORTTEXT data type is to be used for character strings of a given length (similar to NVARCHAR), whereas TEXT represents a *large object* (similar to NCLOB—the SQL data type for a string in the ABAP Data Dictionary). In this context, texts are internally fragmented into *tokens* which form the basis for searches and analyses. The following sections provide more detailed information about this subject.

Support in ABAP

Unfortunately, however, there is currently no native support available in ABAP for the TEXT and SHORTTEXT data types. It is therefore not possible to create a table via the ABAP Data Dictionary that uses these data types. And although the fuzzy search function is basically also supported for other data types (VARCHAR and NVARCHAR, for example), this support is not extensive enough—therefore, the fuzzy search is generally not recommended here. Without the ability to split the texts into searchable tokens, the system is not able to recognize a permutation of words, which is a standard in modern search applications.

What you can do, however, is add the functionality offered by the text data types to a specific column by creating a full text index. In this way, you can enable the text search and text analysis functions for the majority of character-type ABAP Data Dictionary types (including CHAR, STRING, DATS, and so on).

Full text index

When you create a full text index for a table column, the system creates an internal, invisible column (*shadow column*) of the TEXT type, which contains the same data, but in a presentation optimized for search requests. In this context, the text is fragmented into tokens and an additional dictionary is generated. Figure 9.2 shows the internal presentation in a schema based on the example of airline names. You should note that the shadow column exists only transiently in the main memory. When you load the table into the memory (for example, after a database restart) this data structure is created anew. Section 9.6 contains further details about the memory consumption of a full text index.

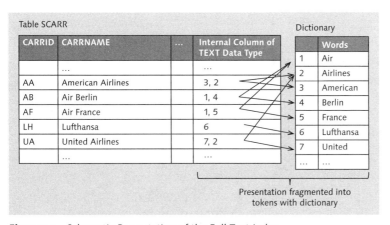

Figure 9.2 Schematic Presentation of the Full Text Index

You can create the full text index using SQL statement CREATE FULLTEXT INDEX. The syntax is as follows:

Using SQL for the creation

```
CREATE FULLTEXT INDEX <index_name>
ON <table_name> ( <column_name> )
[<parameter_list>]
```

Here, you can use numerous optional settings, a description of which would go beyond the scope of this book. But you can obtain a comprehensive documentation from *http://help.sap.com/hana_appliance.* You should also note that the name of the full text index must be unique within a schema, and it therefore makes sense to prefix the index name with the table name in order to avoid name clashes.

Creation in the ABAP Data Dictionary

The following statement defines a full text index for the CARRNAME column of table SCARR:

```
CREATE FULLTEXT INDEX scarr~name ON scarr(carrname);
```

Because you cannot create full text indexes via the ABAP Data Dictionary (Transaction SE11) prior to ABAP release 7.4, these indexes cannot be transported automatically. As of ABAP release 7.4, it is also possible to create a full text index via the ABAP Data Dictionary using a standard configuration. For this purpose, you must define a new index for a table using Transaction SE11, or rather, an *extension index* (for a modification-free extension of an SAP standard table). This contains only the required column as a field and is created exclusively in the HANA database. Figure 9.3 shows this type of index in the CITY column of table SCUSTOM.

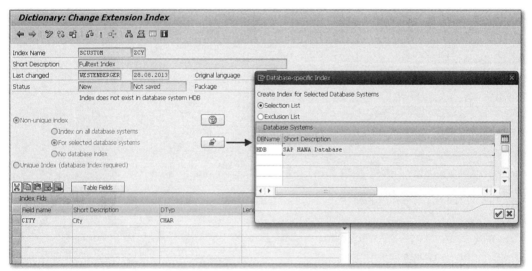

Figure 9.3 Creating a Full Text Index via the ABAP Data Dictionary

You can then activate the full text index via GOTO • FULL TEXT INDEX (see Figure 9.4). The system will then use the default settings of a full text index for text searches.

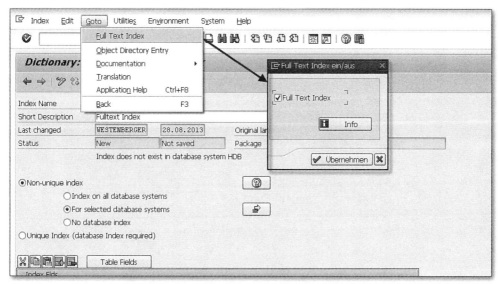

Figure 9.4 Activating the Full Text Index

In addition to using the ABAP Data Dictionary, you can also use Native SQL in an ABAP program to create a full text index. This allows you to use the entire range of options available for a text search; however, this method requires you to manage the index in a system landscape yourself. Listing 9.1 shows how you can create and remove full text indexes using the ADBC interface (ABAP Database Connectivity).

Creation via ADBC

```
REPORT zr_a4h_chapter9_adbc_ft_index.

" Configuration
PARAMETERS:
 table LIKE dd02l-tabname DEFAULT 'SCUSTOM',
 column LIKE dd03l-fieldname DEFAULT 'NAME',
 fzyidx TYPE abap_bool AS CHECKBOX DEFAULT abap_false,
 ta TYPE abap_bool AS CHECKBOX DEFAULT abap_false,
 taconfig TYPE string DEFAULT 'EXTRACTION_CORE',
 drop TYPE abap_bool AS CHECKBOX DEFAULT abap_true,
 create TYPE abap_bool AS CHECKBOX DEFAULT abap_true.
```

```abap
" Index name (<Table>~<Column>)
DATA(lv_idx) = table && '~' && column.

" SQL statement for creating a full text index
DATA(lv_sql) = |CREATE FULLTEXT INDEX { lv_idx } |
            && |ON { table }({ column })|.

" Additional fuzzy search index
IF ( fzyidx = abap_true ).
  lv_sql = lv_sql && ' FUZZY SEARCH INDEX ON'.
ENDIF.

" Text analysis
IF ( ta = abap_true ).
 lv_sql = lv_sql && ' TEXT ANALYSIS ON'.
 " Special configuration of text analysis
 IF ( taconfig IS NOT INITIAL ).
  lv_sql = lv_sql && | CONFIGURATION '{ taconfig }'|.
 ENDIF.
ENDIF.

IF ( drop = abap_true ).
  TRY.
    " Remove index
    cl_sql_connection=>get_connection(
      )->create_statement( )->execute_ddl(
        |DROP FULLTEXT INDEX { lv_idx }|
      ).

    WRITE: / |Full text index { lv_idx } removed|.
  CATCH cx_sql_exception INTO DATA(lo_ex).
    " Error handling
    WRITE: / | Error: { lo_ex->get_text( ) }|.
  ENDTRY.
ENDIF.

IF ( create = abap_true ).
  TRY.
    " Create text index via ADBC
    cl_sql_connection=>get_connection(
      )->create_statement(
      )->execute_ddl( lv_sql ).
```

```
    WRITE: / |Full text index { lv_idx } created|.
  CATCH cx_sql_exception INTO DATA(lo_ex1).
    " Error handling
    WRITE: / | Error: { lo_ex1->get_text( ) }|.
  ENDTRY.
ENDIF.
```

Listing 9.1 Creating a Text Index via ADBC

You can view existing full text indexes when you open a table and click on the INDEXES tab in SAP HANA Studio (see Figure 9.5). Here you can view technical characteristics such as the synchronization behavior.

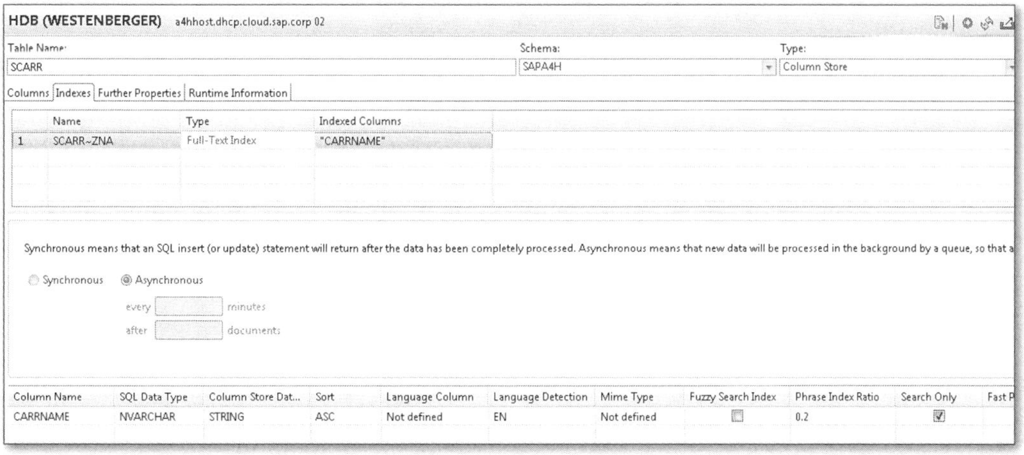

Displaying full
text indexes

Figure 9.5 Displaying a Full Text Index in SAP HANA Studio

9.3   Using the Text Search via SQL

As is the case with the majority of functions in SAP HANA, you can invoke the text search via SQL. To do this, you must use a `SELECT` statement with the key word `CONTAINS`, which enables you to call the manifold variants of the text search. The standard syntax is as follows:

CONTAINS
key word

```
SELECT <field list>
FROM <table or view>
WHERE CONTAINS (<columns>,<search request>,<parameters>);
```

The following example provides an initial idea of how you can use the CONTAINS clause for a fuzzy search:

```
SELECT * FROM scarr WHERE CONTAINS( carrname, 'lusthansa',
FUZZY(0.8));
```

Here, we run a search for airlines whose names are *sufficiently similar* to the search request, 'lusthansa'. Although the search request contains two errors (the search term starts with a lowercase letter and contains one incorrect letter), the system returns the expected data record, "Lufthansa."

FUZZY parameter

The following sections discuss the definition of similarity in greater detail. At this point, you should know that the FUZZY(0.8) parameter defines the threshold value, where a value between 0.7 and 0.8 is usually a good standard value to obtain results that are relatively similar to the search request. In addition to the threshold value, the FUZZY parameter provides many other setting options.

Exact search/
linguistic search

Apart from its use with the FUZZY parameter, you can use the CONTAINS statement in two other variants: EXACT and LINGUISTIC. In searches with the addition EXACT, the system searches for exact matches for the search request with entire words (based on the tokenization of the text in the database). EXACT also represents the default value if you do not enter any parameter. In this case, you can also use wildcards such as '*' in the search request. In contrast to a LIKE in standard SQL, the CONTAINS clause allows you to perform searches across multiple columns. The following example shows an exact search for airlines whose names or web addresses contain "Airlines" or "Airways" or end with ".com."

```
SELECT * FROM scarr WHERE CONTAINS ((carrname,url), 'Airlines
OR Airways OR *.com', EXACT)
```

This example is also useful for demonstrating the effects of a missing full text index. If no full text index exists for the carrname column, the names will not be split into words (tokens); consequently, there will be no exact match between the search request 'Airlines' and an entry like "United Airlines."

If you run an additional analysis of the word stems via a text analysis (see Section 9.5), the LINGUISTIC parameter allows you to obtain additional results in which only the word stems must match.

This book focuses primarily on the subject of fuzzy searches because it is difficult to implement an intuitively usable search function with the exact or linguistic search within an ABAP application. This is because it can easily happen in both cases that fewer results are found than in a classic ABAP input help.

[«]

> **Limitations to the Text Search in SAP HANA SQL**
>
> As already mentioned, you can use SQL for text searches in SAP HANA. However, there are currently several limitations with regard to the supported combinations. These are as follows:
>
> ▶ You can apply the `CONTAINS` clause only to text searches in tables of the column store.
> ▶ You cannot apply the `CONTAINS` clause to text searches in SQL views. Currently, this scenario requires you to use an attribute view. SAP plans to remove this restriction in future versions of SAP HANA.
> ▶ You cannot apply the text search function to calculated attributes of a view.

9.3.1 Fuzzy Search

The following section describes how you can use the fuzzy search function for a simple search run across one or several columns of a table or view. Section 9.3.2 and Section 9.3.3 will then provide details about the specific search variants that utilize additional semantic information about the data.

The examples used in this context involve the airline names (column `CARRNAME` in table `SCARR`) and the locations from the flight schedule (columns `CITYFR` and `CITYTO` in table `SPFLI`). For this purpose, a full text index will be defined for each attribute, as described in Section 9.2. For the examples used here, the variant supported by the ABAP Data Dictionary will suffice.

Searching Across Multiple Columns

The `CONTAINS` statement allows you to specify multiple columns to be considered during the search run. The following example indicates a search in the flight schedule to "Tokio."

Multiple columns within a table

```
SELECT * FROM spfli WHERE CONTAINS ((cityfrom,cityto), 'Tokio',
fuzzy(0.8))
```

The result will contain all flights departing from and arriving in Tokyo, even though the spelling of the city's name deviates slightly (in some languages this is the common spelling of this city). Instead of the individual column names, you can also use an asterisk (*) in order to run the search across all columns that support a text search.

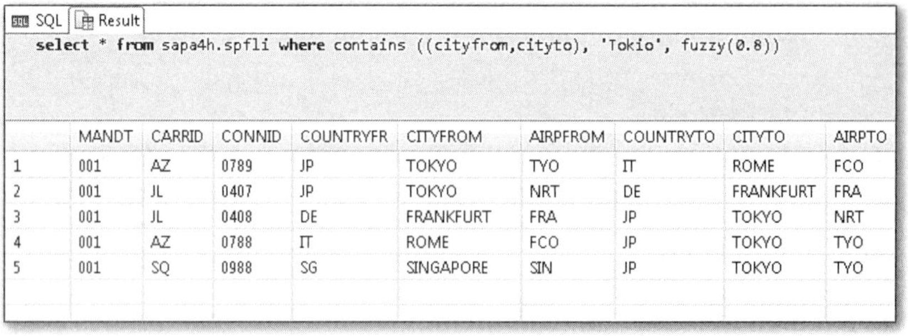

	MANDT	CARRID	CONNID	COUNTRYFR	CITYFROM	AIRPFROM	COUNTRYTO	CITYTO	AIRPTO
1	001	AZ	0789	JP	TOKYO	TYO	IT	ROME	FCO
2	001	JL	0407	JP	TOKYO	NRT	DE	FRANKFURT	FRA
3	001	JL	0408	DE	FRANKFURT	FRA	JP	TOKYO	NRT
4	001	AZ	0788	IT	ROME	FCO	JP	TOKYO	TYO
5	001	SQ	0988	SG	SINGAPORE	SIN	JP	TOKYO	TYO

*select * from sapa4h.spfli where contains ((cityfrom,cityto), 'Tokio', fuzzy(0.8))*

Figure 9.6 Fuzzy Search Across Multiple Columns

Multiple columns in multiple tables

If you want to run the search across multiple columns in different tables that are linked through foreign key dependencies, you can do that in two different ways. You can either write an SQL join or use a view. Concerning the latter, SAP HANA currently supports only the use of attribute views, but the support of normal SQL views is planned for future releases.

In order to include the airline name in addition to the departure and destination names in the flight schedule search, we'll create a simple attribute view, as shown in Figure 9.7.

Fuzzy search in attribute view

In an attribute view, the fuzzy search via SQL is carried out in the same manner as within a table. Thus, the result of the following SELECT statement contains all flights from or to Singapore, as well as all flights operated by Singapore Airlines.

```
SELECT * FROM
  "test.a4h.book.chapter09::AT_FIGHTPLAN_FUZZY"
WHERE CONTAINS(*, 'singapore', fuzzy(0.8))
```

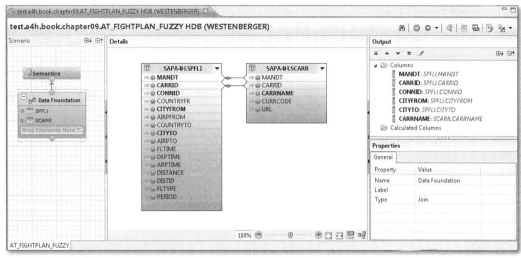

Figure 9.7 Attribute View for Fuzzy Search Across Two Tables

Special Functions

There are special scalar functions available that enable you to retrieve additional information for individual data records in the result set. SAP HANA currently provides the `score()`, `highlighted()`, and `snippets()` functions, which will be described in the following sections.

The `score()` function provides information about the degree of similar- **Score** ity between the search result and the search request. This value ranges between 0 and 1, with higher values indicating a higher degree of similarity. Normally, the function is used for sorting the search results in such a way that results with a higher degree of similarity are displayed further toward the top of the list than those with a lower value:

```
SELECT * FROM scarr WHERE CONTAINS( carrname, 'airways',
fuzzy(0.8)) ORDER BY score() desc;
```

> **Difference Between score() and Threshold Values for Searches** **[!]**
>
> The return value of the `score()` function does not directly correspond to the threshold value in the `fuzzy()` statement. Consequently, it is absolutely conceivable to obtain search results in which the value of the `score()` function is lower than the transferred threshold value.

Highlighted
and snippets In searches through longer texts, it is particularly useful for users if the exact found location of a search request is highlighted in the text. For this purpose, SAP HANA SQL offers the `highlighted()` and `snippets()` functions. If the former is used, the system returns the entire text with the found location highlighted, whereas if `snippets()` is used, only an extract of the text around the found location is returned. Note that there is no difference between the two with regard to shorter texts such as the airline names, for example.

When using these functions, you must specify the column as shown in the following example:

```
SELECT *, highlighted(carrname) FROM sapa4h.scarr
    WHERE CONTAINS( carrname, 'airways', fuzzy(0.8))
    ORDER BY score() desc;
```

The result contains the found location enclosed by *markups* that use the HTML tag `<b>...</b>` (see Figure 9.8). If you plan to implement your own type of search result display, you may want to replace these tags accordingly.

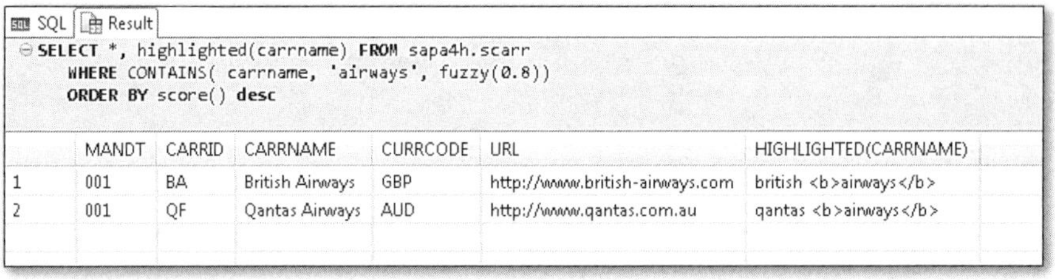

Figure 9.8   Highlighting the Found Location using the highlighted() Function

[»]   **highlighted() and snippets() Only in One Column**

The `highlighted()` and `snippets()` functions can only highlight hits within one column. If you run a search across multiple columns, you can query the value of individual attributes only. Thus, if no found location exists in a column, you won't find any highlight in the value of the function. Unfortunately, there is currently no option available that allows you to directly recognize the column (or columns) that contain the found location.

Other Parameterizations

The parameterization of the fuzzy search has not yet been discussed in detail, and it would go beyond the scope of this book to describe all options and variants related to this topic. However, you should be familiar with some of these aspects, which are essential to a correct usage. These involve, first and foremost, the parameters `similarCalculationMode` and `textSearch`. You must transfer these types of parameter by means of a character string in which you use commas to separate individual parameters, as shown in the following example:

```
SELECT * FROM scarr WHERE
  CONTAINS(carrname, 'lusthansa',
  fuzzy(0.8, 'similarCalculationMode=search'));
```

The `similarCalculationMode` parameter enables you to check how the fuzzy score (i.e., the degree of similarity), is calculated. In this context, you must distinguish between two scenarios. In a text comparison, the request and the text in the database as a whole should be fairly similar; however, in a normal search run, it should be sufficient that the search request is part of the text. For this reason, you should use the `compare` parameter value for text comparisons, and `search` for search runs. The following section describes how you can manually create a specific full text index and discusses the differences between the parameter values.

similar-CalculationMode parameter

In addition, the `textSearch` parameter is important for the description of some of the more complex search options in the following sections; this parameter switches between separate technical implementations in SAP HANA. The details of this parameter and its use will be described in Section 9.3.2.

textSearch parameter

9.3.2 Synonyms and Noise Words

Lists of synonyms and stop words (also called *noise words*) represent an option to implement a more intelligent search. To do this, you must store the additional data in tables of a predefined structure, and the names of these configuration tables must be included in the search requests.

Let us first consider the use of noise words. Names of airlines, for example, frequently contain the word "air," which, compared to other words, presumably plays a minor role in search runs. For this reason, we want to

Stop word table

include this term in the list of stop words. This does not mean that the word will be completely ignored or even that the search will terminate, but merely that less importance will be attached to the term.

The structure of the configuration table is as shown in Table 9.2.

Column	SQL Data Type	Example
stopword_id	VARCHAR(32)	"1"
list_id	VARCHAR(32)	"airline"
language_code	CHAR(2)	
term	NVARCHAR(200)	"Air"

Table 9.2 Structure of Configuration Table for Stop Words

Configuration table columns

Here, the stopword_id field represents the unique key. The list_id column allows for storing multiple individual lists for different usage scenarios in the table. In addition, you can store words that are relevant only for specific languages (this value has been left empty in this example of airline names).

Search within sample table

Figure 9.9 shows a table called ZA4H_BOOK_STOPW in the ABAP Data Dictionary with a matching structure.

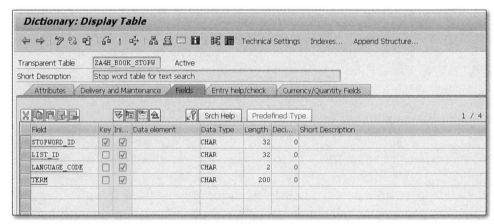

Figure 9.9 Stop Word Table in ABAP Data Dictionary

Now the sample data record from Table 9.2 will be entered into this table. If you want to include the list of stop words in a fuzzy search, you must use the `stopwordTable` and `stopwordListId` parameters. The example in Listing 9.2 shows the search for the terms "air" and "united" and uses the previously generated stop word table.

```
SELECT score(), * FROM scarr WHERE CONTAINS( carrname, 'air OR
united', fuzzy(0.8, 'textsearch=compare, stopwordTable=ZA4H_
BOOK_STOPW, stopwordListId=airline, similarCalculationMode=sear
ch')) ORDER BY score();
```

Listing 9.2 Fuzzy Search with Stop Word Table

The `textsearch=compare` parameter is necessary if you want to use these search variants. The result contains the entry "United Airlines," but not "Air Canada," for example, because due to the stop word table, a lower degree of importance has been attached to the term "Air."

This describes how you can use synonyms in your search requests. To do this, you must map those terms you want to treat as synonyms in a configuration table (*term mapping*). As is the case with stop words, you can store these terms based on individual languages and in multiple lists. In addition, you can store a weighting between 0 and 1 in order to indicate the extent to which the finding of a synonym is supposed to reduce the value of similarity. Table 9.3 shows the structure of the corresponding configuration table.

Lists of synonyms

Column	SQL Data Type	Example
mapping_id	VARCHAR(32)	"1"
list_id	VARCHAR(32)	"airline"
language_code	CHAR(2)	
term_1	NVARCHAR(255)	"Airways"
term_2	NVARCHAR(255)	"Airlines"
weight	DECIMAL	0.8

Table 9.3 Structure of Configuration Table for Synonyms

[»] **Lists of Synonyms Cannot be Stored as ABAP Data Dictionary Tables**

Unfortunately, you cannot create this type of table in the ABAP Data Dictionary because the DECIMAL data type (*floating decimal point*) is not supported in ABAP. However, the following section describes a possible technical alternative that consists of creating a separate table with the appropriate structure in a different schema and synchronizing the synonym data into that table.

The example in Listing 9.3 describes the search for the term, "United Airways."

```
SELECT score(), * FROM scarr WHERE CONTAINS( carrname,
'united airways', fuzzy(0.8, 'textsearch=compare,
termMappingTable=ZA4H_BOOK_SYNTAB, termMappingListId=airline,
similarCalculationMode=search')) ORDER BY score();
```
Listing 9.3 Fuzzy Search with List of Synonyms

The specification of the mapping table via the termMappingTable and termMappingListId parameters causes the fuzzy search to analyze the list of synonyms so that the result contains the expected entry, "United Airlines."

Hypernyms, hyponyms

In addition to terms with identical meaning (i.e., synonyms), you can use the mapping mechanism to include *hypernyms* and *hyponyms*; that is, more general or more concrete terms, which can be particularly useful with large, unstructured texts. This enables you, for example, to recognize the occurrence of the hypernym "airline" when searching for the term "Lufthansa" in a text. To achieve this, you would have to choose a low value (0.2, for example) as weight (WEIGHT).

Moreover, you can use a combination of stop words and synonyms in a search request; in that case, the system calculates the synonymous variants first, followed by the stop words.

9.3.3 Searching Across Date Fields and Address Data

Finally, this section describes some of the more comprehensive options that were introduced in Section 9.1.2 so that you can get an idea of how to use them. This section focuses on fuzzy searches in date fields as well as on the search for ZIP codes. Unfortunately, both options cannot be used directly from within ABAP because they require specific data types and column definitions. These kinds of native developments in the database require additional design concepts.

For this reason, an additional table will be created in a separate database, previously generated schema; we will need this table for our sample scenario. The table will be used to store customer addresses as well as the date and time of the last booking from within the ABAP tables where native HANA types were used. A fuzzy search will then be run across this data in which the semantic characteristics of dates and ZIP codes will be utilized.

Sample scenario

For the sake of convenience, the scenario will be implemented here exclusively via the SQL console in SAP HANA Studio. You can, of course, also execute these native SQL statements from within an ABAP program through the ADBC interface. This will be described in detail in Chapter 13, where a sample application is developed.

The table is created via SQL, as shown in Listing 9.4.

Native database table with SQL

```
create column table custom_fuzzy (
 mandt NVARCHAR(3) DEFAULT '000' NOT NULL ,
 id    NVARCHAR(8) DEFAULT '00000000' NOT NULL ,
 name  NVARCHAR(25) DEFAULT '' NOT NULL ,
 city  NVARCHAR(25) DEFAULT '' NOT NULL ,
 postcode NVARCHAR(10) FUZZY SEARCH MODE 'postcode',
 lastbooking DATE
 );
```

Listing 9.4 Creating a Table with Customer Addresses and Booking Dates via SQL

For the date, we use the native data type DATE, and specify a fuzzy search mode for the ZIP code. Both these settings cannot be used in the same manner for an ABAP Data Dictionary table.

After that, the table is populated based on the data from tables SCUSTOM and SBOOK using the SQL statement in Listing 9.5.

```
INSERT INTO custom_fuzzy
SELECT c.mandt, c.id, c.name, c.city, c.postcode,
       to_date( MIN ( b.order_date ) ) as lastbooking
FROM sapa4h.sbook as b INNER JOIN sapa4h.scustom as c
```

```
            ON b.mandt = c.mandt and b.customid = c.id
        GROUP BY c.mandt, c.id, c.name, c.city, c.postcode;
```
Listing 9.5   Populating the Database Table with Data

In a fuzzy search for a date field, the degree of similarity is impacted by the time difference between the date values, and also by typical typing errors in date entries. You do not need to create a full text index for this kind of fuzzy search, because a fragmentation into tokens (words) is not needed here.

In Listing 9.6, we search for customers whose last booking was carried out *on or around* November 13, 2012. The maxDateDistance=3 parameter specifies the maximum difference in days. In addition, the system will also return results that contain an incorrect number, for example, or in which the day and month have been exchanged.

```
SELECT lastbooking, score() FROM custom_fuzzy
    WHERE CONTAINS(lastbooking, '2012-11-13',
          FUZZY(0.9, 'maxDateDistance=3'))
ORDER BY score() DESC;
```
Listing 9.6   Fuzzy Search for a Date

As described in Section 9.1.2, in the fuzzy search for a ZIP code, the degree of similarity is determined through the geographical proximity, which is indicated by the internal structure of the ZIP codes. Listing 9.7 searches for codes close to "69190."

```
SELECT postcode, score() FROM custom_fuzzy
  WHERE CONTAINS( postcode, '69190', fuzzy(0.7))
ORDER BY score() desc;
```
Listing 9.7   Fuzzy Search for ZIP Codes

Figure 9.10 shows the result of a combined search for customers close to Walldorf, Germany (ZIP code 69190), whose last booking was carried out on or around November 13, 2012.

SQL | Result

```
SELECT * from custom_fuzzy
  where CONTAINS( lastbooking, '2012-11-13', fuzzy(0.9, 'maxDateDistance=3'))
  and   CONTAINS( postcode,    '69190',      fuzzy(0.5))
order by score() desc, postcode
```

	MANDT	ID	NAME	CITY	POSTCODE	LASTBOOKING
1	001	00000003	Hans Bullinger	Heidelberg	69119	13.11.2012
2	001	00003170	Lothar Delon	Walldorf	69180	14.11.2012
3	001	00000794	Florian Buchholm	Wiesloch	69180	14.11.2012
4	001	00001135	Ulla Marshall	Wiesloch	69180	14.11.2012
5	001	00000579	Georg Lautenbach	Walldorf	69190	03.11.2012
6	001	00002858	Lothar Sudhoff	Walldorf	69180	11.11.2012
7	001	00000951	Lothar Dumbach	Walldorf	69180	15.11.2012
8	001	00001700	Lothar Koller	Walldorf	69180	15.11.2012
9	001	00001139	Ulla Weiss	Wiesloch	69180	10.11.2012

Figure 9.10 Fuzzy Search for a Date and ZIP Code

In addition to ZIP codes, you can also run fuzzy searches for house numbers containing specific characteristics such as number ranges (for example, "8–10") or letters ("8a").

9.4 Using the Text Search in ABAP

As you have seen, the fuzzy search function in SAP HANA provides many innovative options to run searches on existing data. Some of these scenarios require you to format or transform the data in order to take advantage of all the options. In the following sections, you'll learn how to use ABAP to call the text search function.

As described in Section 9.1.3, the Embedded Search component enables you to implement independent search applications. The following sections discuss in detail how you can implement searches directly *within* an application such as an input help for a form field, for example.

Mind the lifecycle management

Let us first consider some general remarks. In some scenarios, the direct use of the text search function from within ABAP currently requires a few technical tricks that are not supported by the standard ABAP development model. As a result, you must carefully think about the design of your development before you can use the function in a production system. Some of these design aspects are discussed in Chapter 14 as part of our recommendations on using the advanced SAP HANA functions.

9.4.1 Calling the Text Search from ABAP via SQL

Because the text search function in SAP HANA is not part of the standard features of a traditional database, the CONTAINS statement is unfortunately not yet supported in Open SQL. However, you can still employ the text search directly from within ABAP if you use Native SQL.

Access via ADBC Using the text search via ADBC is pretty simple. To do this, all you need to do is include the CONTAINS statement in the Native SQL statement, as shown in the example in Listing 9.8.

```
REPORT ZR_A4H_CHAPTER9_ADBC_CONTAINS.
" Variables for ADBC call and result
DATA: lv_sql  TYPE string,
      lt_result TYPE TABLE OF scarr.

" Search request
PARAMETERS: search TYPE string LOWER CASE.

" Use of CONTAINS in Native SQL
lv_sql =
    | SELECT * FROM SCARR |
 && |   WHERE mandt = '{ sy-mandt }' and |
 && |   CONTAINS(carrname, '{ search }', fuzzy(0.8))|.

TRY.
    " Prepare SQL connection and statement
    DATA(lo_result) =
            cl_sql_connection=>get_connection(
                )->create_statement(
                )->execute_query( lv_sql ).

    lo_result->set_param_table( REF #( lt_result ) ).

    " Get result
    lo_result->next_package( ).
    lo_result->close( ).
  CATCH cx_sql_exception.
    " Error handling
ENDTRY.

" Result output
LOOP AT lt_result ASSIGNING FIELD-SYMBOL(<line>).
```

```
  WRITE: / <line>-carrid , <line>-carrname.
ENDLOOP.
```

Listing 9.8   Using the Text Search via ADBC

Similarly, you can also run search requests across attribute views. Although the access via OpenSQL is not possible here, either—due to the lack of support for the CONTAINS statement—it is advisable that you first define an external view based on the respective attribute view. This will facilitate the processing of data types because there is already a representation available in the ABAP Data Dictionary.

Search request via attribute views

9.4.2   Freely Defined Input Helps

As mentioned at the beginning of this chapter, input helps provide multiple options for use of the text search in SAP HANA. Figure 9.11 shows this on the basis of a free text search for a passenger based on the passenger's name and place of residence. In this section, you'll learn how to implement this type of input help.

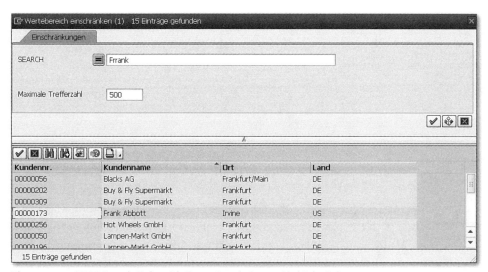

Figure 9.11   ABAP Search Help with Fuzzy Search Across Multiple Columns

You define an input help in the ABAP Data Dictionary. In general, these input helps can then be used in both classic Dynpro-based applications

409

and in application interfaces that have been created using Web Dynpro ABAP or the Floorplan Manager. In this context, you can either create single (so-called *elementary*) search helps, or combine multiple input helps into a *collective search help*. The individual search helps are then usually displayed on separate tabs. Collective search helps are particularly useful if you want to extend an existing search help by an optimized variant in SAP HANA (this variant will then be hidden in other databases).

Search help exit A search help can be defined declaratively in such a way that you specify the name of a table or view and select the fields for the dialog. In addition, you can also implement the data retrieval process by yourself using a *search help exit*. We will use this variant in the following sections to implement the fuzzy search function.

To define a search help exit, you must first create a function module that contains the interface shown in Listing 9.9. A simple search help exit is contained in function module F4IF_SHLP_EXIT_EXAMPLE in the standard SAP system.

```
FUNCTION z_a4h_book_chapter9_exit_cust
  CHANGING
    VALUE(shlp) TYPE shlp_descr
    VALUE(callcontrol) LIKE ddshf4ctrl
  TABLES
    shlp_tab TYPE shlp_desct
    record_tab LIKE seahlpres.

    " ....

ENDFUNCTION.
```

Listing 9.9 Interface for Search Help Exits

Creating and testing an input help Prior to implementing the function module, you should familiarize yourself with the processes of creating and testing an input help in the ABAP Data Dictionary, including the specification of such an exit. For this purpose, all you have to do is open Transaction SE11 and create a new search help. Then enter the relevant display and search help exit parameters. Figure 9.12 shows the configuration of the search help from Figure 9.11.

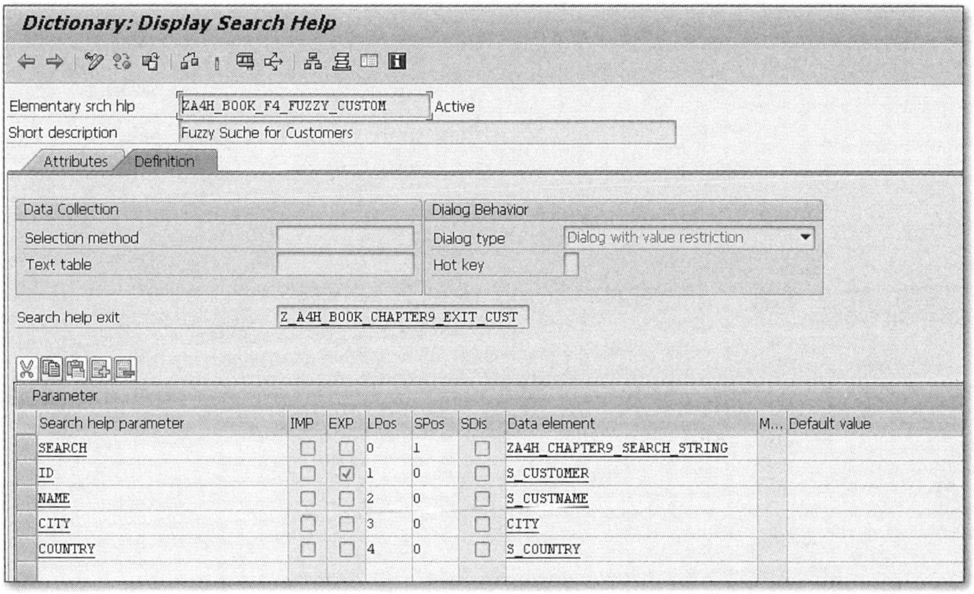

Figure 9.12 Configuring the Search Help in Transaction SE11

The function module is called at several times by the search help framework, and it is during these phases that you can manipulate the behavior of the system. The `callcontrol-step` value allows you to query the current phase. Table 9.4 provides an overview of the phases with a focus on those operations that are available in the context of a fuzzy search.

Call times for search help exits

Phase	Explanation
SELONE	This phase is relevant only for collective search helps. It enables you to manipulate the number and sequence of elementary search helps. In particular, it allows you to hide HANA-specific search helps in systems running on other databases.
PRESEL	This step enables you to manipulate the selection conditions so that you can replace certain special characters (such as a "*") in the context of a fuzzy search, for example.
SELECT	In this phase, you can implement your own selection of data and thus run a fuzzy search via ADBC, for example.

Table 9.4 Phases of a Search Help Exit

Phase	Explanation
DISP	This phase once again allows you to manipulate the data and run an authorization check, for example, or change the presentation mode. The following examples do not use this phase.

Table 9.4 Phases of a Search Help Exit (Cont.)

Implementing a search help exit

Listing 9.10 shows the complete implementation of the search help exit from Figure 9.11. The system reads the data during the SELECT phase (the Dictionary structure ZA4H_CHAPTER9_CUSTOM represents a simple projection of table SCUSTOM) and writes it into the target structure using function module F4UT_RESULTS_MAP.

```
FUNCTION z_a4h_book_chapter9_exit_cust.
*"----------------------------------------------------
*"*"Local Interface:
*"  TABLES
*"      SHLP_TAB TYPE  SHLP_DESCT
*"      RECORD_TAB STRUCTURE  SEAHLPRES
*"  CHANGING
*"     VALUE(SHLP) TYPE  SHLP_DESCR
*"     VALUE(CALLCONTROL) LIKE  DDSHF4CTRL STRUCTURE
DDSHF4CTRL
*"----------------------------------------------------

  DATA: lt_data TYPE TABLE OF za4h_chapter9_custom.

  IF callcontrol-step <> 'SELECT'.
    EXIT.
  ENDIF.

*"----------------------------------------------------
* STEP SELECT    (Select values)
*"----------------------------------------------------
  IF callcontrol-step = 'SELECT'.
    " Search request
    DATA: lv_value type string.
    TRY.
      lv_value =
```

```
      shlp-selopt[ shlpfield = 'SEARCH' ]-low.
  CATCH cx_sy_itab_line_not_found.
   " Ignore
  ENDTRY.

  DATA(lv_sql) =
     |SELECT id, name, city, country FROM scustom|
  && | WHERE CONTAINS(*, '{ lv_value }', |
  && | fuzzy(0.8,'similarCalculationMode=search')) |
  && | AND mandt = '{ sy-mandt }' |
  && |ORDER BY score() desc, id|.

  TRY.
    DATA(lo_result) =
       cl_sql_connection=>get_connection(
                  )->create_statement(
                  )->execute_query( lv_sql ).

    lo_result->set_param_table( REF #( lt_data ) ).
    lo_result->next_package( ).
    lo_result->close( ).
  CATCH cx_sql_exception INTO DATA(lo_ex).
    " Error handling ...
  ENDTRY.

  CALL FUNCTION 'F4UT_RESULTS_MAP'
    EXPORTING
      source_structure = 'ZA4H_CHAPTER9_CUSTOM'
    TABLES
      shlp_tab          = shlp_tab
      record_tab        = record_tab
      source_tab        = lt_data
    CHANGING
      shlp              = shlp
      callcontrol       = callcontrol.

   callcontrol-step = 'DISP'.
  ENDIF.

ENDFUNCTION.
```

Listing 9.10 Search Help Exit with Fuzzy Search Across Name and Place of Residence

Usage in Web
Dynpro ABAP

To conclude this section, the following paragraphs describe how you can use search helps created in the ABAP Data Dictionary in Web Dynpro ABAP. This is a standard Web Dynpro functionality, independent of SAP HANA, and we can only introduce some of the details in the following sections. Moreover, you should also have some basic development knowledge using Web Dynpro ABAP.

Data model of
a Web Dynpro
component

The data model of a Web Dynpro component must be defined using the so-called *context*, which in turn can be defined either manually or based on a Dictionary structure (table or view). When you define the context, the system transfers the associated search helps by default; however, you can also use your own Dictionary search help for an attribute in the Web Dynpro context. Figure 9.13 shows a Web Dynpro context with an attribute for the customer ID (SCUSTOM-ID). At this point, we are using the new Eclipse-based development environment for Web Dynpro ABAP. However, you can make the setting as well via Transaction SE80.

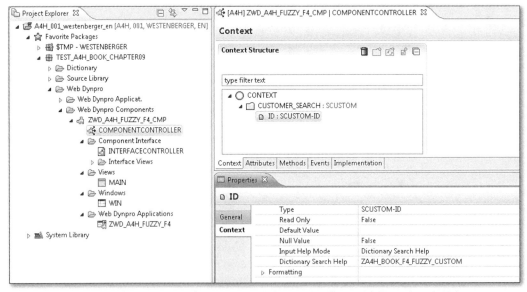

Figure 9.13 Web Dynpro ABAP Context Attribute with Fuzzy Search Help

Web Dynpro ABAP Development in Eclipse [«]

In addition to tools that are used for pure ABAP developments, the ABAP Development Tools for SAP NetWeaver also contain other tools that are integrated natively in Eclipse—one of them being the development environment for Web Dynpro ABAP. You can use this tool in the same manner as other ABAP development objects: There are specific editors available for the Web Dynpro objects (for instance, Web Dynpro components) as well as for the related sub-objects (such as *views* or *windows).* These can be created or opened through the PROJECT EXPLORER view in Eclipse, similar to the way you work with ABAP reports or classes.

If you link this context attribute to an input field in a Web Dynpro view, you will obtain a Web Dynpro application with similar functionality as the one shown in Figure 9.11. Figure 9.14 shows this Web Dynpro application.

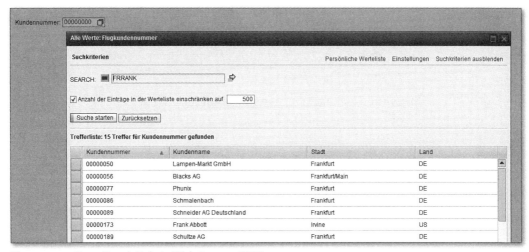

Figure 9.14 Fuzzy Search Help in Web Dynpro ABAP

In addition, you can also view default values directly via Web Dynpro ABAP at the same time the user enters data (*value suggest*). This combination of functions enables you to create search helps that behave like modern Internet searches. This feature will be used for the creation of the sample application in Chapter 13.

Suggesting values

415

9.5   Text Analysis

Semantic characteristics

In addition to running pure searches, you can use the text analysis to extract further insights. Based on the splitting of texts into *tokens*, these tokens are then assigned additional semantic characteristics (see Section 9.1). The semantic principles include, for example:

▶ Which language does the term come from? What is the word stem or basic grammatical form? Is it an abbreviation?

▶ Is the term a technical term? If so, from which subject area or industry does it come?

Does the term implicitly contain an emotional statement—that is, does the term have a positive (e.g., "ideal") or negative (e.g., "unbearable") connotation?

For the purpose of the text analysis, it is necessary for the system to know the characteristics and specifics of the respective language pretty well. SAP HANA is provided with dictionaries containing terms from more than 20 languages. Then, in a text analysis, the system extracts and categorizes metadata from the texts.

You can use the text analysis function for all types of data that allow for the creation of a full text index (such as columns of the following types: NVARCHAR, VARCHAR, CLOB, NCLOB, and so on). Note that when creating a full text index, you must specify the TEXT ANALYSIS ON option as well as an option for the analysis.

Text analysis options

SAP currently supports the options listed in Table 9.5. You can find information on the language(s) supported by each option in the developer documentation at *http://help.sap.com/hana_appliance/*.

Option	Description
LINGANALYSIS_BASIC	Fragments a text into its components (individual words with normalization of umlauts, accented characters, and so forth).
LINGANALYSIS_STEMS	Fragments a text into its components and identifies the word stem of each word.
LINGANALYSIS_FULL	Similar to LINGANALYSIS_STEMS, with additional grammatical categorization of terms.

Table 9.5 Text Analysis Options

Option	Description
EXTRACTION_CORE	Extracts terms from the text and categorizes them semantically (for example, into persons, organizations, locations, and so on).
EXTRACTION_CORE_ VOICEOFCUSTOMER	Analyzes texts according to patterns that indicate emotions and desires of the writer (*sentiment analysis*).

Table 9.5 Text Analysis Options (Cont.)

Basically, you can employ the text analysis function in two different ways—a linguistic and a semantic variant. The linguistic analysis is useful in scenarios where you want to analyze texts according to grammatical aspects. In particular, this variant is a prerequisite for the linguistic search described in Section 9.3. The semantic analysis, in turn, can be used to extract additional information. In many cases, the EXTRACTION_CORE option is sufficient for this.

Linguistic and semantic analysis

The following example defines a full text index with text analysis for the airline names. For the creation, the example uses the ABAP report from Listing 9.1 and the settings shown in Figure 9.15.

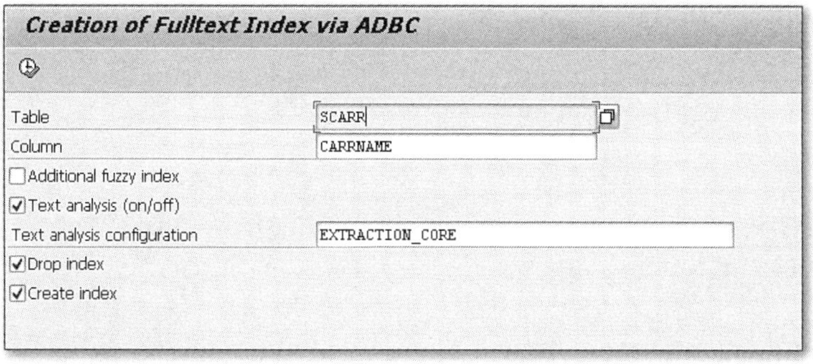

Example: Full text index with text analysis

Figure 9.15 Full Text Index with Text Analysis via ADBC

When you create a full text index with text analysis, the system creates a technical table with prefix $TA_ in the same schema, whose content is shown in Figure 9.16. In addition to the extracted information, this table also contains the primary keys of the original table, so that it can be easily embedded in joins and used accordingly.

Table $TA_*

417

	MANDT	CARRID	TA_RULE	TA_COUNTER	TA_TOKEN	TA_LANGUAGE	TA_TYPE
1	000	AF	Entity Extraction	1	Air France	en	ORGANIZATION/COMMERCIAL
2	001	AA	Entity Extraction	1	American Airlines	en	ORGANIZATION/COMMERCIAL
3	001	AF	Entity Extraction	1	Air France	en	ORGANIZATION/COMMERCIAL
4	001	AZ	Entity Extraction	1	Alitalia	en	ORGANIZATION/COMMERCIAL
5	000	AC	Entity Extraction	1	Air Canada	en	ORGANIZATION/COMMERCIAL
6	000	LH	Entity Extraction	1	Lufthansa	en	ORGANIZATION/COMMERCIAL
7	001	AC	Entity Extraction	1	Air Canada	en	ORGANIZATION/COMMERCIAL
8	001	BA	Entity Extraction	1	British Airways	en	ORGANIZATION/COMMERCIAL
9	001	FJ	Entity Extraction	1	Air Pacific	en	ORGANIZATION/COMMERCIAL
10	001	CO	Entity Extraction	1	Continental Airl...	en	ORGANIZATION/COMMERCIAL
11	001	DL	Entity Extraction	1	Delta Airlines	en	ORGANIZATION/COMMERCIAL
12	001	AB	Entity Extraction	1	Air Berlin	en	ORGANIZATION/COMMERCIAL
13	001	NG	Entity Extraction	1	Lauda Air	en	ORGANIZATION/COMMERCIAL
14	001	JL	Entity Extraction	1	Japan Airlines	en	ORGANIZATION/COMMERCIAL
15	001	SA	Entity Extraction	1	South African Air	en	ORGANIZATION/COMMERCIAL
16	001	LH	Entity Extraction	1	Lufthansa	en	ORGANIZATION/COMMERCIAL
17	001	NW	Entity Extraction	1	Northwest Airli...	en	ORGANIZATION/COMMERCIAL
18	001	QF	Entity Extraction	1	Qantas Airways	en	ORGANIZATION/COMMERCIAL
19	001	SQ	Entity Extraction	1	Singapore Airlin...	en	ORGANIZATION/COMMERCIAL
20	001	SR	Entity Extraction	1	Swiss	en	PEOPLE
21	001	UA	Entity Extraction	1	United Airlines	en	ORGANIZATION/COMMERCIAL

Figure 9.16 Result of a Text Analysis for Airline Names Using the EXTRACTION_ CORE Configuration

Analysis result The system has recognized that the data is related to commercial organizations (column TA_TYPE in Figure 9.16). However, one entry was misinterpreted due to ambiguity, which is a clear indication that most of the time you cannot rely on a completely automatic treatment of the results. In general, one can say that the text analysis function is a powerful tool that enables you to detect indicators and trends, but that the results must always be analyzed and calibrated by a data scientist.

9.6 Resource Consumption and Runtime Aspects of the Text Search

In this chapter, we have discussed the basic architecture and use of the text search and text analysis functions in SAP HANA. You have learned that the column store contains specific data types (TEXT and SHORTTEXT) that provide powerful functions for searching and analyzing unstructured data. For ABAP text types, you can use a full text index to create a virtual column of the TEXT type. And if you employ an additional fuzzy search index, you can accelerate a fuzzy search run.

The following sections provide essential background information on the functionality of the text data types, as well as recommendations concerning the use of indexes. You will learn in particular how to use SQL queries to analyze the memory consumption.

Depending on the configuration, special dictionaries are created for text data types and full text indexes. These store the fragmentation into tokens and linguistic information (such as word stems, for example) in an efficient way. Basically, this process involves the same mechanisms and memory structures as other functions of the column store. If you want to learn more about the technical details of building and accessing such dictionary structures, you can find additional information in Appendix C.

Functionality of text data types

As described in Section 9.2, texts are fragmented into words (tokens), then normalized and stored in the dictionary vector of the column (*word dictionary*). In addition to this, word stems can optionally be stored in a second dictionary, where inflected verbs (for example) are reverted to their basic form or umlauts are replaced. All this information is not persisted on the disk, but generated only when the table is loaded into the main memory.

Additional (optional) memory structures can be used to further accelerate text searches; however, this would have an impact on the required memory size. Currently, there are two options available: an additional fuzzy search index, or an increase of the *phrase-index ratio*. Using a fuzzy search index means that certain data is pre-calculated instead of being determined at the start of a search request. Additionally, in the *phrase index*, frequently occurring word constellations (*phrases*) are stored in a separate dictionary. The higher the specified phrase-index ratio value, the more storage space is reserved in relation to the actual memory consumption of the column (currently, the default value of this ratio is 0.2, i.e., one to five).

Fuzzy search index/ phrase-index ratio

As you can see, there are many setting options available. Using the search and analysis options described here will increase the memory requirements for the required columns, and usually ABAP-based text data requires twice as much memory space. Therefore, it is advisable to use the default settings first, and to employ additional tuning options—such as fuzzy search indexes or changing the phrase-index key figure—only after you encounter performance problems.

Recommendations

Monitoring views

In order for you to get a better picture of the aforesaid, the following paragraphs describe how you can use *monitoring views* via the SQL console to obtain detailed information on the indexes and system memory consumption.

The FULLTEXT_INDEXES view in SAP HANA enables you to view the configuration of all full text indexes in the system. Figure 9.17 shows the full text indexes for the flight model tables created in the preceding sections, as well as some other predefined indexes in the SAP HANA Repository.

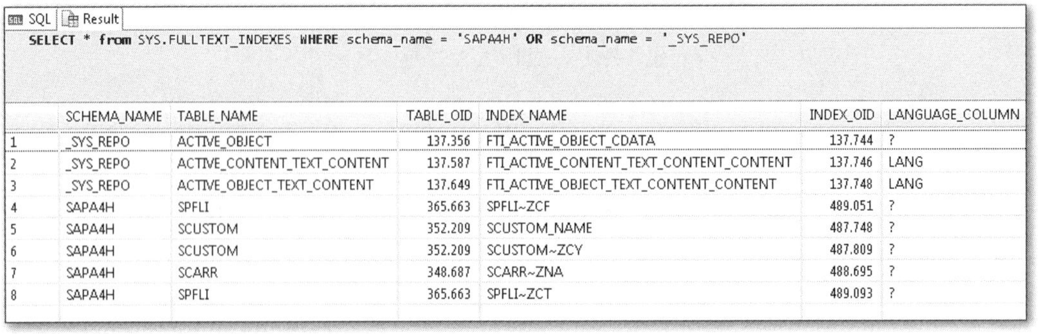

```
SQL   Result
SELECT * from SYS.FULLTEXT_INDEXES WHERE schema_name = 'SAPA4H' OR schema_name = '_SYS_REPO'
```

	SCHEMA_NAME	TABLE_NAME	TABLE_OID	INDEX_NAME	INDEX_OID	LANGUAGE_COLUMN
1	_SYS_REPO	ACTIVE_OBJECT	137.356	FTI_ACTIVE_OBJECT_CDATA	137.744	?
2	_SYS_REPO	ACTIVE_CONTENT_TEXT_CONTENT	137.587	FTI_ACTIVE_CONTENT_TEXT_CONTENT_CONTENT	137.746	LANG
3	_SYS_REPO	ACTIVE_OBJECT_TEXT_CONTENT	137.649	FTI_ACTIVE_OBJECT_TEXT_CONTENT_CONTENT	137.748	LANG
4	SAPA4H	SPFLI	365.663	SPFLI~ZCF	489.051	?
5	SAPA4H	SCUSTOM	352.209	SCUSTOM_NAME	487.748	?
6	SAPA4H	SCUSTOM	352.209	SCUSTOM~ZCY	487.809	?
7	SAPA4H	SCARR	348.687	SCARR~ZNA	488.695	?
8	SAPA4H	SPFLI	365.663	SPFLI~ZCT	489.093	?

Figure 9.17 FULLTEXT_INDEXES Monitoring View

Memory consumption

Moreover, you can query the memory consumption of the special fuzzy search indexes separately using the M_FUZZY_SEARCH_INDEXES monitoring view. The memory consumption depends on various factors, but predominantly on the number of different values within the column. The following SQL statement allows you to query the current memory consumption of all data structures available for the fuzzy search in the system:

```
SELECT * FROM m_heap_memory WHERE category LIKE '%FuzzySearch%'
```

Write operations

To conclude this chapter, we'll briefly discuss the topic of write operations, especially in the context of tables—which are both frequently modified, and can be used for text searches and analyses. Full text indexes can be updated synchronously and asynchronously. If an index is updated synchronously, write operations take slightly longer because the creation of dictionary and index structures is part of the write operation. Usually, the effects should be minimal with small data types (for example, with character strings of a fixed length). For larger documents that are stored as *large objects* in the database (for example, STRING), an asynchronous update can be advantageous.

In addition, when write operations are carried out in the column store, the data is first stored in the so-called *delta store* and is automatically integrated into the *main store* only at specific *merge* times (see also Appendix C). The bigger the delta store gets in this process, the more costly the merging of results in SQL queries. This can significantly impact the system runtime, particularly in complex operations such as those described in this chapter. If you want to run text analyses across large datasets that are carried out asynchronously at fixed points in time; for example, it makes sense to manually implement *delta merge,* which is supposed to be executed on the relevant tables prior to the text analyses. For this purpose, you could for example use SQL statement MERGE DELTA OF <Table>.

Delta store

Using SAP HANA, you can expand transactional applications through analytical functionality. A great variety of technologies and tools are available for this purpose, which—in many cases—allow you to add analytical functions with very little programming effort.

10   Integrating Analytical Functionality

In Chapter 1, you learned that you can combine transactional and analytical functionality or add analytical capabilities to existing transactional applications using SAP HANA. This chapter describes this topic in more detail. From our point of view, this is important to avoid investments in the development of analytical functionalities that are already provided *out of the box*.

In a short introduction, we will start by explaining important concepts and terms used in this context. We will then introduce possible architectures that can be used to expand transactional, ABAP-based systems by analytical functionality, and also list their advantages and disadvantages. To conclude this chapter, we describe a few technologies and tools that we consider important.

Due to space constraints, however, the presented technologies and tools cannot be explained in detail. Therefore, you will not be able to immediately use all of the methods presented for integrating analytical functionality in transactional applications after reading this chapter.

10.1   Introduction

To understand the options described in this chapter, you need to understand what we mean by *analytical functionality* and how the integration of analytical capabilities in transactional applications differs from a *data warehouse*.

Moreover, you should be familiar with some of the basic concepts in connection with SAP NetWeaver Business Warehouse (BW) to understand the explanations in the following sections.

10.1.1 What is Analytical Functionality?

Reporting vs. data analysis

Analytical functionality is more than just *reporting*. Reporting helps you present and format data. Data analysis should then help you understand correlations and causes so you can determine necessary measures based on this information (*insight to action*). Ideally, these measures should have a positive impact for your organization (e.g., higher revenues, lower cost, improved customer retention). Figure 10.1 shows how these concepts are correlated.

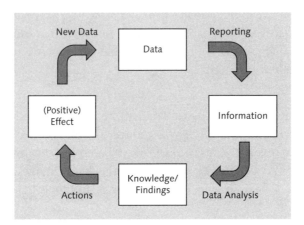

Figure 10.1 Overview of Analytical Functionality

Levels of reporting and data analysis

Reporting and data-analysis tasks can be performed at different levels (Figure 10.2):

▶ **Strategic level**
The strategic level deals with basic questions that have a long-term impact on an organization. Using the SFLIGHT data model from the previous chapters, possible strategic questions for an airline are: Which flight connections should be expanded? How should the miles program be enhanced?

▶ **Tactical level**

The tactical level deals with questions that have a medium-term impact on the organization or individual areas within the company. Possible tactical questions are: How should ticket prices be adjusted starting January 1 of the following year if kerosene prices continue to develop as they have in the last three months? How will the operating result in the next three years be affected by the new air-traffic tax?

▶ **Operational level**

The operational level deals with short-term questions regarding day-to-day operations. Possible operational questions are: Which duty-free products should be replaced due to lack of demand? Which customers should be approached to improve the business-class utilization of a certain flight connection?

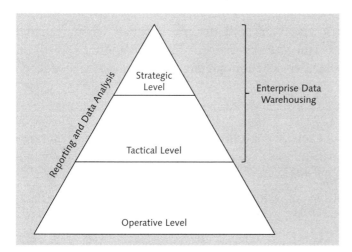

Figure 10.2 Levels of Reporting and Data Analysis

While (small) time delays in data provisioning are usually not problematic for reporting and data analysis at the strategic and tactical level—and it may not be possible to avoid such delays, as data from different systems must be consolidated—latency-free data provisioning is often of paramount importance at the operational level. Imagine a travel agent who is on the phone with a customer who wants to book a flight. Ideally, the travel agent should not only know the current use of the desired flight, but should also be able to offer alternative flights on other dates

Time delay in data provisioning

and possibly on better terms. Moreover, the travel agent should know the current status and bonus-mile count of the customer, the discounts granted, etc. In this example, time delays when provisioning this data are not acceptable.

In addition to *transactional systems* for their business processes (e.g., SAP ERP), organizations often use separate *analytical systems* referred to as *data warehouses* (e.g., SAP NetWeaver BW). Transactional systems are systems for *Online Transactional Processing* (OLTP). As a synonym for analytical systems, the term *Online Analytical Processing* (OLAP) is often used. The latter is not entirely correct, since OLAP describes multi-dimensional analyses based on a star schema, while data in a data warehouse can also be organized in flat database tables (in the case of SAP NetWeaver BW, for example, in the form of so-called *ODS objects*—see Section 10.1.2). Moreover, some background information on OLAP is provided in Section 4.2.

In recent years, SAP NetWeaver BW was not only used for strategic and tactical analyses in the SAP environment, but often also for operational reports and data analyses. In our opinion, this was done for the following reasons:

▶ Load reduction on transactional systems

▶ No significant enhancements of Report Painter, drilldown reporting, Logistics Information System, and other existing reporting tools within transactional systems

▶ Extensive BI content (i.e., preconfigured data transformations and information models for SAP NetWeaver BW)

This meant that the required data was not always provided in *real time* for the end users.

Today, you have the option to implement operational reporting where it belongs: within the transactional systems. Analyses that could only be run during the night and after several data transformations in the past can now be done *on the fly* based on the original data and, for instance, using the tools of the *SAP BusinessObjects portfolio*.

| Will SAP HANA Replace SAP NetWeaver BW? | [«] |

You may be asking yourself now if SAP NetWeaver BW will become superfluous when using SAP HANA. There is a clear answer to that question: no. Even though SAP HANA is more than just a database, it is not a data warehouse.

However, some scenarios that were implemented using SAP NetWeaver BW in the past will be possible without this data warehouse in the future. Instead of setting up *ETL processes* for these scenarios, you will use the original data from the transactional systems (if SAP HANA is the primary database) or you will replicate the required data to a secondary SAP HANA database (i.e., you use SAP HANA as a *data mart*).

Other scenarios will still benefit from the capabilities of a data warehouse in the future. Using SAP NetWeaver BW (based on a traditional database or an SAP HANA database), you can:

▶ Reduce the load of transactional systems
▶ Create data models that are better suited than the original data for strategic and tactical reports and data analyses
▶ Harmonize and integrate data from different data sources
▶ Keep historical data available without using capacity of transactional systems

From our point of view, SAP HANA should be used instead of SAP NetWeaver BW in particular for operational reports and data analysis, and in some cases for system landscapes where only a single transactional system is connected to the data warehouse today. For *enterprise data warehousing* at the tactical and strategic level, you should still use SAP NetWeaver BW (based on SAP HANA, if possible).

10.1.2 Digression: SAP NetWeaver Business Warehouse

In the further course of this chapter, many terms and concepts from SAP NetWeaver BW will be used. If you have never worked with SAP NetWeaver BW, Figure 10.3 provides an overview of the most important concepts. This section briefly describes these concepts.

InfoProviders are used for data access in SAP NetWeaver BW. The system differentiates between InfoProviders where data is actually loaded physically via ETL processes, and InfoProviders that only provide a logical view of the data. Examples for InfoProviders are *InfoCubes*, *ODS objects*, *InfoObjects*, *transient* and *virtual InfoProviders*, and *MultiProviders*.

InfoProviders

InfoObjects
Put simply, *InfoObjects* can be subdivided into *key figures* (e.g., revenue) and *characteristics* (e.g., an airline). InfoObjects are used to model InfoProviders. However, characteristics can also be used as InfoProviders themselves (and usually provide access to master data in this case).

DataSources
DataSources transfer data in SAP NetWeaver BW (e.g., from a transactional system like SAP ERP).

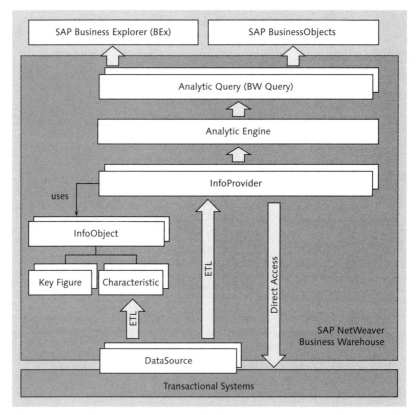

Figure 10.3 SAP NetWeaver Business Warehouse

BW queries
Analytical queries (also referred to as *BW queries*) describe data queries executed on InfoProviders. They define rows and columns, filters, threshold values (to highlight specific records), etc. To define analytical queries, you use the BEx Query Designer, which is part of the *SAP Business Explorer* (*BEx*). Analytical queries are executed via the *Analytic Engine*.

The SAP Business Explorer provides reporting and analysis tools for SAP NetWeaver BW. In particular, these are:

▶ *BEx Query Designer* (to define BW queries)

▶ *BEx Analyzer* (for analyses based on BW queries in Microsoft Excel)

▶ *BEx Web Application Designer* (to create browser-based analytical applications based on BW queries)

As an alternative to the BEx Analyzer and the BEx Web Application Designer, you can also use the tools provided by *SAP BusinessObjects*:

▶ *Analysis, edition for Microsoft Office* is an alternative to the BEx Analyzer (see Section 10.3.2).

▶ An alternative to the BEx Web Application Designer is *SAP Design Studio* (also described in Section 10.3.2).

For further information on the SAP Business Explorer, please refer to *http://scn.sap.com/community/business-explorer*.

10.2 Overview of Possible Architectures

This section describes possible architectures used to add analytical functionality to transactional, ABAP-based systems. When doing so, we'll focus only on the operational level for reporting and data analysis and differentiate between two approaches:

▶ *Direct access* to analytical functions in SAP HANA and integration of analytical functionality in a transactional, ABAP-based application via user-interface integration (e.g., using the SAP NetWeaver Portal or SAP NetWeaver Business Client).

▶ Access to analytical functions *via the SAP NetWeaver AS ABAP*, in particular through the Analytic Engine in SAP NetWeaver BW, and integration of analytical functionality in a transactional, ABAP-based application at different levels. In this case, the SAP NetWeaver BW infrastructure is used via the Analytic Engine without having to operate a separate BW system.

For the information provided in this chapter, it's assumed that SAP HANA is used as the primary database. In some cases, however, the two approaches can also be used if SAP HANA is implemented as a secondary database.

10.2.1 Direct Access to Analytical Functionality in SAP HANA

Direct access to analytical functionality in SAP HANA refers to data analysis via SAP BusinessObjects tools without using an SAP NetWeaver AS ABAP. Moreover, this also includes the provisioning of analytical functionality via *SAP HANA Extended Application Services* (XS Engine, which is described in Section 10.3).

Direct communication The architecture for direct access to analytical functions in SAP HANA is displayed in Figure 10.4. In this architecture, end-users communicate with the SAP HANA database either directly or via the SAP BusinessObjects portfolio, but without using the ABAP application server.

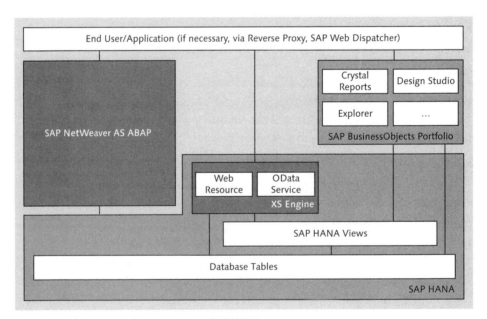

Figure 10.4 Direct Access to SAP HANA

[«]

> **Background Information: SAP HANA Live**
>
> One scenario for direct access to SAP HANA for operational reporting is the implementation of *SAP HANA Live* (previously *SAP HANA Analytics Foundation*).
>
> Put simply, SAP HANA Live provides a virtual, multi-level data model (*Virtual Data Model*) consisting of SAP HANA views based on the database tables of the SAP Business Suite.
>
> SAP HANA Live can be accessed using the SAP BusinessObjects tools or using special HTML5-based applications that are based on SAP HANA Extended Application Services. You can use SAP HANA Live both with a primary and a secondary SAP HANA database.

In the following section, we'll first explain how SAP HANA is accessed using the SAP BusinessObjects tools and then briefly describe the SAP HANA Extended Application Services. Next, we'll describe the advantages and disadvantages of the architecture.

SAP BusinessObjects Portfolio

Besides tools for reporting and data analysis, the SAP BusinessObjects portfolio also contains functions for *Enterprise Information Management* (EIM), *Enterprise Performance Management* (EPM), and *Governance, Risk, and Compliance* (GRC).

The tools for reporting and data analysis usually belong to the *SAP Business-Objects Business Intelligence (BI) platform* (also known as *SAP BusinessObjects Enterprise*). However, some of these functions can also be used without this platform (as shown in Figure 10.5).

SAP Business-Objects Business Intelligence platform

The SAP BusinessObjects BI platform comprises server and client components. To install the server components, a Java server supported by SAP BusinessObjects BI is required (e.g., SAP NetWeaver AS Java). Figure 10.5 shows how the SAP BusinessObjects tools (Release 4.x) are used. This figure shows which tools require server components and how the tools communicate with the SAP HANA database. Basically, there are three options:

Communication options

- Using a *relational universe* (an abstraction layer to translate business data from one or multiple data sources into a language that is well understood by the end users)

431

▶ Using the *BI Consumer Services* (*BICS*), an SAP-proprietary interface for OLAP

▶ Access without server components (Analysis, the edition for Microsoft Office, can for example contact the SAP HANA database directly via ODBC)

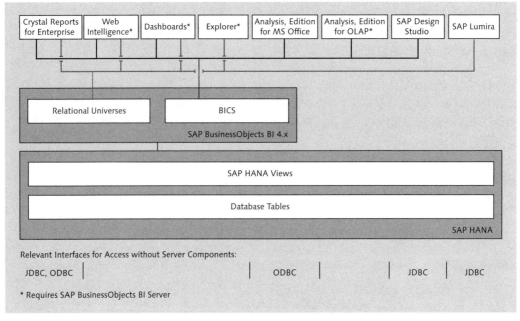

Figure 10.5 SAP BusinessObjects Tools and SAP HANA

Advantages and disadvantages

One of the biggest advantages of the SAP BusinessObjects portfolio is that many of the requirements with regard to reporting and data analysis are met by default (a short description of each tool can be found in Section 10.3.2). Reports can be created without any programming efforts, and you can save the generated reports in a central repository to make them accessible to a large number of end-users. Alternatively, end users can create their own reports and data analyses (provided they were assigned the necessary authorizations). The disadvantage of this approach is that for certain tools a Java server (with its own administration and lifecycle management) is needed in addition to the SAP NetWeaver AS ABAP.

You can use Single Sign-On to integrate the SAP NetWeaver AS ABAP and the SAP BusinessObjects BI platform. The generated reports can be published and thus be made available in the SAP NetWeaver Portal.

Integration

SAP HANA Extended Application Services

Alternatively, you can access and visualize the data in the SAP HANA database via the SAP HANA Extended Application Services (*XS Engine*). As described in Section 10.3, this is an application server that is integrated into the database and addressed using the HTTP protocol. The XS Engine provides far more options than just creating reports and data analyses.

XS Engine

Using SAP HANA Extended Application Services, you can easily define *OData services* based on SAP HANA views and database tables. You can then develop a browser-based user interface based on these OData services. To develop this user interface, you can for example use the *UI Development Toolkit for HTML5* by SAP (also known as *SAPUI5*). This toolkit is integrated in SAP HANA.

OData and SAPUI5

OData and HTML5   [«]

OData (Open Data Protocol) allows you to access data using an HTTP-based protocol. Since communication via OData is stateless, this protocol is especially useful for developing lightweight web applications and mobile applications. Further information on OData can be found at *http://www.odata.org/*.

To use OData for communication with an ABAP-based system, you can use the *SAP NetWeaver Gateway*. As of release 7.4, the SAP NetWeaver Gateway functionality is integrated directly into the SAP NetWeaver AS ABAP.

HTML5 is the combination of *HTML*, *Cascading Style Sheets*, and *JavaScript* to develop user interfaces. To develop HTML5-based user interfaces, SAP offers a library of UI controls—the *UI Development Toolkit for HTML5* (SAPUI5). You can use SAPUI5 in combination with different platforms, such as the ABAP application server. Detailed information on SAPUI5 can be found at *http://scn.sap.com/docs/DOC-31625*.

To visualize business data, SAPUI5 provides a set of presentation graphics (e.g., bar charts, pie charts, and line charts).

One of the advantages is that, in contrast to using the SAP BusinessObjects tools, no Java server is needed to use the XS Engine (in combination with SAPUI5). Moreover, this approach gives you great flexibility and you can align analytical user interfaces exactly to the end users' requirements. A disadvantage is that hardly any functions for reporting and data analysis are provided out of the box, since SAPUI5 is not a platform for Business Intelligence (but merely a library of UI controls).

Integration   To integrate the SAP NetWeaver AS ABAP and the XS Engine, Single Sign-On can be used. User interfaces developed with SAPUI5 can be incorporated into the SAP NetWeaver Portal or the SAP NetWeaver Business Client.

Advantages and Disadvantages of the Architecture

You may be wondering now what the advantages and disadvantages of direct access to analytical functionality in SAP HANA are. First of all, direct access to SAP HANA offers a simple and flexible way to provide access to analytical functionality for end users. Especially when using SAP HANA as a secondary database, this approach has already proven itself in practice, since this architecture was used in many of the first customer projects with SAP HANA (SAP HANA as a data mart).

User administration   A disadvantage of this approach in connection with ABAP-based applications is that users and authorizations have to be administered in several systems. After all, every end user needs not only a user account for the SAP NetWeaver AS ABAP, but also a corresponding user account for SAP HANA, which is assigned the required authorizations for accessing the relevant data models, and possibly also a user account for the SAP BusinessObjects BI server.

10.2.2 Access via the SAP NetWeaver AS ABAP

Instead of using the SAP BusinessObjects portfolio or the XS Engine to directly access SAP HANA, you can provide analytical functions via the SAP NetWeaver AS ABAP. In addition to the SAP BusinessObjects tools, you can use further options to add analytical functions to transactional applications when choosing this approach. A central infrastructure component of this approach is the Analytic Engine we already mentioned.

The architecture for accessing analytical functions via the SAP NetWeaver AS ABAP is shown in Figure 10.6. With this architecture, the application server is used for all communications with the SAP HANA database.

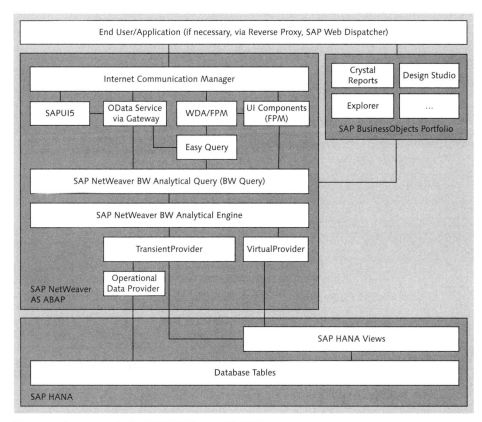

Figure 10.6 Access via the SAP NetWeaver AS ABAP

In the following sections, we'll first explain how the SAP BusinessObjects portfolio is used via the SAP NetWeaver AS ABAP and then describe the Analytic Engine and some of the further options you can use. Subsequently, the advantages and disadvantages of the architecture will be described.

SAP BusinessObjects Portfolio

If you use the SAP BusinessObjects tools via the SAP NetWeaver AS ABAP, you have two options (similar to the approach for direct access to the

SAP HANA database). One of the reasons why these two options (shown in Figure 10.7) are available is that SAP and BusinessObjects used to be two independent companies:

▶ Using a relational universe which can be defined (e.g., referring to *classic InfoSets,* which are described later in this section), function modules, or future tables of the ABAP Data Dictionary

▶ Using the BI Consumer Services (BICS) and thus the Analytic Engine of SAP NetWeaver BW

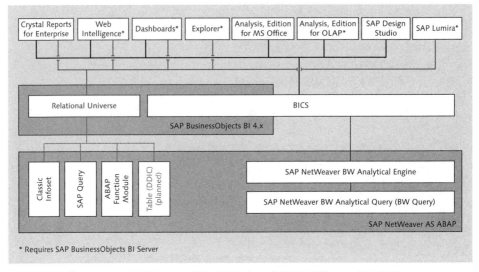

Figure 10.7 SAP BusinessObjects Tools and SAP NetWeaver AS ABAP

From our point of view, using the Analytic Engine, which (as you can see in Figure 10.7) is supported by most of the SAP BusinessObjects tools, provides an especially great variety of options. For this reason, we will describe this approach in more detail.

Using the Analytic Engine

As described in Section 10.1.2, the Analytic Engine is part of the SAP NetWeaver BW infrastructure. It supports reporting and multi-dimensional analyses. In addition, the Analytic Engine also provides planning functions.

Since every SAP NetWeaver AS ABAP includes the `SAP_BW` software component as of release 6.40, every up-to-date ABAP system (this also includes SAP ERP or SAP CRM) comprises the Analytic Engine from SAP NetWeaver BW. This means that you can use BW functionality directly in the OLTP system. This way of using the BW is referred to as *Embedded Reporting* (as opposed to Enterprise Data Warehousing) and is especially suitable for operational reports and data analyses.

For Embedded Reporting, you don't necessarily have to model so-called *InfoProviders* in the *Data Warehousing Workbench* of SAP NetWeaver BW (as is usual in case of Enterprise Data Warehousing). By using transient (*TransientProvider*) and virtual InfoProviders (*VirtualProvider*), and BW queries that are based on these providers, you can directly access data without ETL processes. These types of InfoProviders are discussed in more detail in Section 10.3.1.

TransientProviders, VirtualProviders

Additional Options

Besides access to BW queries via the SAP BusinessObjects portfolio, the SAP NetWeaver AS ABAP infrastructure provides further options for using the Analytic Engine. To integrate analytical functions in transactional applications, the following solutions are particularly useful:

▶ **Easy Query**
Using the *Easy Query interface*, you can expose the result of BW queries via function modules, web services, or the OData protocol (the latter is done in connection with the SAP NetWeaver Gateway). The Easy Query interface is described in Section 10.3.3.

▶ **SAP NetWeaver Gateway**
The SAP NetWeaver Gateway allows you to make business data available as an OData service. Within OData services, you can address the Analytic Engine either via MDX (not described in any detail within this book) or via the Easy Query interface (also described in Section 10.3.3). Based on an OData service and using SAPUI5, you can implement HTML5-based user interfaces.

▶ **User-interface building blocks**
And lastly, the SAP Business Suite (or, more precisely, the software component `SAP_BS_FND`) comprises some reusable user-interface

building blocks for Floorplan Manager that allow you to directly access BW queries (when performing your development tasks in an SAP Business Suite system). User-interface building blocks are described in Section 10.4.

These options that go beyond the tools of the SAP BusinessObjects portfolio are particularly suitable to extending existing applications easily and without risk, such as by providing analytical side panels in the SAP NetWeaver Business Client for your end users.

Advantages and Disadvantages of the Architecture

In our opinion, access to SAP HANA via the SAP NetWeaver AS ABAP and using the Analytic Engine provides some important advantages over direct access to SAP HANA in order to integrate analytical functionality in transactional applications.

User administration

Firstly, in contrast to direct access to SAP HANA, users and authorizations can be maintained and administered in a single system when accessing analytical functionality via the Analytic Engine. End users need only one user account for the SAP NetWeaver AS ABAP. As described in Section 3.1.2, communication with the SAP HANA database is done via a technical database user. In addition, you might have to create users in the SAP BusinessObjects BI server.

Functional scope of the Analytic Engine

Secondly, when using the Analytic Engine, you benefit from some additional functions that are not currently provided by SAP HANA. These include:

► **Hierarchy processing**
As already described in Chapter 4, SAP HANA provides basic support for simple hierarchies. If your hierarchy-processing requirements are not met by this basic support, you can probably meet them by modeling the hierarchy using the functionality of the SAP NetWeaver Business Warehouse. The following functions are currently provided via BW, but are not available directly in SAP HANA: hierarchy versions, time-dependent hierarchies, plus/minus sign reversal, and elimination of internal business volume.

▶ **Formulas**

The BEx Query Designer provides some functions that are not available directly in SAP HANA when defining calculated fields and key figures. In the BEx Query Designer, you can for instance use functions to calculate the percentage share of a result in an interim result or in the overall result of the BW query. Or you might want to display both the absolute sales per flight connection and the relative percentage share of the sales in the total sales of the respective airline.

▶ **Report-report interface**

The *report-report interface* (RRI) allows you to navigate from a BW query to other BW queries, transactions, and reports of an ABAP system or any web address. No comparable function is provided directly in SAP HANA.

Thirdly, the Easy Query interface and the user interface building blocks based on BW queries especially facilitate a very easy integration of analytical functions in existing transactional user interfaces.

Simple integration

10.3 Selected Technologies and Tools

Now that you have an overview of possible architectures for integrating analytical functionality in transactional, ABAP-based applications, we'd like to examine some of these functions in more detail. When doing so, the focus will be on the Analytic Engine. However, the information regarding the SAP BusinessObjects tools in S n 10.3.2 is in principle also valid for direct access to SAP HANA and when using a relational universe.

As in the previous chapters, our example will once again be based on the SFLIGHT data model. Like the other examples, this example is again kept rather simple to make sure we focus only on the important concepts.

Example for this section

Figure 10.8 shows the analytic view AN_FLIGHT (from the test.a4h.book. chapter10 package) that is used as the basis for our example. This view uses the two attribute views AT_AIRLINE and AT_CONNECTION. Based on this foundation, we will create InfoProviders and BW queries, which will then be used for reports and data analysis.

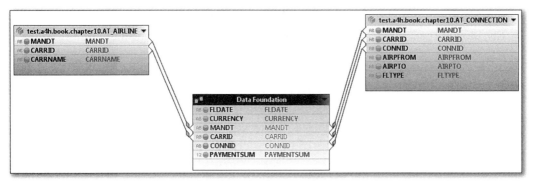

Figure 10.8 Analytic View for the Example

10.3.1 InfoProviders when Using SAP HANA

This section explains how you can access data views in SAP HANA using transient and virtual InfoProviders. In addition to that, we will introduce further transient InfoProviders.

Transient InfoProviders Based on Views

Transient InfoProviders are InfoProviders that are generated based on a data source at runtime and without modeling in the Data Warehousing Workbench. This type of InfoProvider does not contain any data. When accessing transient InfoProviders, the system reads the data from the underlying data source.

Publishing When using SAP HANA as a primary database, you can access SAP HANA views via transient InfoProviders. To do so, you must first publish the views. Suitable candidates are analytic views and calculation views (see Chapter 4).

Use Transaction RSDD_HM_PUBLISH to publish SAP HANA views. This transaction creates an *analytical index* for an SAP HANA view and subsequently a transient InfoProvider @3<Name of the analytical index> based on this index. In case of an analytic view, the characteristics and key figures of the transient InfoProvider are derived from the fact table (*data foundation*) and the dimension tables (e.g., the linked attribute views).

Figure 10.9 shows the analytical index and the transient InfoProvider for the analytic view AN_FLIGHT.

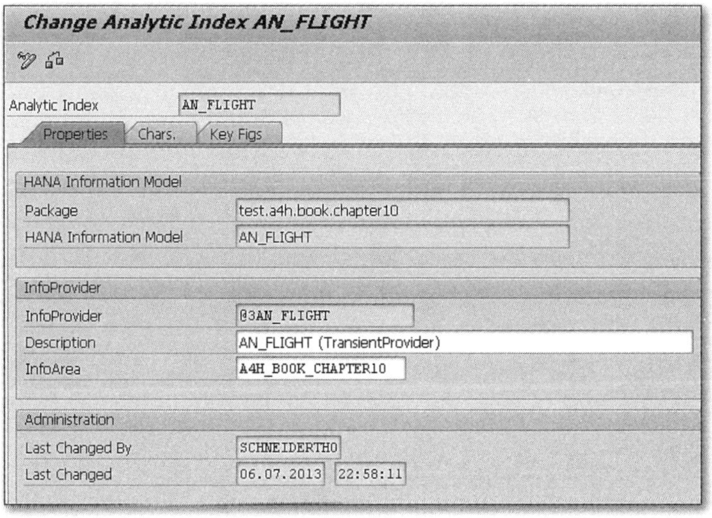

Figure 10.9 Creating an Analytical Index

Optionally, you can assign *InfoObjects* defined in the Data Warehousing Workbench to the characteristics and key figures of the transient InfoProvider. You can thus add further metadata to the InfoProvider that can, for example, be used for authorization checks. It is currently not possible to use the navigation attributes of the referenced InfoObjects.

Assigning InfoObjects

The biggest advantage of a transient InfoProvider is that it is regenerated at runtime by the system if necessary. This means that the InfoProvider and the BW queries that are based on this provider are usually changed automatically if you modify the underlying analytic view or calculation view.

Advantages and disadvantages

A disadvantage is that transient InfoProviders cannot be transported. They must therefore be created manually in every system (development, quality assurance, production).

Virtual InfoProviders Based on Views

Instead of working with a transient InfoProvider, you can also define a virtual InfoProvider. In contrast to transient InfoProviders, virtual Info-Providers are modeled in the Data Warehousing Workbench (Transaction RSA1). Like transient InfoProviders, virtual InfoProviders do not contain any data. When accessing virtual InfoProviders, the system reads the data from the underlying data source. When using SAP HANA as a primary database, you can use virtual InfoProviders to access analytic and calculation views.

Creating a virtual InfoProvider

The example in Figure 10.10 shows how the virtual InfoProvider AN_FLIGHT is created after selecting CREATE VIRTUAL PROVIDER... in the context menu of an InfoArea in the Data Warehousing Workbench. To assign the underlying analytic view AN_FLIGHT to the InfoProvider, click DETAILS below the selection field BASED ON A HANA MODEL.

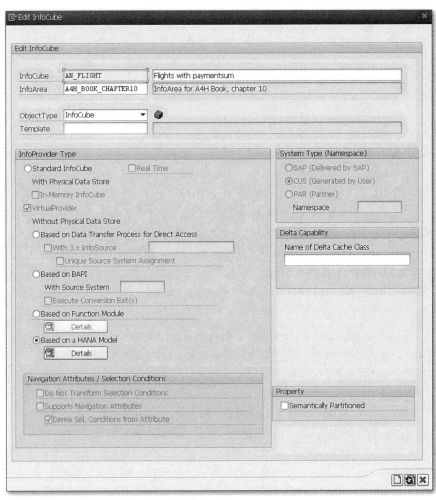

Figure 10.10 Creating a Virtual InfoProvider

Subsequently, you assign the relevant InfoObjects as characteristics and key figures to the InfoProvider. There are two options for this step:

▶ You can have the system propose the required InfoObjects and the assignment to the attributes of the SAP HANA view. To do so, you click ASSIGN HANA MODEL ATTRIBUTES (shown in the upper right of Figure 10.11).

▶ You first manually define the desired InfoObjects as characteristics and key figures of the InfoProvider and then manually assign them to the attributes of the SAP HANA view.

Figure 10.11 shows the InfoProvider AN_FLIGHT after assigning the characteristics and key figures.

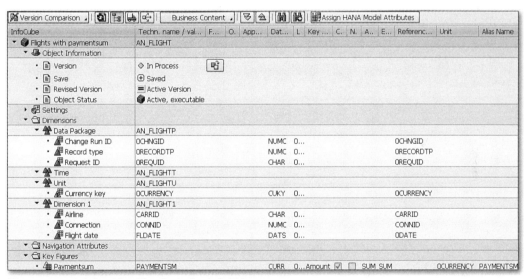

Figure 10.11 InfoProvider After Assigning InfoObjects

If you want to access virtual master data when defining a virtual InfoProvider, you can use *virtual InfoObjects*. Like virtual InfoProviders, virtual InfoObjects are modeled in the Data Warehousing Workbench, but do not contain any data. When accessing virtual InfoObjects, the system reads the data from the underlying data source.

When defining a virtual InfoObject, you can refer to an attribute view in the primary SAP HANA database. The example in Figure 10.12 shows how this is done using the InfoObject `CARRID` and the attribute view `AT_AIRLINE`.

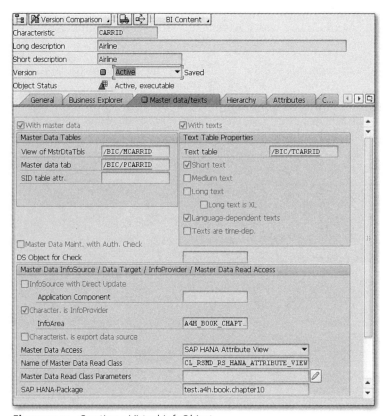

Figure 10.12 Creating a Virtual InfoObject

Advantages and disadvantages

Virtual InfoProviders have several advantages over transient InfoProviders: They support navigation attributes, can be transported, and can be used in MultiProviders.

A disadvantage is that virtual InfoProviders must be modeled in the Data Warehousing Workbench. If you modify the underlying analytic view or calculation view, you might also have to change the virtual InfoProvider. The effort is thus a little greater than in the case of a transient InfoProvider.

Other Transient InfoProviders

For the sake of completeness, we would like to mention that there are further transient InfoProviders. These are also available in traditional databases.

▶ Transient InfoProviders based on classic InfoSets

▶ Transient InfoProviders based on Operational Data Provisioning

Long before developing SAP NetWeaver BW, SAP already provided the reporting tool *SAP Query*. In contrast to other reporting tools (e.g., Report Painter and Drilldown Reporting for financials and controlling, or the Logistics Information System for purchasing and sales), SAP Query can be used universally.

Classic InfoSets

Reports created with SAP Query (so-called *queries*, which must not be confused with BW queries) are based on *classic* InfoSets (not to be confused with the InfoSets in SAP NetWeaver BW). Classic InfoSets provide a view of certain data. The data sources used for classic InfoSets are often database tables or *joins* defined for several database tables. However, classic InfoSets can also be based on a logical database or on a data-retrieval program.

If you release a classic InfoSet for use via the Analytic Engine in Transaction SQ02 via the menu path ENVIRONMENT • BI PROPERTIES, the system creates a transient InfoProvider @1<Name of the classic InfoSet> based on the classic InfoSet.

Operational Data Provisioning is part of the infrastructure that is provided for *Search and Operational Analytics* as of release 7.31 of the SAP NetWeaver AS ABAP.

Operational Data Provisioning

In the context of Enterprise Data Warehousing, *DataSources* (see Section 10.1.2) are used to load data from transactional systems in SAP NetWeaver BW.

The basic idea of Operational Data Provisioning is to define a search-and-analysis model by linking and enhancing DataSources by analytical properties in the transactional system. You can then create an *Operational Data Provider* based on this search-and-analysis model. This Operational Data Provider is made available via a transient InfoProvider for operational reports and data analyses without having to perform an extraction to a data warehouse. Optionally, the data can be indexed in a secondary SAP HANA database or in the *SAP NetWeaver Business Warehouse Accelerator* (*BWA*) based on the infrastructure of the ABAP application server.

Using the InfoProviders in BW Queries

All InfoProviders described above can be used when creating a BW query. A BW query describes a data query to an InfoProvider. BW queries are defined using the BEx Query Designer.

The example in Figure 10.13 shows the BW query AN_FLIGHT_QUERY1 (PAYMENTSUM PER CONNECTION) that is based on the transient InfoProvider AN_FLIGHT. The BW query describes a report that indicates the sales per flight connection. You can run a first test for your query in Transaction RSRT.

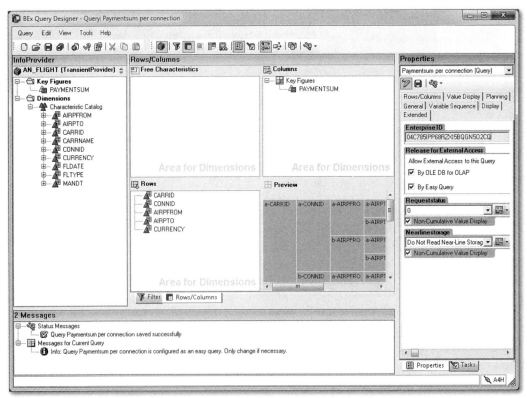

Figure 10.13 BW Query Based on the InfoProvider AN_FLIGHT

10.3.2 SAP BusinessObjects Portfolio

We have now presented some options for defining InfoProviders based on SAP HANA views, and for creating BW queries based on those InfoProviders. This section will give you an overview of the tools for reporting and data analysis provided by the SAP BusinessObjects portfolio.

Overview of the Tools

The SAP BusinessObjects portfolio provides numerous tools for the different levels of reporting. Each tool is used for different application cases and has specific advantages and disadvantages. A detailed description of all tools would go beyond the scope of this chapter. We will therefore only categorize the tools and give you a general overview. A detailed description of the SAP BusinessObjects portfolio can be found in the book *Reporting and Analysis with SAP BusinessObjects* by Ingo Hilgefort (2nd edition, SAP PRESS 2012).

In Table 10.1, the tools of the SAP BusinessObjects portfolio are subdivided into three categories: reporting, data analysis, and data exploration.

Categorization

Reporting	Data Analysis	Data Exploration
SAP Crystal Reports	SAP BusinessObjects Analysis, edition for Microsoft Office	SAP BusinessObjects Explorer
SAP BusinessObjects Web Intelligence	SAP BusinessObjects Analysis, edition for OLAP	SAP Lumira
SAP BusinessObjects Dashboards		
SAP Design Studio		

Table 10.1 Overview of the SAP BusinessObjects Portfolio

Reporting

The reporting tools will help you gather and format data. The most commonly known tool used for this purpose is probably *SAP Crystal Reports*. Using SAP Crystal Reports, you can create formatted reports and (if necessary) format and print these reports with precise pixel values. This tool is the de facto standard for formatted reporting.

SAP Crystal Reports

Figure 10.14 shows the preview of a report created with SAP Crystal Reports for Enterprise that breaks down the sales of the airlines by connection.

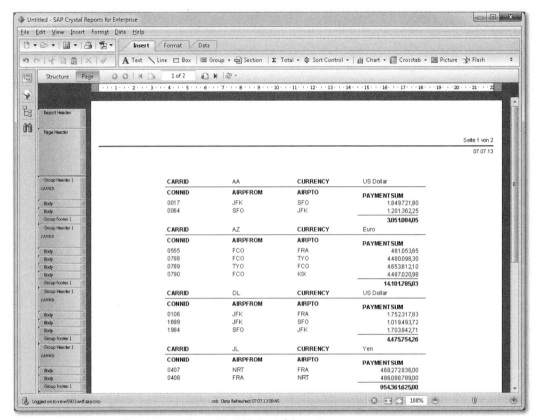

Figure 10.14 Report in SAP Crystal Reports

Web Intelligence *SAP BusinessObjects Web Intelligence* can also be used to generate formatted reports. However, this tool does not provide the same scope of formatting and printing options as SAP Crystal Reports. Web Intelligence, however, is better suited if end-users from the individual departments want to create their own reports (*Self-Service Business Intelligence*).

Dashboards *Dashboards* summarize important key figures for decision-makers. SAP BusinessObjects Dashboards provides a series of components that can be used to create appealing dashboards. Using these dashboards, you can visualize *what-if scenarios* as well as use them offline, if necessary.

Alternatively, you can create dashboards using *SAP BusinessObjects Design Studio*.

Data Analysis

And this brings us to the tools for data analysis. With *Analysis, edition for Microsoft Office*, you can analyze multi-dimensional datasets interactively and based on Microsoft Excel. This makes this tool particularly useful for employees in individual departments who are often well-practiced with Microsoft Excel. The basic idea and design of Analysis, edition for Microsoft Office is similar to the *BEx Analyzer* (please read the background information on the SAP Business Explorer in Section 10.2.2). However, Analysis, edition for Microsoft Office provides more functions and a better user experience. In addition to Microsoft Excel, data can also be embedded in Microsoft PowerPoint.

Analysis, edition for MS Office

Figure 10.15 shows the formatted view of a BW query using Analysis, edition for Microsoft Office based on a query that in turn is based on the virtual InfoProvider AN_FLIGHT.

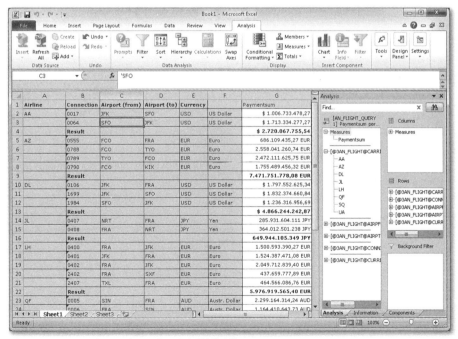

Figure 10.15 Analysis, Edition for Microsoft Office

Analysis, edition
for OLAP
The web-based variant for analyses of multi-dimensional datasets is *Analysis, edition for OLAP*. Alternatively, you can also analyze multi-dimensional datasets in SAP Design Studio.

SAP Business-
Objects Design
Studio
SAP BusinessObjects Design Studio is a tool used to create analytical applications and dashboards. Using Design Studio, you can create pixel-perfect analytical applications and dashboards. This tool provides a variety of charts and comprehensive *theming*. In addition, it also supports mobile scenarios. In the medium-term, Design Studio will replace the SAP BusinessObjects Dashboards and form the technological basis for Analysis, edition for OLAP.

Figure 10.16 shows the design of a simple analytical application in Design Studio that is based on a BW query, which in turn is based on the transient InfoProvider AN_FLIGHT.

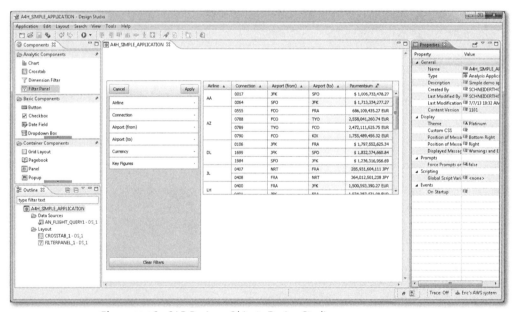

Figure 10.16 SAP BusinessObjects Design Studio

Data Exploration

SAP Business-
Objects Explorer
and SAP Lumira
A special case of data analysis is data exploration (i.e., the interactive analysis of a dataset). For data exploration, end users need tools that can be used intuitively and provide high-quality visualizations. The

SAP BusinessObjects portfolio includes two tools: SAP BusinessObjects Explorer and SAP Lumira (the latter was formally known as *SAP Visual Intelligence*).

10.3.3 Easy Query Interface

In Section 10.3.1, we already described the special InfoProviders that are available for operational reports and data analyses based on SAP HANA. You may be asking yourself how InfoProviders and the BW queries that are based on those providers can be used outside of the SAP BusinessObjects portfolio, and how they can be integrated into existing user interfaces.

The Easy Query interface provides one option to integrate the result of BW queries into existing user interfaces (e.g., Web Dynpro ABAP or SAPUI5). Using the Easy Query interface, you can address a BW query via a (remote) function module, a web service (i.e., via the *Simple Object Access Protocol*, SOAP), or via an OData service.
— **BW Query in User Interfaces**

For a BW query to be called via the Easy Query interface, certain requirements must be met (details can be found in the SAP NetWeaver BW documentation). Moreover, access must be granted explicitly in the BEx Query Designer. The corresponding checkbox BY EASY QUERY can be found on the EXTENDED tab of the BW query properties (shown in Figure 10.13).
— **Requirements**

Once you marked a BW query for access via the Easy Query interface, the system automatically generates an RFC-enabled function module. This generation process can be controlled using Transaction EQMANAGER.
— **EQMANAGER**

The example in Figure 10.17 shows that the RFC-enabled function module /BIC/NF_2 was created for the BW query AN_FLIGHT_QUERY1 that is based on the InfoProvider AN_FLIGHT.
— **RFC**

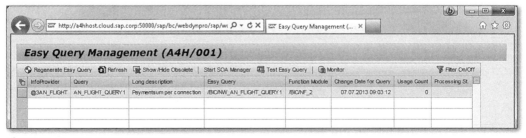

Figure 10.17 Easy Query Management

Transaction EQPREVIEW

You can use Transaction EQPREVIEW to test the generated function module. Figure 10.18 shows the formatted result for the function module /BIC/NF_2.

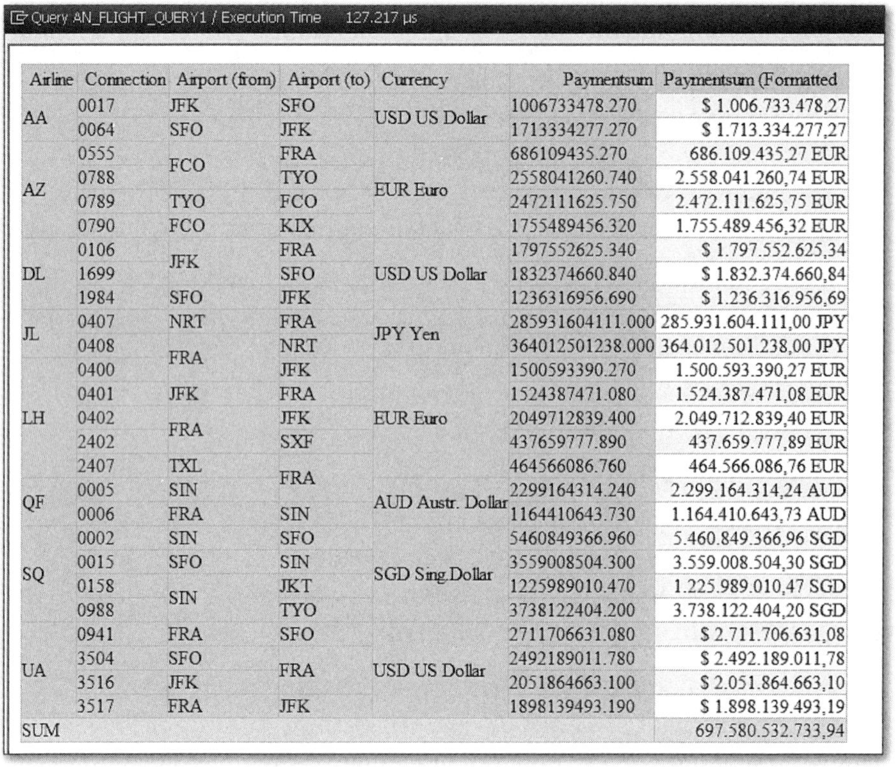

Airline	Connection	Airport (from)	Airport (to)	Currency	Paymentsum	Paymentsum (Formatted
AA	0017	JFK	SFO	USD US Dollar	1006733478.270	$ 1.006.733.478,27
	0064	SFO	JFK		1713334277.270	$ 1.713.334.277,27
AZ	0555	FCO	FRA	EUR Euro	686109435.270	686.109.435,27 EUR
	0788		TYO		2558041260.740	2.558.041.260,74 EUR
	0789	TYO	FCO		2472111625.750	2.472.111.625,75 EUR
	0790	FCO	KIX		1755489456.320	1.755.489.456,32 EUR
DL	0106	JFK	FRA	USD US Dollar	1797552625.340	$ 1.797.552.625,34
	1699		SFO		1832374660.840	$ 1.832.374.660,84
	1984	SFO	JFK		1236316956.690	$ 1.236.316.956,69
JL	0407	NRT	FRA	JPY Yen	285931604111.000	285.931.604.111,00 JPY
	0408	FRA	NRT		364012501238.000	364.012.501.238,00 JPY
LH	0400		JFK	EUR Euro	1500593390.270	1.500.593.390,27 EUR
	0401	JFK	FRA		1524387471.080	1.524.387.471,08 EUR
	0402	FRA	JFK		2049712839.400	2.049.712.839,40 EUR
	2402		SXF		437659777.890	437.659.777,89 EUR
	2407	TXL	FRA		464566086.760	464.566.086,76 EUR
QF	0005	SIN		AUD Austr. Dollar	2299164314.240	2.299.164.314,24 AUD
	0006	FRA	SIN		1164410643.730	1.164.410.643,73 AUD
SQ	0002	SIN	SFO	SGD Sing.Dollar	5460849366.960	5.460.849.366,96 SGD
	0015	SFO	SIN		3559008504.300	3.559.008.504,30 SGD
	0158	SIN	JKT		1225989010.470	1.225.989.010,47 SGD
	0988		TYO		3738122404.200	3.738.122.404,20 SGD
UA	0941	FRA	SFO	USD US Dollar	2711706631.080	$ 2.711.706.631,08
	3504	SFO	FRA		2492189011.780	$ 2.492.189.011,78
	3516	JFK			2051864663.100	$ 2.051.864.663,10
	3517	FRA	JFK		1898139493.190	$ 1.898.139.493,19
SUM						697.580.532.733,94

Figure 10.18 Easy Query Preview

OData service

In addition to the function module, the system automatically generates a web-service definition: /BIC/NW_AN_FLIGHT_QUERY1 in the example shown in Figure 10.17. To call the BW query via an OData service, an additional step is necessary: The function module must be exposed via SAP NetWeaver Gateway. To do this, you use the *SAP NetWeaver Gateway Service Builder* (Transaction SEGW).

10.4   User Interface Building Blocks

Finally, we would like to briefly describe user interface building blocks that are available to consume the result of BW queries in Floorplan Manager for Web Dynpro ABAP.

Floorplan Manager is a framework for creating applications using Web Dynpro ABAP. Using user interface building blocks, you can create model-driven user interfaces and make sure that the user interfaces created with this approach have an identical look and feel.

Floorplan Manager

SAP provides special user-interface building blocks for the SAP Business Suite that can be used to visualize BW queries. These building blocks are part of the SAP_BS_FND software component. In this section, we would like to briefly describe the *analytics list component* and the *chart component*.

Using the analytics list component WDC_BS_ANLY_LIST_ALV, you can display the data from a BW query as a table. For this purpose, either the ABAP List Viewer or SAP Crystal Reports is used. An example is shown in Figure 10.19.

Analytics list component

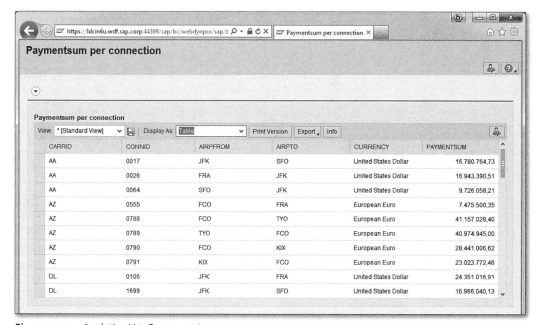

Figure 10.19   Analytics List Component

Chart component   Using the chart component `BS_ANLY_CHART_UIBB`, you can display the data from a BW query in graphic form. This graphic is created via Business Graphics. For more information on the user interface building blocks for visualization of BW queries, please refer to the documentation for SAP ERP 6.0, Enhancement Package 6.

Many of the technologies and tools mentioned in this chapter could only be described very briefly. We still hope that we could help you with some ideas for adding analytical functions to transactional, ABAP-based applications.

Decoupling decision rules from the actual program logic is an important trend in modern business applications. By providing options for modeling decision tables, SAP HANA makes it easy to flexibly control parts of an application via rules.

11   Decision Tables in SAP HANA

Because parameters of business processes are often changed, business applications must be modified from time to time throughout their lifecycle. The complexity—and thus, the cost—of such modifications is often higher than the original cost of introducing the software into an environment. This is especially true if the application was not designed to support flexible adaptation. In addition to the cost, the speed of implementations and adjustments are also a decisive factor. If a business unit must first submit a development request to the internal IT team, which is then implemented and validated in practice, the *turnaround times* are often too long for today's business environment. That is why *business rule management systems* are gaining more and more importance, as they make it possible to control and easily adjust certain parts of an application via rules. *Decision tables* are a typical element of such systems. These tables are used to define simple "if-then" rules. As of SPS5, SAP HANA supports the modeling of decision tables, which is introduced in this chapter. In addition, you will learn how to integrate these decision tables in an ABAP development based on SAP HANA. SAP plans to continuously expand this functionality and to offer further rule-management options in the future. Even though decision tables are an important element in this process, they only represent one option for expressing a set of rules. Other options include decision trees or formula-based decisions. Providing an extensive introduction to business rules is not possible within the scope of this book. If you are interested in further information on this subject, we recommend the book *BRFplus—Business Rule Management for ABAP Applications* by Thomas Albrecht and Carsten Ziegler (SAP PRESS 2011).

BRFplus and SAP NetWeaver Decision Service Management

With BRFplus, the SAP NetWeaver AS ABAP provides a powerful tool for defining and executing business rules. Using the *SAP NetWeaver Decision Service Management* tool, you can distribute and use these rules in a heterogeneous landscape. A large number of operations can then be executed by specialist departments without help from the IT department.

SAP plans to incrementally facilitate the use of SAP HANA capabilities in BRFplus and to particularly offer an integration of the modeling options described in this chapter with BRFplus.

11.1 Basic Principles of Decision Tables

The concept of decision tables will be explained through an example. If you, for example, need to verify whether an air passenger's profile data is complete, you can specify the conditions for this check via ABAP code. The example in Listing 11.1 shows how to check if a private customer has both an email address and a phone number, while business customers need only either an email address or a phone number.

```
METHOD is_profile_complete.
  IF ( is_customer-custtype = 'B' ).

    " Business customers
    IF ( is_customer-email IS NOT INITIAL ).
      rv_complete = abap_true. " Complete
    ELSEIF ( is_customer-telephone IS NOT INITIAL ).
      rv_complete = abap_true. " Complete
    ELSE.
      rv_complete = abap_false. " Incomplete
    ENDIF.

  ELSE.

    " Private customer
    IF ( is_customer-email IS NOT INITIAL ).
      IF ( is_customer-telephone IS NOT INITIAL ).
        rv_complete = abap_true. " Complete
      ELSE.
```

```
        rv_complete = abap_false. " Incomplete
      ENDIF.
    ELSE.
      rv_complete = abap_false. " Incomplete
    ENDIF.

  ENDIF.
ENDMETHOD
```

Listing 11.1 Decision Rule as ABAP Code

If a company changes its criteria for verifying an air passenger's profile's completeness, the code would need to be modified. As a first step to avoid such complicated changes, you can decouple the parameters via a configuration (e.g., via Customizing settings). Even if this would already provide some advantages, the implementation process for changes would still be complex and the structure of the rules would still be inflexible in this Customizing approach.

Decision tables can be used to clearly describe the decisions (*actions*) to be taken based on several parameters (*conditions*). Table 11.1 shows a decision table using the same criteria as Listing 11.1. The last column CUSTOMER PROFILE represents the action; the other columns define the conditions. When changing the rules or parameters, only the structures and values in the decision table must be modified. **Decision tables**

Customer Type	E-mail Address	Phone Number	Customer Profile
Business customer	Present	Any	Complete
	Missing	Present	Complete
		Missing	Incomplete
Private customer	Present	Present	Complete
		Missing	Incomplete
	Missing	Any	Incomplete

Table 11.1 Simple Decision Table to Check the Completeness of Customer Profiles

Decision tables are basically a structured case distinction for mapping input parameters (conditions) and decision values (actions). Conditions **Conditions and actions**

457

can either be columns of a database table or the result of calculations. The actions that constitute the decision table's output are determined by applying certain regulations (*rules*). This set of rules is represented by a table, as shown in Table 11.1. One of the main goals of decision tables is to clearly and consistently define the dependencies of conditions and actions. Each rule management system provides different options for defining rules. The current options available in SAP HANA are described in detail in Section 11.2.

Decision table as a view or procedure In SAP HANA, decision tables are development objects that can be created via the MODELER perspective in SAP HANA Studio, similar to views and procedures. Tables or views can be used as a data basis. The conditions and actions are physical or calculated fields of these objects. When activating a decision table, runtime objects (e.g., views or procedures) are generated.

There are basically two alternative scenarios:

1. Column values of a database table are to be changed using a decision table.

2. The value of a view's calculated column is to be determined using a decision table.

In the following section, we will focus mostly on the second alternative. This is because we recommend in general to modify ABAP tables only from ABAP, and also because it is often not necessary to persist such results on SAP HANA (just like it is not necessary to always materialize aggregates on SAP HANA). Accessing decision tables using ABAP is described in more detail in Section 11.5.

Limits Decision tables in SAP HANA are somewhat limited, because rules can be based only on table content (or views). It is currently not possible to make decisions based on rules *prior* to saving a data record. Furthermore, no direct integration in process management systems is possible. For special scenarios, SAP offers the *SAP NetWeaver Operational Process Intelligence* tool.

> ### SAP NetWeaver Operational Process Intelligence
>
> SAP NetWeaver Operational Process Intelligence powered by SAP HANA is a tool for intelligent process analysis. This analysis covers process visibility (current state of the processes) and decision support for continuous improvement. The tool is integrated with different data sources like SAP Process Observer, SAP NetWeaver BPM, and SAP Business Workflow. Decision tables are an important tool used internally by SAP NetWeaver Operational Process Intelligence.

[«]

In this chapter, we will first create a simple decision table DT_PASSENGER_ PROFILE that can be used to classify the air passengers from table SCUSTOM in Table 11.1. In the second example, the decision table DT_DISCOUNT, we will use a view as the data basis to implement a more complex scenario. We will determine a proposed value for a new discount for air passengers based on the customer type (private customer, business customer), the frequent flyer miles earned in the last year, and the present discount value. For the required calculations (especially for calculating the miles), we will create an analytic view AN_MILES used for unit conversion of flight routes into miles, as seen in Chapter 8.

Reference examples for this chapter

11.2 Creating Decision Tables in SAP HANA Studio

Like other development objects, decision tables are created via the MOD-ELER perspective in SAP HANA Studio. To do so, you select NEW • DECI-SION TABLE in the context menu of a package as shown in Figure 11.1.

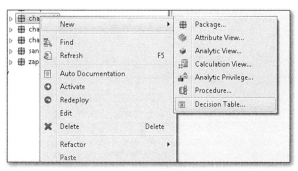

Figure 11.1 Creating a Decision Table (Part 1)

In the next step, you specify the name for the decision table and a description (see Figure 11.2).

Figure 11.2 Creating a Decision Table (Part 2)

Selecting a data basis — As with view modeling (see Chapter 4), you now have to select the data basis for the decision table. You can choose between tables or previously defined views (e.g., an attribute view).

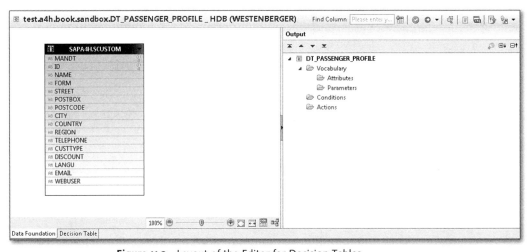

Figure 11.3 Layout of the Editor for Decision Tables

The editor for decision tables (Figure 11.3) consists of two sections that are opened via the tabs DATA FOUNDATION and DECISION TABLE. The DATA FOUNDATION tab is used to define the conditions and actions used in the decision table, the DECISION TABLE pane is used to maintain the actual rule values.

To get started, we want to classify air passengers directly based on columns of the SCUSTOM table, and add them to the DATA FOUNDATION tab. Since we want to access the attributes CUSTTYPE, EMAIL, and TELEPHONE in addition to the name of the passenger, we add these as attributes of the decision table. To use the named attributes as conditions, they must be flagged as such (context menu item ADD AS CONDITION).

Flagging attributes as conditions

In our example, we want to determine a classification with the help of a calculated attribute. To do so, we first define a new parameter via the context menu of PARAMETER, for which we specify a data type CHAR(1) and static fixed values—T for "True" (Complete) and F for "False" (Incomplete)—as shown in Figure 11.4.

Defining actions

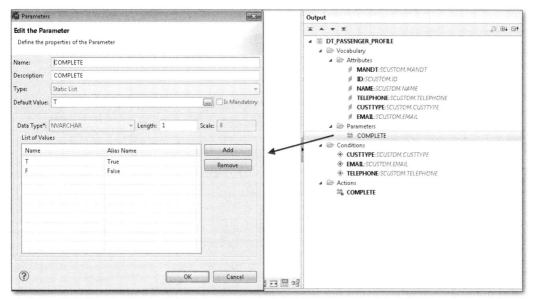

Figure 11.4 Defining a Parameter for the Output Value

Because this parameter should be used as the result, we flag it as ACTION (context menu item ADD AS ACTION). The final structure of the decision table is shown in Figure 11.5.

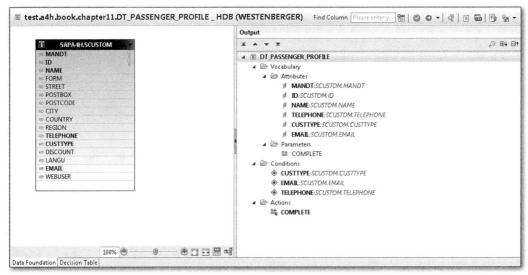

Figure 11.5 Structure of the Decision Table

Specifying rules

Using the DECISION TABLE tab, you can now specify the classification rules for the decision table, as seen in Table 11.1. To define the conditions (e.g., CUSTTYPE), you select a cell and then choose ADD CONDITION VALUES from the context menu. This opens a dialog where you can either enter a condition or select a fixed value from a list. To specify actions (in our example, "COMPLETE"), you can select either SET INITIAL VALUE for fixed values or SET DYNAMIC VALUE for calculated values from the context menu. Figure 11.6 shows a resulting set of rules where the completeness of a profile is determined based on the customer type and the presence of an email address or a phone number. With this rule set, the expression Like _* is used to verify if a non-empty string is present. The static action values "True" and "False" were set using SET INITIAL VALUE.

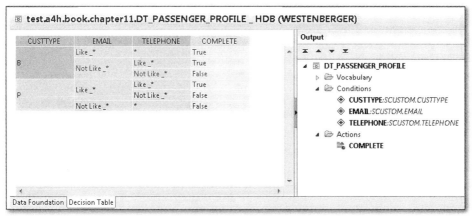

Figure 11.6 Rules of the Decision Table

After saving and activating the decision table, you can display the result using the DATA PREVIEW. Decision tables are activated the same way as views. Figure 11.7 shows that, according to the defined rules, 6% of the system's roughly 4,800 customer profiles are incomplete.

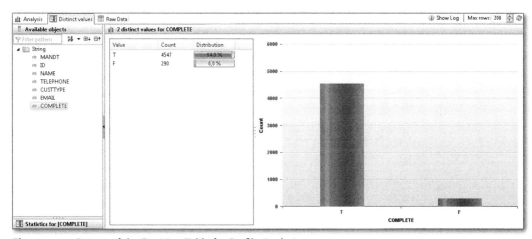

Figure 11.7 Output of the Decision Table for Profile Analysis

You can also export or import the values for decision tables to or from Microsoft Excel. This especially facilitates collaboration between IT experts

Exporting and importing values

463

and business departments. To export or import values, use the context menu in the editor pane DECISION TABLE.

Expressions for
decision rules

SAP HANA currently supports the expressions listed in Table 11.2 to define decision rules.

Expression	Supported SQL Data Types	Example
Not equal (!=)	Any	!= Lufthansa
Greater Than (>), Greater Than Or Equals (>=), Less Than (<), Less Than Or Equals (<=)	Strings and numeric types	Greater Than 20
In, Not In	Strings and numeric types	In AA;LH
Like, Not Like	Strings	Like Lufthansa*
Between	Numeric types	Between 100 and 200
After, Before	Date (DATE)	Before 2013-01-01

Table 11.2 Available Expressions for Decision Rules

Data types

This means that once again, correct handling of data types can be somewhat tricky and ignoring these aspects may cause problems. In particular, you must first convert data types in some cases. For example, to compare dates (After, Before) with an ABAP date (DATS, i.e., NVARCHAR(8) in the database), you first have to convert this date into a field of type DATE. To do so, you create a calculated field in a suitable view type (e.g., an attribute view) and use a conversion function like to_date().

Another example is numeric data stored in a character-type field. If you used the data type NUMC for a numeric value in your ABAP data model, for instance, this is a NVARCHAR type in the database (see Section 3.1.3). An example for this is the DISCOUNT column in the SCUSTOM table. As a result, a rule like >20 is interpreted as a comparison of strings by the decision table, i.e., as >'20' instead of a numeric comparison. Once again, the value must first be converted.

> **Consider Data Types when Designing Decision Tables** **[!]**
>
> To avoid unexpected consequences when evaluating rules, the structure and semantics of a decision table must be carefully defined. For a successful design, you must have the required development skills and understand the technological aspects and semantics of the data structures and types. In combination with a thorough documentation, this makes it possible for the specialist department to correctly define the set of rules.

11.3 Decision Tables Based on SAP HANA Views

Rules are often based on different parameters from several database tables, with certain calculations and expressions potentially also playing a role. Let's consider the following example: To determine the discount for a flight customer, the miles earned within the last year should be considered in addition to the customer type. Based on the current discount, either a higher or a lower discount should then be proposed.

Customer Type	Miles Earned within the Last Year	Current Discount	Proposed Discount Change for the Next Year
Business customer	<10,000 MI	<5%	reduced discount rate of 0%
		between 5% and 15%	–1%
		>15%	–2%
	>=10,000 MI	<15%	+1%
		>=15%	unchanged
Private customer	<20,000 MI	0%	unchanged
		>0%	–1%
	>=20,000 MI	<20%	+1%
		>=20%	unchanged

Table 11.3 Decision Table for Passengers Based on Calculated Key Figures

Calculating
frequent flyer miles To determine the frequent flyer miles, we will once again use the bookings
and flight plan from Chapter 8 and convert the flight route into miles. To
do this, we will use the techniques described in Section 4.2 to create a
new analytic view: AN_MILES. This view is called from a calculation view,
CA_MILES_LAST_YEAR, where we determine the air miles per passenger
within the last year using SQLScript. Listing 11.2 shows the SQLScript
coding and uses the known columns from the tables SBOOK and SPFLI,
in addition to the distance_mi column (containing the distance in miles)
and the discount_dec column (containing the current customer discount
as decimal value—type DECIMAL).

```
var_out =
  select mandt, name, country, city,
          custtype, sum(distance_mi) as miles,
          discount_dec as discount
    from "test.a4h.book.chapter11::AN_MILES"
    where year(fldate) = year(current_utcdate) - 1
    group by mandt, name, country, city,
            custtype, discount_dec;
```

Listing 11.2 Determining Miles Earned Within a Year

We will now create a new decision table DT_DISCOUNT and add the calculation view CA_MILES_LAST_YEAR to the DATA FOUNDATION. Subsequently,
we will define the conditions and actions as described in the previous
section. When doing so, we will define a parameter DISCOUNT_NEW of type
DECIMAL as action.

Dynamic values To determine the proposed value for the new discount, we need to access
the existing discount value. To do so, you specify a dynamic value for the
calculated column (using the context menu item SET DYNAMIC VALUE).
Figure 11.8 shows the resulting decision table with dynamic values for
the DISCOUNT_NEW column (e.g., "DISCOUNT" -1).

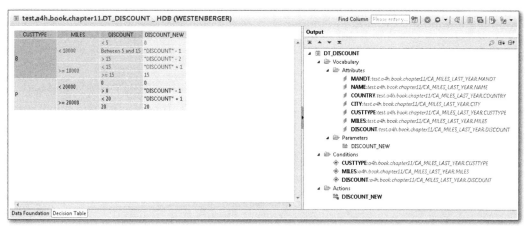

Figure 11.8 Decision Table Based on a Calculation View with a Dynamic Action Value

After successfully activating the decision table, the proposed values for a new discount are displayed as the result (see Figure 11.9).

MANDT	NAME	COUNT...	CITY	CUSTTYPE	MILES	DISCOUNT	DISCOUNT_NEW
001	Eastland Trade	CA	Vancouver	B	3.506.347	18	15
001	Compu Tech	US	San Fransisco	B	3.407.565	18	15
001	Roberta Energy Ltd	CA	Calgary	B	2.895.695	18	15
001	PH Keyboard Corporation	US	Boston	B	3.715.827	17	15
001	Infix Co.	US	San Mateo	B	3.092.348	17	15
001	ABC Dienstleistungen Gm...	DE	Kaiserslautern	B	3.418.927	17	15
001	British Railways	GB	Manchester	B	3.431.930	16	15
001	Marta Buchholm	ES	Barcelona	P	3.475.776	15	16
001	Sophie Kramer	DE	Schifferstadt	P	2.930.768	15	16
001	Theresia Jacqmain	DE	Gaertringen	P	3.508.064	15	16
001	Johann Lindwurm	DE	Berlin	P	3.326.360	15	16
001	Peter Hoffen	DE	Potsdam	P	3.396.326	15	16
001	Irmtraut Sudhoff	DE	Heusenstamm	P	3.240.690	15	16
001	Astrid Buehler	DE	Mannheim	P	3.576.481	15	16
001	Stephen Montero	DE	Schwetzingen	P	3.362.443	15	16
001	Andrej Goelke	SI	Ljubljana	P	3.327.847	15	16
001	Fabio Detemple	IT	Roma	P	3.539.698	15	16
001	Kurt Sessler	DE	Kurt	P	3.278.721	15	16
001	Florian Illner	DE	Wiesloch	P	3.501.449	15	16
001	Adam Eichbaum	DE	Wald-Michelba...	P	3.391.883	15	16
001	Fabio Cesari	IT	Roma	P	3.381.861	15	16

Figure 11.9 Result of the Decision Table Based on Calculated Key Figures and Dynamic Action Values

In the following sections, we will show you how this result is embedded into an ABAP application.

11.4 Runtime Artifacts and SQL Access for Decision Tables

When activating a decision table, several objects are created in the database catalog (schema _SYS_BIC). To start, a database procedure to implement the rules in SQLScript and the corresponding table types are created. If the actions are virtual parameters so that the database procedure does not modify any data, a result view is also created (i.e., a column view that contains the result of the decision table and that can be addressed via standard SQL in SAP HANA like other views).

Result view   The name of this result view is composed of the package name, the name of the decision table, and the suffix RV. Example: "test.a4h.book. chapter13/DT_PASSENGER_CLASS/RV"

If the data basis of the decision table itself is a column view, the same limitations apply for accessing the decision table via SQL as for the view (see Chapter 4).

11.5 Access to Decision Tables from ABAP

Because the result views generated from a decision table and other views can be addressed via SQL, they can also be accessed from ABAP using Native SQL. Unfortunately, it is not currently possible to directly define an external view in the ABAP Data Dictionary for result views. Instead, you must first *wrap* the result view via a calculation view. This can also be necessary for other reasons, such as to remove an unsupported data type from the projection list. For simple scenarios, you can graphically model the calculation view so that you simply add the generated view (via drag-and-drop from the database catalog) and select the desired column (see Section 4.3.2). The example in Figure 11.10 shows how our sample result view is wrapped by another calculation view CA_DISCOUNT_PROPOSAL.

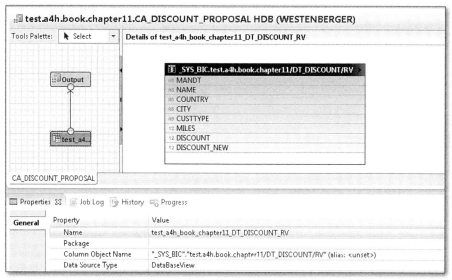

Figure 11.10 Wrapping a Result View as a Calculation View

As described in Section 4.5.2, you can now define an external view for this additional calculation view in the ABAP Data Dictionary, which can be accessed via Open SQL. Alternatively, you can also embed the decision table's view in an SQLScript procedure (or in an SQLScript calculation view), which can then be accessed from ABAP.

For our example, we will define the external view ZEV_A4H_DISCOUNT and display the results in an ALV list (SAP List Viewer). When doing so, we will use a new variant of the ALV grid with integrated data access that moves all operations to the database layer (see information box, "ALV with Integrated Data Access"). Listing 11.3 shows the coding for the *PBO module (Process Before Output)* when initializing the dynpro.

Decision table
in ALV list

```
MODULE pbo OUTPUT.

  " Create ALV with external view as data basis
  DATA(lo_alv_display) =
    cl_salv_gui_table_ida=>create(
      iv_table_name = 'ZEV_A4H_DISCOUNT'
      io_gui_container =
```

469

```
            NEW cl_gui_custom_container( lv_container ) ).

    " Initial sorting
    lo_alv_display->default_layout( )->set_sort_order(
        VALUE #( ( field_name = 'DISCOUNT_NEW'
                   is_grouped = abap_false
                   descending = abap_true ) )
    ).

    ENDIF.
ENDMODULE.
```

Listing 11.3 Using the ALV with Integrated Data Access

As a result, the proposed discounts are displayed in an ALV list (see Figure 11.11). To further enhance this scenario, we could add an option to accept or adjust the proposed values. This option will be dealt with in Chapter 13.

Proposals for discount adaptation

Customer name	Country	City	B/P customer	Old discount	New discount	Miles
Helmle	US	chicago	P	20,00	20,00	2.564.285,42
Andreas Klotz	DE	Walldorf	P	20,00	20,00	2.686.584,22
Tom Peterson	US	Pascadenia	P	20,00	20,00	2.506.358,63
Jean Cosman	CA	Kitchener	P	20,00	20,00	2.626.146,57
Laura Deichgraeber	DE	Mainz	P	15,00	16,00	2.631.673,07
Roland Hansmann	DE	Waldshut	P	15,00	16,00	2.512.746,45
Adam Koller	DE	Wald-Michelbach	P	15,00	16,00	2.506.038,20
Salvador Henry	ES	Sevilla	P	15,00	16,00	2.388.808,27
Anneliese Rahn	DE	Buxtehude	P	15,00	16,00	2.552.791,77
Mathilde Weiss	DE	St. Leon-Rot	P	15,00	16,00	2.498.420,39
Johann Heller	DE	Berlin	P	15,00	16,00	2.372.632,26
Guillermo Koller	ES	Madrid	P	15,00	16,00	2.847.052,88
Annemarie Sessler	DE	Kaiserslautern	P	15,00	16,00	2.342.770,99
Lee Barth	US	Boulder	P	15,00	16,00	2.860.875,31
Guillermo Benz	ES	Madrid	P	15,00	16,00	2.564.367,61
Laura Meier	DE	Mainz	P	15,00	16,00	2.436.550,95
Fabio Henry	IT	Roma	P	15,00	16,00	2.672.419,00
Juan Mechler	ES	Madrid	P	15,00	16,00	2.619.877,98

Figure 11.11 Output of the Proposed Discounts in an ALV List

Background Information: ALV with Integrated Data Access [«]

The *SAP List Viewer* (*ALV*) is a powerful component for displaying data in the ABAP application server; just about every SAP user and ABAP developer has already worked with ALV lists. In addition to the display functionality, the SAP List Viewer offers many other functions (e.g., for sorting, aggregation, personalization, and data export). When using this viewer, you can choose between several display variants for different scenarios and user interfaces (SAP GUI, Floorplan Manager for Web Dynpro ABAP). However, the same programming model is used in all cases: The data is first read into an internal table and then passed on to the SAP List Viewer.

As of ABAP 7.4, a new option is available, allowing you to only describe the data source for the SAP List Viewer and let the viewer make the selections independently on the database. We have used this option in Listing 11.3 by displaying the discount information of all passengers, whereas end users can only see a portion of the list. When scrolling or sorting the result list, the system determines the required portion of the result data.

To conclude this chapter, we would like to briefly mention the transport of decision tables. Like views and procedures, you can transport decision tables within an ABAP system landscape using the SAP HANA transport container introduced in Chapter 6. Since the transport container automatically includes all package contents, there are no special aspects to consider.

Transport of decision tables

As mentioned at the beginning of this chapter, decoupling rule maintenance and rule usage within an ABAP application represents an important aspect of these decision tables. The interface is defined by the structure of the generated result view. For this reason, structural changes to a decision table should only be implemented in the development system and transported consistently.

Function libraries add specific business and mathematical operations to the functionality of SAP HANA. They are integrated into special products, but can also be directly used within an application using SQLScript. This provides new analysis options, especially in the context of statistical predictions.

12   Function Libraries in SAP HANA

This book has already presented several options for efficiently analyzing operational business data using SAP HANA. Depending on the usage scenario, you can use direct native database functions in SAP HANA (see Chapter 4) or benefit from the advanced SAP NetWeaver BW infrastructure (see Chapter 10). Regardless of the technology, such analyses allow decision makers to respond to developments based on available data. It is a relatively new trend in *business intelligence* to take this approach one step further by using statistical models to make *predictions on future developments*. Such *predictive analysis* is used to enable decision-makers to *act* before an event occurs, rather than to *react* after the fact. The mathematical models are quite complex, and the interpretation and calibration of the results generally requires a good understanding of the business domain as well as the statistical algorithms. For this reason, *data analysts* have taken on increasingly important roles in recent years.

For many usage scenarios, you currently have to use special third-party software. Particularly for operational scenarios where time is of the essence, this approach introduces a number of challenges. Especially due to the required data extraction and conversion, a significant time delay and complexity is introduced to the process chain. SAP HANA uses special *function libraries* (Application Function Libraries; AFL) to provide an integrated option for some scenarios, which are based directly on the business data from the ABAP system. Before we discuss these libraries in more detail, we'll present three specific application scenarios.

Forecast creation

A classic usage scenario for statistical models is the creation of forecasts, such as predictions on the development of revenue, sales, or costs. Certain scenarios can also be created using forecasts for customer movements or business environments, which can play an important role within the strategic planning of a company.

Integration of risk assessment and planning

The assessment and response to risks in live operations plays a major role nowadays in many industries. You can imagine, for example, assessing the likelihood of potential defaults on payments, but also analyzing the risks in a complex production process. Here, frequent use is made of *key performance indicators* (KPIs) and *scorecards*, which define limits and assess impacts. The use of statistical predictions enables early detection of exceptional situations and signals in running business processes. This results in new options for closer integration of operational planning, risk analysis, and control options, which opens up great potential for increased efficiency.

Deriving business rules

Another trend that is currently increasing in importance is related to the derivation of business rules from existing business processes (*business rule mining*). This approach can particularly support the modernization of a legacy application by identifying execution patterns and decision points. This allows the use of a service-oriented approach within the application that is controllable via business rules. An integrated solution has the advantage of being able to base itself directly on the existing application code.

Application Function Libraries

The required functions are implemented in SAP HANA in *function libraries*. These libraries are written in C++ and provide highly optimized access to functions for advanced calculations and data-analysis scenarios. With SAP HANA SPS5, the AFL package provides two such libraries, which have been released for customer developments. You can find details of the release in SAP Note 1705650.

BFL and PAL

We will begin this chapter with a brief overview of these two libraries:

▸ The *Business Function Library* (BFL) contains a variety of complex business functions (for example, for determining annual depreciation) as well as reusable basic functions (for example, a weighted average).

▶ The *Predictive Analysis Library* (PAL) contains statistical functions with which you can recognize patterns based on historical datasets (for example, customer groups with similar purchasing behavior) and make predictions (for example, about the development of revenue).

We cannot present the full range of functions within the scope of this book. The number of functions is too great and, as mentioned, some of the algorithms are quite complex or require mathematical knowledge of the statistical models. We will thus limit ourselves to individual examples to give you an overview of these functions' use.

Objective of the chapter

> **Background Information: SAP Predictive Analysis and SAP Lumira**
>
> SAP provides powerful tools via *SAP Predictive Analysis* and *SAP Lumira* (formerly *SAP Visual Intelligence*), particularly for the creation and visualization of forecasts that can be based on the functions of the Predictive Analysis Library in SAP HANA. These tools allow even non-developers easy access to these new techniques. Since this involves separate products that are subject to licensing, we will not discuss these solutions in further detail in this book.

As an application scenario, we will again consider simple examples from the flight-data model in this chapter. We will determine a special key figure for seat utilization in a database procedure LINEAR_AVERAGE_UTILIZATION using a BFL function to illustrate the development of utilization over time by placing more emphasis on recent results than those of the past. Furthermore, we will perform a segmentation of passengers in the CUSTOMER_SEGMENTATION procedure using a PAL function, which could provide helpful information, for example, in an airline's customer rewards program.

Reference examples

We will first give you a brief overview of the functions and installation of AFL in Section 12.1. Here, we will discuss one function in more detail from the BFL and PAL, respectively, and explain the corresponding input and output parameters. Based on this, we will show you in Section 12.2 how to use these functions in your own implementation in SAP HANA. At the end of the chapter, we will explain how to use them in an ABAP application in Section 12.3.

Structure of the chapter

12.1 Basics of the Application Function Library

In this section, we will give you a technical overview of the functions of the AFL and introduce an example of one function from each of the two libraries: BFL and AFL.

12.1.1 Technical Basics

Installation of AFL

The AFL library is dynamically linked into the index server of the SAP HANA database. Although it is part of the delivery and license of the SAP HANA appliance, the hardware partner does not preinstall it by default. However, it can be set up on the customer side using the *SAP HANA on-site configuration tool*. You will find the necessary documentation in the HANA installation guide at *http://help.sap.com/hana_appliance*. After the installation, you as an administrator have to perform some configuration steps, which we will discuss briefly in the following text.

Activating script server

You must configure a separate *script server,* because the AFL functions for large datasets may take up a lot of resources (see SAP Note 1650957 for more information). The script server is a special index server process that does not perform any tasks during normal database operation. This ensures that the execution of AFL functions does not interfere with the operation of a standard application on SAP HANA.

authorizations

The installation of the AFL results in the creation of a technical schema _SYS_AFL, which contains the AFL procedures. In addition, the administrator must assign a user (the database user of the SAP NetWeaver AS ABAP, in the case of access via ABAP) the following two roles for the execution of AFL functions in SAP HANA:

▸ AFL__SYS_AFL_AFLBFL_EXECUTE (for the BFL)

▸ AFL__SYS_AFL_AFLPAL_EXECUTE (for the PAL)

Generating AFL functions

Some functions of the BFL and virtually all functions of PAL are implemented as *generic functions*; that is, the structure of the input and output parameters (number of fields, column names, data types) are not defined a priori. This allows flexible usage, but has the disadvantage that you, as a developer, cannot call these functions directly after the installation. Instead, you first have to generate a special form of the function—known as a *wrapper function* — using a special database procedure (`AFL_WRAPPER_GEN-ERATOR`). We will show you this based on a PAL function in Section 12.1.3.

12.1.2 Business Function Library

The *Business Function Library* (BFL) provides a range of specific business functions mainly from the internal *cash flow statement*. Table 12.1 contains some examples of calculations that are implemented in the BFL.

Examples of functions

Function	Corresponding Database pProcedure
Annual Depreciation	`AFLBFL_DBDEPRECIATION_PROC`
	`AFLBFL_SLDEPRECIATION_PROC`
	`AFLBFL_SOYDEPRECIATION_PROC`
Internal Rate of Return	`AFLBFL_INTERNALRATE_PROC`
Rolling Forecast	`AFLBFL_FORECAST_PROC`

Table 12.1 Some Functions of the Business Function Library

The underlying algorithms and data models are quite extensive, and it is beyond the scope of this book to introduce them in detail. In addition to calculations based on a fixed process, the BFL also exposes specific mathematical functions that are used within complex algorithms, but which can also be called independently.

An example of such a function is `LINEAR_AVERAGE`, which can be used to determine a *weighted average* and which we want to look at as an example. The individual variables are weighted differently here compared to the standard arithmetic average. Thus you can, for example, let values from the recent past play a greater role in the result than older values, which can be useful for some forecasts.

Example: weighted average

The mathematical definition of the weighted average of the numeric values x1 to xn with the corresponding weights w1 to wn is:

$$(w1 \times x1 + \dots + wn \times xn) / (w1 + \dots + wn)$$

Let's take as an example the seat utilization of flights of a fixed flight connection with sample data from Table 12.2.

Period	Month	Average Use (Percent)
1	January	87.5%
2	February	95%
3	March	91%
4	April	60%

Table 12.2 Sample Data for Weighted Average

We use the period as a weighting factor and thus get the following weighted average, while the normal average is approximately 83%.

$(1 \times 0.875 + 2 \times 0.95 + 3 \times 0.91 + 4 \times 0.6) / (1 + 2 + 3 + 4)$
$= 0.7905 \sim 79\%$

The lower value is due to the low utilization during the last month, which has more of an impact on the weighted average. The interface of the LINEAR_AVERAGE function has the structure shown in Table 12.3.

Parameter	Explanation	Column Structure (Name, Type)	
Input: Database table	Original data	VALUE	DOUBLE
Output: Result	In row N, the weighted average of the values up to the period N	AVERAGED_ RESULT	DOUBLE

Table 12.3 Interface of the LINEAR_AVERAGE Function from the BFL

We will use this function in Section 12.2 to determine the (weighted) chronological sequence of the seat utilization and use it as the basis for a forecast.

12.1.3 Predictive Analysis Library

Examples of functions

In comparison to the BFL, the *Predictive Analysis Library* (PAL) provides a series of generic, statistical algorithms that can be used on any data models. Table 12.4 contains some examples of algorithms that can be implemented in PAL.

Function	Description	Sample Scenario
Anomaly detection	Determination of outliers	Detecting unusual system behavior: long response times despite normal system load
A priori	Detection of correlations for deriving rules	Analysis of purchasing behavior: "Customers who have purchased products A and B often purchase product C also."
K-means	Classification of data into groups	Segmentation of a customer base into target groups for promotions

Table 12.4 Some Functions of the Predictive Analysis Library

Not all PAL functions are provided for direct use. For example, some of the more complex PAL functions provide as a return value a description in the *Predictive Model Markup Language* (PMML) format, a standardized XML format for statistical models. Such functions are aimed at usage in the context of a specialized product such as SAP Predictive Analysis.

Predictive Model Markup Language

In this section, we would like to use a function of the PAL that you can use to segment general datasets: the *K-means function*. Here, a dataset is divided into a specified number (K) of groups (or *clusters*). We won't discuss the underlying mathematical algorithm in detail at this point. However, the basic idea is based on assigning an initial selection of centers of data records to the cluster whose center is closest. This enables you to identify patterns and classify datasets (for example, customers, products, and so on). Figure 12.1 displays values and the corresponding cluster. As sample values, you can imagine that each point represents a flight connection, and the values on the axes represent the average seat utilization (Y-axis) and the percentage share of bookings with excess baggage (X-axis) in a period of time. Via the segmentation, you get a classification of flights into different categories. Flight connections with a high utilization and low excess baggage may indicate, for example, very frequent usage by business travellers (left upper cluster).

Example: clustering via K-means

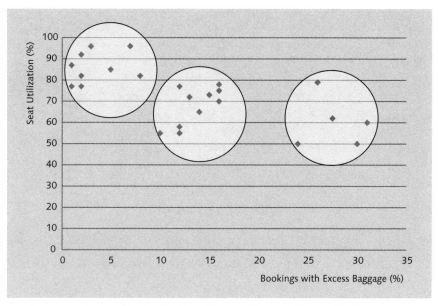

Figure 12.1 Schematic Visualization of Dataset Segmentation via the K-Means Function

Interface

Table 12.5 shows the input and output parameters of the interface of the K-means function, where this segmentation is based on two numeric values (V000 and V001).

Parameter	Explanation	Column Structure	
Input: Database table	The dataset to be classified, consisting of ID and numeric values	ID	INTEGER
		V000	DOUBLE
		V001	DOUBLE
Input: Parameter table	Parameterization of segmentation by name/value pairs, for example, cluster number (GROUP_NUMBER)	NAME	NVARCHAR (50)
		INTARGS	INTEGER
		DOUBLEARGS	DOUBLE
		STRINGARGS	NVARCHAR (100)

Table 12.5 Interface of K-Means Function from PAL

Parameter	Explanation	Column Structure	
Output: Cluster assignment	Assignment of data records to a cluster	ID	INTEGER
		CENTER_ ASSIGN	INTEGER
		DISTANCE	DOUBLE
Output: Cluster data	List of centers of the groups (Cluster ID and coordinates of the center)	CENTER_ID	INTEGER
		V000	DOUBLE
		V001	DOUBLE

Table 12.5 Interface of K-Means Function from PAL (Cont.)

As described in Section 12.1.1, you as an administrator must first generate this interface. In this case, you execute the SQL statements from Listing 12.1 via the SQL console in SAP HANA Studio with the user SYSTEM. Here, table types for the input and output parameters from Table 12.5 are first created in the schema _SYS_AFL, and then the desired interface is created using the database procedure AFL_WRAPPER_GENERATOR. After the successful execution of these SQL statements, the schema _SYS_AFL contains a procedure with the name PAL_KMEANS. For more information on generating database procedures for the BFL and PAL libraries, see the reference documentation of these libraries at *http://help.sap.com/hana_appliance.*

Generating the K-means function via the SQL console

```
SET SCHEMA _SYS_AFL;

-- Create table types for interface
CREATE TYPE PAL_KMEANS_RESASSIGN_T AS TABLE(
"ID" INT,
"CENTER_ASSIGN" INT,
"DISTANCE" DOUBLE);

CREATE TYPE PAL_KMEANS_DATA_T AS TABLE(
"ID" INT,
"V000" DOUBLE,
"V001" DOUBLE,
primary key("ID"));

CREATE TYPE PAL_KMEANS_CENTERS_T AS TABLE(
"CENTER_ID" INT,
"V000" DOUBLE,
```

```
"V001" DOUBLE );

CREATE TYPE PAL_CONTROL_T AS TABLE(
"NAME" VARCHAR (50),
"INTARGS" INTEGER,
"DOUBLEARGS" DOUBLE,
"STRINGARGS" VARCHAR (100));

-- Define interface
DROP TABLE PDATA;
CREATE COLUMN TABLE PDATA(
"ID" INT,
"TYPENAME" VARCHAR(100),
"DIRECTION" VARCHAR(100) );

INSERT INTO PDATA VALUES (1, '_SYS_AFL.PAL_KMEANS_DATA_T',
'in');
INSERT INTO PDATA VALUES (2, '_SYS_AFL.PAL_CONTROL_T', 'in');
INSERT INTO PDATA VALUES (3, '_SYS_AFL.PAL_KMEANS_RESASSIGN_T',
'out');
INSERT INTO PDATA VALUES (4, '_SYS_AFL.PAL_KMEANS_CENTERS_T',
'out');

-- Generation of the K-means function
call SYSTEM.AFL_WRAPPER_GENERATOR ('PAL_KMEANS', 'AFLPAL',
'KMEANS', PDATA);
```

Listing 12.1 Generation of an Interface for the K-Means Function

We will use the K-means function in Section 12.2 to perform a segmentation of the flights.

[»] **Additional Information: R-Integration**

In addition to PAL, SAP HANA also contains an adapter for integrating the open-source software system R (*http://www.r-project.org/*). You have an additional range of statistical operations available via this adapter. We will not discuss R-integration in detail within this book. However, it is used in a similar manner to how the AFL functions are used via database procedures in SAP HANA. You must note, however, that the R server is not part of SAP HANA for licensing reasons, and must be installed separately on a dedicated server. For more information, see the *SAP HANA R Integration Guide* at *http://help. sap.com/hana_appliance/*.

12.2   Use of Application Function Library Functions in SQLScript

In this section, we will discuss the calling of AFL functions via SQLScript and explain this by means of the two sample functions, weighted average and K-means, which we presented in the previous section.

As a first example, we would like to determine the weighted average of seat utilization for all flights of one airline. The result should be a time-based progression over the years, which can provide a better data basis for a flight-utilization forecast than the normal calculation of the average because the current data is valued higher than historical results of the past. To determine the required values, we use the analytic view AN_SEAT_UTILIZATION as the data source, which we defined in Section 4.2.

Weighted average of seat utilization

Figure 12.2 shows the interface of the database procedure LINEAR_AVER-AGE_UTILIZATION. As inputs, we transfer the client and the airline. As output, we expect a table with the normal as well as the weighted average of the seat utilization for all years for which data is available in the system.

Interface

Figure 12.2 Interface of the LINEAR_AVERAGE_UTILIZATION Procedure

In Listing 12.2, you see the SQLScript implementation for calling the BFL function AFLBFL_LINEARAVERAGE_PROC. We first select the average seat use using the analytic view AN_SEAT_UTILIZATION grouped by year that was created in Section 4.2, and thus call the BFL function. Finally, we use the CE function CE_VERTICAL_UNION (see Section 5.2.4) to transfer the columns of the two internal tables to the result structure.

Implementation

483

```
/********* Begin Procedure Script ************/
BEGIN

  lt_data = select
   100 * to_double(avg(utilization)) as "VALUE", year
     from "test.a4h.book.chapter04::AN_SEAT_UTILIZATION"
     where mandt = :iv_mandt and carrid = :iv_carrid
     group by year_int;

  call _SYS_AFL.AFLBFL_LINEARAVERAGE_PROC(
                      :lt_data, :lt_avg );
  et_utilization = CE_VERTICAL_UNION(
    :lt_data, [ "YEAR", "VALUE" as "AVERAGE"],
    :lt_avg,  [ "AVERAGED_RESULT" as "LINEAR_AVERAGE"]);
END;
 /********* End Procedure Script ************/
```

Listing 12.2 Implementation of the LINEAR_AVERAGE_UTILIZATION Procedure

Segmentation of flight customers   In the second example, we want to perform a segmentation of flight customers using the K-means function in a CUSTOMER_SEGMENTATION procedure, while considering the following input variables:

► Total of booking prices (EUR) in one year

► Total of baggage weight (KG) in one year

To determine the required values, we also use the analytic view AN_BOOKING as the data source from Section 4.2. As a result of this application, we expect a division of flight passengers into groups (with gradations and combinations), of which passengers are more likely to be business (many flights, little baggage) or private (fewer flights, more baggage). From this information and its corresponding time-based development, an airline could design a bonus system that is tailored to the needs of these groups (for example, higher baggage allowance for frequent travelers).

Interface   Figure 12.3 shows the interface of the CUSTOMER_SEGMENTATION procedure. As inputs, we transfer the clients (IV_MANDT), the year (IV_YEAR), as well as the number of clusters (IV_GROUPS). The output should contain the assignment to the clusters as well as the coordinates of the cluster as described in Table 12.5.

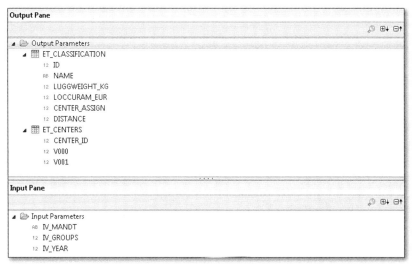

Figure 12.3 Interface of the CUSTOMER_SEGMENTATION Procedure

Listing 12.3 shows the implementation with the call of the PAL function PAL_KMEANS. In this case, we first fill the parameter table (see Table 12.5), where we apply a trick that we would like to describe briefly.

Implementation

Building Internal Tables in SQLScript

If you have to fill a table variable with certain values in an SQLScript implementation, but cannot map this via a SELECT statement in an existing table or a view, you have the option of selecting fixed values of the dummy virtual object.

select 'GROUP_NUMBER' as name from dummy;

Using this approach, you can build any kind of table content using aliases, type conversions, and unions.

In the parameter table, we set the value for GROUP_NUMBER (number of groups) based on the input parameter IV_GROUPS (see Figure 12.3), select the data of the analytic view AN_BOOKING and then call the database procedure PAL_KMEANS from the schema _SYS_AFL. In the final step of Listing 12.3, we read the names of the passengers from the SCUSTOM table and also include the previously calculated values for baggage weight and booking prices in the result.

```
lv_count   INT := 0;
 /********* Begin Procedure Script ************/
```

```
BEGIN

/* Fill the parameters of the table */
lt_control = select 'GROUP_NUMBER' as name, :iv_groups as
intargs, to_double(0) as doubleargs, '' as stringargs from
dummy;

/* Select data of analytic view */
lt_data =
    select
        to_int(customid) as id,
        to_double( sum(luggweight_kg) ) as v000,
        to_double( sum(loccuram_eur)  ) as v001
    from "test.a4h.book.chapter04::AN_BOOKING"
    where mandt = iv_mandt and year_int = :iv_year
    group by customid;

select count(*) into lv_count from :lt_data;

IF lv_count > :iv_groups THEN
    /* Call K-means function from PAL */
    CALL _SYS_AFL.PAL_KMEANS(:lt_data, :lt_control,
                    :lt_classification, :et_centers );

    /* Build result structure */
    et_classification =
        select l.id,
               c.name,
               to_decimal(d.v000) as luggweight_kg,
               to_decimal(d.v001) as loccuram_eur,
               l.center_assign,
               l.distance
            from :lt_classification as l
            inner join scustom as c on l.id = c.id
            inner join :lt_data as d on l.id = d.id
            order by l.center_assign, l.distance;

END IF;

END;
/********* End Procedure Script ************/
```

Listing 12.3 Implementation of the CUSTOMER_SEGMENTATION Procedure

> ### Separation of Technical Settings and Application Parameters [!]
>
> The parameters of many AFL functions contain a mixture of technical settings and real usage parameters. For example, you can set the desired number of clusters (application parameters) for the K-means function in the control table and also configure the number of threads that SAP HANA may use for the execution (technical setting). We recommend that you clearly separate these aspects in separate interfaces and work with default values if possible for technical settings.

12.3 Integration of Function Libraries in ABAP

Now that you have seen how you can call functions of the AFL from SQLScript procedures, we'll discuss their use from an ABAP program in the last section of this chapter. We will invoke these functions using the *database procedure proxies* that were introduced in Section 5.3.

To invoke the database procedure CUSTOMER_SEGMENTATION from the previous section, you create a proxy (see Figure 12.4) using the ABAP development tools in Eclipse. We thus map the fields of the output table ET_CLASSIFICATION to existing or specially created ABAP Data Dictionary database types. This will obtain the corresponding short texts, in particular when the table is created.

Creating database procedure proxy

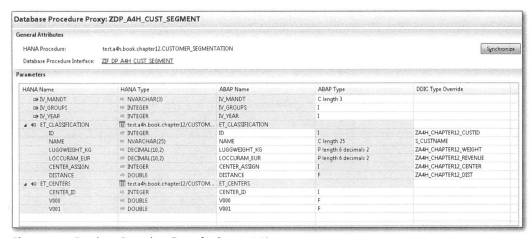

Database Procedure Proxy: ZDP_A4H_CUST_SEGMENT

General Attributes

HANA Procedure: test.a4h.book.chapter12.CUSTOMER_SEGMENTATION   [Synchronize]

Database Procedure Interface: ZIF_DP_A4H_CUST_SEGMENT

Parameters

HANA Name	HANA Type	ABAP Name	ABAP Type	DDIC Type Override
IV_MANDT	NVARCHAR(3)	IV_MANDT	C length 3	
IV_GROUPS	INTEGER	IV_GROUPS	I	
IV_YEAR	INTEGER	IV_YEAR	I	
ET_CLASSIFICATION	test.a4h.book.chapter12/CUSTOM...	ET_CLASSIFICATION		
ID	INTEGER	ID	I	ZA4H_CHAPTER12_CUSTID
NAME	NVARCHAR(25)	NAME	C length 25	S_CUSTNAME
LUGGWEIGHT_KG	DECIMAL(10,2)	LUGGWEIGHT_KG	P length 6 decimals 2	ZA4H_CHAPTER12_WEIGHT
LOCCURAM_EUR	DECIMAL(10,2)	LOCCURAM_EUR	P length 6 decimals 2	ZA4H_CHAPTER12_REVENUE
CENTER_ASSIGN	INTEGER	CENTER_ASSIGN	I	ZA4H_CHAPTER12_CENTER
DISTANCE	DOUBLE	DISTANCE	F	ZA4H_CHAPTER12_DIST
ET_CENTERS	test.a4h.book.chapter12/CUSTOM...	ET_CENTERS		
CENTER_ID	INTEGER	CENTER_ID	I	
V000	DOUBLE	V000	F	
V001	DOUBLE	V001	F	

Figure 12.4 Database Procedure Proxy for Segmentation

Following this preparatory work, we can very easily access the procedure for segmenting the customer data. The ABAP program in Listing 12.4 allows the year and desired number of groups to be entered and calls the database procedure with these parameters. The result is displayed in a simple ALV table (see Figure 12.5).

```
REPORT zr_a4h_chapter12_cust_seg.

PARAMETER: groups TYPE i,
           year TYPE i.

DATA: lt_class  TYPE TABLE OF
         zif_dp_a4h_cust_segment=>et_classification,
      lt_center TYPE TABLE OF
         zif_dp_a4h_cust_segment=>et_centers.

" Call procedure
CALL DATABASE PROCEDURE zdp_a4h_cust_segment
    EXPORTING
      iv_mandt  = sy-mandt
      iv_groups = groups
      iv_year   = year
    IMPORTING
      et_classification = lt_class
      et_centers        = lt_center.

" Display in ALV table
cl_salv_table=>factory(
    IMPORTING r_salv_table = DATA(lo_alv)
    CHANGING    t_table    = lt_class
).
lo_alv->display( ).
```

Listing 12.4 Call of Procedure for Segmentation from ABAP

Segmentation of customer data via database procedure

Customer Id	Customer name	Luggage weight	Revenue in EUR	Group	Distance
286	N.I.C. HiTech	7.668,00	727.030,56	0	2,4836310107840984E-01
1.148	Jean-Luc Heller	8.212,00	849.537,27	0	2,7475844472131389E-01
4.123	Thomas Meier	8.254,00	852.087,72	0	2,8986650996575414E-01
434	Ulla Rahn	8.408,00	820.631,36	0	3,4522106679493136E-01
449	Friedrich Jacqmain	6.835,00	786.001,94	1	2,0505848661727345E-03
3.652	Benjamin Pratt	6.837,00	783.919,18	1	3,4512575990974558E-03
2.355	Dominik Illner	6.831,00	784.411,83	1	3,6906071445656973E-03
3.075	Stephen Jacqmain	6.823,00	785.238,36	1	6,2256485002180530E-03
3.118	Christoph Jeremias	6.847,00	781.733,23	1	8,2564318515369849E-03
3.410	Benjamin Hansmann	6.829,00	781.368,73	1	9,2579961385404457E-03
478	Friedrich Sisko	6.874,00	784.467,91	1	1,2099064302251132E-02
2.331	Matthias Pratt	6.809,00	789.016,10	1	1,2364674836067234E-02
82	Metal Container Inc.	6.875,00	786.121,23	1	1,2439745992063420E-02
82	Schumacher Beratung	6.875,00	786.121,23	1	1,2439745992063420E-02
1.339	Jean-Luc Heller	6.830,00	791.584,35	1	1,3479664698705845E-02
3.906	Andrei Kreiss	6.861,00	791.357,06	1	1,3657093920410047E-02

Figure 12.5 Output of Customer Flight Data Segmentation in an ALV Table

Graphical representations play an important role in understanding the results of statistical operations. To this end, SAP provides different approaches and tools. In Chapter 13, we will use the *SAP UI Toolkit for HTML5* (SAPUI5) as an example to implement a simple visualization of a segmentation.

Visualization

You can break new ground with the development of innovative ABAP applications on SAP HANA. The combination of transactional data with the powerful analysis functions of SAP HANA results in new options for intelligent business processes in a combined system. A modern application design should be ready for this.

13   Sample Scenario: Development of a New Application

Within this book, you have encountered a variety of new techniques and tools that are available for the ABAP development on SAP HANA. In this chapter, we would like to use these options in a clear overall scenario.

We will start here with a fictitious initial situation and formulate a set of requirements from a business perspective on this basis. We will then create a design for the implementation and explain the essential implementation steps. You will find the documented application as part of the source-code examples associated with this book for download (see Appendix E).

13.1   Scenario and Requirements

We will continue to progress with the sample application in the scenario of a travel agency who makes customers an offer for a desired flight based on flight schedule and ticket prices, and who can make the booking for them (see also Section 8.2).

As an initial situation, we assume that the current IT system already provides an option for the employees of the travel agency to create or change flight bookings (cancellation, for example). Furthermore, it is also possible to manage the master data of the passengers, which includes the current discount given on the normal price as well as address data.

Initial situation

Finally, a simple reporting application about the flight bookings is available, where flights can be evaluated by airline and time period.

Change requests (business)

To differentiate himself from the competition, the travel company owner wants to serve his customers in a personalized manner and to develop customer loyalty. To this end, he wants to create opportunities to offer personalized pricing offers based on a customer's earlier bookings, including discounts or other benefits (for example, increased baggage allowance). These conditions are stored in the form of predefined *discount variants*, for which a passenger can decide if he meets the prerequisites. For the passenger himself, an overview is to be available that presents his current data and options in an attractive mobile application. In order to assess the effectiveness of this marketing initiative, the owner would like to be able to compare customer behavior before and after the introduction, as well as a segmentation of customers in target groups. In addition, he'd like improved efficiency from employees by shortening the interaction times with the system.

Change requests (technical)

As discount offers would be based on defined rules, the system should be able to make most decisions automatically. In exceptional cases, a manual confirmation by a company employee is necessary.

13.2 Application Design

We create an architecture for the planned application in this section and explain the fundamental design decisions and components in use. We will then discuss the specific implementation and the corresponding development objects in Section 13.3.

Application parts

We divide our application scenario into three independent ABAP developments, which use current SAP user-interface technologies:

▶ A Web Dynpro ABAP application ZA4H_DISCOUNT_MANAGER through which a tour-operator employee can search quickly for customers and approve or adjust special discount changes.

▶ An HTML5 application ZA4H_BOOK_PANEL, which displays a side panel containing more information about the flight bookings of a selected passenger and his membership in a customer group with similar behavior. The *side panel* is a special area in an SAP application frame such as

SAP NetWeaver Business Client, which a user can expand and in which he can show *widgets*; that is, small user-interface components. A user can add this side-panel view, if necessary, to the Web Dynpro ABAP application ZA4H_DISCOUNT_MANAGER to obtain analytical data to assist with decisions about discount changes.

▸ The third application part is an HTML5 application ZA4H_PASSENGER_APP, which is designed specifically for mobile devices. It displays information for a passenger about his previous flight bookings, and allows him to choose his personal discount scheme from the options available.

13.2.1 Management of Discounts by the Travel Company Owner

To manage discounts, we create a simple web application ZA4H_DISCOUNT_MANAGER with Web Dynpro ABAP. This consists of a search function for searching for air passengers ❶ and a result list ❷ which represents the miles flown per passenger, as well as the selected and the recommended discount scheme. The travel agent can perform actions in the toolbar to select a passenger and adjust the discount scheme. Figure 13.1 shows the user interface of the application.

Structure of application

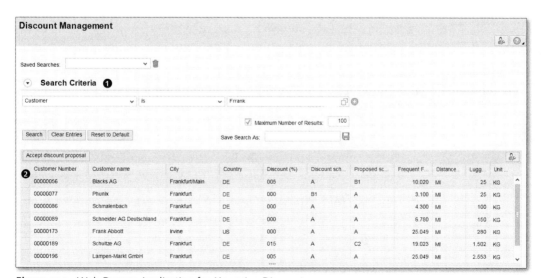

Figure 13.1 Web Dynpro Application for Managing Discounts

Elements used   In the application, the following techniques are used:

- For the search function, we use the fuzzy search in SAP HANA (see Chapter 9) to enable a fault-tolerant search for passenger data with suggesting of values while the user is typing.

- For an efficient representation of a dataset in the results display, we use the ALV with integrated data access (see the information box in Section 11.5).

- The miles flown are determined via an SAP HANA view (similar to Chapter 8), and the recommended discount scheme is determined via a decision table (see Chapter 11).

13.2.2   Additional Evaluations via a Side Panel Application

In addition to managing discounts, our application contains a side panel ZA4H_BOOK_PANEL, which includes an overview of an air passenger's bookings, as well as a graphical representation of the segmentation of all customer data. An employee can quickly obtain an overview of the customer—based on both his own flights as well as his relation to the booking behavior of all other customers in the system.

Structure of
application   A user can show this side panel for the previously described application for discount management in SAP NetWeaver Business Client (on the right in Figure 13.2). If you select a row—that is, a customer—on the left in the results list, the side-panel display is updated automatically.

Elements used   To implement the side-panel application, we use the following techniques, which we discuss in more detail in Section 13.3:

- We create the side panel as a *CHIP* (or *"Collaborative Human Interface Part"*), which consists internally of a small HTML5 application. Using a menu configuration in ABAP role management (Transaction PFCG), we create the connection to the ZA4H_DISCOUNT_MANAGER application.

- For the HTML5 application, we use *SAP UI Development Toolkit for HTML5* (*SAPUI5*) and create an OData service for data access using *SAP NetWeaver Gateway*. As we do not explain the use of these two relatively new SAP components in more detail in this book, we have compiled some background with references to further reading in the information box at the end of this section.

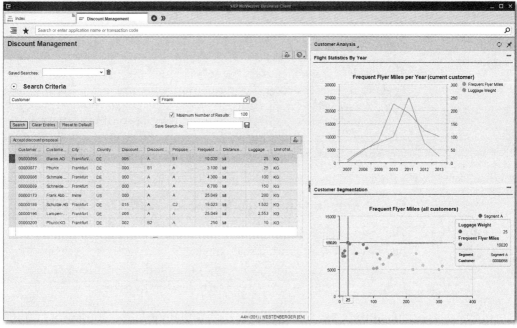

Figure 13.2 Additional Information in Displayed Side Panel

▶ We read the flight statistics for a passenger via the same SAP HANA views as the data used in the Web Dynpro application in the previous section, only with different filter values and aggregations. To segment the customer data, we create a database procedure and use the Predictive Analysis Library, which we presented in Chapter 12.

Using SAPUI5 and SAP NetWeaver Gateway   [«]

SAPUI5 is a rendering library, initially independent of the server technology, that's used to create HTML5 applications. In particular, it supports the web browsers of current mobile devices. When you use it on the Application Server ABAP, the *BSP Framework* (Business Server Pages) is used on the backend side. The SAPUI5 library is included directly in SAP NetWeaver AS ABAP 7.4, while it is available as an add-on for earlier ABAP releases (as part of *User Interface Add-ons for SAP NetWeaver*). Eclipse-based tools are available for the development with SAPUI5. Extensive information about the use of SAPUI5 can be found in the SAP Community Network at *http://scn.sap.com/community/developer-center/front-end*.

> SAP NetWeaver Gateway provides a development environment for the creation of RESTful web services based on the OData standard (*http://www.odata.org*). Similar to the SAPUI5 library, SAP NetWeaver Gateway is also part of SAP NetWeaver AS ABAP 7.4, while the framework is available in the form of add-ons in earlier releases. The development of services is done with the help of the *Service Builder* (Transaction SEGW). Furthermore, Eclipse-based tools are available, which are actually independent of the ABAP technology. You can also find more information on development with SAP NetWeaver Gateway in the SAP Community Network at *http://scn.sap.com/community/netweaver-gateway*.

13.2.3 Mobile Application for the Air Passenger

The ZA4H_PASSENGER_APP application is aimed at the air passengers. It is a browser-based application that is specifically designed for use on mobile devices (specifically tablets) in terms of resolution and interaction model. It can also be fully used in a modern desktop browser.

Structure of application
An initial screen shows an overview with the available functions. Furthermore, a passenger can browse the flight plan and look at existing bookings. He also sees his accumulated personal airline miles ❶, information on his baggage weight ❷, and the discount scheme currently chosen ❸. Before changing the discount scheme, a simulation of the impact can be done in an additional dialog, based on the historical booking data. Figure 13.3 shows a section of the application.

Elements used
For the implementation, we use the following techniques:

► For the development of the HTML5 application, we use SAPUI5 combined with SAP NetWeaver Gateway.

► We read the flight statistics as well as the available and recommended discount options via the same views or decision tables as in the Web Dynpro application described in Section 13.2.1. To simulate the impact of a change in the discount scheme, we create an additional database procedure in SAP HANA.

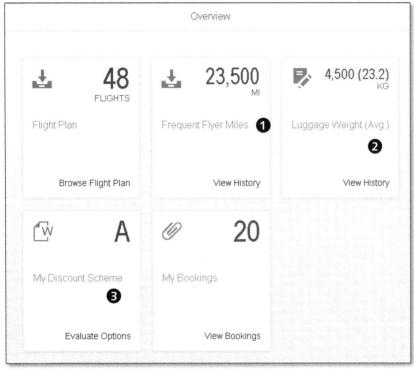

Figure 13.3 Mobile Application for the Air Passenger

13.3 Implementation of the Application

The implementation of the sample application consists of the following three layers:

Levels

▸ The implementation of data views and operations in SAP HANA forms the backbone of the applications (in addition to a small enhancement of the SFLIGHT data model for the discount settings). We describe the enhanced data model as well as the general implementation of the development objects in SAP HANA in Section 13.3.1.

▸ For accessing the read and write operations from a user context (for example, if you change the discount settings), we create a simple ABAP interface using ABAP Objects without using any special business framework. Access to the native HANA objects takes place via external views

497

and database procedure proxies. We have summarized the rough interaction of components in Section 13.3.2.

- ▶ For the user interfaces, we use Web Dynpro ABAP (including the *Floorplan Manager* for Web Dynpro ABAP) and SAPUI5 (with access to an OData service generated via SAP NetWeaver Gateway). We access the data via the aforementioned ABAP interfaces.

Packaging We provide all developments in a specific development package. In other words, this chapter's application is not a separate unit, but a part of the downloadable examples for this book (see Appendix E). Our application consists of the ABAP developments from the subpackage TEST_A4H_BOOK_ CHAPTER13 as well as the objects from the SAP HANA Repository from subpackage test.a4h.book.chapter13.

13.3.1 SAP HANA Views and Procedures

Enhancement of the data model To implement our scenario, we enhance the SFLIGHT data model minimally by storing additional data about a flight customer (for example, the selected discount scheme, see Table 13.1) in an additional database table ZA4H_BOOK_CUST_EXT. The details of the available discount options (prerequisites and benefits) are stored in another Customizing table ZA4H_BOOK_DIS_CONF, which we will not discuss in more detail at this point. You will find both as part of the ABAP development objects corresponding to this chapter.

Column	Data Type	Description
MANDT	MANDT	Client
ID	S_CUSTOMER	Customer number (foreign key for table SCUSTOM)
DISCOUNT_SCHEME	ZA4H_DISCOUNT_ SCHEME	Identifier for discount scheme (foreign key for Customizing table ZA4H_BOOK_DIS_CONF)

Table 13.1 Structure of Table ZA4H_BOOK_CUST_EXT

Development objects To determine key figures and to perform other analysis operations, we use the development objects that are explained in Table 13.2.

Development object	Description
AT_FLIGHT_PLAN	Attribute view of the flight plan with the support for fuzzy searches.
AT_CUSTOMER	Attribute view of customer data with the support for fuzzy searches.
CA_FLIGHT_STATISTIC	Calculation view to determine the frequent flyer miles and baggage weights for passengers.
CUSTOMER_SEGMENTATION	Database procedure for segmenting the customer data by frequent flyer miles and baggage weight. The customer base in question can be restricted to a type of customer (private or business customer), a country, or a discount scheme.
SIMULATE_DISCOUNT	Database procedure for simulating the impact of a discount scheme on a flight customer, based on data from the previous year.
DT_DISCOUNT_PROPOSAL	Decision table for determining default values for a discount scheme, based on airline miles, type of customer, and existing discount scheme.

Table 13.2 Description of Created Views and Procedures

For the fuzzy search, we create full-text indexes for the text columns of the tables SPFLI, SCUSTOM, SCARR, and SAIRPORT using the ABAP Data Dictionary (see Section 9.2).

13.3.2 Core of the ABAP Application

At its core, the ABAP application uses the SAP HANA views and procedures from the previous section for read accesses. Since these accesses take place from different applications (using Web Dynpro ABAP or HTML5), we create a common ABAP *interface*. The same interface also enables access to the write operations, for example, changing the discount settings.

Common ABAP interface

Table 13.3 provides an overview of the most important ABAP development objects for the data access.

Development Object	Description
ZEV_A4H_CA_STATISTIC	External view for the calculation view CA_FLIGHT_STATISTIC
ZDP_A4H_CUS_SEG	Proxy for the database procedure CUSTOMER_SEGMENTATION
ZDP_A4H_SIM_DIS	Proxy for the database procedure SIMULATE_DISCOUNT
ZIF_A4H_BOOK_DATA_PROV	ABAP interface for the data access (read and write)
ZCL_A4H_BOOK_DATA_PROV_HANA	Implementation of the interface ZIF_A4H_BOOK_DATA_PROV with access to the native HANA development objects for the read operations

Table 13.3 Description of ABAP Development Objects

Data interface

The interface ZIF_A4H_BOOK_DATA_PROV abstracts the required accesses to the views and procedures from the planned user interfaces and provides service methods for changing the discount settings within a transaction. We will not present the individual interface methods at this point, but will only give you an impression of the interaction of development objects based on an example.

Example: flight statistics for passengers

For both HTML5 applications, we require access to the flight statistics for a selection of air passengers. In this case, there is a method GET_FLIGHT_STATISTIC in the interface ZIF_A4H_BOOK_DATA_PROV, which—based on a selected table of customer numbers (input parameter lt_custom_sel)—provides the data on airlines and baggage weights based on the bookings of the corresponding customer (output table et_flight_statistic). The implementation of the data interface in ZCL_A4H_BOOK_DATA_PROV_HANA then takes place via the external view ZEV_A4H_CA_STATISTIC as shown in Listing 13.1.

```
METHOD zif_a4h_book_data_prov~get_flight_statistic.
  CLEAR et_flight_statistic.

  SELECT * FROM zev_a4h_ca_statistic
    INTO TABLE et_flight_statistic
```

```
    WHERE custom_id IN lt_custom_sel.

ENDMETHOD.
```

Listing 13.1 Access to the Flight Statistics of a Passenger via an External View

---

Using a Factory Class [+]

The use of an interface allows a simple decoupling of data access and the creation of alternative implementations. In our example, we create the required implementation of the data interface ZIF_A4H_BOOK_DATA_PROV using a *factory class*, which provides either an instance of ZCL_A4H_BOOK_DATA_PROV_HANA or a class-based exception for ABAP systems that do not run on SAP HANA. This exception is caught in the application and converted into an error message specific to the UI technology (for example, as error text in the *message area* in the case of Web Dynpro ABAP).

We will explain how to program such a factory class for the encapsulation of native HANA implementations in Section 14.1.2. In our sample package, you will also find another implementation of the data interface in the class ZCL_A4H_BOOK_DATA_PROV_TEST, which is based on static test data and can be used for simple application tests.

13.3.3 User Interfaces

In this section, we present the implementation of the three user interfaces using the Floorplan Manager for Web Dynpro ABAP, the HTML5 library SAP UI5, and SAP NetWeaver Gateway, as well as the side-panel technology. The use of these components would require a detailed introduction in each case, which is beyond the scope and topic of this book. For this reason, we will only discuss the basic concepts for implementing the specific user interface. If you are already familiar with the components, the descriptions should provide sufficient information to navigate in the implementation. If you were unable to attain any previous experience with these technologies, you will learn some options, including what type of applications can be implemented using these development tools. In addition, you can try out the downloaded sample applications from the user's perspective (see Appendix E).

Web Dynpro ABAP with the Floorplan Manager

For Web Dynpro ABAP applications, we use the Floorplan Manager (FPM), which allows the easy creation of a standard component user interface. Similar to the normal Web Dynpro development, you can also create Floorplan Manager-based applications (FPM applications) using the ABAP development environment in Eclipse (see Figure 13.4).

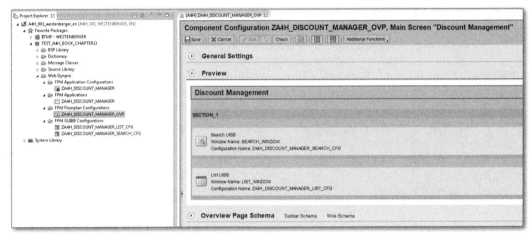

Figure 13.4 Web Dynpro ABAP Development with the Floorplan Manager in Eclipse

Feeder classes

The required data operations (data selection, actions, and so on) within an FPM application take place via *feeder classes*. These are normal ABAP classes that implement specific interfaces and are used in the configuration of an FPM application. The feeder classes that we create for our application internally use, in turn, the data interface ZIF_A4H_BOOK_DATA_PROV from Section 13.3.2.

Example: feeder class for a list

To roughly illustrate the interaction with this interface, you see a section of a feeder class for a simple list view in Listing 13.2. There, we create an instance of the data interface during the initialization via the factory class, which we then call within the data collection that takes place via the GET_DATA method.

```
CLASS zcl_a4h_book_list_feeder DEFINITION
  PUBLIC
  FINAL
  CREATE PUBLIC.
```

```
PUBLIC SECTION.
  " FPM Feeder Interfaces for Lists
  INTERFACES if_fpm_guibb.
  INTERFACES if_fpm_guibb_list.

PROTECTED SECTION.
PRIVATE SECTION.

  DATA mo_data_provider
       TYPE REF TO zif_a4h_book_data_prov.
ENDCLASS.

METHOD if_fpm_guibb_list~get_data.
  " [...]

  " Read data via data interface
  lt_data = mo_data_provider->get_flight_statistic(
      lt_selection_criteria
  ).

  " [....]
ENDMETHOD.

METHOD if_fpm_guibb~initialize.
  " Create data provider via factory class during the
  " initialization of the feeder class
  mo_data_provider =
      zcl_a4h_book_factory=>get_instance( ).

  " [...]
ENDMETHOD.
```

Listing 13.2 Section of the Feeder Class for a List View

Gateway Service Builder

Both the side-panel application ZA4H_BOOK_PANEL and the mobile applica-   Service generation
tion ZA4H_PASSENGER_APP access the data from the ABAP system from
the browser using an OData service via the HTTP protocol. We use the
Gateway Service Builder (Transaction SEGW) to create this service. The
OData service provides various data for the two applications, such as
the flight plan, an overview of the passenger's air miles, the result of the

segmentation function, as well as the discount simulation. The structure of the service is shown in Figure 13.5.

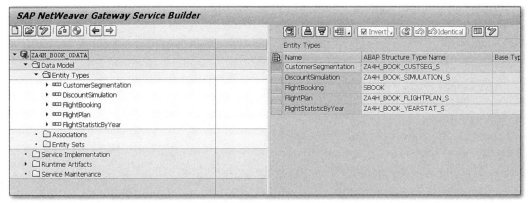

Figure 13.5 Structure of the OData Service in the Gateway Service Builder

Based on the service modeling, the Service Builder generates an ABAP class per entity in which you have to implement the data retrieval in turn (similar to the FPM feeder class from the previous section). Here, we access the classes from Section 13.3.2 again. An abstraction via an ABAP interface that is independent from the UI technology pays off especially well when using an application logic in different user interfaces.

SAPUI5 Interfaces

To create the SAPUI5-based user interfaces (side-panel and mobile-application), we use the standard development tools for web development in Eclipse, which provide support for the development of HTML pages and JavaScript. You receive these tools together with SAPUI5 development environment for Eclipse, which you can obtain free of charge via the website *https://tools.hana.ondemand.com.* Figure 13.6 shows the structure of our SAPUI5 application ZA4H_BOOK_PANEL as an Eclipse project. The application consists of a series of HTML and JavaScript files that contain the layout and the client-side logic of the application.

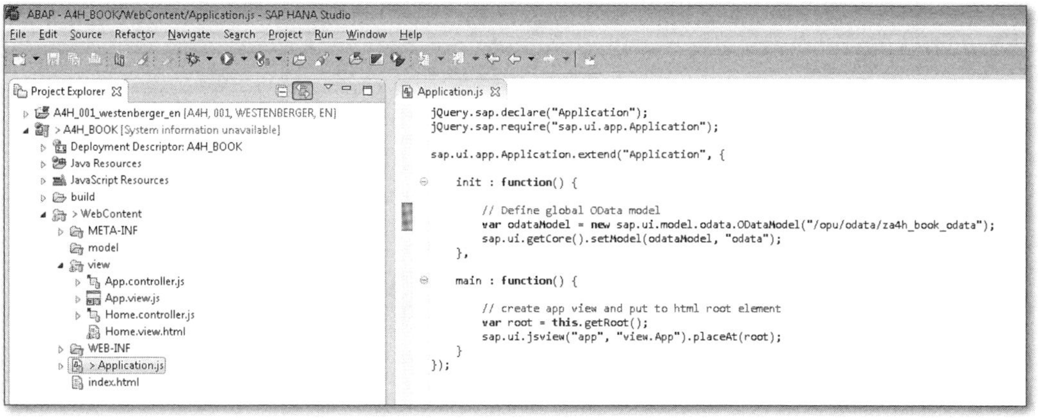

Figure 13.6 SAPUI5 Development Tools in Eclipse

As the data model of the application, we use the class `sap.ui.model.` **Connection to**
`odata.ODataModel` of the SAPUI5 library in JavaScript, through which **OData service**
we establish access to the OData service that was created. Here, we only
have to specify the ICF path (Internet Communication Framework) of
the service. The entity structure (attributes, associations, and so on) is
automatically derived from the metadata of the OData service.

We create the side-panel application `ZA4H_BOOK_PANEL` as a simple HTML **MVC pattern**
page using the user-interface elements provided by the SAPUI5 library. The
more comprehensive mobile application `ZA4H_PASSENGER_APP`, designed
for passenger use, is based on the *Model View Controller concept* (MVC
concept) of SAPUI5. This design pattern allows to declaratively define the
individual areas of the user interface and manage the navigation paths
between the areas. For more information on using the MVC pattern, see
the development documentation for SAPUI5 (see *https://sapui5.hana.
ondemand.com/sdk*).

Side Panel Configuration

The side panel is configured via the menu maintenance of a user role in **Transaction PFCG**
Transaction PFCG. In this case, you create `menu` entries for the side panel
and specify the references to those applications for which the side panel
is to be available. Figure 13.7 shows the configuration for the side panel
`ZA4H_BOOK_PANEL`.

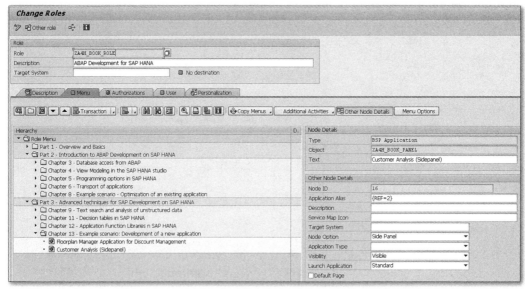

Figure 13.7 Side Panel Configuration in Transaction PFCG

You will find a predefined role ZA4H_BOOK_ROLE as part of the download package for this book. For more information on creating and configuring side panels, please refer to the SAP documentation at *http://help.sap.com/ nw74* and search for *Implementing Side Panels*.

13.4   Using the Applications

Requirements

Finally, we would like to briefly explain how to launch the applications. You primarily require an Internet browser, and in particular a current version of a standard browser is recommended for the HTML5 applications. To use the side panel, we recommend the current Version 4.0 of SAP NetWeaver Business Client; you can find information about this in the SAP Community Network at *http://scn.sap.com/community/ netweaver-business-client*.

Use in the
Business Client

If you use SAP NetWeaver Business Client and have installed the samples from the book (see Appendix E), you only have to assign the above role ZA4H_BOOK_ROLE to your application user. If you then log on to SAP

NetWeaver Business Client in the system with this user, you have direct access to the implemented applications, including the side panel.

For direct invocation in the browser, it is best to use Transaction SICF of the Internet Communication Framework (filter for the part of the name *A4H*). The context menu entry TEST SERVICE opens the browser with the Internet address associated with the service.

Call in the browser

Best practices play an important role, especially when using new technologies. Even if something is technically possible, it may not be practical or useful in each scenario. Old rules should be reviewed, and new design patterns should be explored.

14   Practical Tips

We have presented a variety of options within this book for calling functions in SAP HANA from ABAP systems. In addition to normal database access, you have been introduced to the modeling of views, SQLScript-based views, and database procedures, as well as some advanced technologies such as text analysis, function libraries, and decision tables.

In this chapter, we'll present some practical tips on topics that are particularly important when developing ABAP applications on SAP HANA. These are subdivided into the following topic areas:

▸ **General recommendations**
We'll first provide you with some general recommendations for developing ABAP on SAP HANA. We primarily discuss details that you should consider for the migration and optimization of ABAP programs.

▸ **Conventions**
We present some conventions which, from our perspective, are useful but optional. These include naming conventions, conventions for encapsulating and packaging, guidelines for distributed development, and similar topics.

▸ **Quality aspects**
For implementations in the database, non-functional criteria such as robustness, testability, and security should play an important role in addition to performance. We introduce some measures that will help ensure high quality in development.

▸ **Performance guidelines**
The execution speed of programs naturally plays a crucial role in the

context of SAP HANA. Many usage scenarios involve real-time access to large datasets. A solid understanding of the guidelines and techniques for achieving optimal performance is essential here. We provide an overview of existing and new recommendations, and we particularly discuss changes in comparison to traditional databases.

We will also enhance programming recommendations via positive and negative examples.

14.1 General Recommendations

In this first section, we have compiled some general recommendations that you should follow for migration and development on SAP HANA. This involves functional aspects in particular. We will return to nonfunctional topics such as conventions, quality aspects, and performance in subsequent sections.

We'll start with recommendations for the use of column or row stores in SAP HANA. We will then discuss possible design patterns for the encapsulation of HANA-specific implementations and provide a checklist for relocating calculations to SAP HANA.

14.1.1 Recommendations for Column and Row Store

You can look in the ABAP Data Dictionary's technical settings to see whether a table should be created in the row store or column store of SAP HANA (see Section 3.2.1). The column store is the default setting here.

Column store
The analysis of large datasets can be performed more efficiently in the column store. Thus SAP recommends that you store every table in the column store, as long as there is no dedicated reason for storing it in the row store. Tables that contain application data are always stored in the column store, because it is very likely that this data is also to be used in analysis scenarios. This applies particularly to tables that contain a large number of data records, because the column store provides better compression properties. This also applies to tables that are to be used for text searches (see Section 9.2).

Still, you have reason to use the row store if, for example, a table is accessed predominantly by time-critical DML statements (Data Manipulation Language; that is, UPDATE, INSERT, or DELETE). In addition, this must not be an application table on which you subsequently want to perform analyses. Therefore, primarily technical, internal SAP tables are eligible for row store. Examples include tables for update processing (STSK package) or for RFC processing (SRFC package). These tables are typically accessed with a SELECT SINGLE.

Row store

> **Use the Column Store!**
>
> In general, you should store all tables in column store for SAP HANA unless more technical tables are involved, as described above.

[+]

14.1.2 SAP HANA-Specific Implementations

With the ABAP development on SAP HANA, we must distinguish between two scenarios:

- Database-independent implementations (for example, Open SQL).
- Implementations using SAP HANA-specific functions (for example, Native SQL, column views, and procedures).

Scenarios

In the first case, you do not have to consider anything special from a software logistics perspective. You use SAP HANA like any other database, but benefit directly from the high processing speed of SAP HANA in many scenarios. Your developments are executable on all database systems supported by SAP.

When using native HANA functions, the same implications as usual initially apply if you define parts of an application specifically for a database system (for example, via Native SQL, hints, or other techniques). When designing the application, you should consider the following questions:

HANA-specific implementations

- Are there systems with a different database system in my landscape or in my customers' landscapes? Is an alternative implementation of the functions required for other database systems?

▶ How fundamental are database-specific functions to my application scenario? Is the central quality of the application involved, or is it just the "teasing out" of the optimal performance?

▶ Is the development in SAP HANA to be called solely via ABAP-based applications or via other channels as well (for example, SAP Business-Objects tools)?

Pure optimization initially via Open SQL

It's difficult to give a general recommendation as to when exactly it makes sense to use a database-specific implementation. For pure performance optimization of an existing ABAP application, we recommend that you initially proceed by using standard tools (for example, via an optimal use of Open SQL). In Section 14.4, we provide special performance recommendations for the use of Open SQL on SAP HANA.

ABAP interface

If you use the techniques in this book to relocate operations to SAP HANA and ensure that they can be called via ABAP, it is often useful to encapsulate access to these functions via an interface in ABAP (thus, an ABAP interface). This enables the use of the *factory pattern* — a standard design pattern in software development — which is used for decoupling. Listing 14.1 shows a sample code in which a data retrieval was abstracted via an interface lif_data_provider (the exact appearance of this interface is irrelevant to understanding this example). The factory class provides a method that transfers an instance of a HANA-specific implementation (lcl_hana_provider) to a HANA system, while an alternative implementation is created in systems with a classic database. The test on SAP HANA is done via the class CL_DB_SYS, which has advantages over a test on the system field sy-db because you can easily make a "where-used" list for a class to find all parts of the program that perform such a distinction.

```
" Factory class
CLASS lcl_factory DEFINITION.
  PUBLIC SECTION.
    CLASS-METHODS: get_instance
                     RETURNING VALUE(ro_instance)
                       TYPE REF TO lif_data_provider.
ENDCLASS.

" Implementation of the factory class
CLASS lcl_factory IMPLEMENTATION.
  METHOD get_instance.
```

```
    IF ( cl_db_sys=>is_in_memory_db = abap_true ).
      ro_instance = NEW lcl_hana_provider( ).
    ELSE.
      ro_instance = NEW lcl_standard_provider( ).
    ENDIF.
  ENDMETHOD.
ENDCLASS.
```

Listing 14.1 Example of Factory Design Pattern Use for Decoupling HANA-Specific Implementations

This approach can also be combined with *BAdIs* (Business Add-Ins), because the concept of an (abstract) factory class is also used in this case. The optimization has thus been implemented in SAP Business Suite powered by SAP HANA because alternative implementations can be activated and deactivated using this technique.

BAdIs

> **Optimization Procedure**   **[+]**
>
> Try to implement local performance optimization initially via Open SQL. For major program changes and relocation of operations to SAP HANA, invest in decoupling—for example, via the aforementioned factory approach.

14.1.3 Checklist for Database-Specific Implementations

In this section, we'll provide a checklist of what you should consider when relocating program code to the database. This helps you avoid errors related to internationalization or localization.

Dates play an important role in business data and processes (for example, when a booking was made). You must of course pay attention to using the respective time zones correctly. If you use the time zone to which the server is set, you must note that the database server's time zone is used for SQLScript, while the time zone of the ABAP application server is crucial in ABAP implementations. SAP recommends that you always make sure these time zones are identical during the installation.

Date/time

To determine the period between two calendar dates, there are special calculation rules for some business processes and in some global regions (for example, using a fiscal year with 360 days or combining the days of a weekend into one day). Depending on the context, you must ensure

Calculating with date fields

513

that such calculations are interpreted correctly from a business perspective. The SQL function days_between supported by SAP HANA does not know these specifics.

Currencies and units When handling currencies, you must ensure that some amounts are stored in the database with displaced decimal places (for example, for Japanese yen). When calculating with such values, you must ensure that this displacement is taken into account before an output for an end user. This takes place in ABAP, for example, via specific conversion functions or the WRITE statement. If you work with currencies in analytical models in SAP HANA and want to consume them externally, you should mark these key figures as such and specify that the decimal displacement is to be taken into account (see Section 4.2.4). In SQLScript procedures, you should clearly define whether you are working with internal or external formats in the definition of the interface, so each user knows how to interpret the values.

Conversion exits There may be differences between internal and external presentations for other data types also. An example of this is the flight time in the flight plan of our sample data model (column FLTIME in the table SPFLI). The flight time is stored internally in minutes as an INTEGER in the database, while it is presented externally via a conversion exit as a character string consisting of hours and minutes. If you are thus using a data model in different user interfaces, we recommend that you ensure that it is treated uniformly.

Rounding behavior When calculating with decimals, rounding behavior plays an important role, especially for monetary amounts. Small rounding differences can have a major impact on totals, so you should make sure to minimize rounding errors. When converting a currency, you should, if possible, only perform the conversion after an aggregation, which is also advantageous from a runtime perspective.

Text sorting The sorting of texts depends on the current language settings. In the ABAP command SORT, therefore, the addition AS TEXT will sort the character strings alphabetically according to the set text environment. If you sort content in an SQL statement via the addition ORDER BY, however, it is sorted in a binary manner according to the internal presentation. Figure 14.1 shows an example using German umlauts. Here, the name

"Möller" appears after "Muller," although it should appear alphabetically after "Moller." For this reason, we recommend that you usually sort texts, which you present in an ABAP application for an end user, in an application server.

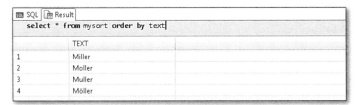

Figure 14.1 Sorting Texts in the Database

> **Handling Data Correctly from a Business Perspective**
>
> For time stamps, currencies, units, and texts, pay particular attention to the correct treatment of the business data in the context of native implementations in the database.

[+]

14.1.4 Recommendations for Migration

In this section, we give you some tips to consider when migrating an existing system to SAP HANA. A basic rule is that ABAP applications are fully compatible. There are a few fine points to note, which we would like to discuss here:

▶ **Database-dependent ABAP code**
  If you use database-dependent ABAP code in existing developments, you must test it as with any data migration and adjust it for the HANA database if necessary.

▶ **Converting pool and cluster tables**
  When converting pool and cluster tables to transparent tables, problems may occur if you have relied on an implicit sort behavior in your developments or if you directly accessed the internal physical clusters or pools.

▶ **Sort behavior**
  If no ORDER BY was specified in the SQL statement, the sequence in which the records are read is unpredictable.

Database-Dependent Code

If your existing applications have database-dependent code — for example, native SQL via the statement EXEC SQL, the interface ABAP Database Connectivity (ADBC), or database hints — these positions in the code must be checked. While database hints are no longer executed on the new platform when you migrate to another database, an exact check is always required for database-dependent SQL, because errors may occur here unless you intervene.

Hints

Hints to the database (or also the database interface) are given a database indicator in ABAP. This generally looks as follows:

```
SELECT ... %_HINTS <DB> 'db_specific_hint'.
```

The hint is sent only to the database specified instead of the <DB> place-holder. This means that, when the additional statement to the optimizer of the old database platform is converted to the new platform, it is no longer sent to the optimizer of the new database. This concerns not only hints for the database, but also specific instructions to the database interface. For a conversion, you must thus check whether the desired behavior on the old database platform should also be defined again by a hint on the new database platform. This is generally unnecessary for SAP HANA due to the modified architecture. Usually, no adjustment is necessary for the hints to the database interface, either. Here, we recommend that you use the default values for SAP HANA for the database interface.

Native SQL

Database-dependent code must always be checked for a conversion. The code should be tested even if standard SQL is involved. For database-specific SQL, you must first clarify the code is to achieve. An SQL statement must then be written to deliver the same result on SAP HANA. If possible, you should use Open SQL for it.

Sort Behavior

Pool and cluster tables

Access to former pool or cluster tables, which we have already discussed in Section 7.3, is a point that should be emphasized separately. For pool and cluster tables, an implicit sorting is always performed by the database interface. This is lost after the conversion to a transparent table, because no automatic ORDER BY is added here to the statement. Access to pool and cluster tables must therefore be analyzed with regard to their sorting during a migration. In this case, the Code Inspector provides a separate check—"Find SELECT for Pool/Cluster Tab without ORDER BY"—so you can quickly and easily find such critical points in your own developments.

However, changes can also occur in the implicit sort behavior for existing transparent tables. Classic row-oriented databases are usually accessed via a primary or secondary index. Here, the data is often read in the desired sequence, because it is read from the database in the sequence stored there when you use an index. However, this is not guaranteed, and this behavior is not a documented feature of Open SQL. The selected access path and the associated sorting can thus change at any time. You must use the addition ORDER BY instead if the data is to be selected in a specific sorting. This rule applies in particular to SAP HANA because there the data is column-oriented, there is no secondary index, and the data can be read in parallel. Thus, such places involve a programming error that you should correct regardless of a migration to SAP HANA.

Sort explicitly when sorting is necessary

Problems may occur if a certain sorting is assumed in program sequences. This is the case, for example, when working with searches in internal tables with the addition BINARY SEARCH, because a relevant sorting is essential there. However, there may also be surprises with the output of data if it is suddenly not appearing in the desired sort order.

Possible effects

Don't Rely on Implicit Sortings	**[+]**
If you require a specific sorting of data when you access a database, use the addition ORDER BY explicitly.	

14.1.5 Development in Landscapes

In a standard SAP development scenario, multiple systems are generally used, and even entire landscapes are often included in larger developments. To ensure that no problems occur during the transition from a development system to another system (for example, a test or production system), you should follow some guidelines for implementations in the database.

First, we would like to remind you of the correct handling of schema
names and the client field, which we have already discussed in Section
4.5.4. During modeling or SQLScript implementation, avoid referencing
schema names directly, because these names are no longer valid after a
transport to a different system. Thus, for procedures and calculation views,
use the settings for a standard schema and define appropriate schema
mappings as described in Section 6.1.2. As with SQLScript and Native
SQL, you should always ensure that you handle the client field correctly.
One option is to store different data configurations in various clients in
the development or test system, and test them explicitly. For SAP HANA
views, you should generally select the setting DYNAMIC DEFAULT CLIENT
to use the current client of the ABAP session (see Section 4.5.4).

For the transport of ABAP applications that directly reference HANA
objects such as views or procedures, we recommend the techniques
described in Chapter 6. You should use a common transport to ensure that
inconsistencies do not occur in a target system (for example, a missing
database procedure that is accessed from ABAP). When using external
views, database procedure proxies, and HANA transport containers,
you should also ensure that you have synchronized the content prior to
a transport.

If you have mixed development landscapes in which some systems do
not (yet) run on SAP HANA, you can transport ABAP developments on
SAP HANA through these systems without any problems. We recommend
that you always ensure that SAP HANA-specific implementations—which
cannot run in such systems—do not lead to uncontrolled program terminations if they are called (also see Section 14.3.2).

[+]   **Development in System Landscapes**

Avoid direct accesses to schema names in SQLScript, and ensure correct client
handling. Dependent ABAP and HANA developments should be transported
together consistently.

14.1.6 Modifying Data in SQLScript or Native SQL

We recommend in general that you largely avoid write operations on
ABAP tables via SQLScript or Native SQL (EXEC SQL or ADBC). If you

nevertheless modify database contents via these mechanisms, you should be particularly careful. We will give you some important relevant information in this section.

Such accesses are sent virtually unchanged via the database interface (DBI) to the database, so the SAP services on the application server—for example, for locking (see Section 3.1) and table buffering (see Section 3.2)—and their synchronization are completely bypassed. Such changes may lead to inconsistent data, as the following examples show.

Bypassing ABAP services

If, for example, data that is in the SAP table buffer is changed via SQLScript or Native SQL, the change is made only in the database. The data in the local table buffer (on the server on which the change was made) will not be changed. Neither will synchronization entries be written in the table DDLOG, where other application servers would be informed of changes in buffered tables and then be able to synchronize them. The data in the table buffer is no longer consistent with the data in the database, because the changes were made directly via Native SQL or SQLScript while bypassing the table buffer. Thus, tables that are in the SAP table buffer must always be changed via Open SQL, because otherwise the data cannot be changed or synchronized in the buffers.

Changes to buffered tables

In Figure 14.2, you can see the differences between changes via SQLScript (or Native SQL) and the standard variant via Open SQL statements. In the former case, the calls are forwarded directly via the database interface to the database, while bypassing the table buffer, and the changes are made in the database.

The system behavior is similar for locks. Data that is protected from change in parallel in the ABAP system via the enqueue service can still be changed directly in the database if SAP lock management is bypassed. This can also lead to inconsistent data if, for example, an ABAP application has set a lock to perform consistent calculations while another application is covertly changing this data directly in the database. Changes that were already made may also be lost if a lock on data records is ignored.

Changes without enqueue service

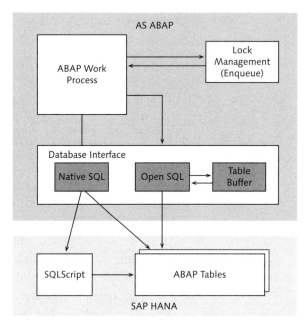

Figure 14.2 Changing Accesses via SQLScript or Native SQL

[+]   **Avoiding Modification of ABAP Tables via SQLScript and Native SQL**

You should avoid changing data via SQLScript or Native SQL if possible. If you can't avoid this, ensure that the data isn't subject to table buffering or protected via the SAP enqueue service. Otherwise, data inconsistencies may occur.

14.2 Conventions

Conventions can help, particularly when distributing development projects among one or more teams. In this section, we will discuss the following topics:

▶ Possible naming conventions for HANA objects, including parameters in interfaces and ABAP proxies.

▶ Recommendations for the encapsulation of developments, such as use of packages in SAP HANA Repository and granularity of the HANA transport container.

14.2.1 Naming Conventions

In contrast to ABAP, the names of development objects in SAP HANA Repository have to be unique only within a package (see Section 6.1.2). Some types of artifacts share a namespace: For example, it is not possible to create an attribute view and an analytic view with the same name in a package.

For this reason and for easy readability, we recommend that you use *prefixes* for HANA development objects. The naming conventions shown in Table 14.1 have been established.

Naming Conventions for HANA Development Objects

Artifact	Prefix	Example
Attribute view	AT_	AT_FLIGHT
Analytic view	AN_	AN_BOOKING_AMOUNTS
Calculation view	CA_	CA_PASSENGER_MILES
Procedure	–	EXECUTE_SEGMENTATION
Decision table	DT_	DT_PASSENGER_CLASS

Table 14.1 Naming Conventions for HANA Development Objects

The package in SAP HANA Repository assumes the role of the namespace. You will find the SAP standard development in subpackages of the package `sap`.

The corresponding ABAP objects (external views, procedures) are subject to the ABAP naming restrictions. This includes the ABAP namespace concept in addition to the global uniqueness of names. Due to the length of name restrictions for ABAP development objects, the names of HANA objects (including the package) cannot always be adopted. Often, they must be abbreviated. Table 14.2 includes our recommendations for naming ABAP objects (Z namespace).

Naming conventions for ABAP proxies

Artifact	Prefix	Example
External view	ZEV_	ZEV_AT_FLIGHT
Database procedure proxy	ZDP_	ZDP_EXECUTE_SEGMENTATION

Table 14.2 Naming Conventions for ABAP Proxies for HANA Objects

Artifact	Prefix	Example
Interface for the database procedure proxy	ZIF_	ZIF_EXECUTE_SEGMENTATION

Table 14.2 Naming Conventions for ABAP Proxies for HANA Objects (Cont.)

Simple assignment

We recommend that you create only one corresponding external view or procedure proxy for each HANA object and reuse them in ABAP. This facilitates the necessary adjustments, particularly in the event of changes.

Input and output parameters

For naming input and output parameters of a database procedure, we use the same naming convention as for interface parameters of ABAP methods and function modules (see Table 14.3).

Type	Prefix	Example
Scalar input parameter	IV_	IV_CLIENT
Tabular input parameter	IT_	IT_FLIGHT
Scalar output parameter	EV_	EV_CARRNAME
Tabular output parameter	ET_	ET_FLIGHT
Local scalar variable	LV_	LV_COUNT
Local table variable	LT_	LT_FLIGHT

Table 14.3 Naming Conventions for Input and Output Parameters

14.2.2 Encapsulating Packages

Delivery unit

In principle, you can create objects anywhere in SAP HANA Repository (outside the SAP namespace). However, we recommend that you clearly encapsulate components of applications in packages. Here, you should pay attention to the following aspects:

▸ Local developments and developments to be transported must be in separate packages because delivery units always contain full packages.

▸ A delivery unit should ideally include a package tree—that is, a super-package and all subpackages.

▶ Cyclical dependencies between delivery units must be avoided because otherwise an automatic import is not possible. Cyclical dependencies between packages should also be avoided.

▶ Those objects that are accessed externally (for example, via ABAP code) should be marked, because changes to the interface usually require adjustments and synchronization of the user. One option is to encapsulate these objects in a separate package.

14.3   Quality Aspects

In this section, we have compiled some recommendations you can use when implementing native views and procedures in SAP HANA; these guidelines will help increase the quality of your own developments. We will discuss three aspects here: testing views and procedures, robust programming, and security aspects.

14.3.1   Testing Views and Procedures

It is particularly important to ensure a stable design and good test coverage for the definition of data models and implementations near the database. First, functional errors can have potentially expensive implications (such as data inconsistencies or incorrect business results). Additionally, changes to database objects are always more complex than small adjustments to a user interface. For this reason, you should pay great attention to these design aspects, especially for SAP HANA views and database procedures.

Design

Tests are an essential tool for verifying whether the interfaces are usable and cover all special cases. We have already discussed the technical options for testing views and procedures in Section 7.2.1. At this point, we would like to remind you once again of the two most important recommendations:

▶ Enable the writing of unit tests for individual parts of your application by modularization and decoupling. If parts of the application cannot be automatically tested, testing becomes more difficult and you run the risk of overlooking important special cases.

Test recommendations

523

▸ Create appropriate test data in realistic dimensions. You can either use (anonymous) copies from a production system or data generators.

Comparison after optimization

If you optimize an existing implementation and would like to make sure that the optimized version is the functional equivalent of the old version, the system provides automatic tests that compare the results of both implementations. You can also determine runtime improvements here.

[»] **Testing**

Especially for larger refactorings, investing in high-quality tests and test data is justified.

14.3.2 Robust Programming

If an implemented function is used in practice, configurations can always occur for which the function was not intended (for example, a call with invalid parameters). Such situations can be dealt with via *robust programming*. This should be an important design goal for implementations near the database, because problems can have potentially serious consequences for data consistency or system stability. We will give you some recommendations in the following text for robust programming within the context of SAP HANA.

Well-defined behavior

More robust programming guarantees well-defined and deterministic behavior in all situations. Assumptions with regard to the value range of input parameters should be tested explicitly. If an input table of an SQLScript procedure shouldn't be empty, it must be clearly defined whether this is to lead to a program termination or a specific output (for example, an empty output table). In other words, the interfaces of database functions should be fully defined. Using unit tests, you should review the behavior for invalid input data as well.

Error handling

In addition to well-defined behavior, dealing with error situations is essential for a robust implementation. Terminations should not lead to unwanted side effects on data consistency, system stability, or other users. Such situations can potentially arise, particularly with write accesses to ABAP tables outside of the LUW concept (logical unit of work) in ABAP systems, which we have already discussed in Section 14.1.6. Even when calling read operations only, you should always provide clear error handling—even if, from an ABAP code perspective, it is only a simple call such as a SELECT statement on an external view. You should decide whether there must be a controlled program termination (*dump*) or whether a meaningful error message for the user (along with a log entry for subsequent analysis) is possible.

In SQLScript, there is the option of using the EXEC command to execute a programmatically-generated SQL statement in the form of a character string. This is a powerful tool for generating flexible and generic instructions at runtime, but has disadvantages with regard to robustness, security (see Section 14.3.3), and performance (see Section 14.5.3). We recommend that you largely avoid dynamic SQLScript, particularly to ensure robust behavior.

EXEC command

Robust Programming	**[+]**
Pay particular attention to robustness for implementations in the database. Every possible data configuration should lead to a well-defined result or error. Program terminations should be avoided.

14.3.3 Security Aspects

If you follow the classic ABAP development model and the associated guidelines, this will provide you with protection against most security risks.

When changing to native implementations for SAP HANA, and using native database calls from ABAP, you should always incorporate security considerations. We would like to discuss two aspects at this point: authorization checks and SQL injection attacks.

Security for native implementations

With critical business data, you must always ensure that no user has access to data for which he has no authorization. To do this, you must know and protect the possible access channels. For ABAP applications, you should implement authorization checks via ABAP authorization objects and the assignment to roles. If you relocate operations via views and procedures to SAP HANA, you should secure the call paths in ABAP using appropriate AUTHORITY-CHECK statements. If you would also like to release these data models in SAP HANA directly for end users (for example, via the

Access channels and authorization

Excel client presented in Section 4.4, or via the SAP BusinessObjects tools presented in Chapter 10), you should restrict access by means of analytical authorizations (see Section 2.4.3). For information about authorization checks in the context of native developments in SAP HANA using SAP HANA Extended Application Services (XS), see the development documentation at *http://help.sap.com/hana_appliance*.

Avoiding SQL injection

Especially when using Native SQL or SQLScript, you should always check or mask external inputs (for example, by a user or via an external interface) to avoid an injection of unwanted SQL code (SQL injection) by an attacker. We recommend that you keep the level of free input of such Native SQL statements as small as possible, and check them against *white lists* as much as possible. For Native SQL accesses via ADBC, the use of prepared statements (see Section 3.2.4) can provide certain protection here. In SQLScript implementations, as for any other interface, you should take care that the authorizations necessary for execution are clear from a business perspective. We would advise you against creating excessively "powerful" procedures that read a combination of business data, which no end user may see in this form.

[!] **Secure Programming**

Native implementations increase the responsibility for ensuring security. All access paths should be protected with authorization checks and all user input should be checked.

14.4   Performance Recommendations for Open SQL

In this section, we will provide performance recommendations for developing ABAP applications on SAP HANA. We will discuss the most important, frequently asked questions related to SAP HANA. If you want to delve more extensively into the topic of SAP or ABAP performance, we recommend the books *SAP Performance Optimization Guide: Analyzing and Tuning SAP Systems* by Thomas Schneider (7th edition, SAP PRESS 2013) and *ABAP Performance Tuning* by Hermann Gahm (SAP PRESS 2009), in which the topic of performance is discussed in great detail. Here, we will describe the most important rules and any changes in the context of SAP

HANA. In addition, there are some new performance topics with SAP HANA that we will consider here.

First, we will discuss the golden rules for database programming and whether or how these change for SAP HANA. The time-tested golden rules for database programming are as follows:

Golden rules for database programming

1. Keep the result set as small as possible.

2. Keep the transferred dataset as small as possible.

3. Reduce the number of query executions as much as possible.

4. Minimize the search effort as much as possible.

5. Reduce the load on the database as much as possible.

In the next sections, we will describe each rule and illustrate some with examples. We will then explain the extent to which these rules are relevant for SAP HANA or what has changed.

14.4.1 Rule 1: Keeping Result Sets Small

The first golden rule recommends that you keep the result set (that is, the number of selected rows) as small as possible when reading data from the database. You can minimize the result set using various measures. We would like to discuss three aspects:

Minimizing result set

▶ Using a WHERE clause

▶ Working with the HAVING clause

▶ Transferring only required rows

WHERE condition

In ABAP, the number of transferred data records is controlled by the WHERE condition. You should read only those data records that you actually need. The WHERE condition may be waived only if all records are required for each access. Waiving the WHERE clause is particularly problematic for database tables that increase over time, because increasing volumes of data are then transferred over time.

The following examples show this in comparison. All customers are selected in Listing 14.2, and then the selection is restricted to the data records actually required. In Listing 14.3, only the data records actually required are read from the database.

```
SELECT id name discount custtype
    FROM scustom
    INTO (lv_cust-id, lv_cust-name,
    lv_cust-discount, lv_cust-custtype).
      IF lv_cust-custtype = 'B'.
        WRITE: / lv_cust-id,
         lv_cust-name, lv_cust-discount.
           ENDIF.
ENDSELECT.
```

Listing 14.2 Missing WHERE Clause

```
SELECT id name discount
    FROM scustom
    INTO (lv_cust-id, lv_cust-name, lv_cust-discount)
    WHERE custtype = 'B'.
        WRITE: / lv_cust-id,
         lv_cust-name, lv_cust-discount.
ENDSELECT.
```

Listing 14.3 Query with WHERE Clause

HAVING Clause

Use of the HAVING clause provides another option to reduce the transferred rows. It's used if there is a GROUP BY clause and you would like to transfer only certain groups by making restrictions to the grouped rows; for example, in the aggregate values.

GROUP BY expression with and without HAVING

The following examples illustrate this option. In Listing 14.4, the minimum use of all flight connections is determined and transferred. In Listing 14.5, only the flight connections with a minimum use greater than zero are transferred.

```
SELECT carrid connid MIN( seatsocc )
  FROM sflight
  INTO (lv_sflight-carrid, lv_sflight-connid, lv_min)
  GROUP BY carrid connid.
    IF lv_min > 0.
      WRITE: / lv_sflight-carrid,
       lv_sflight-connid, lv_min.
```

```
      ENDIF.
ENDSELECT.
```

Listing 14.4 Missing HAVING Clause

```
SELECT carrid connid MIN( seatsocc )
  FROM sflight
  INTO (lv_sflight-carrid, lv_sflight-connid, lv_min)
  GROUP BY carrid connid
  HAVING MIN( seatsocc ) > 0.
    WRITE: / lv_sflight-carrid,
    lv_sflight-connid, lv_min.
ENDSELECT.
```

Listing 14.5 GROUP BY Expression with HAVING Clause

Transferring Only Required Rows

You should always transfer only data records that you actually require. You should never remove data that you do not require in application server in the ABAP program and thus transfer it unnecessarily from the database.

Two examples were listed previously. Another example that falls under this rule concerns the selection of data in internal tables, from which unnecessary data records are then deleted using DELETE (see Listing 14.6). CHECK statements or filtering by means of IF may also indicate the transfer of too many rows. In the example of Listing 14.7, the selection is restricted instead to the required data.

Selecting specific data instead of deleting

```
SELECT id name discount custtype
FROM scustom
    INTO CORRESPONDING FIELDS OF TABLE lt_scustom
    WHERE country = 'DE'.
DELETE lt_scustom WHERE custtype = 'P'.
LOOP AT lt_scustom INTO ls_cust.
  WRITE: / ls_cust-id, ls_cust-name,
  ls_cust-discount, ls_cust-custtype.
ENDLOOP.
```

Listing 14.6 Subsequent Deleting

```
SELECT id name discount custtype
FROM scustom
    INTO CORRESPONDING FIELDS OF TABLE lt_scustom
```

```
        WHERE country = 'DE'
        AND custtype <> 'P'.

LOOP AT lt_scustom INTO ls_cust.
  WRITE: / ls_cust-id, ls_cust-name,
  ls_cust-discount, ls_cust-custtype.
ENDLOOP.
```

Listing 14.7 Selecting Only Required Data

Summary and Significance for SAP HANA

A consistent application of this rule for classic databases leads to reduced I/O effort, optimized memory consumption in the cache, reduced CPU consumption and, last but not least, to an optimized network transfer because less data is transferred.

[»]

Significance of Rule #1 for SAP HANA

This rule applies unchanged and with the same priority to SAP HANA. CPU and main memory resources are also conserved on SAP HANA if fewer data records have to be read. There is no change in the transfer of data via the network.

The Code Inspector (see Section 7.3) provides support here with the following checks:

- ► Analysis of the WHERE condition for a SELECT
- ► Analysis of the WHERE condition for the statements UPDATE and DELETE
- ► Search for SELECT statements with DELETE
- ► SELECT statements with subsequent CHECK

These checks are described in more detail in Section 7.3.1.

14.4.2 Rule 2: Keeping Transferred Datasets Small

The second golden rule recommends that you transfer as little data as possible between the database and the application server. The data is transferred from the database to the application server in blocks. The network load can be reduced by transferring fewer blocks.

Number of selected rows and columns

As a programmer, you can do this by influencing the number of selected rows and columns via restrictions that go beyond the WHERE condition. We would like to discuss these aspects in the following subsections:

- Using the addition UP TO n ROWS
- Working with DISTINCT
- Reducing the number of columns
- Using aggregate functions
- Performing existence checks efficiently
- Changing only required columns

Using UP TO n ROWS

If you require only a certain number of rows, you can use the UP TO n ROWS addition to further restrict the number of rows. The following examples illustrate how you can use UP TO n ROWS to further reduce the number of transferred data records. The business customers with the highest discounts are selected. In Listing 14.8, the system terminates in a loop after the tenth data record (example of a bad process). Since SELECT ... ENDSELECT reads the data in blocks from the database, however, more data records than necessary were already transferred in the first block. In Transaction ST05 (see Section 7.4.3), you can see how many data records were transferred in the first block (corresponds to a FETCH).

```
SELECT id name discount
    FROM scustom
    INTO (ls_cust-id, ls_cust-name, ls_cust-discount)
    WHERE custtype = 'B'
    ORDER BY discount DESCENDING.
  IF sy-dbcnt > 10. EXIT.
    ENDIF.
  WRITE: / ls_cust-id, ls_cust-name, ls_cust-discount.
ENDSELECT.
```

Listing 14.8 No UP TO n ROWS

Exactly 10 records are transferred in Listing 14.9, because the statement — the statement saying only 10 records were required — was transferred to the database (example of a good process).

```
SELECT id name discount
    FROM scustom UP TO 10 ROWS
    INTO (ls_cust-id, ls_cust-name, ls_cust-discount)
    WHERE custtype = 'B'
```

```
    ORDER BY discount DESCENDING.
  WRITE: / ls_cust-id, ls_cust-name, ls_cust-discount.
ENDSELECT.
```

Listing 14.9   With UP TO n ROWS

Using DISTINCT

If the system calculates with a certain WHERE condition that has unnecessary duplicate entries regarding the selected columns, the DISTINCT statement should be used to remove the duplicate entries already in the database.

Example with and without DISTINCT

In the following example, a list is created of discounts that were granted. In Listing 14.10, the duplicate entries are deleted after the selection. In Listing 14.11, only the required data is read from the database.

```
SELECT custtype discount
    FROM scustom
    INTO CORRESPONDING FIELDS OF TABLE lt_scustom
    WHERE discount > 0
    ORDER BY custtype discount DESCENDING.

DELETE ADJACENT DUPLICATES FROM lt_scustom.

LOOP AT lt_scustom INTO ls_cust.
  WRITE: / ls_cust-custtype, ls_cust-discount.
ENDLOOP.
```

Listing 14.10   Query without DISTINCT

```
SELECT DISTINCT custtype discount
    FROM scustom
    INTO CORRESPONDING FIELDS OF TABLE lt_scustom
    WHERE discount > 0
    ORDER BY custtype discount DESCENDING.

LOOP AT lt_scustom INTO ls_cust.
  WRITE: / ls_cust-custtype, ls_cust-discount.
ENDLOOP.
```

Listing 14.11   Query with DISTINCT

Reducing Number of Columns

You should select only columns in a database table that are also required in the ABAP program. Here, you should list the columns individually in the field list after SELECT, if possible. The selection of all columns using SELECT * should only be used if all columns are really required.

Although the addition INTO CORRESPONDING FIELDS OF selects only the columns that are also in the above objective when * is specified, extra effort is involved in comparing names in the database interface. Thus this addition should be only be used sparingly and for larger result sets because the effort involved in comparing names can be relatively high for very quick SELECT statements.

Addition INTO CORRESPONDING FIELDS OF

In the following example, the system determines the days on which a certain flight connection exists in 2013. In Listing 14.12, all columns of the SFLIGHT table are read, although only the flight date is required. In Listing 14.13, only the required column is read.

SELECT specific columns

```
SELECT * FROM sflight
    INTO ls_sflight
   WHERE carrid = 'LH'
     AND connid = '0300'
     AND fldate LIKE '2013%'.
  WRITE: / ls_sflight-fldate.
ENDSELECT.
```
Listing 14.12 Query without Field List

```
SELECT fldate FROM sflight
    INTO (lv_sflight-fldate)
   WHERE carrid = 'LH'
     AND connid = '0300'
     AND fldate LIKE '2013%'.
  WRITE: / lv_sflight-fldate.
ENDSELECT.
```
Listing 14.13 Query with Field List

Another option for reducing the dataset is the use of aggregate functions.

Using Aggregate Functions

If data is required only for calculations, it is better to perform these calculations in the database and transfer the results rather than transferring all data and performing the calculation in the ABAP program. The available aggregate functions are: COUNT, MIN, MAX, SUM, and AVG for the number, the minimum value, the maximum value, the sum of the values, and the average value, respectively.

Determining data with and without aggregate function

In the following example, the system determines the sum of the reserved seats of an airline in a specific year. In Listing 14.14, all reservations of flights are selected and added up in the ABAP program. In Listing 14.15, the sum of the reservations is calculated in the database and only this sum is transferred to the ABAP program.

```
lv_sum = 0.
SELECT seatsocc
    FROM sflight INTO lv_seatsocc
    WHERE carrid = 'LH'
        AND fldate LIKE '2013%'.
    lv_sum = lv_sum + lv_seatsocc.
ENDSELECT.
WRITE: / lv_sum.
```

Listing 14.14 Query without Aggregate Function

```
SELECT SUM( seatsocc )
    FROM sflight INTO lv_sum
    WHERE carrid = 'LH'
        AND fldate LIKE '2013%'.
WRITE: / lv_sum.
```

Listing 14.15 Query with Aggregate Function

Performing Existence Checks Efficiently

You should use these aggregate functions only if you need such a calculation. To determine whether there is a data record for a specific key, for example, you should not use SELECT COUNT(*) because the number is irrelevant in this case. For such an existence check, you require only a single field of the data record you seek. This should be a field of the index that is in use.

In the example, the system is to check whether there were flights for a specific flight connection in a specific year. In Listing 14.16, this is checked using a COUNT(*). Here, all data records in the database that meet the condition are counted. The addition UP TO 1 ROWS does not change anything because it is only executed after counting. In Listing 14.17, the data records are not counted because the number of records is irrelevant. Only one field is selected—there should be no SELECT * here either—and the result set is restricted to one row with UP TO n ROWS. This ensures that only one data record is read. Once the database has determined a record that meets the conditions, the processing is terminated.

Existence check without counting the data records

```
SELECT count(*) UP TO 1 ROWS
    FROM sflight INTO lv_cnt
    WHERE carrid = 'LH'
      AND connid = '0400'
      AND fldate LIKE '2013%'.
IF lv_cnt > 0.
...
```

Listing 14.16 Existence Check with COUNT(*)

```
SELECT carrid INTO lv_sflicht-carrid
    UP TO 1 ROWS
    FROM sflight
    WHERE carrid = 'LH'
      AND connid = '0400'
      AND fldate LIKE '2013%'.

ENDSELECT.
IF sy-subrc = 0.
...
```

Listing 14.17 Existence Check without COUNT(*)

Changing Only Required Columns

For changes with the UPDATE statement, only the desired columns are to be changed with the SET statement. When changing rows from work areas, too much data is usually transferred and columns that have not changed are also overwritten.

The connection number of a specific flight is to be changed in the example. In Listing 14.18, the rows to be changed are first read, then a column is

Complete and specific change

changed with a new value in the work area, and finally the entire row is written back to the database. Here, an unnecessarily large number of columns is transferred and all columns are overwritten in the database, even if their values have not changed. In Listing 14.19, an UPDATE ... SET overwrites only the desired column with a new value. The records are thus not read at all and far less data is transferred to the database. In addition, the database has to change only the transferred column.

```
SELECT * FROM sbook
    INTO ls_sbook
    WHERE carrid  = 'LH'
      AND connid  = '0400'
      AND fldate >= '20140101'.
  ls_sbook-connid = '0500'.
  UPDATE sbook FROM ls_sbook.
ENDSELECT.
```

Listing 14.18 Changing the Entire Row

```
UPDATE sbook
  SET connid = '0500'
  WHERE carrid  = 'LH'
    AND connid  = '0400'
    AND fldate >= '20140101'.
```

Listing 14.19 Changing the Desired Columns

Summary and Significance for SAP HANA

The effects of rule #2 are very similar those of rule #1. The consistent application of these rules leads to reduced resource consumption in the classic database.

[»] **Significance of Rule #2 for SAP HANA**

This rule applies unchanged to SAP HANA because the resources are conserved in a similar manner here. The priority of the rule is slightly higher than for other databases. This can be attributed to the different storage of data. If data records are stored in a row-based manner, all columns in a block are close together. In column-oriented storage, each column is a separate storage structure. Although these storage structures can be processed in parallel, the time required for multiple columns is slightly higher. Even if the differences are not very large, you should pay special attention to these rules and check time-critical applications for optimization with regard to this rule.

The Code Inspector (see Section 7.3) provides support here with the following checks:

▶ Problematic SELECT * statement

▶ EXIT or no statement in SELECT ... ENDSELECT loop

These checks are described in more detail in Section 7.3.1.

With regard to the aggregate functions, it must be emphasized that these are very well supported by SAP HANA. However, you should only use them where you actually require the calculations.

14.4.3 Rule 3: Reducing Number of Queries

The third rule recommends reducing the number of queries to the database. Each SQL statement in an ABAP program that is sent to the database involves a certain degree of effort in the database. Thus, the statement itself and its associated parameters are transferred to the database. It must analyze the statement in terms of the syntax and search by hash function in the SQL cache, or store it there when it is first executed. In addition, authorizations and the existence of database objects (tables, views, and so on) must be checked to ensure they are present. The results of the query must also be transferred. To reduce the load on the database, you should thus keep the number of accesses as low as possible.

Processing effort for SQL statements

In ABAP programs, you can influence the number of statements by the following measures:

▶ Using set operations instead of individual operations

▶ No longer performing multiple accesses

▶ No longer using nested SELECT loops

▶ Not executing SELECT statements in the LOOP via internal tables

▶ Using buffers

Using Set Operations Instead of Individual Operations

When reading with SELECT, you should choose the addition INTO TABLE instead of the SELECT ... ENDSELECT loop if all the data to be read must fit into the main memory. The SELECT ... ENDSELECT also reads the data in blocks from the database to the database interface. From there, the

Read

data is transferred in single records to the ABAP program. The SELECT ... ENDSELECT loop is thus useful if the available memory is insufficient for all data or if the read data is accessed once only.

Set operations with internal tables

For write accesses, you should rely wherever possible on set operations with internal tables. The number of database queries is thus greatly reduced, and the database can perform more optimizations with the data that was transferred all at once.

Loop or set operation

In the following two examples, data records are inserted in the SBOOK table. In Listing 14.20, the data records are inserted record by record in a loop. In Listing 14.21, all data records are inserted at once in a set operation.

```
LOOP AT lt_sbook INTO ls_sbook.
  INSERT INTO sbook VALUES ls_sbook.
ENDLOOP.
```

Listing 14.20 Inserting in a Loop

```
INSERT sbook FROM TABLE lt_sbook.
```

Listing 14.21 Inserting in a Set Operation

No Longer Performing Multiple Accesses

Deleting without SELECT statement

You should make sure you do not repeatedly access the same data. For example, avoid a SELECT before a DELETE for the same data record (see Listing 14.22). You have already seen an example with UPDATE in Listing 14.18. Listing 14.23 shows a delete operation without a preceding SELECT statement.

```
SELECT SINGLE * FROM sflight INTO lv_sflight
  WHERE carrid = 'SQ' AND connid ='0002'.

IF sy-subrc = 0.
  DELETE FROM sflight
  WHERE carrid = 'SQ' AND connid = '0002'.
    IF sy-subrc = 0.
      COMMIT WORK.
    ENDIF.
  ENDIF.
```

Listing 14.22 Deleting after SELECT

```
DELETE FROM sflight
  WHERE carrid = 'SQ' AND connid = '0002'.

IF sy-subrc = 0.
  COMMIT WORK.
ENDIF.
```

Listing 14.23 Deleting without SELECT

No Longer Using Nested SELECT Loops

For nested SELECT loops, the inner SELECT statement is executed once for each data record that the outer SELECT loop returns. The number of records in the outer data records' result set thus determines the executions of the inner SELECT statement. Therefore, such a construct should only be used if the result set of the outer loop contains very few rows.

For merging data sets, we recommend that you use the following options:

▸ Views (see Chapter 3, Section 3.2.3 and Chapter 4)

▸ Joins

▸ FOR ALL ENTRIES

▸ Subqueries

▸ Cursors

Views and joins

The runtime of views and joins depends greatly on the execution plan selected by the database optimizer. Accesses to views and joins are still usually faster than nested loops. If this is not the case, the execution plan must be analyzed more precisely, which requires good knowledge of the respective database. The optimizer may not be able to optimally determine the sequence of the tables. Joins and views have a disadvantage in that the data of the outer table is redundant in the result set with a 1:n relationship between the outer and inner table. Thus more data than necessary may be transferred. You must make sure to select only the fields that are actually required. In extreme cases, a FOR ALL ENTRIES (see next section) can be better.

SELECT loop and inner join

The following is an example where the data from the tables SFLIGHT and SBOOK is merged. All bookings from the table SBOOK for a specific aircraft type are to be read from table SFLIGHT. In Listing 14.24, this is implemented via nested SELECT loops. Here, the SELECT statement is executed once in the table SBOOK for each data record that was read from the table SFLIGHT. In Listing 14.25, the data is read using a join, and only one statement is sent to the database.

```
SELECT carrid connid fldate FROM sflight
    INTO (lv_carrid, lv_connid, lv_fldate)
    WHERE planetype = '727-200'.
  SELECT bookid FROM sbook INTO lv_bookid
      WHERE carrid = lv_carrid
        AND connid = lv_connid
        AND fldate = lv_fldate.
    WRITE: / lv_carrid, lv_connid, lv_bookid.
  ENDSELECT.
ENDSELECT.
```

Listing 14.24 Nested SELECT Loops

```
SELECT f~carrid f~connid b~bookid
    INTO (lv_carrid, lv_connid, lv_bookid)
    FROM sflight AS f INNER JOIN sbook AS b
        ON f~carrid = b~carrid AND
           f~connid = b~connid AND
           f~fldate = b~fldate
    WHERE planetype = '727-200'.
  WRITE: / lv_carrid, lv_connid, lv_bookid.
ENDSELECT.
```

Listing 14.25 Inner Join

FOR ALL ENTRIES   Nested loops can also be avoided via the FOR ALL ENTRIES construct. Here, the data of the outer table is stored in an internal table, and then the inner SELECT statement is executed once with the addition FOR ALL ENTRIES. The internal table is thereby divided into blocks and a statement is executed for each block. That means the transfer of redundant data from the outer table can be avoided, which can lead to better performance in certain cases. Generally, a JOIN should be selected wherever possible, because the number of statements sent to the database is smaller than with FOR ALL ENTRIES. You will find an example of a FOR ALL ENTRIES statement in the following section.

With subqueries, you can also access multiple tables in a single statement. **Subqueries** The data of the subquery is not transferred at all, but is used only within the query in the database itself.

The following example shows the flight data of the busiest flights, based **Nested and** on the maximum number of occupied seats. In Listing 14.26, the inner **subquery** SELECT statement is sent for each data record of the outer to the database. For Listing 14.27, only a single statement is sent to the database.

```
SELECT carrid connid MAX( seatsocc )
  FROM sflight
  INTO (lv_carrid, lv_connid, lv_max)
  GROUP BY carrid connid.
    SELECT fldate FROM sflight
        INTO lv_fldate
      WHERE carrid  = lv_carrid AND
            connid  = lv_connid AND
            seatsocc = lv_max.
      WRITE: / lv_carrid, lv_connid, lv_fldate.
    ENDSELECT.
ENDSELECT.
```

Listing 14.26 Nested SELECT Statements

```
SELECT carrid connid fldate
    FROM sflight AS f
    INTO (lv_carrid, lv_connid, lv_max)
    WHERE seatsocc IN
    ( SELECT MAX( seatsocc ) FROM sflight
      WHERE carrid = f~carrid
        AND connid = f~connid ).
  WRITE: / lv_carrid, lv_connid, lv_fldate.
ENDSELECT.
```

Listing 14.27 Subquery

Not Executing SELECT Statements in the LOOP via Internal Tables

Similar to nested loops, you should not execute SELECT statements in the LOOP via internal tables. Here, the addition FOR ALL ENTRIES is useful for reducing the number of executions. In this case, you should ensure that the internal table is never empty and does not contain duplicates with FOR ALL ENTRIES.

In the example, the corresponding booking data is determined for all flights that are in the internal tables LT_SFLIGHT. In Listing 14.28, a SELECT is executed for each data record in the LOOP via the internal table LT_SFLIGHT. In Listing 14.29, the number of executed SELECT statements is reduced by FOR ALL ENTRIES.

```
LOOP AT lt_sflight INTO lv_sflight.
    SELECT SINGLE bookid customid FROM sbook
    INTO lv_sbook
      WHERE carrid = lv_sflight-carrid
        AND connid = lv_sflight-connid
        AND fldate = lv_sflight-fldate.

        WRITE: / lv_sflight-carrid,
        lv_sflight-connid, lv_sflight-fldate,
        lv_sbook-bookid, lv_sbook-customid.
ENDLOOP.
```

Listing 14.28 SELECT in the LOOP

```
IF lines( lt_sflight ) > 0.
  SELECT carrid connid fldate bookid customid
  FROM sbook
  INTO CORRESPONDING FIELDS OF TABLE lt_sbook
  FOR ALL ENTRIES IN lt_sflight
    WHERE carrid = lt_sflight-carrid
      AND connid = lt_sflight-connid
      AND fldate = lt_sflight-fldate.
  ENDIF.
```

Listing 14.29 Restriction with FOR ALL ENTRIES

Using Buffers

The use of the SAP table buffer and other buffers (see Section 14.4.5) also contributes to minimizing the number of SQL statements that are sent to the database.

Summary and Significance for SAP HANA

The consistent application of this rule leads to reduced CPU consumption for classic databases. Network resources are also used better because the number of sent blocks can be optimized.

[«]

> **Significance of Rule #3 for SAP HANA**
>
> This rule has a higher priority for SAP HANA than for other databases. The effort involved in the execution of a statement is currently slightly higher in SAP HANA than in classic databases. However, this will be optimized in the future. Applications that send a very large number of quick queries to the database are thus to be examined in terms of optimization potential, based on the approaches presented in the examples in this section.
>
> The Code Inspector provides support here with the following checks:
>
> ▶ Searching for `SELECT ... FOR ALL ENTRIES` clauses to be transformed
>
> ▶ Searching for database operations in `LOOPS` within modularization units
>
> ▶ Changing database accesses in loops
>
> These checks are described in more detail in Section 7.3.1.

14.4.4 Rule 4: Minimizing Search Effort

This section is about the effort involved in selecting the dataset that was restricted via the `WHERE` and `HAVING` clauses. You can minimize the effort of the data search with an index. As in the previous sections, we will first discuss the recommendations for classic databases before we turn to the recommendations for SAP HANA.

Database Index in Classic Databases

An index consists of selected fields of the database table, which are copied in a sorted sequence into a separate structure. A distinction is made between the *primary index* and the *secondary index*. The primary index contains the primary key fields. Thus this index is *unique*, and there can be only one data record for any combination of the fields of this index. It is always created automatically in SAP systems when you create a table.

Primary vs. secondary

Then there are the secondary indexes, which can be unique or non-unique. Secondary indexes are created in the ABAP Data Dictionary. They are usually used to optimize performance, but can also have semantic motives in the case of unique indexes if, for example, only unique values may be in a column that is not part of the primary key.

The correct formulation of WHERE or HAVING clauses and a suitable second-ary index definition can minimize the search effort significantly because only part of the data has to be read.

Our recommendations for creating indexes are as follows:

▶ Secondary indexes are to be created only for database tables where the read accesses are more time-critical than the write accesses, since each created index has to be maintained for write accesses.

▶ The number of created indexes and fields in the index should be kept as small as possible. Otherwise, it takes more effort to change database accesses, and the optimizer is likelier to make wrong decisions.

▶ The fields on which indexes are created should only be in one index if possible. Overlaps should be avoided.

▶ The fields in a secondary index should be fields through which you often select. These fields should also be selective, that is, the percent-age of data records selected by the index should be small.

▶ The fields that are most likely to be queried with the = operator should be at the beginning of the index.

To formulate the WHERE clauses, these are our main recommendations:

▶ The = operator or EQ operator and AND links are always supported effi-ciently in the index. That is, the optimizer can thus reduce the I/O effort whenever it is technically possible. An IN list also falls into this category because it represents, in principle, a multiple = for the col-umn. Thus you should use = and IN conditions wherever possible.

▶ Avoid negative conditions (<>, NE, NOT) because they cannot be sup-ported efficiently in the index. If possible, rewrite such conditions as positive conditions. If this is not possible, you should still specify the conditions in the WHERE condition and not omit them completely. This is the only way in which the required data records will be selected. Otherwise, you would read unnecessary records that you would then have to remove in the ABAP program, which would contradict the first golden rule.

▶ If you do not specify all fields in the index, make sure that you enclose the initial section of the index in the WHERE condition. Otherwise, the use of an index is not possible in many cases.

Database Index in SAP HANA

There has been much development in this area for SAP HANA. This section involves the question of how and when indexes should be created in SAP HANA. In Appendix C, we explain the background of read accesses and write accesses for column-based data storage. There, we also explain why it is no longer necessary in many cases to create an index here, even though an index had to be created in other databases. With SAP HANA, we distinguish between *inverted* and *composite indexes* (see Appendix C).

Composite indexes have a higher memory requirement due to the memory structures for an additional internal column. Thus, we recommend that you work as much as possible with inverted indexes. That is, an index should be created in each case for the column that has the most selective condition. Composite indexes should be created only in exceptional cases—for example, when data from different columns correlates to such an extent that only certain combinations are selective. The maintenance of indexes results in increased costs for write accesses in SAP HANA also. However, these costs are significantly less for inverted indexes than for composite indexes, for which multiple memory structures must be maintained.

Inverted versus composite index

If you are migrating an existing system to SAP HANA, all existing secondary indexes for column store tables are no longer created. Technically, they are included in the exclusion list for SAP HANA in the ABAP Data Dictionary (see Section 3.2.1).

Index creation in SAP HANA

In principle, additional indexes should only be created if the access times are insufficient without an index. In this case, an index should be created for the selective conditions, provided these are not already covered by the primary index.

SAP Note for Analyzing and Creating Column Store Indexes

[+]

SAP Note 1794297 describes a method recommended by SAP for analyzing and creating indexes in column store tables. The note also provides the necessary programs for analyzing and creating the indexes. We recommend you use this method when creating additional secondary indexes.

Summary and Significance for SAP HANA

A consistent application of this fourth rule for classic databases leads to reduced I/O effort, optimizes memory consumption in the cache, reduces CPU consumption and, last but not least, optimizes the network transfer because less data is transferred.

[»] | **Significance of Rule #4 for SAP HANA**

The fourth rule changes in SAP HANA, and its observance has a lower priority. This is because no index at all is required in SAP HANA in many cases. If an index is required for very large tables, the rules for the index definition change. In these cases, the CPU consumption is reduced by the index.

In SAP HANA, indexes are usually created for individual columns. Indexes that span multiple columns are the exception. The Code Inspector supports you here with the "Analysis of the WHERE condition" check.

14.4.5 Rule 5: Reducing Load on Database

The fifth rule summarizes the aforementioned rules and also recommends to reduce the load on the database wherever possible. The database is a central resource in the SAP system. For this reason, you should keep the load for repeated operations on the database as small as possible. We will describe some measures below that contribute to reducing the load on the database:

▶ Using buffers

▶ Sorting

▶ Avoiding identical accesses

Using Buffers

Cross-user buffer Since the data for SAP HANA is stored in the main memory, you may have wondered whether the buffers on the application server or in programs are still required. The following cross-user buffers are available on the application server:

▶ Shared objects

▶ Shared buffer

▶ Shared memory

▸ Table buffer

The following user-specific buffers are also available within a user session: User-specific buffers

▸ SAP Memory

▸ ABAP Memory

▸ Program-specific buffering in internal tables

The most important properties of this buffer are summarized in Table 14.4.

Cross-User Buffering				
	Table Buffer	**Shared Objects**	**Shared Memory**	**Shared Buffer**
Possible Purpose	Simple tables data	Complex data, object networks	Extracts, metadata	Extracts, metadata
Copy-Free Access	No	Yes	No	No
Compression	No	No	Optional	Optional
Synchronization	Yes	No	No	No
Displacement	Yes	No	No	Yes
ABAP Statement	Open SQL	Methods of the class `cl_shm_area`	`EXPORT TO SHARED MEMORY` `IMPORT FROM SHARED MEMORY` `DELETE FROM SHARED MEMORY`	`EXPORT TO SHARED BUFFER` `IMPORT FROM SHARED BUFFER` `DELETE FROM SHARED BUFFER`

User-Specific Buffering			
	Internal Tables	**ABAP Memory**	**SAP Memory**
Possible Purpose	Smaller amounts of master data	Extracts, metadata	Parameter
Copy-Free Access	Yes, if implemented appropriately	No	No
Compression	Yes, if implemented appropriately	Optional	No

Table 14.4   Properties of Cross-User and User-Specific Buffers

User-Specific Buffering			
	Internal Tables	**ABAP Memory**	**SAP Memory**
ABAP Statement	Statements for internal tables (READ, LOOP, and so on)	▸ EXPORT TO MEMORY ID ▸ IMPORT FROM MEMORY ID ▸ DELETE FROM MEMORY ID	▸ SET PARAMETER ID ▸ GET PARAMETER ID

Table 14.4 Properties of Cross-User and User-Specific Buffers (Cont.)

Basically, there are no changes to the recommendations for buffering data when using SAP HANA. Accessing the buffer on the application server is still faster than accessing the database, also in the case of SAP HANA. This is because, among other things, the main memory in the application server is on the same server on which the ABAP program is running. For the main memory in the database, however, a network is located between the application server and the database. In addition, several software layers are involved in accessing the database. We will highlight the table buffer in particular below because it is one of the most important buffers.

Table buffer Accessing the table buffer is approximately 10 times faster than accessing data in the database. Tables that are frequently read, rarely changed, and are not too big should be buffered. When doing so, you should consider the following:

Buffer considerations
▸ Due to the synchronization between the application servers, there may be a delay in the availability of the changed data for other users. This must be acceptable from the application perspective. Thus, tables where the latest level is always required should not be buffered.

▸ Tables that are frequently changed (> *0.1% to 1% of all accesses*) should be not buffered, because performance tends to deteriorate rather than improve due to the synchronization effort and reloading.

▸ A buffered table should only occupy a small percentage (up to 5%) of the table buffer.

▸ In SAP NetWeaver 7.4, both primary and secondary keys are used efficiently in the table buffer for the search. In earlier releases, this was true only for the primary key, and accesses via the secondary key were not optimized.

When accessing buffered tables, you must ensure that the SQL statements can use the buffer. Basically, accesses pass the table buffer if the WHERE condition applies to more than one buffer object. Thus, all fields of the generic key must be specified for generically buffered tables. All fields of the primary key must be specified for single-record buffered tables. In addition, there are still a number of statements that read past the buffer:

Accesses that read past the buffer

▶ Accesses with the addition BYPASSING BUFFER

▶ Accesses with IN lists in key fields that contain more than one element

▶ Accesses with the addition FOR UPDATE in the SELECT clause

▶ Accesses with aggregate functions

▶ Accesses with the addition DISTINCT

▶ Accesses with the IS NULL operator

▶ Accesses with subqueries

▶ Accesses with ORDER BY (except ORDER BY PRIMARY KEY)

▶ Accesses with JOIN

▶ Accesses with the addition CLIENT SPECIFIED if the client is not specified

▶ Accesses that were written in Native SQL

▶ Accesses that are executed after calling the function module DB_SET_ ISOLATION_LEVEL (see SAP Note 1376858)

The Code Inspector helps you search for such statements with the check "SELECT statements that bypass the buffer."

The rules remain the same also for the other buffers (for example, shared objects, shared memory, shared buffer, internal tables, ABAP Memory, and SAP Memory). This means you should continue to store in such buffers any data that is time-consuming to obtain or calculate, or which is used more than once, in order to relieve the database of repeated costly queries. These include, for example, the results of analytic views or database procedures which you have created using code pushdown.

Other buffers

If you need the results several times in the application context, it is better just to read the data once from the database and then to buffer it in the application server. The buffers you choose will depend on whether the data is required across multiple users or only within an application. You will find the most important properties of the various buffers in Table 14.4 at the beginning of this section. Through this, you can relieve the database of unnecessary multiple accesses that are repeated with the same parameters.

Sorting To Improve Performance

Sorting in database or application server

In Section 14.1.4, we discussed the functional aspects of sorting for the database migration. The question remained open as to whether you want to sort in the database or in the ABAP program. The rules have not changed here. If the sorting in the database cannot be mapped via an index that is used for the selection, you should sort in the ABAP application server—especially if the total dataset to be sorted is required by the application. If, however, the sorting of a large dataset is required to calculate a smaller result (for example, determining the five best customers in relation to order value), the sorting should be left to the database. If the sorting is part of the calculation or can be performed cost-effectively in the database, it should also take place in the database.

Avoiding Identical Accesses

Another measure is avoiding identical accesses—that is, you should avoid the multiple reading of identical data. This reduces not only the number of accesses to the database (see golden rule #3), but avoids especially unnecessary load on the database. Usually, internal tables or even buffers are used to avoid identical accesses.

Summary and Significance for SAP HANA

A consistent application of this fifth rule for classic databases leads to reduced CPU consumption and to a reduced load on the network. The I/O effort may also be reduced by avoiding multiple accesses.

Buffering calculations to be frequently called

Also with SAP HANA, the buffers on the application server continue to be justified because they offer faster access times and can relieve the database of unnecessary accesses. This means, for example, that you can in fact execute complex calculations via code pushdown in the database on SAP HANA, but you only call these calculations as often as necessary. If a result has to be queried multiple times, it should be stored in a buffer.

Significance of Rule #5 for SAP HANA   **[«]**

The strongest feature of SAP HANA is the execution of complex calculations on large sets of data. These calculations should be done on the database. On the other hand, it does not make sense to send the same calculations or access commands to the database over and over again. Thus, the fifth rule can be worded as: "Relieve the database of unnecessary accesses." Thus formulated, this rule applies unchanged and with the same priority to SAP HANA, because CPU and network resources can be relieved here, too.

The buffering rules also remain unchanged when using SAP HANA. All buffers continue to be used in those places where the database can be relieved from repeated accesses. Sortings can also provide relief if they are executed on the application server, where this is useful. Identical requests should always be avoided, because this also relieves the database.

14.4.6 Summary of Rules

As you have seen in the previous sections, most golden rules for database programming also apply to SAP HANA. Only a few priorities change. Therefore, the number of accesses to the database is more important for SAP HANA than it is in classic databases. Thus rule #3 has a higher priority. On the other hand, indexes are required on SAP HANA only under certain circumstances, so rule #4 has a lower priority. To sum up, it can be said that observing the golden rules means fewer adjustments to ABAP programs for performance optimization.

Same rules, changed priorities

14.5 Performance Recommendations for Native Implementations in SAP HANA

After having discussed performance recommendations for working with Open SQL in the previous section, we would now like to provide some recommendations for working with Native SQL, modeled and implemented SAP HANA views, as well as SQLScript.

14.5.1 Recommendations for Native SQL

In connection with the use of Native SQL via ADBC, we would like—in addition to the recommendations for Open SQL, which apply in the same way as Native SQL—to refer to two topics separately. This involves the use of Prepared statements and mass operations. We have presented both in Section 3.2.4, so we only want to discuss the performance aspects here. For the topics presented here (and for others), there is an example in the subroutines INSERT_ROWS and INSERT_ITAB in the ABAP test program ADBC_DEMO, which is provided with the standard SAP.

Prepared Statements

Unlike Open SQL, which is optimized for performance by the SAP kernel, the programmer must ensure optimal use when using Native SQL via ADBC. If the class CL_SQL_STATEMENT is used, this involves a dynamic statement that is transferred to the database for each execution with the method EXECUTE_QUERY, which analyzes the SQL statement in turn as a character string. The parameters are included in the analysis. The following two SQL statements are thus different for the database because two different character strings are involved:

```
SELECT * FROM scarr WHERE carrid = 'AA';
SELECT * FROM scarr WHERE carrid = 'UA';
```

For each of these two statements, the database must perform, among other things, the following steps:

Prepare phase
- Parse the statement (for example, for the syntax).
- Reserve memory for the statement and the execution plan.
- Create the execution plan and store it in the SQL cache.

These steps are known as the *prepare phase* because the statement for execution is prepared here. If a very large number of SQL statements is sent to the database, which differ only in the parameters that are used, the database has to make a relatively large effort in preparing each statement. The time required can lie in the mid-three-digit microsecond range and thus may be as high as the time required for actually executing the statement. Frequent executions therefore quickly involve additional effort, which can constitute a significant part of the runtime.

If only the parameters of an SQL statement change, the SQL statement can be transferred to the database using the class CL_PREPARED_STATEMENT with a *parameter marker*. The transferred statement looks, for example, as follows:

Advantage of prepared statements

```
SELECT * FROM scarr WHERE carrid = ?;
```

This statement is prepared once only and is stored in the SQL cache. Immediately before execution, the parameters that were set with the method SET_PARAM are used instead of the parameter marker when you call the method EXECUTE_QUERY of the class CL_PREPARED_STATEMENT. That means you can reduce the effort in preparing the SQL statements to the bare minimum. Once you no longer require the prepared SQL statement, you should use the method CLOSE to close the class CL_PREPARED_STATE-MENT, so you can release the resources required by the SQL statement as soon as possible.

You should use the class CL_SQL_STATEMENT to execute statements that are executed only once. For SQL statements that you want to execute several times, you should use the class CL_PREPARED_STATEMENT, and pass the different parameters seperately. That helps keep the effort in preparing SQL statements as low as possible and contributes to relieving the database.

Recommendation for use

Mass Operations

As of SAP NetWeaver AS ABAP 7.4, an array interface is available for modifying SQL statements via ADBC. You can add, for example, multiple rows at once and do not have to proceed row by row. Since a reduced number of statements has a positive effect on the performance of an application, we recommend that you use this option not only for read accesses, but also for write accesses. As discussed in Section 14.1.6, however, you should modify data via the ADBC interface only in exceptional situations.

14.5.2 Recommendations for SAP HANA Views

In Chapter 4, you learned about different view types. When modeling and implementing SAP HANA views, you can make certain errors that have a particularly adverse effect on performance. We would like to provide a few basic recommendations for modeling SAP HANA views.

Selecting the Correct View Type

First, it's incredibly important to select the correct view type when modeling in SAP HANA Studio. Your options are shown in Figure 14.3.

Figure 14.3 is derived from the SAP HANA SQLScript Reference and supports you in decision-making.

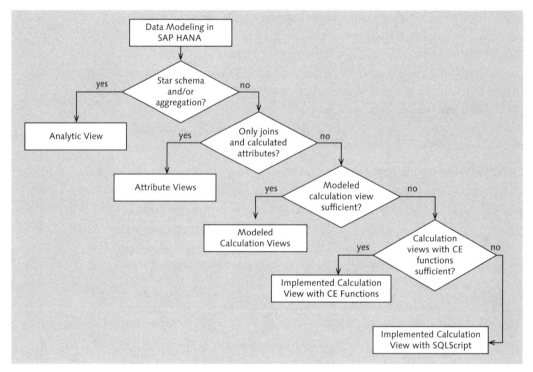

Figure 14.3 Selecting the View Type in SAP HANA

Analytic and attribute views

When selecting the view type, you should first check whether you need a star schema to map a given requirement and/or would like to aggregate a large number of data records. If this is the case, we recommend that you use an analytic view. Otherwise, you can first use an attribute view. An attribute view allows you to relate multiple tables to each other using joins. If necessary, you can also define calculated fields.

Calculation views

If you cannot map a given requirement through an analytic view nor an attribute view, use a calculation view. You can use a modeled calculation view if you want to use only the operations JOIN, PROJECTION, AGGREGA-TION, and UNION. Otherwise, you must implement the calculation view and either use only CE functions or rely on the additional options of SQLScript.

Modeling/Implementation

In addition to selecting the correct view type, you should consider some other recommendations for modeling and implementing SAP HANA views to achieve optimum performance.

You very often need several SAP HANA views (see Figure 14.4) to solve a given requirement, as in the following situation:

Combination of several views

▶ You aggregate various key figures with different analytic views (that could be, for example, an analytic view based on the SFLIGHT table and a second analytic view based on the SBOOK table; the first analytic view determines the load, while the second determines the sum of baggage weights per flight connection).

▶ You then combine the interim results of the analytic views for the final result (by using the UNION operation within a calculation view).

▶ Finally, you can enrich the final result with additional master data (for example, by using the JOIN operation and an attribute view based on the SPFLI table within the calculation view to read the master data of the flight connections).

In such a case, several engines (see Section 1.3) are involved in calculating the final result. This is illustrated schematically in Figure 14.4.

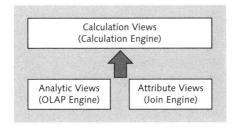

Figure 14.4 Combination of SAP HANA Views

You can support the engine involved in solving a given task by following some rules:

Support engine in solving tasks

▶ **Keeping datasets small**

As when using Open SQL within ABAP applications, we recommend that you minimize the dataset that is read *and* exchanged between the engines for modeling SAP HANA views. You achieve this by filtering data as soon as possible (by defining a suitable filter or WHERE conditions) and aggregating (especially via analytic views). In addition, you should read only the columns that are actually required.

▶ **Aggregating data as soon as possible and performing calculations on aggregated data**

By aggregating data as soon as possible and performing calculations on aggregated data, you achieve two things: First, you reduce the dataset for further processing and thus also the dataset which must, for example, be transferred from the *OLAP Engine* to the *Calculation Engine*. Secondly, you minimize the number of calculations under certain circumstances (for instance, to convert amounts to a single currency).

▶ **Avoiding complex joins**

Avoid complex joins—that is, long concatenations of JOIN operations and joins between very large database tables. These can be very expensive. Alternatively, in some cases, you can first aggregate key figures from different fact tables independently of each other via different analytic views, and then combine the interim results via the UNION operation.

▶ **Reading master data as late as possible**

Read master data as late as possible, if it is not required for the previous calculation steps.

▶ **Recommendations for SQLScript**

When using implemented calculation views, also note the recommendations for SQLScript in the following section.

14.5.3   Recommendations for SQLScript

If you have to use SQLScript to implement a requirement (because the requirement cannot be mapped by modeling an SAP HANA view), note the following rules. We have already discussed them to some extent in Chapter 5:

- **Minimizing complexity of SQL statements**

  You can break down complex SQL statements using table variables. This makes it easier for you to read the code, and also facilitates the work of the HANA database optimizer. It makes it easier in some cases, for example, by decomposing complex database queries, to identify redundant subqueries and to avoid calculating them several times.

- **Avoiding dependency of SQL statements**

  As described in Chapter 5, multiple SQL statements within a database procedure or a calculation view are executed in parallel by the database as often as possible. However, this assumes that these SQL statements are independent of each other. Thus, avoid *unnecessary* dependencies between SQL statements.

- **Avoiding mixture of SQL and CE Plan Operator functions**

  SQL and CE Plan Operator functions are optimized independently of each other. Avoid mixing both if possible.

- **Avoiding imperative programming**

  Imperative language elements (especially loops and cursor processing) make the parallelization more difficult or may prevent it completely. Try to work with declarative language elements. For data-intensive calculations, use loops and cursors in particular only if you cannot solve a requirement differently.

- **Using strengths of OLAP and Join Engine**

  If you need SQLScript to implement a requirement, it doesn't necessarily mean that you have to implement the requirement solely with SQLScript. You can often delegate parts of the task within a database procedure or a calculation view to analytic views and attribute views. Check this option, because it allows you to use the strengths of OLAP and Join Engine.

- **Avoiding dynamic SQL**

  The optimization options of dynamic SQL are restricted. Dynamic SQL must be re-compiled for each call under certain circumstances. Avoid dynamic SQL where it is not necessarily required.

For more information, refer to *SAP HANA SQLScript Reference* in the SAP online help.

14.6 Summary of Recommendations

At the end of this chapter (and the book), we would like to compile again the five main recommendations for successful ABAP development on SAP HANA in a more concentrated and striking form:

▶ **Tip 1: Not seeing the database as a black box**
Our first recommendation is more theoretical and involves the interaction between application server and database. You should no longer see the database as a pure black box that provides only the basic CRUD functions (create, read, update, delete) for you as a developer. Instead, it provides a rich platform that offers a variety of services.

There are various channels for using these services, of which SQL is the most important. For this reason, the SQL knowledge and related database programming concepts, which you have acquired within this book, are very important.

Another change from the past is that the database platform is no longer used solely by an ABAP system, but also by other users such as business intelligence tools or the XS Engine.

▶ **Tip 2: Performing performance optimizations as much as possible with standard tools**
For an optimization, we always recommend that you proceed gradually. After an analysis of the status quo, the optimization potential of Open SQL and standard ABAP programming (and standard ABAP components) should be used in the first step. Ideally, you can already change the ABAP code in this step so that further potential optimization of database accesses can be easily performed by a native implementation.

The performance recommendations for Open SQL in ABAP do not change fundamentally on SAP HANA, but are mainly weighted differently (see Section 14.4). Familiarize yourself with the rules and also get to know the new tools for performance analyses.

▶ **Tip 3: Encapsulation and testing are essential for implementations in the database**
If you cannot solve a requirement (whether in terms of performance or functions) with standard tools, use HANA-specific functions.

Bear in mind that a clean encapsulation and good test coverage are important, especially for implementations near the database. Define appropriate test cases, provide appropriate test data, and run automated tests if possible to make sure that the system still responds correctly, even after an adjustment is made to an SAP HANA view or a database procedure.

▶ **Tip 4: Maintainability, correctness, and robustness are ultimately more important than optimal performance**
The relocating of application code from the application layer to the database layer provides a lot of potential. However, it may also increase the complexity of ABAP programs—for example, if you also have to reserve an implementation for traditional databases in addition to the optimized implementation of a program for SAP HANA.

In addition, the result of a program can change due to the relocation of the application code in the database, if you are not careful (see Section 14.1.3). Always ensure that the data is handled correctly from a business perspective.

We recommend that you not relocate application code unnecessarily in SAP HANA views and database procedures. Only do so where there is a real benefit in terms of performance and functions. Not every ABAP program is performance-critical and must provide a result within a fraction of a second.

▶ **Tip 5: New opportunities and application patterns beyond performance optimizations**
Consider SAP HANA as more than a technology to accelerate programs. Particularly in the third part of this book, you encountered a number of techniques through which you can gain new insights from existing databases. OLTP and OLAP become blurred due to the possibilities of SAP HANA, and new application patterns emerge. These sometimes allow companies far more than solely performance improvements—they can develop new business models and differentiate themselves from competitors.

The opening of the ABAP programming model with regard to SAP HANA's native database technologies is a major step and will create new

Opening of the ABAP programming model

559

opportunities for ABAP developments together with further innovations in SAP HANA. We hope that, with the recommendations in this book, we've made it easier for you to get the maximum out of the HANA platform within ABAP developments or enhancements.

Appendices

A   Flight Data Model

In this book, we use the SAP NetWeaver flight data model as our data basis (with some slight extensions). Therefore, information about the structure of the flight data model is provided in this appendix as reference material.

The flight data model, often known as the SFLIGHT model, is a simple example of classic application development using SAP NetWeaver AS ABAP. It also provides the basis for numerous specialist books, training courses, and documentation relating to SAP software. Essentially, the data model comprises a set of database tables. An understanding of these tables and their content is helpful in order to understand the examples in this book.

As an ABAP developer, you have almost certainly worked with the SFLIGHT model at some time or another. Therefore, we will focus our attention on the relationships that exist between the tables used in this book and classify them in the context of HANA data modeling, which was introduced in Chapter 4.

First, we will briefly outline the simple underlying business process. Then, we will explain the structure of and relationships between the most important database tables used in this book. Finally, we will discuss the various options associated with generating mass data.

A.1   Basic Principles of the Flight Data Model

The flight data model can be used to simulate various business scenarios within the context of bookings for scheduled flights. Essentially, two scenarios can be considered here:

Scenarios

▶ **Operating an airline**
An airline operator sells tickets either directly to customers or through a travel agent. The system contains only data relating to this airline, albeit for all bookings.

▶ **Simulating a travel agency**
A travel agency sells tickets on behalf of multiple airlines. The system

563

contains the complete flight schedule. Furthermore, bookings for all flights can be made here. This scenario is based on the assumption that the system contains the latest booking information from the airlines so that the number of seats available on a flight is always known locally. Only bookings made through a travel agent are held in the system.

The flight data model is fully presented and documented in the *Data Modeler* (Transaction SD11) for the `BC_TRAVEL` model. In addition to individual flights, this model also makes it possible to combine multiple flights (for example, flights with stops en route). However, this variant is beyond the scope of this book.

Business scenario in this book

Note that with regard to the simple implementation examples contained in this book, we will not always exactly pursue a business process. In the two end-to-end examples in Chapter 8 and Chapter 13, we will focus on the second scenario, namely the scenario involving the travel company.

A.2   Database Tables for the Flight Data Model

There are approximately 25 database tables for business data that relates to the flight data model. Standard configurations and Customizing also play a role (for example, the client configuration, customizing for currencies, and so on). These are stored in additional tables.

In this section, we will discuss the structure of and relationships between approximately 10 tables used in this book. We will classify these tables on the basis of Customizing, master data, and transaction data.

Once we have introduced you to the main tables associated with the `SFLIGHT` model, and their role within the business scenario, we will discuss some general design decisions in relation to the data model, and evaluate them in the context of SAP HANA.

A.2.1   Customizing

Settings for the ABAP application server

The flight data model uses the following settings for the ABAP application server:

▶ The client configuration, which is stored in the table T000 and is used as a check table for the client field associated with other tables.

▶ Customizing for currencies and conversion variants, which are stored in the tables TCURR and TCURX. At this point, we must mention that for training purposes, the flight data model uses a separate currency-conversion variant based on the tables SCURR and SCURX. Since the currency conversion in SAP HANA—which was introduced in Section 4.2.4—uses the standard variant, we will not discuss the special variant of the flight data model. Instead, we will implicitly assume that the data (for example, the currencies available) is identical.

▶ Customizing for units of measurement (lengths, weights, and so on) from the table T006.

A.2.2 Master Data

In this book, we use the SFLIGHT model master data listed in Table A.1.

Table	Description	Important Content
SCARR	Airlines	Airline code and name
SPFLI	Flight schedule	Flight connection with information about the origin/destination as well as the flight duration
SAIRPORT	Airports	Airport names and time zones
SGEOCITY	Cities	Cities, including their geographical data (longitude and latitude)
SCUSTOM	Customer data	Name, address, email address, and authorized price reduction
SAPLANE	Aircraft	Information about the number of seats available, as well as aircraft usage and speed

Table A.1 Master Data for the Flight Data Model

Since this book primarily considers the scenario involving a travel agent who sells tickets directly to customers, we will not use the tables for configuring different travel agents (for example, table STRAVELAG) and business partners (for example, SBUSPART), which would be important in the scenario that simulates operating an airline.

From a master data perspective, an important relationship exists between the flight schedule, the airlines, the airports, and the cities. Figure A.1 shows the relevant tables and foreign key relationships in the form of an attribute view in SAP HANA Studio.

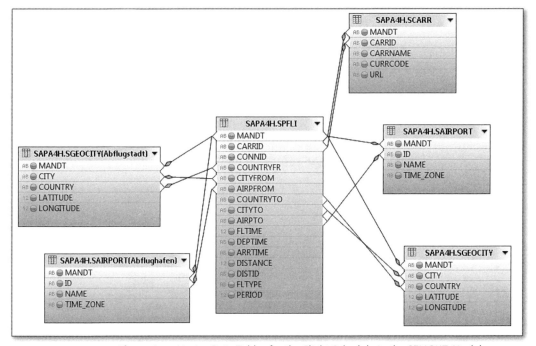

Figure A.1 Master Data Tables for the Flight Schedule in the SFLIGHT Model

The other two tables—namely SCUSTOM and SAPLANE—have, above all, connections to the transaction data, which we will show in the next section as dimensions of a star schema.

A.2.3 Transaction Data

The flight data model primarily has two tables that contain transaction data—namely, the flight bookings table (SBOOK) and the flights table (SFLIGHT). Table A.2 summarizes the contents of each.

In certain respects, the table SFLIGHT plays a dual role here. On the one hand, it contains transaction data because it represents an actual flight. On the other hand, it can also be regarded as a dimension of the bookings.

Table	Description	Important Content
SFLIGHT	Flights	Information about a specific flight (flight connection, time, and seats occupied) **Key performance indicators:** ▶ Flight price ▶ Seats occupied/available
SBOOK	Flight bookings	Information about a flight booking in relation to passenger information **Key performance indicators:** ▶ Booking price ▶ Luggage weight

Table A.2 Transaction Data in the Flight Data Model

The business logic for creating transaction data is relatively simple. In the case of a flight booking for a customer, both the flight and the customer must exist in the system. Then, before making a flight booking, a check is performed to determine whether any seats are available and, if so, the number of seats available is reduced over the course of the transaction. The booking price is also calculated from the passenger discount and the previously configured flight price. This logic is encapsulated in a business application programming interface, or BAPI (FlightBooking business object), and can be called within function modules.

Business logic

At this point, we will not discuss the transaction logic in any further detail. Instead, we will consider how it interacts with the master data. The cardinality of the transaction data (❶ in Figure A.2) with respect to the master data is n:1, because the master data is used in different transactions (Each booking ❷ for a flight ❸ involves a customer ❹ who can make multiple bookings). Figure A.2 shows a section of the data model in which the additional master data associated with a flight schedule in ❺ (previously in Figure A.1) is not shown again.

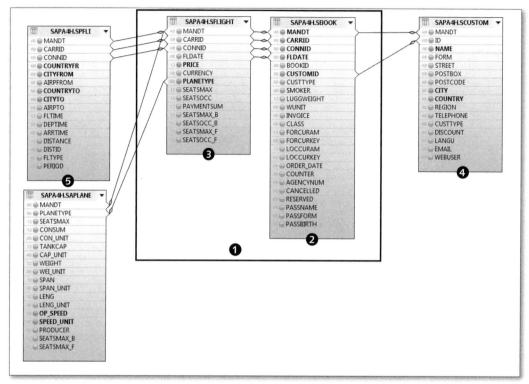

Figure A.2 Transaction Data in the Flight Data Model

The model shown here is a simple, graphical representation of the relationships between the tables. When analyzing the transaction data in real life, it is better to use an analytic view in SAP HANA (see Section 4.2).

A.2.4 Designing the SFLIGHT Data Model

In this section, we will discuss some design considerations associated with the SFLIGHT data model. It is very obvious that the tables used here were developed prior to SAP HANA, which is the case with most tables in an SAP system. Next, we will discuss the technical structure of the tables (primary and foreign keys, data types, indexes, and normalization) along with the semantics of their contents.

Table structure   Technical modeling of the SFLIGHT tables is typical of SAP R/3. This includes the following structural characteristics:

▶ Tables generally have a set of character-like key fields. No GUIDs (*Globally Unique Identifiers*) are used as generated, technical keys. Foreign key relationships therefore comprise multiple conditions (see Figure A.1 and Figure A.2).

▶ A date is recorded in the date and time fields (DATS, TIMS). Time stamps are not used (TIMESTAMP and TIMSTAMPL data elements).

▶ Some numeric fields are recorded as a character-like field (NUMC) in order to ensure that the display is formatted consistently (including leading zeros). One example of this is the customer number in the table SCUSTOM.

▶ The model is not completely normalized. In other words, the tables contain certain redundancies. In particular, this is a direct consequence of avoiding technical keys. For example, a flight is defined using three attributes (CARRID, CONNID, and FLDATE), which also exist in other tables.

Newer SAP Business Suite modules have pursued other approaches. Interestingly, however, the aforementioned structural characteristics are also well-suited to the SAP HANA architecture. On the other hand, GUIDs, which often exist in the database as RAW types, do not have an optimal compression behavior, and also the performance of join operations can be negatively impacted. In the SFLIGHT data model, however, there are also some design decisions that are not recommended unreservedly for new developments within the context of SAP HANA.

For example, some calculated values are materialized as physical columns. The booking price, for example, is stored twice in the table SBOOK, once in the airline currency and once in the local currency. Such a field can also be recorded as a calculated field within a view. You learned about this in Section 4.1.3. Furthermore, numerical values that potentially play a role for calculations should not be modeled as character strings (NUMC) because the database cannot differentiate between these and other texts. The DISCOUNT value in the table SCUSTOM is one such example.

Table content

A.3 Data Generation

To become familiar with the opportunities presented by SAP HANA, you should always work with large volumes of data. Even though the SAP

NetWeaver flight data model is a very simple data model, there are, in reality, extremely large volumes of data in the underlying business scenario. In 2011, for example, approximately 56 million flight passengers passed through Frankfurt Airport (source: The Statistics Office for the State of Hesse).

Data generator · In order to have a large volume of data available during training, the development of a prototype (or any productive development) tools for data generation are often used. These tools help to generate a consistent and realistic volume of records for a data model. The ABAP report SAPBC_DATA_GENERATOR is available in the flight data model for this purpose. At present, however, it cannot generate data volumes of arbitrary size (for example, the number of bookings is currently limited to a maximum of 1.4 million).

Mass data · Therefore, for this book, we developed a data generator that was suitable for our examples—namely, the ABAP report ZR_A4H_BOOK_GENERATE_MASS_DATA. It draws on data generated by the ABAP report SAPBC_DATA_GENERATOR, and generates additional flights and flight bookings. In other words, you must call this ABAP report first. At present, our data generator works as follows:

- In the first step, the data generator deletes the flights and flight bookings generated by the ABAP report SAPBC_DATA_GENERATOR.

- It then generates flights (that is, entries in the database table SFLIGHT). For each connection (each entry in the database table SPFLI), the program generates one flight for each day that falls within the dates entered on the selection screen. Flight capacity fluctuates between 70% and 100%. In some months (for example, during the Christmas period), a higher average capacity is assumed than in other months. During these months, the flight price is also higher than in other months.

- Finally, the program generates the flight bookings in the database table SBOOK and uses a random algorithm to determine the customers and travel agencies associated with the bookings. The data generator determines the booking date on the basis of three hard-coded distribution functions that are selected at random for each flight. There is a maximum of 180 days before the flight date.

The ABAP report ZR_A4H_BOOK_GENERATE_MASS_DATA generates, on average, approximately three million bookings each year. Therefore, if you schedule the program for a period of 10 years, you obtain a volume of data that equates to approximately 30 million bookings. Since these are distributed across approximately 4,500 customer master records, many more bookings are accepted here for individual customers than would be the case in reality. However, this is not a problem for our examples. For more information about generating data, see Appendix E.

B What's New in ABAP in SAP NetWeaver 7.4

SAP NetWeaver 7.4 provides a number of compatible enhancements to the ABAP programming language. Thanks to a greater orientation towards expressions, these enable you to write shorter, more legible ABAP code.

One example is *string templates*. These were introduced in ABAP 7.02 and provide an elegant, powerful option for defining compound character strings that go far beyond the possibilities associated with CONCATENATE or WRITE statements. In this appendix, we will provide a brief introduction to some new features in ABAP 7.4, which are used throughout this book. For comprehensive information about ABAP release 7.4, please refer to the ABAP language documentation (see *http://help.sap.com/abapdocu_740/en/*).

In the context of ABAP development on SAP HANA, the new options associated with expressions make it possible to reduce ABAP code to the essential intention: The code pushdown paradigm discussed in this book can be used to perform calculations within the database and (by using the components contained in the ABAP Application Server) the application can be orchestrated using considerably less application code.

B.1 Inline Declarations

Previously in ABAP, you always had to use a DATA statement to declare variables before you could use them. Furthermore, you always had to specify the data type—even if, during an assignment, this was canonical from the context. Let's take a look at the example in Listing B.1.

Variables

```
" Data declaration without inline declaration
DATA: lo_alv TYPE REF TO cl_salv_table,
      lo_exc TYPE REF TO cx_salv_msg.

TRY.
    " Generate table ALV in factory
    cl_salv_table=>factory(
      IMPORTING r_salv_table = lo_alv
```

```
        CHANGING t_table = lt_data ).

    " Display ALV
    lo_alv->display( ).
  CATCH cx_salv_msg INTO lo_exc.
    MESSAGE lo_exc TYPE 'I' DISPLAY LIKE 'E'.
ENDTRY.
```

Listing B.1 Classic Example without Inline Declaration

To define the corresponding variables, you have to know or find out the names of the classes CL_SALV_TABLE and CX_SALV_MSG.

DATA() statement

With an inline declaration using the DATA() statement, you can make an implicit declaration and specify a type for a variable directly (inline) during the assignment. Listing B.2 demonstrates this using the same example.

```
" Data declaration with inline declaration
TRY.
    " Generate table ALV in factory
    cl_salv_table=>factory(
      IMPORTING r_salv_table = DATA(lo_alv_inline)
      CHANGING t_table       = lt_data ).

    " Display ALV
    lo_alv_inline->display( ).
  CATCH cx_salv_msg INTO DATA(lo_exc_inline).
    MESSAGE lo_exc_inline TYPE 'I' DISPLAY LIKE 'E'.
ENDTRY.
```

Listing B.2 Example with Inline Declaration

Here, the variables for the ALV table and the exception CX_SALV_MSG in the CATCH block are defined directly (inline) during the assignment. Inline declarations can be used not only for classes and interfaces but also for structures, table types, data references, and so on.

Field symbols

It is also possible to declare field symbols inline, as shown in Listing B.3.

```
LOOP AT lt_data ASSIGNING FIELD-SYMBOL(<line>).
  " ...
ENDLOOP.
```

Listing B.3 Inline Declaration of a Field Symbol

When using inline declarations, you must consider the following:

▸ Inline declarations do not change the *scope* of ABAP variables. Therefore, it is not possible to use the same variable name multiple times within a method, even if you seem to define it locally—as is the case with the variables `lo_exc_inline` in Listing B.2, for example.

We recommend that you continue to define, at the very start of a method implementation, variables that you want to use in several places within an extensive method. Inline declaration is useful for variables with a local, limited usage context (for example, the loop in Listing B.3).

▸ Inline declarations cannot be used in all situations. In particular, it is not possible yet to use an inline declaration to define the result of a `SELECT` statement (`INTO`, `INTO TABLE`).

B.2   Constructor Expressions

Constructor expressions enable you to create and initialize ABAP objects, data structures, and data references by means of an expression. The benefit of such expressions lies in the reduction of statements needed, as well as compatibility with inline declarations.

Traditionally, ABAP objects can be created using the following statement:

```
CREATE OBJECT <variable> [ TYPE <type> ].
```

Of course, the variable must be declared beforehand and adjusted to the instantiation. When we introduced you to inline declaration in the previous section, you may have asked yourself whether it can be used in connection with creating an object instance. In ABAP 7.4, this can be done using the `NEW` operator, which enables you to declare an object instance directly inline. The parameters for the constructor are transferred when the method is called. For example, the following assignment is possible:

```
DATA(lo_object) = NEW lcl_my_class( iv_param = 1 ).
```

Of course, you can also define the variable `lo_object` separately.

VALUE operator In addition to objects, you can also use expressions to initialize structures and even internal tables. In this case, the VALUE operator shown in the example in Listing B.4 is used.

```
DATA: ls_carr TYPE scarr.

" Classic initialization of a structure
ls_carr-carrid   = 'LH'.
ls_carr-carrname = 'Lufthansa'.

" Alternative using the constructor expression
ls_carr = VALUE #( carrid   = 'LH'
                   carrname = 'Lufthansa' ).
```

Listing B.4 Using "VALUE" to Initialize a Structure

One benefit of the VALUE expression is that it can be combined with an inline declaration. In this case, however, you must specify the exact data type:

```
DATA(ls_carr) = VALUE scarr( carrid   = 'LH'
                             carrname = 'Lufthansa').
```

You can also use the VALUE operator to initialize internal tables, as shown in Listing B.5.

```
DATA: lt_carrier TYPE TABLE OF scarr.
lt_carrier = VALUE #(
    ( carrid = 'AA' carrname = 'American Airlines' )
    ( carrid = 'LH' carrname = 'Lufthansa' ) ).
```

Listing B.5 Using "VALUE" to Initialize an Internal Table

In this example, it's particularly evident that less code is needed, and code is more legible, compared to using multiple APPEND statements to perform a classic initialization of structures or to set up an internal table.

REF operator The final new element we wish to mention is the REF operator, which is an expression-oriented alternative to generating a data reference (TYPE REF TO DATA) with the ABAP statement GET REFERENCE. The example in Listing B.6 uses this operator and inline declarations for an ADBC access (ABAP Database Connectivity, see Listing 3.12 in Section 3.2.4).

```
TRY.
 " Prepare SQL connection and statement
 DATA(lo_result_set) =
         cl_sql_connection=>get_connection(
               )->create_statement(
               )->execute_query( lv_statement ).

 lo_result_set->set_param_table( REF #( lt_result ) ).

 " Obtain result
 lo_result_set->next_package( ).
 lo_result_set->close( ).
CATCH cx_sql_exception INTO DATA(lo_exc).
 " Error handling
ENDTRY.
```

Listing B.6 ABAP 7.4: Expressions in an ADBC Context

In addition to NEW, VALUE, and REF, ABAP 7.4 has other new operators such as conversions (CONV) or type conversions (CAST). For more information, refer to the documentation at *http://help.sap.com/abapdocu_740/en/*.

When you use constructor expressions, you should not overlook runtime considerations or the elegance of the code. If, for example, you require an object in several places, you should not initialize it twice.

Performance considerations

B.3   Internal Tables

Traditionally, READ TABLE statements were used to access the content of internal tables, which facilitated the use of a key or line index to read individual lines.

In ABAP release 7.4, this can be done using expressions that you assign directly or process further. Listing B.7 shows an example of such use.

Access via an index or key

```
DATA: lt_carrier TYPE TABLE OF scarr WITH KEY carrid.
lt_carrier = VALUE #(
    ( carrid = 'AA' carrname = 'American Airlines' )
    ( carrid = 'LH' carrname = 'Lufthansa' ) ).

" Read first entry from the internal table
DATA(ls_carrier)  = lt_carrier[ 1 ].
```

```
" Access with a key and use of an
" attribute
DATA(lv_name) = lt_carrier[ carrid = 'LH' ]-carrname.
```

Listing B.7 Expressions for Access to Internal Tables

These new expressions also facilitate direct access in the case of multidimensional structures—that is, if an internal table in a column also
contains a table.

Performance
considerations

As is the case with constructor expressions, you should always bear performance in mind and avoid unnecessary accesses with expressions for
internal tables. The following example demonstrates *unfavorable* usage of
table expressions because the same line is read multiple times. Instead,
you should temporarily store the line in a variable.

```
DATA(lv_carrid)   = lt_carrier[ 1 ]-carrid.
DATA(lv_carrname) = lt_carrier[ 1 ]-carrname.
```

C Read and Write Access in the Column Store

Having some technical background knowledge of the structure of the column store will help you understand the concept of read and write access in SAP HANA. In this appendix, we will give you some key information about the column store, as well as some background information about processing accesses in the column store. First, we will examine the concept of accesses without indexes. Then, we will outline the basic principles of indexes in SAP HANA and explain how to use indexes to optimize accesses.

C.1 Basic Principles

In Section 1.2.2, you learned that a column in a column store is stored internally in at least two structures: the dictionary vector and the attribute vector.

Dictionary and attribute vectors

Figure C.1 shows a sample table that comprises three columns: *ID*, *Name*, and *Gender*. The data stored in this table is contained in Table C.1.

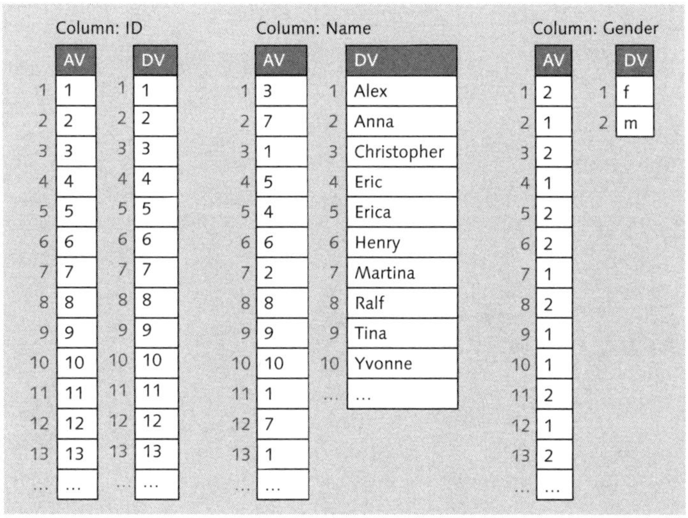

Figure C.1 Column Store with a Dictionary Vector and Attribute Vector

ID	Name	Gender
1	Christopher	M
2	Martina	F
3	Alex	M
4	Erica	F
5	Eric	M
6	Henry	M
7	Anna	F
8	Ralf	M
9	Tina	F
10	Yvonne	F
11	Alex	M
12	Martina	F
13	Alex	M

Table C.1 Sample Data for this Appendix

Each column has one dictionary vector and one attribute vector. In the dictionary vector, the distinct contents of the column are saved once. The data is held in the dictionary vector in sorted order, thus making it possible to quickly find relevant entries through a binary search. A value is assigned to an entry's position in the dictionary vector, and this value is stored in the attribute vector instead of the actual value. In our example, the name "Martina" occupies seventh position in the dictionary vector. In the attribute vector, the number 7 occupies second and twelfth position because "Martina" is both the second and the twelfth data record in Table C.1's data.

C.2 Read Access without an Index

The dictionary vector and attribute vector make it possible to store data very efficiently and therefore process this data quickly. Very little data needs to be transferred from the main memory to the CPU (central processing unit). Consequently, in SAP HANA, indexes are not required in many cases that previously would have needed them. In this section, we will explain how a read access in the column store is processed and how the dictionary vectors and attribute vectors are used.

We will now use an example that illustrates the column store's search function in greater detail. Figure C.2 shows a table that comprises the following three columns: *ID*, *Name*, and *Gender*. The dictionary and attribute vectors are shown for each column. To make it clearer, we have displayed the row ID for each vector on the left-hand side of the figure. This is implicitly determined by value's position in the vector. It is not persisted and it does not use any memory. Furthermore, no indexes are defined. For the purpose of our example, we will use the condition WHERE NAME = 'Alex.'

Read access in the column store

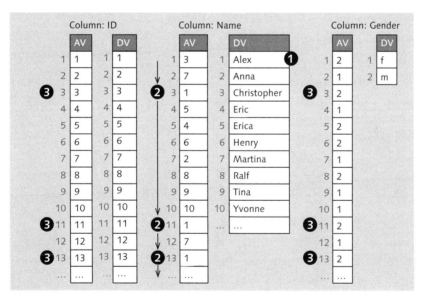

Figure C.2 Column Store Table with Three Columns

1. First, a binary search is performed in the dictionary vector to determine the value for "Alex." Since the dictionary vector has been sorted, an optimized binary search can be used. "Alex" occupies first position in the dictionary vector ❶. Therefore, the value for Alex is 1.

2. The attribute vector is then searched for the value 1 ❷.

3. Then, the row IDs are used to reconstruct the rows for all hits. In other words, in our example, the third, eleventh, and thirteenth entries in the other columns are read ❸.

Performance

Thanks to data compression, a relatively small volume of data needs to be searched, and the search mainly compares integers. Since you can parallelize the search across multiple CPU cores, the speed is usually sufficient, and an index is not required. In the case of tables with fewer than half a million entries, there is very little difference between having an index and not having an index. If, on the other hand, the table has hundreds of millions of entries, accessing a highly selective column without an index is slower by a factor of 100 or more compared to accessing it with an index. This factor increases as the table grows in size. If such an access is performed very frequently, as may be the case, in an OLTP system, for example, an index is vital for good performance.

Main store and delta store

Up to now, we have discussed only the concept of the *main store*, which has been optimized for read accesses (see also Section C.2.2). However, data can also be stored in a *delta store*, which is generated by write accesses and has been optimized for such accesses. In the next section, we will discuss the differences between the main store and the delta store. We will also explain how to transfer data from one to another.

C.3   Write Access without an Index

Write accesses in the delta store

Since the dictionary vector in the main store has been sorted and this data needs to be held in sorted order, it would be very time-consuming to have direct write accesses to the main store. If the name "Adrian" was inserted in the example in Section C.2, all existing values in the dictionary vector would have to move one place. Therefore, the value for "Alex" would change from 1 to 2 and the value for "Anna" would change from 2 to 3, and so on. Then, the entire attribute vector would have to be changed to include the new values.

To prevent this, write accesses are executed in the delta store. As is the case with the main store, good data compression is facilitated by having one dictionary vector and one attribute vector for each column in the delta store. Unlike the main store, however, the dictionary vector in the delta store is not sorted. As a result, a new value can be inserted quickly by simply appending it to the end of the dictionary vector. However, a binary search can no longer be performed in the dictionary vector. For this reason, each column has a B* tree index that makes it possible to quickly find existing values in the dictionary vector. These structures also make it possible to insert and compress data quickly. A schematic representation of a main store and delta store is provided in Figure C.3. To improve legibility, we have abbreviated the dictionary and attribute vectors and omitted the implicit row IDs for each vector.

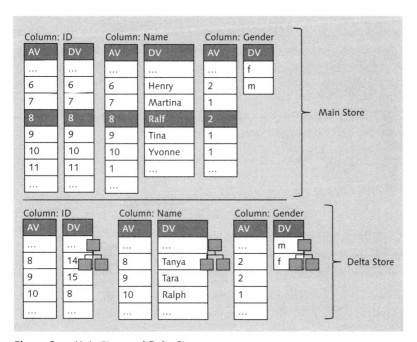

Figure C.3 Main Store and Delta Store

All change accesses are processed in the delta store. In the example shown in Figure C.3, the following data records were added to in Table C.1: ("14—Tanya—F" and "15—Tara—F").

The following change was made to the data record "8—Ralf—M": "Ralf" was changed to "Ralph." In SAP HANA, such an UPDATE is made using the following sequence: SELECT (to find the old data record and mark it for deletion) and INSERT. This action is known as INSERT ONLY because a change to a data record only ever results in a new version of the data record being inserted. The deletion indicators are managed in another internal structure not shown in Figure C.3. The old version of the data record is deleted later when the merge action is performed.

Read accesses in the delta store

Once a read access has searched the main store (as described earlier), it must then search the delta store because data records that correspond to the search request may have been written to the delta store. Since the delta store has been optimized for write accesses, searches performed in the delta store are more time-consuming. This is because, for example, the delta store contains an additional memory structure—the B* tree—which references the unsorted dictionary vector. It is therefore desirable to keep the delta store quite small and to regularly transfer it to the main store. This action is known as *merge*.

Merge action generates a new main store

When the merge is performed, the data in the delta store is transferred to the main store asynchronously. Old versions of data records are deleted if there are no open transactions for these records.

During the merge process, data from the delta store is incorporated into the main store's dictionary and attribute vectors, so these vectors are reorganized and assigned a new structure. A new main store (Main 2) is generated from the old main store (Main 1) and delta store (Delta 1). Data records that have an open transaction are not transferred to the new main store but to a new delta store (Delta 2). Once this transfer is complete, the old main store (Main 1) and old delta store (Delta 1) are discarded.

Write accesses in the new delta store

This process occurs at table level. During the merge, the data from the old main store and delta store is transferred to a new main store, and data from the old main store is still readable. However, write accesses occur in the new delta store (Delta 2) while the merge is still running and Delta 1 is being processed. A schematic representation of the merge is shown in Figure C.4.

You can use different parameters to configure the execution times for merge processes. Such parameters can take into consideration, for example, the size of the delta store, the system load, and the number of entries or the time since the last merge was performed. Therefore, a new main store is created on a regular basis, and changes are bundled together and transferred as efficiently as possible from the delta store to the main store.

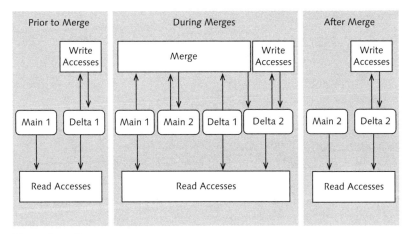

Figure C.4 Merge

Figure C.3 and Figure C.5 in the next section show the dictionary and attribute vectors both before and after the merge.

C.4 Read Accesses with an Index

Now that you have learned about accesses without an index, we will now turn our attention to accesses with an index. As mentioned, read accesses involving very large tables can, despite compression and parallelism, be too slow if these are executed very frequently. In such cases, an index should be created so you won't have to scan the entire column. In SAP HANA, a distinction is made between the following two types of indexes:

▶ **Inverted index**
Inverted indexes refer to only one column. Here, the index data is stored in internal memory structures that belong to the respective column—namely, the index offset vector and the index position vector. For each value in the dictionary vector, the index offset vector stores the position of this value's first occurrence in the index position vector. The index position vector contains the row ID assigned to the data record in the attribute vector. The index position vector is sorted according to the indexed column and uses the row ID to reference the attribute vector.

▸ **Composite index**

Composite indexes refer to more than one column. First, the contents these columns are grouped together in an internal column, and an inverted index is then created for this internal column.

Let's discuss read accesses for these two index categories.

Inverted index As an example, we will create an index for the *Name* column. Since it concerns only one column, we will create an inverted index as shown in Figure C.5. We will continue to use the example from the previous sections, namely the condition WHERE NAME = 'Alex'. When there is no index, the entire attribute vector must be searched for the value determined from the dictionary vector.

Column: ID		Column: Name		Invert Index: Name		Column: Gender	
AV	DV	AV	DV	IO	IP	AV	DV
1	1	3	Alex	1	3	2	f
2	2	7	Anna	4	11	1	m
3	3	1	Christopher	5	13	2	
4	4	5	Eric	6	7	1	
5	5	4	Erica	7	1	2	
6	6	6	Henry	8	5	2	
7	7	2	Martina	9	4	1	
8	8	8	Ralph	11	6	2	
9	9	11	Tanya	12	2	1	
10	10	12	Tara	13	12	1	
11	11	1	Tina	14	8	2	
12	12	7	Yvonne	15	14	1	
13	13	1	...	...	15	2	
14	14	9			9	1	
15	15	10			12	1	
...	...	...			...	...	

Figure C.5 Inverted Index for the "Name" Field

Search process With an inverted index, however, this is no longer necessary. The search process is then as follows:

1. First, in the dictionary vector, a binary search is performed to determine the value for "Alex." This concerns the value "1" because "Alex" occupies first position in the dictionary vector.

2. Then, the index offset vector is checked to see which value occupies first position (and therefore contains information about the first value in the dictionary vector). In this case, the number "1" is stored there, which means that the positions of the value we require are stored in the first position in the index position vector.

3. Here, you find the following values in succession: "3" (in first position), "11" (in second position), and "13" (in third position). These values are the positions (row IDs) in the attribute vector occupied by "Alex" (the value "1").

4. The search ends with the fourth entry in the index position vector because position 4 describes the end of the section being searched within the index offset vector. In other words, the value that lies after the value "Alex" in the dictionary vector occupies position 4 in the index position vector. Now, only the required columns from the other attribute vectors need to be read using the predetermined row IDs.

In the next example, we will create a composite index for the *Gender* and *Name* columns. In this case, an additional column is created in SAP HANA and the contents of the *Gender* and *Name* columns are stored there together. As described earlier, an inverted index is created for this internal column which is not visible in the ABAP Data Dictionary. In our example, we will search the database table using the condition WHERE GENDER ='F' AND NAME = 'Tina'. When there was no index, the entire attribute vector for the *Name* column had to be searched.

Composite index

This is no longer necessary. The search process is as follows:

Search process

1. In the dictionary vector for the internal column composed from the *Gender* and *Name* fields, a binary search is performed to determine the position. The required value occupies position 6.

2. In the index offset vector, the reference to the position in the index position vector (position 7 in our example) is obtained from position 6.

3. In the index position vector, the reference to the position in the attribute vector (position 9 in our case) is at position 7.

4. We have now determined row IDs for the attribute vectors whose columns are required for the SELECT.

Column: ID		Column: Name		Column: Gender		Concat. Index: Gender, Name			
AV	DV	AV	DV	AV	DV	AV	DV	IO	IP
1	1	3	Alex	2	f	9	fAnna	1	7
2	2	7	Anna	1	m	3	fErica	2	4
3	3	1	Christopher	2		8	fMartina	3	2
4	4	5	Eric	1		2	fTanya	5	12
5	5	4	Erica	2		10	fTara	6	14
6	6	6	Henry	2		11	fTina	7	15
7	7	2	Martina	1		1	fYvonne	8	9
8	8	8	Ralph	2		12	mAlex	9	10
9	9	11	Tanya	1		6	mChristopher	12	3
10	10	12	Tara	1		7	mEric	13	11
11	11	1	Tina	2		8	mHenry	14	13
12	12	7	Yvonne	1		3	mRalph	15	1
13	13	1	...	2		8	..	...	5
14	14	9		1		4			6
15	15	10		1		5			8
...	...	...		...		...			...

Figure C.6 Composite Index for the "Gender" and "Name" Fields

[»] **Write Accesses with an Index**

Inverted and composite indexes occur in both the main store and the delta store. As with classic databases, write accesses in the delta store are more labor-intensive because the indexes have to be maintained. In the case of a composite index, write accesses require more time and effort than with an inverted index, because composite indexes require that more memory structures be maintained.

D SAP Business Application Accelerator Powered by SAP HANA

Using the SAP Business Application Accelerator powered by SAP HANA, you can accelerate existing programs by executing specific SQL accesses on SAP HANA without having to change the programs. Since the redirection is done via Customizing, there is no need to change the program itself. This appendix explains how to use the SAP Business Application Accelerator.

SAP Note 1694697 details how to obtain the software, which comprises the SAP kernel and add-on.

Technical Requirements	[«]

To install the SAP Business Application Accelerator, SAP kernel version 7.21 or higher and the SAP Business Application Accelerator add-on SWT2DB are required. For the kernel, please check SAP Notes 1713986 and 1716826; for the add-on, please read SAP Notes 1694697 and 1597627.

To use the SAP Business Application Accelerator, you'll need an SAP HANA database connected to your SAP system via a secondary connection (side-by-side scenario). SAP Note 1597627 explains how to create a secondary connection.

Moreover, tables are needed on SAP HANA that are replicated by the SAP system which is to be used with the SAP Business Application Accelerator. This is usually done via the SAP Landscape Transformation Replication Server.

One of the prerequisites for redirecting a program using the SAP Business Application Accelerator is a large database time-share in the program runtime. Only programs reading from the tables that are replicated by the SAP system can be redirected. These are typically programs used in reporting. When reading from replicated tables, it must be noted that the data is presented in *near real-time*; i. e., there may be smaller delays until the data is replicated. Since it is possible that position data is replicated prior to header data, transactional consistency cannot be guaranteed for short periods of time. You should therefore carefully assess which programs are suitable candidates for redirecting access to the data replicated in SAP HANA. You should then evaluate which accesses would greatly benefit from being redirected to SAP HANA.

Programs and accesses for redirection

To identify programs that are good candidates for redirection, we recommend the service *SAP HANA Feasability Check* (*HFC*) from SAP Active Global Support (please also check SAP Note 1694697). Based on the above criteria, this service identifies the programs where redirection is possible and useful.

Customizing   In Customizing, you can maintain a so-called *context* for the program to be redirected. This is where entries for the combination of program, background job, and table/view are entered. For example, for each program, you specify the tables for which reading accesses should be redirected. By maintaining a background job, you can also specify whether this should only be done if the program runs in the background. This customizing is evaluated during runtime and all accesses are redirected accordingly. Figure D.1 illustrates this process.

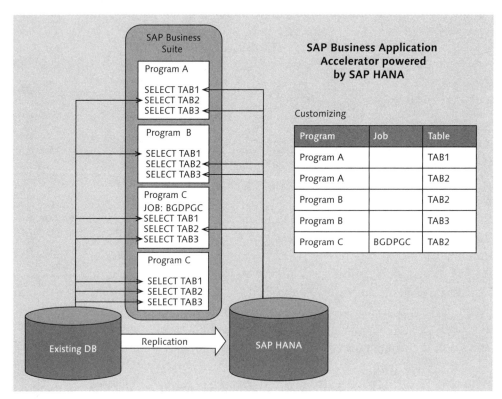

Figure D.1   Redirecting Specific Table Accesses

Technical details

Redirection can only be done on application servers with the profile parameter `rsdb/rda = on` set. If this parameter is set, access to the following objects can be redirected:

▶ Transparent tables

▶ Cluster tables (converted into transparent tables during replication)

▶ Database views (if all underlying tables are replicated and the view exists in SAP HANA)

Access to pool tables, table pools (the actual database tables containing the pool tables), and table clusters (the actual database tables containing the cluster tables) cannot be redirected.

Limitations

Moreover, there are limitations with regard to the statements that can be redirected. The following Open SQL statements can be redirected:

▶ `SELECT` statements

▶ `OPEN CURSOR ... FETCH`

However, the following accesses cannot be redirected:

▶ `SELECT` statements with the addition `CONNECTION` (secondary connections)

▶ `SELECT ... FOR UPDATE`

▶ `OPEN CURSOR WITH HOLD...`

See SAP Note 1694697 for further details on the customizing of the SAP Business Application Accelerator.

The SAP Business Application Accelerator can be used to accelerate programs where the runtime is dominated by read accesses without having to change the program itself. The extent to which accesses can be accelerated depends on the specific SQL statement. In several projects, customers observed performance increases of 20 to several hundred percent compared to the original performance.

E   Installing the Sample Programs

Together with this book, several sample programs are available to help you better understand the explanations and contents provided in each chapter. These sample programs can be found in the download area for this book at *www.sap-press.com*. In this download area, you'll find the code used in this book. Moreover, it details the subsequent steps that must be executed for your system.

All ABAP development objects are included in the TEST_A4H_BOOK package, all SAP HANA development objects are included in the test.a4h.book package. These packages include subpackages for each chapter of this book.

Packages

For all sample programs, SAP NetWeaver Application Server (AS) ABAP 7.4 (Support Package 2), ABAP Development Tools for SAP NetWeaver 2.7, and SAP HANA 1.0 (Support Package Stack 5) are required. For our tests, SAP HANA 1.0 Revision 52 was used.

Requirements

If your system does not meet these requirements, you can also install the sample programs on a hosted test system. Since July 2013, you can have an IaaS provider (currently *Amazon Web Services*) provision such a test system as a virtual appliance for you. This system is comprised of SAP NetWeaver AS ABAP 7.4 and the SAP HANA database. This offer is based on a free 90-day *Test and Evaluation License Agreement*. However, you must pay for all costs incurred for the infrastructure services of the IaaS provider. For further information, please refer to the SAP Community Network at *http://scn.sap.com/docs/DOC-41566*.

Hosted test system

After importing the code, you should make sure to generate sufficient data for your tests. For this purpose, use the ABAP report ZR_A4H_BOOK_GENERATE_MASS_DATA. Details can be found in the download area.

Test data

F   The Authors

Thorsten Schneider is a product manager in the Product & Innovation HANA Platform department at SAP AG. In this position, he deals with application development using the new in-memory database technology. His main focus is the implementation of business applications based on ABAP and SAP HANA. Prior to working as a product manager, Thorsten was a consultant at SAP Deutschland AG & Co. KG for several years. During this time, he advised national and international organizations on product lifecycle management and project portfolio management matters.

Eric Westenberger studied mathematics at the University of Kaiserslautern, Germany, where he was awarded his doctorate degree in the field of singularity theory. Since 2005, he has been working for SAP AG, where he is currently a product manager for SAP HANA and SAP NetWeaver. Prior to this, he was involved in the development of several components of the SAP NetWeaver basis technology as a developer and software architect for several years.

 **Hermann Gahm** is a principal consultant in the performance CoE of SAP Global IT Application Services. In this position, he is primarily responsible for performance analysis and optimization of the internal SAP ABAP systems powered by SAP HANA. Between 2006 and 2012, Hermann worked as an SAP technology consultant at SAP SI AG and as an SAP support consultant in the Technology & Performance division of the Active Global Support department at SAP AG. In this position, his main responsibilities were helping major SAP customers solve performance problems in the context of ABAP developments and system, database, and ABAP program tuning. During his in-service studies of information management, he worked as an ABAP developer in one of the largest commercial enterprises in Germany and as an SAP system administrator for a market-leading industrial mortgage company between 1998 and 2006. During this time, his main responsibilities were performance analysis and optimization of mass data processing in SAP systems.

Index

■ Implement SAP HANA as a
standalone data warehouse

■ Integrate SAP Data Services and
the SAP BusinessObjects BI tools
with SAP HANA

■ Benefit from step-by-step
instructions, technical details, and
downloadable data for every step

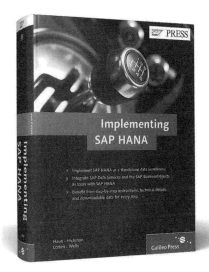

Jonathan Haun, Chris Hickman, Don Loden, Roy Wells

Implementing SAP HANA

You know what SAP HANA is—now you need to see it in action. Look no
further than this book, which will steer you through a real-life implementation
of the standalone version of SAP HANA. You'll find step-by-step instructions
and screenshots that show you how to implement real data in a real system,
from concept to go-live.

837 pp., 2013, 69,95 Euro / US$ 69.95
ISBN 978-1-59229-856-3
www.sap-press.com

Galileo Press

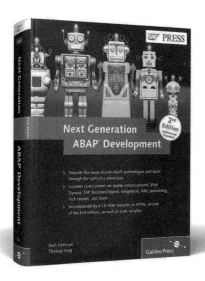

■ Presents the most recent ABAP technologies and tools through the eyes of a developer

■ Includes new topics like syntax enhancements, ABAP Test Cockpit, AJAX, SAP BusinessObjects integration, XML processing, Rich Islands, NWBC 3.0, and many more

■ Covers an entire upgrade project from release 4.6C to 7.0 EHP2

Rich Heilman, Thomas Jung

Next Generation ABAP Development

If you're a seasoned developer, you know that it's important to keep up with the latest ABAP changes. This second edition of our best-selling title follows along with a lead ABAP developer as he learns how to employ tools and features new to recent ABAP releases. Experience the entire process of building applications—design, development, and testing of all areas—and walk away with a firm understanding of techniques and technologies that were not previously available. With this book, you're learn how to keep your ABAP fresh.

735 pp., 2. edition 2011, with CD, 69,95 Euro / US$ 69.95
ISBN 978-1-59229-352-0
www.sap-press.com

■ Provides 100 little-known, time-saving tips and tricks

■ Features step-by-step instructions and guiding screenshots

■ Helps you use the ABAP Workbench more effectively

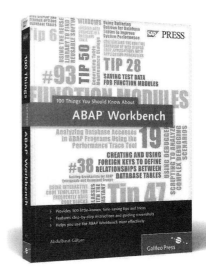

Abdulbasıt Gülşen

ABAP Workbench

100 Things You Should Know About...

Don't hesitate in learning how to perform ABAP Workbench tasks more easily and efficiently than ever before! Whether you're a beginner or advanced user, this book provides tips and tricks that give you different and valuable ways of working with the tool. Based on your specific needs, you'll easily navigate the 100 tips and workarounds to help you increase productivity, save time, and improve the overall ease-of-use of working with the ABAP Workbench.

341 pp., 2012, 49,95 Euro / US$ 49.95
ISBN 978-1-59229-427-5
www.sap-press.com

Galileo Press

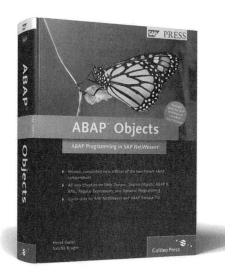

■ Second, completely new edition
of the benchmark ABAP
compendium

■ All-new chapters on Web Dynpro,
Shared Objects, ABAP & XML,
Regular Expressions, Dynamic
Programming, and more!

■ Up-to-date for SAP NetWeaver
2004s (ABAP release 7.0)

Horst Keller, Sascha Krüger

ABAP Objects

ABAP Programming in SAP NetWeaver

This completely new third edition of our best-selling ABAP book provides
detailed coverage of ABAP programming with SAP NetWeaver. This outstanding
compendium treats all concepts of modern ABAP up to release 7.0. New topics
include ABAP and Unicode, Shared Objects, exception handling, Web Dynpro
for ABAP, Object Services, and of course ABAP and XML. Bonus: All readers will
receive the SAP NetWeaver 2004s ABAP Trial Version ("Mini-SAP") on DVD.

1059 pp., 2. edition 2007, with DVD 5, 79,95 Euro / US$ 79.95
ISBN 978-1-59229-079-6
www.sap-press.com

■ Teaches you all you need to know about the central repository of information for ABAP data

■ Provides an introduction to ABAP Data Dictionary components, as well as specific technical information

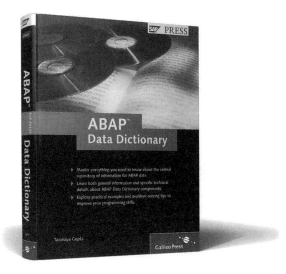

Tanmaya Gupta

ABAP Data Dictionary

If you work regularly with the ABAP Data Dictionary, this is the reference you need. Suitable for both beginners and advanced users, this book will answer all your questions about the central repository of information for ABAP data. You'll learn basic background information as well as details about the specific functionality of Data Dictionary elements (domains, tables, views, etc.), both of which will help you enhance your programming skills. The book also provides coverage of more complex topics, such as lock objects.

403 pp., 2011, 69,95 Euro / US$ 69.95
ISBN 978-1-59229-379-7
www.sap-press.com

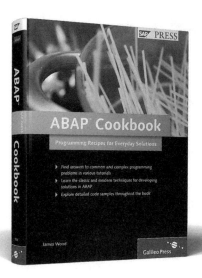

- Find answers to common and complex programming problems in various tutorials

- Learn the classic and modern techniques for developing solutions in ABAP

- Explore detailed code samples throughout the book

James Wood

ABAP Cookbook

Programming Recipes for Everyday Solutions

This book is intended to quickly provide answers to typical ABAP development problems or tasks: persistence programming, interface programming, security and tracing techniques, etc. You'll discover best practices in developing solutions, and you can use this book to broaden your skills and see how to apply ABAP to solve various types of problems. The complexity of the „recipes " ranges from the simple starter plates to the complex main courses – and some sweet deserts, of course! Each chapter is a short tutorial in itself, all organized and consolidated into an easy-to-read format. Many code samples, screenshots, and different icons will help you to follow the best practices provided. Enjoy your ABAP meal!

548 pp., 2010, 69,95 Euro / US$ 69.95
ISBN 978-1-59229-326-1
www.sap-press.com